THE STATE OF
BLACK AMERICA 1990

Published by **National Urban League, Inc.**
January 1990

THE STATE OF BLACK AMERICA 1990

Editor

Janet Dewart

Copyright © National Urban League, Inc., 1990
Library of Congress Catalog Number 77-647469
ISBN 0-914758-11-X

Price $19.00

The cover art is "The Reception" by Jonathan Green. "The Reception" is the third in the "Great Artists" series of limited edition lithographs on black Americans created for the National Urban League through a donation from the House of Seagram.

National Urban League, Inc.

The Equal Opportunity Building ▪ 500 East 62nd Street ▪ New York, New York 10021

Founded in 1910, the National Urban League is the premier social service and civil rights organization in America. The League is a nonprofit, community-based agency headquartered in New York City, with 113 affiliates in 34 states and the District of Columbia. Its principal objective is to secure equal opportunity for blacks and other minorities.

Dedication

This fifteenth edition of *The State of Black America* is dedicated to the memory of Clarence Coleman, former Vice President of the National Urban League, who died July 7, 1989. Among his many notable accomplishments is the creation of *The State of Black America* series.

TABLE OF CONTENTS

About The Authors

DR. CARL C. BELL
Psychiatrist/Lecturer
Executive Director
Community Mental Health Council, Inc.

Dr. Bell is a distinguished psychiatrist specializing in mental health issues. He is currently Medical Director and Executive Director at the Community Mental Health Council, Inc., in Chicago. He is also Associate Professor at the University of Illinois School of Medicine and lecturer for the department of psychiatry at the University of Chicago, and Chicago Medical School. Moreover, he has a private practice and represents black psychiatrists of America on the issue of black-on-black murder.

Dr. Bell is a member of a variety of organizations; among them are the American Psychiatric Association, Black Psychiatrists Committee, National Medical Association, and American Board of Psychiatry and Neurology.

He has written over 80 articles on mental health issues and co-authored a textbook chapter on mental health and people of color as well as a chapter on the misdiagnosis of black alcoholics in *The Treatment of Black Alcoholics*. He has also participated in countless interviews and news articles concerning his view on preventing homicide; among the most prominent are *The New York Times, Chicago Tribune Magazine, People* magazine, the *Chicago Reporter, Ebony, Jet,* and *Essence*. Additionally, he has appeared on Ted Koppel's "Nightline," where his expert opinion was utilized.

Dr. Bell received his B.S. degree in biology from the University of Illinois, Chicago Circle Campus, and his M.D. from Meharry Medical College.

* * * *

ESTHER J. JENKINS is professor of psychology at Chicago State University and research associate at the Community Mental Health Counsel. She earned her bachelor's degree in psychology from Northwestern University; her masters and Ph.D. degrees in Social Psychology from the University of Michigan; and she successfully completed postdoctoral work at the Department of Behavioral Sciences, University of Chicago and the Institute for Social Research, University of Michigan.

DR. ANDREW BILLINGSLEY
Professor and Chairman
Department of Family and Community Development
University of Maryland—College Park

Dr. Andrew Billingsley is a renowned educator and scholar. Currently he is Professor and Chairman of the Department of Family and Community Development at the University of Maryland, College Park. Dr. Billingsley was previously Professor of Sociology and Afro-American Studies at the University of Maryland, President and Professor of Sociology at Morgan State University from 1975 to 1984, and Scholar in Residence at Fordham University, as well as Vice President for Academic Affairs and Graduate Professor of Social Sciences at Howard University.

Dr. Billingsley is the author of several major publications on the black American family and child welfare. His two major books are *Black Families in White America* and *Children of the Storm* (with Jeanne Giovannoni). His most recent publications include "Families: Contemporary Patterns," *Encyclopedia of Social Work, 1987;* "Black Families in a Changing Society," *The State of Black America 1987* (National Urban League); and "The Impact of Technology on African-American Families," *Family Relations,* 1988.

He is recipient of the 1988 Marie Peters Award given biannually by the National Council on Family Relations for outstanding scholarship on minority issues. Additionally, he was awarded grants totaling $375,000 from the Ford Foundation and the Lily Endowment to conduct a two-year national study of the impact of the black church on black families.

Dr. Billingsley received his B.A. in political science from Grinnell College, his M.A. in sociology from the University of Michigan, and his Ph.D. in social policy/social research from Brandeis University. He holds memberships in the National Council on Family Relations, The Groves Conference on Marriage and the Family, the Association of Black Sociologists, and the National Association of Social Workers.

JULIUS L. CHAMBERS, ESQ.
Director-Counsel
NAACP Legal Defense and Educational Fund, Inc.

Attorney Chambers is a distinguished attorney and lecturer. Presently, he is director-counsel of the NAACP Legal Defense and Educational Fund, Inc., and a lecturer at the University of Pennsylvania School of Law and Columbia University School of Law.

He belongs to numerous bar associations and boards, among them the American Bar Association; National Bar Association; New York State Bar Association; Board of Directors, Legal Aid Society of New York; Board of Editors, American Bar Association *Journal;* and Board of Directors of the Children's Defense Fund.

Attorney Chambers is a member of numerous social and honorary organizations, including: Order of the Golden Fleece, Prince Hall Masonic Lodge, and Alpha Phi Alpha fraternity.

Attorney Chambers graduated *summa cum laude* from North Carolina Central University with a B.A. degree in history and earned a M.A. degree in history from the University of Michigan, where he received the Woodrow

Wilson Scholarship. He received a J.D. degree from the University of North Carolina at Chapel Hill, where he graduated as a member of the highest honor society at the university; he was awarded his LL.M. degree from Columbia University School of Law.

He has received honorary degrees from Amherst College, Northeastern University, North Carolina Central University, St. Augustine College, and Johnson C. Smith University. Additionally, he has received the Distinguished Alumni Award from the University of North Carolina at Chapel Hill and the Columbia University Medal for Excellence. He is an honorary fellow of the University of Pennsylvania Law School.

DR. PHILLIP L. CLAY
Associate Professor of City Planning
Department of Urban Studies and Planning
Massachusetts Institute of Technology

Dr. Clay is currently an associate professor of City Planning at Massachusetts Institute of Technology. He teaches courses on housing, urban demographics, and community development. He is author of *Neighborhood Renewal* (with Robert Hollister) and *Neighborhood Planning and Politics*.

Dr. Clay has served on many task forces and national and local committees. He has also presented congressional testimony on the issue of national housing policy and served as a federal court expert in a major and successful fair housing case.

Dr. Clay earned an undergraduate degree with honors from the University of North Carolina at Chapel Hill and a Ph.D. degree in city planning from Massachusetts Institute of Technology.

DR. RAMONA H. EDELIN
President and Chief Executive Officer
The National Urban Coalition

Ramona Hoage Edelin is President and Chief Executive Officer of the National Urban Coalition, an urban action and advocacy organization.

Dr. Edelin has been associated with the Coalition since 1977, after an outstanding career as a social activist, scholar, and academic administrator at some of the nation's leading institutions. Prior to her appointment as CEO, she served the organization as Senior Vice President of Program and Policy where she directed programs in advocacy, housing and economic development, and health and urban education.

While gaining respect for insight into a broad spectrum of urban issues, Dr. Edelin has been especially identified with the development and implementation of the NUC's Say YES to a Youngster's Future™ program—an early intervention, family learning program aimed at exposing African-American, Latino,

Native American, and female children, ages 4 to 19, to mathematics, science, and computer technology to help prepare them for the high tech jobs of the 21st century.

Under her leadership as president and CEO, the NUC has instituted the M. Carl Holman Leadership Strategy Series, a project that periodically brings together leaders from national organizations, labor, business, Capitol Hill, foundations, academia, community-based and youth groups for strategic sessions on timely issues of public policy and organizational development.

Before her tenure with the NUC, Dr. Edelin was founder and chair of the Department of African American Studies at Northeastern University in Boston. She has taught at Brandeis University, Emerson College, and the European Division of the University of Maryland.

A Phi Beta Kappa graduate of Fisk University, Dr. Edelin performed undergraduate work at Harvard University, earned a M.A. degree in philosophy from the University of East Anglia in Norwich, England, and a Ph.D. in philosophy from Boston University.

DR. LENNEAL J. HENDERSON
Distinguished Professor of
Government and Public Administration
The University of Baltimore

Dr. Henderson is currently a Distinguished Professor of Government and Public Administration, a Senior Fellow in the William Donald Schaefer Center for Public Policy, and a Henry C. Welcome Fellow at the University of Baltimore. He was formerly Head and Professor of Political Science at the University of Tennessee, Knoxville, a Senior Faculty member at the Federal Executive Institute in Charlottesville, Virginia, and a Professor in the School of Business and Public Administration at Howard University. He was a Ford Foundation Fellow, National Research Council Postdoctoral Fellow at the Johns Hopkins School of Advanced International Studies, a Kellogg National Fellow (1984–87), and a Rockefeller Research Fellow.

He has lectured or consulted in Africa, Egypt, Israel, India, Brazil, Peru, the Caribbean, the USSR, and the People's Republic of China.

He has chaired the Mayor's Budget and Resources Advisory Commission for Washington, DC, and serves on the boards of the Population Reference Bureau, Inc., Decision Demographics, and the National Civic League.

He has published or edited five books and articles in such publications as *Urban League Review, The Review of Black Political Economy, The Annals, Policy Studies Journal, Howard Law Journal, Public Administration Review,* and *The Black Scholar.* He received his A.B., M.A., and Ph.D. degrees from the University of California, Berkeley.

DR. MATTHEW HOLDEN, JR.
Professor of Government and Foreign Affairs
University of Virginia

Dr. Holden is a highly regarded scholar currently serving as the Henry L. and Grace M. Doherty Professor of Government and Foreign Affairs at the University of Virginia. He was formerly Commissioner, Public Service Commission of Wisconsin (1975–77) and Commissioner, Federal Energy Regulatory Commission (1977–1981).

Dr. Holden is the author of *The Divisible Republic, Racial Stratification as Accident and as Policy,* and a variety of other papers on politics and public policy. He is a member of the National Academy of Public Administration, the editorial board of the *American Political Science Review,* and the editorial board of the *Urban League Review.* He has been nominated to be editor of the *National Political Science Review,* a journal sponsored by the National Conference of Black Political Scientists.

Dr. Holden earned his undergraduate and graduate degrees in political science: his bachelor's from Roosevelt University, and both his master's and doctorate from Northwestern University. He has received an honorary Doctor of Laws from Tuskegee Institute.

DR. LASALLE D. LEFFALL, JR.
Surgeon and Professor
Chairman, Department of Surgery
Howard University College of Medicine

Dr. Leffall is a distinguished surgeon, oncologist, and medical educator. His specialty is the effects of cancer on African Americans. He is presently Professor and Chairman of the Department of Surgery at Howard University College of Medicine.

Dr. Leffall has been active in numerous professional and civic organizations, among them president of the American Cancer Society; president of the Society of Surgical Oncology; president, Society of Surgical Chairmen; second vice president, American Surgical Association; and chairman, Executive Committee, Board of Governors, United Way of America.

He has also received many honors and awards including the Presidential Award, DC Chapter, American College of Surgeons; Howard University Distinguished Scholar-Teacher Award; named "Washingtonian of the Year" and listed as one of the "Best Doctors in Washington, DC," *Washingtonian* magazine; and listed as surgical oncologist in *Town and Country's* America's Best Doctors. In 1987, The Biennial LaSalle D. Leffall, Jr. Award was established to recognize contributions to cancer prevention, treatment, and education in minority and economically disadvantaged communities. As recently as 1989, the citizens of Dr. Leffall's hometown (Quincy, FL) named a street and the surgical wing in the Gadsden Memorial Hospital in his honor.

Dr. Leffall graduated *summa cum laude* with a B.S. degree from Florida A&M University and a M.D. degree from Howard University College of Medicine, where he ranked first in his class. He has received honorary degrees from Georgetown University, University of Maryland, Florida A&M University, Meharry Medical College, and Clark University (Worcester, MA).

DR. GENE S. ROBINSON
Associate Professor
Communication Arts and Theatre Department
University of Maryland, College Park

Dr. Robinson is presently an associate professor at the University of Maryland, College Park. He is also a filmmaker; his prize-winning film, "Tar Baby," has been included in the USIA series for foreign distribution. He also scripted "The Class of '52," a documentary detailing the reintegration of Gallaudet University for the Deaf in Washington, DC, and wrote "Inclusionary Mainstreaming," an article for *Black Film Review*. He is currently at work on a documentary series, "The Black Artist in America."

A linguist, Dr. Robinson has conducted many international seminars and edited technical journals including *Electronics and Communications in Japan, Systems and Computers in Japan,* and *Electrical Engineering in Japan.*

Dr. Robinson received his B.A. and M.A. degrees in Radio, Television, Film from the University of Maryland, College Park, and earned his Ph.D. in American Studies from the University of Maryland.

DR. DAVID H. SWINTON
Dean of the School of Business
Jackson State University

Dr. Swinton is a renowned economist and educational administrator. He is recognized as an expert on the economics of social policy and minority groups. He is presently Dean of the School of Business at Jackson State University. Under his direction, the school has implemented a new quality assurance program to ensure that all graduates have the skills, competencies, and attitudes required for success in corporate America.

Prior to coming to Jackson State, Dr. Swinton was Director of the Southern Center for the Study of Public Policy and Professor of Economics at Clark University in Atlanta. While at the policy center, he was the principal fundraiser and architect of the research program.

Dr. Swinton earned his academic degrees in economics: his Ph.D. and M.A. from Harvard University, and his B.A. from New York University. He has served as a Teaching Fellow at Harvard and a lecturer at City College of New York.

His annual economic analysis is a regular feature of *The State of Black America.*

Black America, 1989
An Overview

John E. Jacob
President and Chief Executive Officer
National Urban League, Inc.

During the heady days of the winter revolts against Eastern Europe's totalitarian regimes, a newspaper cartoon appeared that provides a stunningly accurate commentary on the current state of urban and Black America.

The cartoon showed Uncle Sam looking over the Berlin Wall through binoculars. He says: "Gee, isn't it fascinating to watch the way communism is disintegrating." Behind him, on the U.S. side, is an urban landscape of mugging victims, hypodermic needles strewn on the ground, drug addicts, guns, potholed roads, and crumbling houses.

That cartoon punctured the smugness that attended so many comments about the revolution in the East. While it is important to celebrate the spread of freedom, it is also important to be aware of the impediments to freedom here at home.

The international events that marked 1989 offer hope that after a half-century of hot wars and a devastating Cold War, America can get back on track and finally resolve the unfinished business of ending racism and poverty.

For African Americans, 1989 ended on that note of hope—on the assumption that changing world conditions will result in a renewed national concern with critical domestic issues, an enhanced financial capability to deal constructively with those issues, and a reinvigorated passion for democracy at home as well as abroad.

But 1989 also began as a year of hope for African Americans, primarily because the new year brought with it a new administration pledged to greater openness and to a fair-minded approach to our problems. There was confidence that it would not actively erect barriers to black progress as its predecessor had done.

It was heartening to see such signs of new openness as the president's coming to address the Urban League's annual conference, where he pledged to use the weight of his office to fight racial bias, the appointment of African Americans to such positions as Secretary of Health and Human Services and Chairman of the Joint Chiefs of Staff, and legislative proposals in education and other areas of concern.

It is also clear that the thaw in relations between Washington and the African-American community must be followed with much bolder, more imaginative, moves. For the state of Black America remains critical.

In 1989, black poverty and unemployment continued at high levels, and African Americans remain frighteningly vulnerable to a recession.

The decade of the 1980s saw a sharp increase in the proportion of black children living in poverty, in single-parent households, and in homes where the family head is unemployed.

The 1980s also witnessed the crack invasion of our neighborhoods, a virtual epidemic that threatens the future of our young people. Despite the rhetoric about wars on drugs, treatment centers are understaffed and underfunded. The explosion in drug trafficking has resulted in some big-city clinics having backlogs that require waits of 15 months for admission.

AIDS has emerged as a special concern. The dread disease has become a major public health problem, exposing the weaknesses of our social support structures—the severe deficiencies in health care, substance abuse treatment, and housing, as well as the severe shortages of trained health care personnel and social service facilities.

Other pressing needs went unmet in 1989. The growth of poverty and inequality in America could be seen most vividly in the growth of homelessness and the lack of affordable housing in urban America.

Over the past decade, the number of poor households increased by more than 25 percent, while the number of low-rent housing units declined by 20 percent. It is estimated that there are eight million low-income renters competing for four million housing units. That ratio is bound to get worse, as low-income areas become targeted for new developments aimed at the middle-income and affluent. Minorities are hit hardest by the housing crunch. About a third of all poor African Americans live in substandard housing—about two-and-a-half times the proportion of poor whites living in such circumstances.

As the poor got poorer in the 1980s, the share of their shrinking incomes devoted to housing rose sharply. A clear majority of all poor families spend more than half their income on housing, and two out of five of the minority poor spend at least 70 percent of their incomes on housing.

The most visible part of the housing crisis, of course, are the homeless—especially the growth of the homelessness among families with children. The invisible part of the homeless situation is the widespread doubling-up that is happening, as people who cannot afford to maintain their own homes move in with relatives and friends, often shuttling back and forth among several hosts.

The Bush administration announced plans for a $4 billion, three-year housing program. While a federal re-entry into the housing arena is long overdue and very welcome, the package is nowhere near the scale needed. If the housing crisis is to be solved, the first priority should be a vast expansion of the housing stock available to low-income people.

The federal deficit appears to be the all-purpose excuse for not dealing adequately with problems such as drugs, housing, health care, education, and job training. Somehow, the deficit did not impede a $160 billion bailout of the savings and loan industry; nor did it stem the flow of cash into less urgent areas.

There were, however, some signs of a more positive legislative approach to our problems. Congress and the administration boosted federal appropriations for Head Start and for compensatory education programs, but they failed to enact an urgently needed child-care bill. While the minimum wage was increased, that small raise for the working poor was bought with a below-minimum "training wage" for young workers.

Perhaps the biggest negative of 1989 was the continued rollback of civil-rights gains by a Supreme Court that has been highjacked by Reaganite judges hostile to affirmative action. Among their more backward rulings, the justices rolled back local government set-aside programs designed to encourage minority businesses and to compensate for past discrimination, and punched holes in affirmative action programs intended to remedy historic discrimination against African Americans. Julius Chambers, Director-Counsel of the NAACP Legal Defense and Educational Fund, charges that ". . . the Court seemed to ignore both the bitter history and current practice of race discrimination in this country."

A major priority for Congress in 1990 should be passage of legislation that rolls back these decisions and makes reasonable affirmative action programs "court-proof." For this court appears to be comfortable with the myth that we are a "color-blind" society and that racism was buried in the 1960s, even as racism remains a serious and growing threat to America's future.

The vicious murder of an African-American teenager in the Bensonhurst section of Brooklyn, New York, in August was but one of many incidents in a long pattern of racist violence against black people and other minorities.

It is no accident that open and often violent racism has re-emerged in the 1980s, for we live in a climate in which discrimination persists in spite of the laws. Just a week after the Brooklyn murder, for example, the Federal Reserve Bank of Boston released a study that documented pervasive denial of mortgage loans on properties in African-American neighborhoods.

Racism in all its forms has to be stamped out. The Justice Department should take the lead in prosecuting today's subtle discriminators, whether they are employers, mortgage lenders, or government agencies. It must also mount a strong get-tough policy to combat the violent racism that has led to murders of young black men and to attacks on African Americans and other minorities.

It has been estimated that hate crimes have tripled over the past seven years, many of them committed by young people, ranging from dropouts to college students, who think their white skin confers privilege and superiority. There has been a rise in the number of openly racist organizations who preach violence and incite attacks on African Americans and other minorities. The Anti-Defamation league estimates some 3,000 members of neo-Nazi groups are operating in 31 states. Those numbers have grown in recent years, especially among young people who style themselves "skinheads" and glorify racism and violence.

We cannot be so busy applauding the rise of democracy in far-away countries that we ignore the rise of home-grown racism that endangers our own democracy. The way to begin fighting it is to launch a national campaign against racism that educates people to living in a pluralistic society and gets very tough with those who practice and preach the violent racism that brutalizes our society.

Fortunately, such a campaign can be built on the considerable base of good will and racial respect that has been built over the decades. While we press the fight against widespread racism, we also recognize the widespread positive changes that have taken place in our society.

The electoral victories of Douglas Wilder as governor of Virginia and David Dinkins as mayor of New York City were another step in the long process of removing America's racial barriers, indicators that we have come a long way as a nation since the 1965 Voting Rights Act. Only two decades after Virginia led the fight against desegregation in the 1960s, it elected an African-American governor—that is as powerful a sign of the changes that have taken place in America as can be imagined.

The Wilder and Dinkins elections, as well as the electoral victories of other African-American candidates in key cities, will force reassessments of some long-held political beliefs. The first is the dictum that African-American political candidates can win only in jurisdictions where blacks are the majority of voters. That belief always allowed for exceptions—notably districts or cities in which white citizens were presumed to be "enlightened" about race, or districts with so few black voters that blacks were not deemed to constitute a "threat."

The 1989 elections prove that there are enough white citizens who base their votes on the competence and ideas of the candidates, and are willing to vote for African Americans, just as blacks have voted for white political candidates all these years.

There remains a solid core of white voters, however, who will not vote for a black candidate under any circumstance.

That means most African-American candidates start with a serious deficiency and have to build cross-racial coalitions and alliances. A black mayoral or gubernatorial candidate has to be concerned with the interests of more affluent white neighborhoods as well as with the needs of poor inner city neighborhoods. That is a fact of political life, and successful African-American politicians like Douglas Wilder and David Dinkins demonstrated that they know it is the only way to win in jurisdictions where blacks are in the minority.

In one sense, that is a higher standard for blacks, since many white political candidates win elections without stepping foot into a black neighborhood or evidencing any concern about the poor. In another sense, this expectation reflects the growing maturity of black politicians and voters who recognize that you cannot govern without first getting elected, and forging the coalitions necessary to win at the polls. So African-American voters maintained a solid front behind black candidates, preventing an erosion of their political base, while they sought votes in the white community. The 1990s will see more of that, and I am confident that cross-racial coalitions will be built that constructively address America's unmet needs.

Part of the reason for my optimism lies in the growing realization at all levels of leadership that America will become a second rate power with a third-rate living standard if it does not draw on the underutilized human capital represented by its growing minority population. In this volume, distinguished University of Virginia professor Matthew Holden analyzes the strategies of the Wilder campaign and its national significance for other African Americans whose political success will depend upon similar daring and an understanding of how power is acquired and used.

America has to compete in a global marketplace that has changed dramatically. The continued growth of the Japanese economic juggernaut and the impending economic unification of Europe mean that we will be shut out of the world's markets unless our economy becomes more productive. That cannot happen unless America's neglected minorities are brought into the mainstream.

A third of America's future work force will be non-white. African Americans, Hispanics, women, and immigrants will make up 85 percent of new entrants into the work force in the 1990s. By the end of the decade, a majority of jobs will require at least some college education. Although African Americans and Hispanics have increased their high school graduation rates, college enrollment rates among minorities have slipped far below earlier levels.

America cannot compete effectively unless it trains, educates and employs the core of its future work force—minority Americans. It cannot train, educate, and employ those minorities to the maximum, as it must, unless it combats the poverty, health, and housing problems that are barriers to their success.

The National Urban League has called for a national effort directed at racial parity by the year 2000. As the U.S. enters the final decade of this millenium, we have a window of opportunity to follow aggressively policies that lead to racial parity.

No one should think the task will be easy. The National Urban League released a study during the summer of 1989 that documents the extent of the gap separating white and black Americans.

The study asked: how far behind are we and how long will it take to catch up? It pulls together a number of comparative measurements into a Racial Parity Index (RPI). With an RPI of 100 measuring full parity, the scale stands at only 47. That is a drop from 51.2 in 1967, so the gap has widened in the last two decades.

What about specific key items? In unemployment, African Americans have not made any progress at all in lowering their unemployment rate compared to the white rate. In fact, black unemployment has grown worse since 1967. The conclusion—at the current rate of change, African-American workers will never reach parity with white workers. We will just slip farther behind.

The study looked at the ratio of African Americans to whites in executive and managerial jobs. It found that if progress continues at the present pace, it will be 54 years before parity in those jobs is achieved.

The earnings gap: For black men, it will take 73 years at the current rate of progress to close the racial gap in earnings.

Family income: In 1967, black family earnings were about 59 percent of white family earnings. In 1985, they were down to about 57.5 percent. No progress. Family income is becoming more unequal, and unless that changes, there will never be black-white parity.

Poverty: Black family poverty is triple the white rate, and it will take 169 years at the current rate of change for black and white families to have the same poverty rate.

The one economically important area where the gap appears to be closing faster is education. If we continue to improve our high school graduation rates at the same pace that held between 1967 and 1985, in 16 years black and white high school graduation rates will be equal. However, for college completion rates, it will be 40 years.

The National Urban League's study demonstrates both the importance of the parity concept in galvanizing action to change conditions and the size of the gaps that must be closed before parity is achieved. It is going to take strong action by government, business, and civic groups to close those gaps. We must concentrate on those areas where African Americans are slipping farther behind and are in danger of never reaching parity.

At a time when statesmen talk of a new Marshall Plan for eastern Europe and of a new Economic Development Bank to invest in the economies of those countries, we need to remind policy-makers of the still pressing need for an Urban Marshall Plan first introduced by Whitney M. Young and the National Urban League 25 years ago, and an Urban Development Bank that invests in our own people and our own cities.

The opportunity to do that is provided by the end of the Cold War. The opening of the Berlin Wall and the December summit in Malta effectively marked the close of the post-war era that mandated huge defense expenditures and a wartime mentality. The Soviets appear willing to cooperate in constructing a new world order, and they are desperate to shrink their own military burden.

Experts say that, without compromising our national security, our defense costs can be sliced in half over the next several years. Without a viable enemy, there is no need for draining our economy for $500 million-per-plane bombers and multi-billion dollar Star Wars systems that scientists say will not work. With the Soviets slashing troop strengths, allowing their former satellite nations freedom, and the Berlin Wall crumbling, there is no reason for America to foot

Europe's defense bill to the tune of some $160 billion a year, especially when Europe has become wealthier than we have.

In fact, the wealth and power of Europe and Japan are traceable to the fact that their defense expenditures are a fraction of ours, allowing them to invest in becoming economically competitive instead of investing in military equipment that cannot be used without committing suicide. The United States and the Soviet Union, by coming to their senses and ending the Cold War, appear to have finally realized that their military rivalry has just about wrecked their economies. The Soviets' enormous and unnecessary military spending just about ruined them, while ours has led to the erosion of our global economic leadership.

Bringing our defense spending down to levels commensurate with true national security needs would result in defense budgets in the $150 billion area—an annual saving of $150 billion. That $150 billion a year amounts to a giant peace dividend that, used wisely, could spark a significant economic boom and close the racial gap.

If we assume that the lion's share of the savings is applied to deficit reduction—say, $100 billion—interest rates would drop to levels of about four or five percent. That would mean U.S. businesses could borrow at rates similar to those of their foreign competitors. Investment and productivity would rise. The growth in jobs and sales would increase tax revenues and further reduce the deficit to the point where it is no longer significant.

The remaining $50 billion in annual savings realized by ending the Cold War could fund an Urban Marshall Plan that develops our economic infrastructure, renews our cities, and moves people out of poverty.

There is little question that strengthening the nation's weakened infrastructure, both physical and human, is necessary for future growth. Repairing and modernizing roads, railways, bridges, ports, and air links are basic to economic well-being; all were deeply neglected during the 1980s.

But the major investments need to be in the human capital represented by the people at the margins of our society who can and must be drawn into the mainstream to become producers in a productive society. The world economy in the 1990s will be characterized by advancing technology and automation, and no company or country can survive in that environment without highly trained people with technical and communications skills.

We are competing with countries like Japan, where 94 percent of young people graduate from schools that provide advanced technical training and college preparation. In the U.S., our national dropout rate is over one-fourth, and over half in some major cities. While the Japanese make sure all their people get a sound education in the fundamentals, many of our high school graduates need remedial work in the basics.

Along with investments in education, government needs to invest in employment and training programs that work. Past programs were often ineffective;

present ones tend to skim the best-prepared while ignoring those most in need of training. Community-based institutions, in partnership with industry and government, can recruit and train tomorrow's work force.

There are other significant investments that must be made in our people—health, child care, housing, and other important needs can be met through carefully designed Urban Marshall Plan programs targeted to those most in need.

While some deride the so-called "peace dividend," or refuse to consider new government initiatives, it should be clear that America's future prosperity depends on making the investments necessary to provide opportunities to those denied them. In a world of diversity and many cultures, America's great strength lies in its own diversity as a multi-cultural nation. That strength represents a comparative advantage in today's world, and we need to capitalize on it through policies that enable all Americans to contribute to our society.

The thrust for racial parity is part of the process, and the decade of the 1990s is the time to complete the civil rights revolution of the 1960s.

Last November, in Montgomery, Alabama, a memorial carved in black granite was dedicated to the fallen martyrs of the civil rights struggle. They were shot, lynched, bombed, and mutilated because they dared to assert their constitutional rights as free Americans. Their sacrifices were not in vain, for African Americans have made enormous strides forward since the days of segregation and racist terrorism.

The state of black Americans in 1990 suggests that those gains have not been nearly enough; that while half of our people have made advances, the other half are mired in poverty, joblessness, and hardship. The dream that animated the civil rights movement of the past was not some progress, but equality; not improved conditions, but parity.

That dream of parity lives on, and the 1990s offer a window of opportunity in which it can be achieved. The convergence of such factors as the end of the Cold War, the realignment of the global economy, and the changing demographics of our nation's work force create conditions in which the moral imperative to close the racial gap is now also an economic imperative for America.

This edition of *The State of Black America* includes papers from outstanding scholars. Their independent evaluations are intended to inform and to stimulate, but their views do not necessarily reflect the positions or policies of the National Urban League. Our own summation and recommendations appear at the end of this report.

This *State of Black America,* like past ones, contributes to the nation's awareness of the reality of life within Black America and to the decision-making process in 1990. We express our gratitude to the authors.

Black Americans and the Courts: Has the Clock Been Turned Back Permanently?

Julius L. Chambers, Esq.

"One wonders whether the majority still believes that race discrimination—or, more accurately—race discrimination against non-whites—is a problem in our society, or even remembers that it ever was."—Justice Blackmun, dissenting on *Wards Cove v. Atonio*, June 5, 1989[1]

INTRODUCTION

For much of this century, black Americans have relied on the federal courts—especially the Supreme Court—for help in the battle against segregation and discrimination. During the last three decades in particular, the courts have set moral and legal standards that have been crucial to civil rights progress.

The *Brown v. Board of Education*[2] ruling helped to precipitate the dismantling of legally sanctioned segregation in the South, and contributed to the national dialogue on the status of black Americans that sparked the Civil Rights Act of 1964, the Voting Rights Act of 1965, the Fair Housing Act of 1968, and other important civil rights statutes.

In the 1970s, the Supreme Court upheld the constitutionality of race-conscious remedies designed to close economic and educational gaps between the races, and generally gave civil rights laws a liberal, remedial interpretation.[3] During the Reagan administration, the Supreme Court was often a bulwark against the Justice Department's efforts to undermine effective enforcement of civil rights laws and abolish many forms of affirmative relief for victims of discrimination, even though the Court's rulings were not always helpful to black Americans.[4]

However, during the Supreme Court's 1988-1989 term, more than a half-dozen rulings caused minorities and others to question whether the Court would continue to be an ally to the civil rights struggle. In one ruling after another, the Court erected a series of formidable barriers to blacks who must rely on the judicial system to protect them from employment discrimination. In doing so, the Court seemed to ignore both the bitter history and current practice of race discrimination in this country, as Justice Blackmun suggests in the memorable commentary that begins this chapter.

The decisions were so chilling that they have even prompted some to question whether the Court is still an appropriate forum to address the remaining

9

obstacles to equal rights and equal opportunities for black Americans, or even to preserve past gains. But I believe that to react to the rulings by foregoing the judicial system as a forum to effect social change and protect minority rights would not only be ill-advised—it would also be dangerous.

The resources and means available for minorities to address race discrimination—and its twin scourge, poverty—are woefully limited. This chapter will show that, given the limited tools available to us, and despite the Court's recent decisions, the judicial system remains an important forum to help black citizens achieve full participation in all aspects of American life.

After reviewing recent Supreme Court decisions related to employment discrimination and race-conscious remedies, the chapter surveys key legal developments in voting rights, housing, education, and the administration of criminal justice. Each section concludes with a suggested agenda that could help to accelerate the slow, painstaking process of translating constitutional principles into rights, and rights into realities.

SUPREME COURT REVIEW

Most of the 1988-1989 Supreme Court decisions that alarmed black Americans involved employment discrimination and race-based remedies. However, the tone of these rulings and their narrow interpretation of civil rights laws have prompted fears that eventually the Court will create new barriers to minority plaintiffs seeking equal justice in other areas of the law as well.

In a series of rulings, the Court reversed established case law that has evolved from the two most important congressional statutes protecting minority rights in the economic arena: Title VII of the 1964 Civil Rights Act, and section 1981 of the 1866 Civil Rights Act. Before reviewing the rulings, it is important to note the context in which these laws were enacted.

With legislation passed in 1866, 1871, and 1964, Congress acted with the specific, stated intention of addressing the pervasive problem of the exclusion of blacks and other minorities from America's economic mainstream. In interpreting these statutes during the last two decades, courts generally read them as remedial, giving them a broad, liberal interpretation in order to carry out the objectives of Congress.

For example, section 1981 of the 1866 Act prohibits race discrimination in the making and enforcement of contracts. In 1976, the Supreme Court in *Runyon v. McCrary*[5] ruled that this statute could be used to uphold sanctions against a private school that refused to admit blacks. Since then, lower courts have been virtually unanimous in construing section 1981 to forbid all forms of intentional discrimination in contractual relations, including those involving hiring, promotions, treatment of employees while on the job, and dismissals.

Another broad, liberal, and helpful reading of civil rights law was made by the Court in *Griggs v. Duke Power* (1971),[6] when it interpreted Title VII of the 1964 Civil Rights Act, which bars employment discrimination. In *Griggs,* the

Court held that Congress intended Title VII of the 1964 Civil Rights Act to prohibit not only intentional discrimination in employment, but also tests and other devices that disproportionately excluded minorities and women from jobs. Such tests and selection procedures were held to be lawful only when the employer could prove they were business necessities, i.e., essential to effective job performance or the operation of the business. The *Griggs* doctrine has resulted in both court-ordered and voluntary reforms of discriminatory employment practices by public and private employers throughout the country.

In 1988-1989, however, five members of the Supreme Court took a different approach. They did not give the language of civil rights laws the broad interpretation necessary to ensure that the statutes could meaningfully address many forms of discrimination and injustice in contemporary America. Instead, they interpreted the language narrowly, demanding explicit commands from Congress to remedy discrimination in highly specific situations, even situations that Congress could not have anticipated.

More ominously, the Court chose to overlook the problem of race discrimination that led Congress to enact civil rights statutes in the first place. In essence, it asked black plaintiffs to go back and prove the necessity of those statutes once again.

- In *Patterson v. McLean Credit Union*,[7] the Court ruled that section 1981 did not protect a black credit union employee named Brenda Patterson from blatant, on-the-job racial harassment. Ms. Patterson alleged that she had been subjected to abusive comments and treatment because of her race. For example, she was regularly required to do demeaning tasks that were never required of white employees with the same job description, and often given more work than white employees.

Yet, the Supreme Court held that section 1981 doesn't proscribe the on-the-job harassment suffered by Ms. Patterson; rather, the Court held that section 1981 "extends only to the formation of a contract, but not to the problems that may arise later from the conditions of continuing employment."[8] The Court also held that the statute doesn't prohibit discriminatory denials of promotions unless the promotions create "a new and distinct relation between the employer and the employee."[9]

This narrow definition of contractual relations has removed a valuable weapon from the civil rights arsenal. Although Title VII prohibits racial discrimination in the workplace, it limits relief to court injunctions and back pay. The 1866 Act is the only federal law that enables a victim of employment discrimination on the basis of race to sue an employer for damages—a prospective penalty that had effectively deterred racist harassment in the workplace. Now, that deterrent is gone.

Patterson has already had a disastrous effect on federal fair employment litigation. A recent study by the NAACP Legal Defense and Educational Fund shows that between June 15, 1989 (when the decision was announced) and

November 1, 1989, at least 96 employment discrimination claims were dismissed because of *Patterson*, without serious consideration of the merits of those claims.[10]

The problems are not limited to dismissal of the numerous harassment claims which previously would have been covered by section 1981. *Patterson* has also created considerable confusion and disagreement in the lower courts because the decision left unanswered a number of questions concerning the application of section 1981 to other employment practices, such as discharges, demotions, and retaliations.[11] This confusion, and the newly limited scope of the 1866 Act, will make it far more difficult for many victims of even overt race discrimination to get simple, rudimentary justice under federal employment laws. Of equal importance, the Court has removed a deterrent that had prompted many employers to abandon discriminatory practices voluntarily.

• In *Wards Cove Packing Co. v. Atonio,*[12] the Court nearly eviscerated the *Griggs* doctrine, as described above. It shifted the burden of proof in the cases covered by *Griggs* from the employer to the employees. In doing so, the Court made it much more difficult for discrimination victims to show that certain employment practices violated their rights.

Now, when there are statistical disparities between the races in a work force, the majority in *Wards Cove* suggests that it is the *victims* of those disparities who must identify all the criteria responsible for them. That is particularly true when those criteria are entirely subjective (such as an employer's claim that certain employees didn't fit into the "corporate culture"), rather than objective (such as standardized tests). Now, the minority plaintiffs may have to examine each component of an employer's hiring or promotion system in an attempt to show the precise, discriminatory effect of each practice as well as the lack of business justification—an extremely difficult and expensive undertaking.

And if the plaintiffs succeed in identifying the employment practice that disproportionately excludes minorities, now they may have to undertake the difficult task of proving a negative—that the challenged practice does not serve the legitimate employment goals of the employer.

The Court in *Wards Cove* has not only lightened considerably the employer's burden of justifying discriminatory employment practices, it has also placed substantially greater burdens of time and cost on Title VII plaintiffs.

• The Court further lightened the burden of proof an employer must meet when accused of employment discrimination in *Price Waterhouse v. Hopkins.*[13] It ruled that an employer may now escape liability altogether even when forbidden employment discrimination is found, if the employer offers some evidence that there was another, legitimate reason for its action. For example: an employer fires employee "X," not only because she is a black woman, but also because she didn't learn how to use the personal computer efficiently. Even if the first reason—the racist one—was the primary factor in the employer's decision, as long as the second reason is offered as an explanation, apparently the employer is on solid legal grounds. And the Court also made it easier for the employer to prove the legitimate reason for such a discriminatory practice—limiting the burden of proof the employer is required to meet.

One doesn't have to be a legal scholar to believe that the message *Price Waterhouse* sends to employers and minorities is "there is nothing wrong with a little racism or sexism, as long as it isn't the only thing on an employer's mind." I believe that absolutely nothing in today's civil rights laws suggests that Congress or the American people agree with this message.

* The Court has also posed new threats to affirmative action plans and other race-based remedies. In *Martin v. Wilks,*[14] the Court allowed white firefighters in Birmingham, Alabama, to challenge an affirmative action settlement that had been in effect since 1981. The affirmative action plan had been the only effective way to give blacks a fair chance at jobs and promotions in the same department which had turned its firehoses on civil rights demonstrators in the 1960s.

The *Wilks* ruling practically *invited* time-consuming challenges to long-established affirmative action settlements. As a result, employers will be less likely to establish voluntary affirmative action plans, since they will fear lawsuits by white employees.

Wilks is particularly troubling when it is viewed in the context of the Court's earlier decision on race-based remedies. In *City of Richmond v. J.A. Croson Co.,*[15] the Court rejected Richmond, Virginia's program which set aside 30 percent of city contracts for minority businesses. Before this program was instituted, minority contractors received fewer than one percent of the contracts offered by the city, although minorities constitute approximately 50 percent of Richmond's population.

Richmond was the cradle of the Confederacy, yet the Court in *Croson* held that not enough evidence had been shown to demonstrate that minorities had been discriminated against in city contracts. In so holding, the Court applied new, extremely strict requirements to cities or states attempting to establish or defend minority set-aside programs. For one thing, it requires a city or state to give much more evidence than was previously necessary about the history of discrimination in a specific industry before establishing such a program. It also requires that the set-aside program be narrowly tailored to address the identified discrimination.

While *Croson* did not gut minority set-asides entirely, the decision has made it much more difficult and costly to plan, implement, and defend such programs. As a result, the ruling already has had an alarming, adverse effect on minority businesses and set-aside programs. As of December 15, 1989, the set-aside programs in five jurisdictions failed to meet judicial approval under the standards established in *Croson.* Seventeen states or cities have either voluntarily terminated or suspended minority set-asides because of the ruling. Nationally, some 236 state and local programs are in jeopardy.[16]

- On the same day the Court ruled on the *Wilks* case, it also ruled on *Lorance v. AT&T Technologies, Inc.*[17] When viewed together, the rulings demonstrate inconsistencies that seem explicable only in racial or sexist terms.

Lorance involved a seniority system which discriminated against women. Logically enough, the women in that case did not file their complaints against the seniority policy until the policy harmed them, several years after the system was adopted. Yet, the Court held that the women had to bring their claims within 300 days after the adoption of the system.

So the women in *Lorance* were expected to meet a strict deadline. Yet, apparently, there was *no* deadline for the white firefighters in *Wilks*, who had filed their claim against an employment policy that had been adopted in 1981.[18] The apparent double standard is not merely unfair—it is astonishing.

The net result of this decision could be that minorities and women will be forced to file Title VII complaints whenever there is a change in an employment policy that might have been adopted with discriminatory intent—even if they do not know that the policy will harm them in the future.

- Finally, the Court put severe clamps on the resources available to assist victims of employment discrimination who wish to have their day in court. The Court had previously restricted the costs which plaintiffs could recover in employment discrimination proceedings. It held in *Crawford Fittings v. J.T. Gibbons*[19] that fees for expert witnesses, who are usually essential in these cases, cannot be recovered. In the previous term, in *Independent Federation of Flight Attendants v. Zipes,*[20] the Court held that plaintiffs may not recover attorneys' fees if they successfully defend a challenge to a settlement of a Title VII case by intervening white employees.

In short, if a private attorney runs the gauntlet and successfully meets the stricter standards for establishing liability that now exist, his chances of recovering fees for his time are limited, and he cannot recover the costs necessary for putting his case together.[21]

What Is To Be Done

The recent decisions by the Court suggest that: it no longer favors employment discrimination claims; it will require stringent standards for establishing liability of an employer; it will limit the relief available; and it will discourage private attorneys who seek to represent victims of discrimination.

These rulings prompted Justice Thurgood Marshall, in a recent speech, to suggest that the Supreme Court is no longer a friend to civil rights. He said that while we need not and should not give up on the Court, we must realize that the Court has changed, and we must also consider other forums. He advised us to bring pressure on all branches of state and federal governments, urging them to undertake the civil rights battles that must still be won.[22]

Each of the Court's decisions discussed above can be corrected with legislation. Since the Court found some language in the civil rights laws of the past century to be vague and insufficient to prohibit clearly certain forms of discrimination, it is certainly possible for new, congressional legislation to clarify and strengthen that language. It is also possible for Congress to act under the power given to it by post-Civil War constitutional amendments to address the questions and issues raised in *City of Richmond v. Croson*. Efforts are currently underway in Congress to draft such legislation and to gain the endorsement of the president for new civil rights statutes.

In addition, the rulings have prompted a flurry of activities by civil rights attorneys who are shaping new litigation strategies. Even without new legislation, a great many legal options are being explored that could protect the rights of Title VII plaintiffs and others affected by the rulings.

VOTING RIGHTS

The ability of black Americans to have their concerns heard and addressed in the halls of government has increased dramatically since passage of the Voting Rights Act of 1965. Registration of eligible black voters went from 25 percent in 1965 to more than 64 percent in 1988. The number of black elected officials has increased from fewer than 200 before the enactment of the Voting Rights Act to more than 7,200 as of January, 1989.[23]

Despite this progress, there are still significant barriers to black political empowerment and representation. These obstacles include restrictive registration systems and electoral practices that dilute minority voting strength by submerging black votes in a larger pool of white votes, e.g., at-large elections, multi-member districts, and majority-vote requirements.

In 1982, Congress provided an important tool to address these electoral schemes and requirements when it amended Section II of the Voting Rights Act. The amendment requires no proof of intentional discrimination, only discriminatory *results*, for voting requirements and practices to be illegal. In 1986, the Supreme Court affirmed this "results" standard in *Thornburgh v. Gingles,*[24] which greatly simplified the legal standards for proving unlawful discrimination in voting practices.

Since then, Section II has been used successfully to broaden the application of the Voting Rights Act to a wide variety of electoral practices. For example, because of Section II litigation, at-large elections have been ruled illegal in a broad range of jurisdictions, from Springfield, Illinois,[25] to Norfolk, Virginia.[26] Section II has also been extended in recent years to judicial elections, which are held in 31 states, many of which sanction electoral practices that result in the near-segregation of state court judgeships. In the last three years, courts have ruled unequivocally that the "results" test in Section II was violated by judicial electoral practices in Mississippi,[27] Texas,[28] and Louisiana.[29] However, in *Chisom v. Roemer*, after an appellate court ruled that Section II applied to the election of judges to Louisiana's

Supreme Court, a district court ruled that the evidence presented by black plaintiffs did not establish a violation. The case is on appeal.[30]

In a historic ruling in December, 1989, an appellate court held that Section II applied to majority-vote requirements in primary elections in Phillips County, Arkansas. The case, *Whitfield v. Clinton*, was the first to challenge successfully majority-vote requirements as a Section II violation. In Phillips County, where blacks constitute 47 percent of the voting age population, black candidates for several county posts have finished first four times in Democratic primary elections. But because they didn't win more than 50 percent of the votes, they were forced into run-off elections against white candidates, which they lost because of the high degree of racial bloc voting in that county. In the *Whitfield* ruling,[31] the appellate court ruled that the county's majority-vote requirement violated Section II. Ten other states—or subdivisions within 10 states—have majority-vote requirements.[32] This ruling may be helpful in limiting such practices in those states.

Another significant barrier to effective black political representation is the extremely restrictive voter registration system in many states. For example, in many jurisdictions, citizens can only register to vote at county courthouses during business hours. Since many economically disadvantaged blacks lack adequate transportation or are unable to take time off from work without loss of wages, such a system makes it extremely difficult for them to register. Blacks in some states are still exposed to subtle harassment, intimidation, and inconveniences when they attempt to register.

The presidential candidacy of Jesse Jackson, the recent ascendancy of other black elected officials, and the tireless registration efforts of many civil rights activists have played an important role in increasing black voter registration. But legal challenges to restrictive registration systems could be another important tool for this purpose.

For example, largely as a result of the kinds of restrictive practices described above, the black registration rate in Mississippi is only 54 percent of the eligible population, while the white registration rate is 79 percent of the eligible population. In 1987, the registration system in Mississippi was held illegal under Section II in *Mississippi State Chapter, Operation PUSH v. Allain*,[33] the first successful challenge of registration systems under that statute. The parties involved in the case are now attempting to devise an appropriate remedy.

What Is To Be Done

Some of the progress described above could be threatened by the 1990 census, which will determine the boundary lines of congressional and state legislative districts as well as local governments. A study by the Southern Regional Council predicts that "without a miraculous change in population trends or a surprising legal development, the 1990 census will . . . distribute political power away from urban and rural areas to suburbs . . . and away from some predominantly black districts to white-controlled districts. . . . These shifts could likely reduce the number of House members who support legislation favoring the poor [and] civil rights."[34]

Thus, in addition to continuing and expanding legal challenges to discriminatory electoral and registration practices that are barriers to black political empowerment, black Americans must monitor vigilantly the reapportionment that will take place in 1990. They must be active in the state legislative process that determines district boundaries.

Another mechanism for minority involvement in the reapportionment process is provided by Section IV of the Voting Rights Act. This statute requires certain jurisdictions with a history of discrimination in voting practices to submit all changes in election laws and procedures to the Justice Department for review and pre-clearance. After district boundaries are determined in state legislatures, the Justice Department will have thousands of jurisdictions submitting district plans. The Department will have 60 days to review the plans and receive comments from eligible voters. Active participation from civil rights activists in this review process will be essential.

HOUSING

Twenty-two years after passage of the Fair Housing Act of 1968, housing in the United States continues to be characterized by a high degree of racial segregation. Studies based on the 1980 census show that the average level of residential segregation between blacks and whites has declined by only seven percent in the nation's 25 largest cities since 1950.[35] This segregated housing pattern is one of the root causes of a great many associated problems, such as racially isolated schools.

Housing segregation obviously has a variety of causes, but there is considerable evidence that continuing race discrimination plays an important role in perpetuating it. In 1987, the Department of Housing and Urban Development (HUD) estimated that more than two million instances of housing discrimination were still occurring every year.[36]

The 1968 Act (Title VIII) banned most forms of housing discrimination, but its enforcement provisions proved to be too weak to address effectively this stubborn problem.[37] For example, HUD could do little more than negotiate settlements when it received housing discrimination complaints.[38] Furthermore, the Attorney General was authorized to file suits only when there was a "pattern or practice" of discrimination, or in cases that raised "an issue of general importance."[39] Thus, private litigants bore the lion's share of the burden of enforcing Title VIII. But largely because of the time and effort necessary to file such suits—and the limited damages available—during the last 20 years, an average of only 20 housing cases per year has been reported in federal courts.[40]

Recognizing that new enforcement mechanisms were essential to combat housing discrimination, Congress passed the Fair Housing Amendments Act of 1988.[41] The 1988 Amendments to the Act are the most important development in housing discrimination law in 20 years, and could help to fulfill the long overdue promise of fair housing for minorities and other Americans. The new law adds families with children and the handicapped to groups protected under the law, adds new enforcement provisions, and makes other significant improvements to Title VIII.

Under the new law, HUD can issue a charge based on a housing complaint and have it heard by an administrative law judge (ALJ). Among other things, the ALJ can impose civil penalties and can award compensatory damages.[42] Complainants can also bypass the ALJ and go to federal district court, where they will be represented by the Justice Department.[43] The 1988 Act also speeds up the hearing process in housing cases.[44] In addition, it expands the Justice Department's ability to file housing cases on its own and broadens the remedies in such cases.

The 1988 Act provides an impressive array of new legal tools for challenging housing discrimination, and it has already prompted a dramatic increase in new complaints to HUD. In the eight months between mid-March and mid-November, 1989, 5,418 housing discrimination complaints were filed with HUD—in contrast to 4,000 complaints during all of 1987.[45]

However, these complaints have created a backlog in an agency whose budget was slashed by about two-thirds under President Reagan. As of December, 1989, only 19 complaints have been determined to have "reasonable cause" by HUD, and have gone before either administrative law judges or federal district courts.[46]

The new Housing Act has also increased the Justice Department's workload. The Department filed 24 new cases between March 12, 1989, and September 30, 1989—more cases in six months than in any fiscal year during the 1980s.[47]

No discussion of housing and black Americans would be complete without reference to the decreasing availability of affordable, low-income housing. The decline in low-income housing stock has many causes—including gentrification, neglect by private landlords—but it was exacerbated by the low priority given to the construction and maintenance of public housing by the Reagan administration. Between 1980 and 1988, federal spending on housing was reduced from $30 billion to $7.7 billion.[48] There were only 6,000 authorized public-housing units constructed in 1987, as opposed to 33,000 units in 1981.[49] Housing advocates have shown the direct connection between these federal policies and America's homeless epidemic, which has hit minority communities particularly hard.[50]

The Bush administration's recent $7 billion, low-income housing program is certainly a step in the right direction, but it is mainly concerned with stimulating the renovation of existing housing[51]—not the construction of the new housing that is needed to solve the housing crisis for millions of indigent Americans.

What Is To Be Done

Thus far, the serious backlog of complaints filed at HUD under the 1988 Act has caused many private fair housing groups and housing discrimination victims to take their cases to court without HUD's help.[52] There has been only an incremental improvement in the actual enforcement of fair housing laws since the Act went into effect.

But the tools for effective enforcement are in place, and we must ensure that these tools are utilized. The civil rights community must play an active role in monitoring the fair housing enforcement activities of HUD and the Justice Department.

In addition, even in a time of federal budgetary constraints, the black community must press HUD and the Bush administration to create a comprehensive program that will make more federally supported housing available to low-income Americans.

EDUCATION

As the 1990s begin, more black children attend racially isolated schools than at any time since the early 1970s.[53] The increasing resegregation of America's public schools deepens the isolation of black children not only on the basis of race, but also on the basis of economic class—since poor black schoolchildren are increasingly segregated from middle-class blacks as well as whites. Racially isolated schools are often neglected and lack the resources and programs needed to address the special educational problems associated with poverty.[54]

Yet, rather than trying to prevent resegregation and foster the integration of America's public schools, the Justice Department under President Reagan openly tried to undermine many court-ordered integration plans. For example, in February, 1988, the Department announced a campaign to dismiss nearly 300 school desegregation suits and dissolve injunctions requiring school districts to maintain desegregation.

The pretext for the federal action was that these school districts had attained "unitary status"—which means courts consider that the districts have eliminated past discrimination and are operating desegregated schools. Once school districts are declared unitary, the Justice Department has argued that they no longer have the legal duty to eliminate the vestiges of their racially dual school systems; they can literally ignore the lingering effects that decades of discrimination have had on black children; and they can easily return to the segregated patterns of the past.

The Justice Department under Bush has continued this case-closing campaign, although with only limited success thus far, as litigation continues on a district-by-district basis. In several cases in 1989, black plaintiffs have prevented a return to "neighborhood school" plans that would lead to resegregation, or have obtained further relief to eliminate continuing segregation and discrimination in school systems. Some of these school districts include Oklahoma City, Oklahoma;[55] DeKalb County, Georgia;[56] Duval County, Florida;[57] Natchez, Mississippi;[58] Jackson, Tennessee;[59] and Topeka, Kansas.[60]

However, black parents and schoolchildren attempting to preserve past gains have certainly not met with success across the country in recent years. In 1986, the Supreme Court declined to consider an appeal of a court order permitting Norfolk, Virginia, to return to neighborhood schools—a plan which has resulted in nearly a dozen, virtually all-black schools.[61] If this principle is finally approved by the Court, civil rights attorneys involved with education fear that more school districts will emulate Norfolk.

It is quite likely that in its 1990-1991 term, the Supreme Court will consider the question of precisely when a school district has finally dismantled a formerly segregated system and what obligations, if any, remain for such school systems. In two currently pending cases involving Yonkers, New York,[62] and Kansas City, Missouri,[63] the Court will consider the limits on federal authority to direct funding of desegregation efforts.

Efforts to improve opportunities for blacks in colleges and universities were dealt a setback in 1988-1989, as the Department of Education released seven southern and border states from further obligations to increase minority participation in higher education or to improve historically black colleges. Those states are no longer required to provide enhancements to historically black colleges, to recruit black students and faculty to historically white colleges, to eliminate the disparities in college enrollment between the races, and to improve graduation rates for black students. The litigation that required those actions, *Adams v. Cavazos*, has been derailed during appeals pending since 1987.[64]

Steps to increase minority participation in higher education are also likely to be presented to the Supreme Court soon. For example, in a Louisiana case, the Court may decide what specific steps a state must take in order to eliminate the vestiges of segregation in higher education.[65]

It is much too early to predict whether the resegregation and lack of equal educational opportunity in America's schools eventually will be sanctioned by our judicial system. In the meantime, while litigation continues on desegregation issues, other legal options could address educational problems in Black America.

What Is To Be Done

It is imperative that black Americans continue efforts to stave off the resegregation of America's public schools, using the *Brown* ruling and the cases that have evolved from it. While this battle continues, more attention also must be focused on a fundamental right that is as crucial as any of the legal rights black Americans have won since *Brown*: the right to a minimally adequate education.

Educators have begun to develop working definitions of what, at a minimum, schools must provide. At a minimum, they must ensure that students reach young adulthood with the ability to read and write. At a minimum, they must identify students who need remediation and special counseling in order to gain the skills necessary to compete at some level in America's economic arena.[66]

The educational reform movement that has captured the nation's attention could help to ensure that new state laws mandate this adequate education. Prompted by this movement, state commissions and legislatures have proposed and enacted literally hundreds of educational reform initiatives in recent years, including those which enunciate and define state standards for education.[67] We must ensure that these legislative initiatives address the special problems that minorities and the poor bring to America's school systems. Adequate resources and services must be provided to ensure that disadvantaged students have a fair chance to meet educational standards as defined by the states.

In addition, we might find greater relief in the state courts. For example, 48 state constitutions recognize the right to an education. These constitutional provisions may reasonably be construed to require state legislatures to provide for public school systems of a specific quality. We must explore the use of such education clauses to help enforce the provision of adequate education to economically disadvantaged minority students. An important step in this direction was taken by the Texas Supreme Court, in *Edgewood Independent School District v. Kirby* (October, 1989),[68] when the court ruled that education is a fundamental right and that the state must equalize disparate funding between poor and affluent school districts.

ADMINISTRATION OF CRIMINAL JUSTICE/CAPITAL PUNISHMENT

Some of the most important recent developments affecting blacks and the criminal justice system were related to capital punishment. Americans may have differences of opinion about the wisdom and morality of the death penalty. But surely even those in favor of capital punishment want to ensure that racism is never a factor in its application, and that black death-row inmates—who are 40 percent of the condemned population[69]—get the same legal protections as white defendants. Yet racism in the application of the death penalty has now become virtually unchallengeable because of two developments.

In *McClesky v. Kemp*[70] (1987), the Supreme Court was presented with overwhelming evidence of race discrimination in the application of Georgia's death penalty. Data showed that when a white person was murdered, the likelihood that the accused murderer would be sentenced to death was more than four times greater than when a black person was murdered.[71] Yet, the Court held that racial bias in capital sentencing cannot be proven through statistical documentation. Rather, defendants must prove purposeful discrimination by prosecutors, jurors, or judges on a case-by-case basis—a burden of proof that can be met only in rare instances.

Another unfortunate development is the increasing reluctance of federal courts to overturn death sentences imposed in state trials that *clearly* violate the defendant's constitutional rights. Increasingly, courts in the capital review process are less concerned with the substance of justice and more concerned with the states' interests in the finality of death sentences. And that trend, together with *McClesky*, has made it extremely difficult to challenge racial bias in death sentences.

For example, in 1978, Alton Waye, a black man, was tried for the rape and murder of a white woman in Virginia. The trial took place in a rural county courthouse where there was still a memorial to Confederate soldiers and "the cause for which they fought." The trial judge was a wealthy landowner known for sentencing blacks to probation on condition that they work free for his white farmer friends. During Mr. Waye's trial, the judge constantly reminded the jury (10 whites and two blacks) of the "racial problem" underlying the case—i.e., a black man raping a white woman—and referred to Mr. Waye and black witnesses as "colored" or "boy."

The racist environment in which Mr. Waye was tried was never complained about during the trial. Neither were numerous constitutional violations, notably the withholding of evidence from the jury which suggested that Mr. Waye was not the murderer. For example, the prosecutor failed to reveal—though the Constitution required it—that the physical evidence collected at the crime scene, when accurately analyzed, pointed more directly to another man as the murderer; and that this other man was seen with a particular knife shortly before the crime, a knife which was found in the victim's bed after the crime.[72]

Yet, none of these serious violations was known or complained about until Mr. Waye's case was in the federal courts for a second—and final—appeal. By then, no court would even *consider* the issues. Standard procedure dictated that Mr. Waye's counsel should have raised these issues earlier in the appeals process. His failure to do so was the paramount concern, not the egregious injustices Mr. Waye had suffered in what passed for a trial. Mr. Waye was executed in August, 1989.[73]

Unfortunately, the NAACP Legal Defense Fund's Capital Punishment Project has dozens of examples of capital trials with examples of racial bias or other constitutional violations that were not addressed during trial and direct appeals.

Despite this alarming trend in the capital review process, it is still a potentially important way to ensure that lives are not taken simply because of lawyers' mistakes—mistakes often made because of the grossly inadequate legal representation available to indigent capital defendants. Yet, adequate federal review of death sentences has been further threatened by the recommendations of a committee of federal judges who recently advised Congress to impose strict new limits on the multiple appeals currently available to inmates on death row.

The committee, headed by retired Supreme Court Justice Lewis Powell, has proposed that a death-row inmate would have only six months to file a petition in federal court after his direct appeal has been heard in state court. A stay of execution would be in effect during those six months. After that, the federal court would be precluded from granting relief in a second petition or from entering another stay, except in highly unusual circumstances.[74]

The Powell proposal is almost exclusively concerned with speeding up the convictions process. It fails to address adequately another serious problem: the failure of many states to provide competent legal counsel to indigent capital defendants. And it does not ensure that constitutional claims which were not raised at the trial or on appeal will be reviewed before someone is executed. A vocal "death penalty lobby" is trying to turn the Powell Committee's proposals into law. Senator Strom Thurmond (R-SC) has introduced these recommendations as his own bill.[75]

What Is To Be Done

Several legislative options exist which could help to protect black defendants from racial bias in the application of the death penalty. For example, in direct response to the *McClesky* decision, the Racial Justice Act has been introduced in Congress. It would allow an individual to challenge his or her death sentence if statistical evidence showed that it was part of a racially biased pattern of sentencing.

To encourage adequate federal review of death sentences, an alternative to Senator Thurmond's bill (described above) has been introduced by Senator Joseph Biden (D-DE). While providing for greater efficiency in the appeals process, it would also ensure that federal courts have the ability to address racial bias and other constitutional violations when reviewing capital sentences.[76]

These bills attempt to provide at least a semblance of justice and protection to those on death row, many of whom are black, virtually all of whom are poor. While such legislative options are pursued, another objective should be to ensure that states provide independent, competent, and adequately compensated attorneys to capital defendants throughout the trial and appeals process—an obligation the Supreme Court placed on states over 50 years ago in the "Scottsboro Boys" case,[77] yet one that too many states refuse to honor.

CONCLUSION

This chapter has detailed some serious setbacks to black Americans who traditionally have used the judicial system to move closer to the goals of equal rights, equal opportunities, and equal protection under the law.

The ability of some key civil rights statutes to protect blacks from employment discrimination and to remedy that discrimination has been limited severely by a new, conservative Supreme Court majority. The protracted assault of the Reagan administration on court-ordered school desegregation has continued under President Bush. The racist, arbitrary application of capital punishment is increasingly difficult to challenge in the courts.

Yet, it would be a mistake for black Americans to assume that the clock has been turned back permanently in America's courts. While recent Supreme Court rulings have sent an ominous message to minorities, this message is not necessarily the last word on their rights in the workplace. A number of legislative and litigation strategies are being explored that could at least mitigate the potentially disastrous effects of these decisions. Similar strategies have the potential to afford stronger legal protections to capital defendants—protections that, ultimately, will help to safeguard other legal rights that are crucial to minorities. In addition, there have been some promising developments in voting rights, housing, and education that should not be overlooked in an evaluation of black Americans and the law.

Past gains are certainly threatened. But these setbacks need not be permanent, as Black America continues its ongoing struggle for equal justice and equal rights.

The Economic Status of Black Americans During the 1980s: A Decade of Limited Progress

David H. Swinton, Ph.D.

INTRODUCTION

As the 1990s open, it seems appropriate to take a retrospective look at the decade now concluding. The 1980s was an eventful decade. It began with the deepest recession of the post-war period and concluded with the longest peacetime recovery. The role of government in promoting social policy was sharply curtailed and the largest tax decrease was enacted. The twin deficits—budget and balance of trade—reached astronomical heights. The U.S. went from being the world's banker to being the world's largest debtor nation. Major changes took place in the structure of the American economy as the structural transformation from a goods-producing to a service economy continued. Society continued to change as the proportion of single-parent and never-married households continued to rise, and the role of women in the workplace continued to expand. The drug epidemic reached major proportions. Finally, as the decade closed, the geopolitical structure appeared to be undergoing a major change as the movement for freedom and democracy appeared to be transforming the Soviet empire.

Despite the momentous changes taking place in other arenas during the 1980s, the movement to gain economic equality for blacks stalled. Of course as has been pointed out in this volume previously, the stagnation of progress against racial inequality had already begun as we entered the 1980s. In the late seventies the counterattack against affirmative action effectively ended any active strategy to promote racial equality through public policy and collective action. The 1980s heralded a new era in which the personal efforts of individual blacks became the major strategy to promote racial equality. Freedom, personal responsibility, self-help, and *laissez faire* became the new watchwords for the neoconservative strategy to promote greater racial equality in economic life.

Although all of the data are not yet in, it is apparent that this new strategy failed the group as a whole. The 1980s will be recorded as a decade during which progress towards racial equality in economic life for black Americans as a group came to a grinding halt. Indeed, although there is some variation in the trends by region and class, the overall degree of racial inequality in American economic life remained high and may even have increased during the decade.

In the ensuing pages of this essay, we will present the data for the 1980s to support this conclusion. The facts will paint a clear picture of persisting racial inequality in all aspects of economic life. The racial gaps are very large and in most cases have grown over the decade. This is generally true of each measure of economic well-being that we examine. Indeed, the evidence supporting the case for little or no progress in increasing the degree of racial equality in economic life during the 1980s is so overwhelming as to be incontrovertible.

Although the primary purpose of this essay is to present the facts concerning the economic status of blacks during the 1980s, we will also discuss the reasons for the limited progress against racial inequality in economic affairs. The main argument to be advanced in this discussion is that little progress was made in reducing racial inequality because little progress was made in reducing the gaps in wealth, human capital, and economic power that are the main generators of racial inequality in economic life. The neoconservative strategy of *laissez faire* is not enough to bring about significant reductions in racial inequality, given the realities of present-day American economic life.

The paper will conclude with a brief look at prospects for making greater progress in reducing racial inequality in America during the next decade. The major point of this discussion will be that progress against racial inequality will depend on adopting more active and interventionist policies. The discussion will advance the concept of reparations as the basis for more effective policies.

OVERVIEW OF RACIAL INEQUALITY IN ECONOMIC LIFE DURING THE 1980s

Our exploration of racial inequality in economic status will rely primarily on data collected by the U.S. Bureau of the Census. The data to describe the socioeconomic status of groups are collected monthly in the Current Population Survey. Labor market data are collected every month, while income, poverty, and other data are collected only once a year. Since the data are collected from a sample, they are subject to sampling variations. Small year-to-year changes in subcomponents of the data may be attributed to chance variation in the sample. Thus, our concern is primarily with the overall pattern.

In the tables accompanying this discussion of the trends during the 1980s, we will present data for selected years only in the interest of saving space. We will almost always use data for the latest year available and selected other years. We frequently use 1982 because this was the deepest point of the recession. We will also sometimes display data for 1970 and 1978 to have a point of comparison with the 1970s. In any event, the data discussed will be sufficient to provide a general picture of the trends being discussed.

Trends in Per Capita and Aggregate Income

Table 1 contains some summary data on aggregate and per capita or per-person income. As can be seen, in absolute terms, aggregate black income and per-capita black income have risen over the decade. Aggregate black income in 1988 was 242 billion dollars, while per-person income was $8,271. Per capita

Table 1
Per Capita Income, Aggregate Income,
And Income Gaps, Selected Years
(1988$)

	Aggregate Black Income	Per Capita Income			Parity Gap	
		Black	White	B/W	Per Capita	Aggregate
1988	$242 Billion	$8,271	$13,896	0.595	$5,625	$165 Bil
1987	234 Billion	7,961	13,687	0.582	5,726	168 Bil
1986	226 Billion	7,779	13,332	0.583	5,553	161 Bil
1982	179 Billion	6,571	11,679	0.563	5,108	139 Bil
1978	183 Billion	7,319	12,333	0.593	5,014	126 Bil
1970	137 Billion	5,699	10,226	0.557	4,527	105 Bil

Source: U.S. Department of Commerce, Bureau of the Census, *Money Income and Poverty Status in 1988,* Table 16. Calculations of aggregates and gaps done by author.

income for blacks and whites reached all-time highs in 1988. The recovery clearly made up for the lost ground of the early 1980s and had surpassed the peak per-capita income years of the late 1970s.

However, the racial equality did not improve at all during the 1980s by the per-capita income measure, as whites made even greater gains in per capita income than did blacks. The last three columns of Table 1 show three measures of racial equality. B/W is the ratio of black-to-white per capita income. As can be seen, this measure was less than .60 throughout the decade. Thus, blacks typically had less than 60 cents in income for every dollar of income whites had. Moreover, for most of the 1980s, this ratio was below the peak period of the 1970s. Only during the last year, 1988, did the degree of equality by this measure match the peak levels of the 1970s.

The per-capita parity gap shows how much less income is available for each black person on the average than is available to each white person. As is readily apparent, this absolute per-person gap has expanded for each year during the 1980s except during 1988. At the end of the decade, the annual income available on average for each black man, woman, and child, was $5,625 less than was available to the average white. In 1988, this amounted to an aggregate parity gap of 165 billion dollars for the black community as a whole. This aggregate parity gap had also increased each year of the 1980s and was considerably larger than it was during the 1970s. Thus, it is apparent that no progress was made during the 1980s in reducing racial inequality in per capita income.

Trends in Family Income

The data displayed in Table 2 for family income reveal a very similar pattern. The difference here is that median family income for blacks in the 1980s was considerably below their median family income in the 1970s. Even in 1988, after the longest recovery in post-war history, median family income for blacks was still below the 1978 level by about 400 dollars.

Table 2
Median Family Income
Selected Years
(1988$)

| | Median Family Income | | | | Aggregate* |
	Black	White	B/W	B/W	Gap
1988	$19,329	$33,915	57.0	$14,586	$111 Billion
1987	19,168	33,725	56.8	14,557	107 Billion
1986	19,001	33,255	57.1	14,254	104 Billion
1985	18,455	32,051	57.6	13,596	99 Billion
1982	16,670	30,161	55.3	13,491	91 Billion
1980	18,196	31,447	57.9	13,251	83 Billion
1978	19,739	33,327	59.2	13,588	80 Billion
1970	19,144	31,209	61.3	12,065	61 Billion

*Equals (Mean White Family Income – Mean Black Family Income) × Number of Black Families

Source: U.S. Department of Commerce, Bureau of the Census, *Money Income and Poverty Status in 1988,* Table 7. Calculations of aggregates and gaps done by author.

Not only was there no absolute improvement in median family income during the 1980s, but it is also clear that inequality expanded. Black families typically had around 57 cents for every dollar available to white families during the 1980s. The ratio of black median family income to white media family income generally declined during the 1980s. This ratio was only 57.0 in 1988 compared to 57.9 in 1980 and 61.3 in 1970. The absolute gap between black and white median family income was $14,586 in 1988, which is considerably higher than the absolute gap was at any point during the 1970s. In the aggregate, black families had over 111 billion fewer dollars in 1988 than did white families. This aggregate also increased steadily across the decade of the 1980s. By this measure at least, black-white inequality has clearly increased.

Table 3 gives another perspective on income inequality. Here, income distribution data are shown for 1978 and 1988. As can be seen, the black income distribution shifted over this period. The proportion of black families with very low income increased. The proportion with income under $5,000 increased from 8.1 percent in 1978 to 11.9 percent in 1988. Likewise, the proportion with less than ten-thousand dollars income increased from 25.6 percent to 27.3 percent. We should also note that the 1988 figures were the lowest proportion of black families with low income since 1982. The proportion of white families receiving less than five-thousand dollars income also increased since 1978. However, this increase was only from 2.4 percent to 3.0 percent, while the proportion with less than ten thousand dollars was the same in 1978 and 1988. Thus, the disparity between the proportion of white families receiving low incomes increased during the 1980s. For example, while black families were about 3.4 times more likely to receive incomes under $5,000 in 1978, they were almost 4.0 times more likely to receive such low incomes in 1988. The higher rate of receipt of incomes less than $5,000 means that an extra 659,000 black families had such low incomes during 1988.

Table 3
Percentage of Black Families
Receiving Incomes In Selected Ranges

	1988 Blk	1988 Wht	1987 Blk	1987 Wht	1986 Blk	1986 Wht	1978 Blk	1978 Wht	1970 Blk	1970 Wht
Under $5,000	11.9	3.0	12.6	3.0	12.5	3.1	8.1	2.4	8.4	2.3
Less Than $10,000	27.3	8.5	28.5	8.7	28.0	9.1	25.6	8.5	24.6	8.0
$10,000– 34,999	46.7	43.2	46.9	43.3	47.5	44.2	51.2	47.7	56.3	45.4
More Than $35,000	25.9	48.4	24.6	47.8	24.4	46.7	23.3	43.8	19.2	46.6
More Than $50,000	12.6	27.4	10.8	26.8	10.8	25.8	10.0	21.1	6.1	23.2

	1980 Blk	1980 Wht
Under $5,000	10.1	2.6
Less Than $10,000	27.4	9.0
$10,000– 34,999	51.9	48.0
More Than $35,000	20.7	43.0
More Than $50,000	8.0	21.0

Note: Totals may not equal to 100.0 due to rounding.

Source: U.S. Department of Commerce, Bureau of the Census, *Money Income and Poverty Status in 1988,* Table 7-7.

At the other end of the income distribution, the proportion of white families with incomes greater than $35,000 increased more rapidly than the proportion of black families with such incomes between 1978 and 1988. During this period, the percent of blacks with such high incomes increased from 23.3 percent to 25.9 percent, while the percent of whites increased from 43.8 percent to 48.4 percent. Similarly, the proportion of black families with incomes greater than $50,000 increased from 10.0 percent to 12.6 percent, while the proportion of white families in this bracket increased from 21.1 percent to 27.4 percent. Thus, in 1988, 1.1 million fewer black families had incomes above $50,000 than would have had such incomes if parity existed. The degree of inequality also increased at the highest income levels during the 1980s as well.

It is interesting to note that the 1980s saw a reversal of the trend of declining proportions of black families receiving very low incomes that occurred throughout the 1970s. At the same time, since the end of the deep recession, there has been a resumption in the slow growth of the proportion of black families receiving high incomes. Thus, there has been a divergence in the structure of income received by black families. This divergence was also apparent for white family income. However, the trend was more attenuated for blacks, since fewer white families fell into the low-income category and larger proportions rose to the high-income category. In any case, the middle-income group has gotten smaller for both races, and the inequality in the two distributions has increased.

Black families throughout the family income distribution are disadvantaged in comparison to similarly situated white families. This is shown by the data presented in Table 4. As can be seen, in 1988, black families in the lowest quintile had an upper limit that was only 42.5 percent of the corresponding upper limit for whites. This ratio increased as one went up the income distribution at least until the highest income levels were reached. However, black families still need only 70.2 percent as much income to make the top five percent of their income distribution as white families do to make it into the top five percent of their income distribution. It is interesting to note that the upper limits of the three lowest white quintiles all generally equal or exceed the upper limits of the next highest black quintiles. For example, all blacks in the third quintile of the black family income distribution would fall completely within the second quintile of the white income distribution. Inequality clearly was great throughout the family income distribution in 1988.

As shown in the table, this general pattern has persisted since 1970. For the 1980s taken as a whole, there was no progress in closing the gap between black and white family income at any point on the income distribution. In fact, as measured by the ratios of black-to-white quintile limits, inequality generally increased during the 1980s and was generally somewhat higher than it was during the 1970s. The relative level of inequality at all points of the income distribution was higher in 1988 than it was in 1970 and 1980. It is also interesting to note that the absolute level of income going to the lower quintiles

Table 4
Income at Selected Positions of the Income Distribution
1970, 1980, 1988 By Race (Constant 1988 Dollars)

		1988		
		Black	White	Blk/Wht
Upper Limit of				
Lowest Fifth		$ 7,148	$16,814	42.5
Second		14,400	28,000	51.4
Third		24,425	40,000	61.1
Fourth		40,300	57,350	70.3
Lower Limit of Top 5%		65,927	93,900	70.2

1970			1980		
Black	White	Blk/Wht	Black	White	Blk/Wht
$ 9,054	$16,756	.54	$ 8,511	$16,238	.52
15,983	26,588	.60	15,219	26,478	.57
24,069	35,619	.68	25,023	36,584	.68
35,646	48,532	.73	38,477	50,825	.76
56,428	75,927	.74	62,311	79,252	.79

Source: David Swinton, "The Economic Status of the Black Population," Table 3, page 93, in *The State of Black America 1983* (New York: National Urban League); U.S. Department of Commerce, Bureau of the Census, *Money Income and Poverty Status in 1988,* Table 5.

has declined markedly since 1970, while the income going to the upper two quintiles has risen. The declines at the lower quintiles have been somewhat greater for blacks than for whites.

The pattern of income inequality apparent in the national data also persists in each of the four census regions. The data to illustrate this fact are displayed in Table 5. First, as is apparent from the size of the income declines in the various regions between 1978 and 1982, the recession had its greatest impact on black families in the Midwest and Northeast. The impact of the recession in the South was less pronounced, although noticeable in the data. The data for the West tend to be erratic, so the year-to-year fluctuations are harder to interpret.

Perhaps the most striking fact about the regional data is the sharp decline in the relative and absolute position of black families in the Midwest. The recession of the early 1980s really hit black families in the Midwest very hard. Their median family income fell by over $9,000 between 1978 and 1982. While there was some modest recovery between 1982 and 1988, black family income in the Midwest was still $6,000 or 26 percent lower in 1988 than it had been in 1978. The data also reveal that inequality increased dramatically during the 1980s as

Table 5
Median Family Income By Regions

	NORTHEAST			MIDWEST		
	Black	White	Blk/Wht	Black	White	Blk/Wht
1988	$24,495	$37,588	65.2	$17,469	$34,246	51.0
1987	21,534	36,722	58.6	17,449	33,480	52.1
1986	22,533	35,982	62.7	18,732	32,921	56.9
1982	17,891	31,347	57.1	15,025	30,240	49.7
1978	20,946	33,670	62.2	24,572	34,170	71.9
1970	23,685	33,329	71.1	23,514	32,015	73.4
	SOUTH			WEST		
	Black	White	Blk/Wht	Black	White	Blk/Wht
1988	$17,545	$31,475	55.7	$25,840	$33,478	77.2
1987	18,081	32,001	56.3	21,481	33,867	63.3
1986	17,518	31,433	55.7	23,898	33,856	70.6
1982	15,840	28,037	56.5	20,046	30,660	65.4
1980	16,696	29,620	56.4	24,601	32,469	75.8
1978	17,679	30,770	57.5	19,405	33,838	57.4
1970	15,922	28,152	56.6	24,377	31,632	77.1

Source: David Swinton, "The Economic Status of Blacks," in Janet Dewart (ed.), *The State of Black America 1988* (New York: National Urban League, 1989), Table 5, page 135. U.S. Department of Commerce, Bureau of the Census, *Money Income and Poverty Status in 1988,* pages 32–35, Table 6.

well. During the 1970s, blacks in the Midwest typically had median family incomes that were at least 70 percent as large as white median family income. However, during the 1980s, black median family income fluctuated between only 49 and 57 percent of white median family income. Indeed, the turnaround in the position of black families in the Midwest during the 1980s is reflected in the fact that they went from being the region with the highest black income and lowest income inequality in the seventies to the region with lowest black income and highest degree of inequality in the 1980s. The 1980s represent the first decade during which a region other than the South had this distinction.

Although no other region had as dramatic a reversal of black fortunes as did the Midwest, racial inequality in family income did not improve in any of the other regions. The recession had a dramatic impact on black family income in the Northeast. Family income may have been lower on the average in the Northeast for the decade, but the ground lost during the recession was made up by 1988. In general, the level of inequality in the Northeast, as measured by the ratio of black-to-white family income, was much higher during the 1980s than it had been during the 1970s. However, the data for 1988 indicate that the recovery had finally eliminated much of the increased inequality. In any case, black families in the Northeast typically had median incomes that were between only 57 and 65 percent of the median incomes of whites families throughout the decade.

In the South, the median incomes of black families have historically been the lowest of the four regions. As mentioned earlier, the South lost this distinction during the 1980s. This did not occur, however, because of improvement in the South but because of deterioration in the Midwest. In fact, in the South, blacks did not completely recover to the late 1970s peak family income levels until 1987. Moreover, racial inequality in median family income was slightly higher throughout the 1980s in the South than it had been during the 1970s.

The pattern of year-to-year fluctuations in the West are too erratic—due most probably to sampling variation—to discuss a pattern. It would appear that the most consistent interpretation of the data is that there were probably no secular changes in the degree of racial inequality in this region during the 1980s. Except for the West, then, there was a general increase in family income inequality in each region during the 1980s.

Trends in Poverty Rates

Poverty rates give another perspective on black income status during the 1980s. The poverty rate measures the percent of the population with incomes below the level set as a poverty standard by the federal government. This level of income defines the amount that is considered to be the minimum required to obtain a subsistence standard of living. The data showing poverty rate trends for the country as a whole are shown in Table 6 and regional data in Table 7.

The data in the top panel of Table 6 show the percent of the total population with incomes below the official poverty level. As can be seen, this rate for black persons fluctuated within a narrow band during the 1970s and the 1980s, ranging from about 30 to 36 percent. Poverty rates for blacks dropped to their lowest point in the late 1970s, increased during the recession, and attenuated slightly after that. The 1988 poverty rates are based on new processing procedures that lowered the poverty estimates by about one percent for blacks; therefore, the 1988 rates displayed in the table are not strictly comparable to earlier years. However, the change is not large enough to impact significantly our conclusions. In general, poverty rates for both blacks and whites were slightly higher during the 1980s than they were in the previous decade.

Black poverty was consistently substantially higher than white poverty throughout this period. The ratio of black-to-white poverty rates was generally above three to one. This ratio attenuated somewhat during the early 1980s, as the relative increase in white poverty rates brought on by the recession was somewhat larger than the relative increase in black poverty rates. As the recovery proceeded, the traditional three-to-one ratio reemerged.

Table 6
Poverty Rates for Selected Years
(Percent of Population)

| | All Persons | | | |
	Black	White	B/W	All Persons Poverty Gap
1988	31.6	10.1	3.13	6.4 Million
1987	33.1	10.5	3.15	6.6 Million
1986	31.1	11.0	2.83	5.8 Million
1982	35.6	12.0	2.97	6.4 Million
1980	32.5	11.4	2.85	5.6 Million
1978	30.6	8.7	3.52	5.5 Million
1970	33.5	9.9	3.38	5.5 Million

| | Related Children Under 18 | | | |
	Black	White	B/W	Children's Poverty Gap
1988	44.1	14.1	3.06	2.9 Million
1987	45.1	15.0	3.01	*
1986	42.7	15.3	2.79	*
1982	47.3	16.5	2.87	*
1978	41.2	11.0	3.75	*
1970	41.5	10.5	3.95	*

| | Female-Headed Families | | | |
	Black	White	B/W	Female-Headed Families Poverty Gap
1988	49.0	26.5	1.85	725 Thousand
1987	53.8	26.4	2.04	*
1986	52.9	27.9	1.90	*
1982	57.4	28.7	2.00	*
1970	58.8	31.4	1.87	*

*Not calculated.

Source: U.S. Department of Commerce, Bureau of the Census, *Money Income and Poverty Status in 1987,* Table 17.

The last column in this table provides an aggregate perspective on the higher black poverty rates. In 1988, the higher black poverty rate meant that there were an additional 6.4 million poor blacks. As can be seen, the number of extra poor black persons increased during the 1980s: the 1988 number is almost one million higher than the 5.5 million excess poor calculated for 1978. By this absolute measure, inequality increased during the 1980s.

The second panel of Table 6 shows the poverty rate for black children; the pattern follows fairly closely the pattern for the top panel. The rate of poverty for black children is considerably higher than the rate of poverty for all black persons, ranging from about 41 to 47 percent for the years displayed in the table. Again, the poverty rate for children was a little higher for both races during the 1980s. The relative gap was again around three to one. However, the relative ratio declined during the 1980s as the relative increase in poverty among white children rose faster than the relative increase in poverty among black children. In the aggregate there were 2.9 million more poor black children in 1988 than would have existed if racial equality prevailed.

The final panel shows poverty rates among female-headed households. Both black and white female-headed families had substantially higher poverty rates than all persons. The rates were also substantially higher than the rates for married-couple and single male-headed families. Census data not shown in the table show that in 1988, the black married-couple poverty rate was only 12.3 percent and the single male-headed family poverty rate was 24.3 percent. The corresponding figures for white families were 5.2 percent and 10.3 percent, respectively. With poverty rates ranging from 49 to 59 percent for black female-headed families and from 26 to 32 percent for white female-headed families, the female-headed family was obviously disadvantaged. However, the poverty rates for both black and white female-headed families did decline slightly during the 1980s.

Racial inequality in female-headed families' poverty rates persisted throughout the 1980s. Black females experienced about twice the rate of poverty as did white female-headed families. In 1988, this meant an extra 725,000 black female-headed families experienced poverty. In general, there does not appear to be any significant secular trend in the degree of racial inequality for female-headed families. Inequality persisted during the 1980s at about the historical level.

Data describing poverty rates by region are displayed in Table 7. In general, poverty rates for both blacks and whites were somewhat higher during the 1980s in all regions except the South than they were during the 1970s. Even in the South, the level of poverty was slightly elevated in the 1980s in comparison to the late 1970s. Moreover, the recovery did very little to ameliorate the generally higher poverty rates observed in each region. Thus, in 1988, after six years of recovery, poverty was still generally high in all regions in comparison to levels which prevailed during the 1970s.

As was the case with the income trend, the greatest deterioration in the situation occurred in the Midwest. In this region, black poverty rates throughout the 1980s were on the order of 40 to 50 percent higher than the rates that prevailed during the 1970s. Moreover, the level of racial inequality in poverty rates drifted upwards during the 1980s. By 1988, black poverty rates in the Midwest were four times as high as white poverty rates. The Midwest

Table 7
Poverty Rates for Regions: Selected Years

	NORTHEAST			MIDWEST		
	Black	White	Blk/Wht	Black	White	Blk/Wht
1988	22.9	8.4	2.7	34.8	8.7	4.0
1987	28.8	8.9	3.2	36.6	9.9	3.7
1986	24.0	8.9	2.7	34.5	10.6	3.3
1984	32.2	10.7	3.0	37.9	11.5	3.3
1980	30.7	8.9	3.4	33.3	8.9	3.7
1978	29.1	8.2	3.5	24.8	7.4	3.4
1970	20.0	7.7	2.6	25.7	8.9	2.9

	SOUTH			WEST		
	Black	White	Blk/Wht	Black	White	Blk/Wht
1988	34.3	11.6	3.0	23.6	11.3	2.1
1987	34.5	11.5	3.0	24.3	11.5	2.1
1986	33.6	11.8	2.8	21.7	12.3	1.8
1984	33.6	12.0	2.8	26.6	11.8	2.3
1980	35.1	12.2	2.9	19.0	10.4	1.8
1978	34.1	10.2	3.3	26.1	8.9	2.9
1970	42.6	12.4	3.4	20.4	10.6	1.9

Source: U.S. Department of Commerce, Bureau of the Census, *Money Income and Poverty Status . . .:1987, 1988,* and Bureau of the Census, Current Population Reports Series P-60, *Characteristics of the Population Below Poverty Level,* 1984, 1978, 1970.

replaced the South during the 1980s as the region in which blacks experienced the highest poverty rates and the greatest racial disparities in poverty rates.

In the other regions, the increase in poverty was not nearly as dramatic as it was in the Midwest. Indeed, in the Northeast, there had been some recovery by 1988. However, for the decade, poverty was clearly at elevated levels in this region. The degree of racial inequality fluctuated during the decade. Blacks in the Northeast generally continued to experience poverty levels about three times the white level. In the South, poverty for blacks remained below the early 1970s level but generally above the late 1970s level. White poverty in the South relatively increased more than black poverty during the first half of the 1980s. As a result, there was a slight decline in the degree of racial inequality as measured by the ratio of black-to-white poverty rates. However, the ratio continued to be around three to one throughout the decade. The data for the

West suggest little trends in black poverty rates for the decade taken as a whole. Black poverty rates in the West were the lowest for the nation for most of the 1980s. The degree of racial inequality was also lowest with blacks experiencing poverty at roughly a two-to-one ratio in the West rather than the three-to-one ratio experienced in the rest of the nation.

Causes of Income Inequality in the 1980s

The review of income and poverty trends in the last section of this paper makes it clear that racial inequality in economic life probably increased during the 1980s. High levels of racial inequality persisted in all regions of the country and throughout the income distribution. The data in Tables 8 and 9 show that this income inequality originated from every source of income. Blacks had lower overall incomes than whites because a smaller proportion of the black population was of earning age, fewer blacks of earning age received income, and those blacks who received income on average received smaller amounts of income from each source. The only exception to this general pattern was public assistance income.

In 1980, about 71 percent of blacks and about 78 percent of whites were at least 15 years old; in 1987, that population was about 72 percent of blacks and 79 percent of whites. Thus, in each year, only about 91 percent as large a proportion of the black population was at least 15 years old. As the data in Table 8 show, a smaller proportion of this smaller group received each source of income except public assistance income during 1980 and 1987. For example, 59.2 percent of working-age blacks received income from wages and salaries in 1980 and 61.0 percent in 1987. In contrast, 63.3 percent of working-age whites had such income in 1980 and 64.5 percent in 1987. We might note in passing that in 1970, more blacks (62.0 percent) than whites (59.8 percent) received wage and salary income. Blacks were about one-third as likely to receive income from non-farm self-employment and 40 percent as likely to receive property income. Blacks received as high a proportion of income only in public assistance. Although only 8.5 percent of blacks received public assistance and welfare income in 1987, this was over five times the proportion of whites (1.6 percent) receiving public assistance and welfare income. There was little change in this general pattern during the 1980s.

The mean income received by blacks was less than the mean income received by whites for all sources except welfare income. The amount of income received by blacks in 1987 on average ranged from about one-third to four-fifths as much income as received by whites on average from each source except welfare income, where blacks averaged as much as whites. Blacks generally received higher relative incomes from transfer sources, followed by employment sources, with the least equality existing in property sources.

Between 1980 and 1987, inequality widened slightly in transfer and self-employment sources. Inequality remained about the same for wage and property income.

Table 8
Percent With Income, Specified Type,
and Ratio of Black/White Means

| | 1987 | | | 1980 | | |
	Blk	Wht	Blk/Wht	Blk	Wht	Blk/Wht
Wage or Salary	61.0	64.5	.74	59.2	63.3	.73
Nonfarm Self-Empl	2.0	6.5	.55	1.9	5.8	.74
Farm Self-Emplmnt	.1	1.1	NA	.2	1.2	.19
Property Income—All	24.1	61.6	.33	22.3	61.1	.33
Interest Income	22.9	59.9	.33	NA	NA	NA
Transfer & All Other	37.5	34.0	.70	39.1	34.0	.77
Soc Sec or RR Retrmnt	15.8	18.9	.82	16.0	18.3	.81
Pub Asst & Supplmntal	13.2	3.0	1.00	14.3	3.3	1.12
Pub Asst and Welfare	8.5	1.6	.97	NA	NA	NA
Supplemental	5.2	1.5	1.02	NA	NA	NA
Retirement & Annuities	4.5	8.7	.80	3.3	6.8	.87

| | 1970 | | |
	Blk	Wht	Blk/Wht
Wage or Salary	62.0	59.8	.75
Nonfarm Self-Empl	2.3	5.5	.62
Farm Self-Emplmnt	.7	2.3	.30
Property Income—All	5.3	24.3	.48
Interest Income	NA	NA	NA
Transfer & All Other	NA	NA	NA
Soc Sec or RR Retrmnt	10.9	13.6	.91
Pub Asst & Supplmntal	NA	NA	NA
Pub Asst and Welfare	11.2	2.4	1.23
Supplemental	NA	NA	NA
Retirement & Annuities	NA	NA	NA

Source: U.S. Department of Commerce, Bureau of the Census, *Money Income of Households, Families, and Persons in the United States: 1987, Consumer Income,* Series P-60, No. 162.

The net impact of these three factors (smaller working-age proportions, smaller proportions receiving income, and smaller mean receipts for income recipients) on black per capita income is displayed in Table 9. The per capita income received by blacks from every source other than public assistance was significantly smaller than it was for whites. The per capita income received by blacks from wage and salary income was only 63.79 percent as much as received by whites in 1988, and only 61.92 percent as much as in 1980. In 1988, blacks received only 15 percent as much income from self-employment and about 12 percent as much from property sources. Inequality by this measure increased

Table 9
Per Capita Income and Income
Gaps By Source of Income (1987$)

	1987					
	Black Per Capita	White Per Capita	Per Capita B/W	Aggregate Gap	% of Gap	Gap
Wage & Salary	$6,110.09	$9,577.87	63.79	$3,467.78	$101.5 Bil	62.81
Nonfarm Self-Employed	121.11	777.59	15.58	656.48	19.2 Bil	11.88
Farm Self-Employed	4.07	71.64	5.68	71.64	2.0 Bil	1.24
Property	112.59	954.51	11.80	841.93	24.6 Bil	15.22
Transfer and Other Income[1]	1,172.61	1,660.79	70.61	488.18	14.3 Bil	8.85
Soc. Sec. & RR	491.80	792.87	62.03	301.07	8.8 Bil	5.45
Public Asst.	179.21	38.45	466.11	-140.76	-4.1 Bil	-2.54
Ret & Annuities	198.63	527.04	37.69	328.41	9.6 Bil	5.94
Total	7,520.47	13,042.40	57.66	5,521.93	161.6 Bil	100%

	1980					
	Black Per Capita	White Per Capita	Per Capita B/W	Aggregate Gap	% of Gap	Gap
Wage & Salary	$5,388.25	$8,703.55	61.92	$3,314.30	$ 87.7 Bil	68.56
Nonfarm Self-Employed	143.15	647.70	22.10	504.55	13.3 Bil	10.43
Farm Self-Employed[2]	2.36	83.63	2.82	81.27	2.1 Bil	1.68
Property	83.20	745.14	11.17	661.94	17.5 Bil	13.69
Transfer and Other Income[1]	1,190.70	1,462.72	81.41	271.98	7.2 Bil	5.63
Soc. Sec. & RR	539.11	706.65	76.29	167.54	4.4 Bil	3.47
Public Asst.	329.41	74.71	440.92	-254.70	-6.7 Bil	-5.27
Ret & Annuities	146.98	388.91	37.79	241.93	6.4 Bil	5.00
Total	6,807.70	11,641.74	58.48	4,834.04	128.8 Bil	100%

[1]Includes Social Security or Rail Ret. Income, Public Assistance or Welfarc Payments, Suppl. Sec. Income, Ret./Annuities, Veteran Payments, Unemployment and Worker's Comp., Alimony, etc.

[2]Assumes that black income recipients receive the same mean income as white income recipients in this category.

Source: Calculated by author from data in U.S. Department of Commerce, Bureau of the Census, *Money Income of Households, Families, and Persons* . . . 1987, 1986, 1970.

during the 1980s for self-employment but remained about the same for property income. The other numbers in this table show that, in general, inequality in all sources by this measure held steady or increased slightly during the 1980s.

Wage inequality cost each black man, woman, and child an average of $3,467.78 in 1987, or a total cost to the black community of 87.7 billion dollars. The cost-per-person from inequality in self-employment and property income was about $728 and $742, respectively. These two sources generated a combined annual loss of about 45.8 billion dollars. The annual loss per person from social security, retirement, and other transfers except welfare was about $629 per person, or 18.4 billion dollars in the aggregate. Blacks received more welfare income than whites per person. This reduced the per-person gap by $140.76 and the aggregate gap by 4.1 billion dollars.

Comparison of the gap estimates in Table 9 for 1980 and 1987 shows that the absolute level of inequality increased on a per-person and aggregate basis for all sources. The net benefit from welfare income was even, about $114 per person lower in 1987 than in 1980. Thus, blacks failed to make any progress against income inequality during the 1980s because inequality persisted at high levels in all income sources.

Cause 1: Limited Wealth and Business Ownership. The large disparities in receipt of income reflect the persistence of underlying disparities in the basic economic position of blacks in the American economy. As we have repeatedly pointed out in this publication, blacks are disadvantaged economically by owning fewer businesses and smaller amounts of wealth. The disadvantages in current ownership reflect the historical pattern of limited black participation in the American economy. These disadvantages in ownership generate the disadvantages observed in self-employment, property, and retirement income. While we have no data to examine trends in ownership in the 1980s, Tables 10 and 11 show available data on wealth and business ownership in the 1980s reported in earlier editions of *The State of Black America.*

The data in Table 10 clearly show the disadvantages in wealth ownership. Overall, reported mean black net worth was only 23.45 percent of reported net worth for whites. A smaller proportion of the black population owned each type of asset. For example, while over 75 percent of white households reported owning interest-bearing accounts at financial institutions, only about 44 percent of blacks reported holding such assets. As another example, 22 percent of whites compared to 5.4 percent of blacks indicated that they owned stocks and bonds. Similar disparities in ownership existed for all of the other asset classes reported in the table.

The disadvantages were compounded by the fact that, on average, the smaller proportion of blacks owning assets had much smaller mean holdings. This is shown by the data in the first two columns of the table. We see that in each instance, black mean holdings were significantly smaller than white mean

Table 10
Wealth Ownership 1984
($ 1987)

	BLK Mean	WHT Mean	BLK %	WHT %	B/W	BLK AGG	WHT AGG	AGG Gap
Net Worth	$22,141	$99,435.65	100	100	23.45	$210,538.20	$7,115,065	$637,450.40
Interest Earning at Financial Institutions	3429	18448.05	43.80	75.40	10.80	14,282.71	1,048,008.00	117,985.90
Regular Checking	655	1,035.90	3200	56.90	35.56	1,993.71	44,408.83	3,611.04
Stock & Mutual Funds	3,077	30,293.53	5.40	22.00	2.49	1,580.02	502,129.20	61,793.44
Equity in Business	37,188	70,548.90	4.0	14.00	15.06	14,144.89	744,151.10	79,774.02
Equity in Motor Vehicle	3,769	6,242.70	65.00	88.50	44.34	23,298.48	416,253.80	29,236.69
Equity in Home	32,722	56,814.32	43.80	67.30	37.47	136,284.90	2,880,818.00	227,301.50
Equity in Rental Property	41,722	80,761.23	6.69	10.10	33.75	26,184.63	614,564.10	51,379.19
Other Real Estate	15,777	38,386.89	3.30	10.90	12.43	4,950.72	315,330.10	34,846.92
U.S. Savings Bonds	602	2,870.31	7.40	16.10	9.63	423.34	34,817.44	3,970.95
IRA or Keogh	3,764	9,896.21	5.10	21.40	9.06	1.825.38	159,560.50	18,312.67

Source: U.S. Department of Commerce, Bureau of the Census, *Household Wealth and Asset Ownership: 1985*, Tables 1 and 3.

holdings. The same examples used above will illustrate this point. The smaller number of blacks who had interest bearing accounts in financial institutions had average holdings of only $3,429.27 compared to $18,448.08 held by whites. Blacks who owned stocks and bonds had average holdings of $3,077.04, about 10 percent of the average white holdings of $30,293.53.

The tremendous impact of these two factors—lower percentages holding each type of asset and lower mean holdings—is revealed by the data displayed in column five. The B/W ratio represents the ratio of black per-capita holdings to white per-capita holdings. Thus, blacks had only 10.80 percent as much per person invested in interest-bearing accounts at financial institutions as did whites, and only 2.49 percent as much per person invested in stocks and bonds. In other words, white stock and bond holdings per person were roughly 40 times black per-person holdings. These large discrepancies in wealth holdings accounted for the differences in receipt of property and retirement incomes. We should also note in passing that the discrepancies in the ownership of consumer durables such as housing and motor vehicles imply that the use of current income to measure the economic status of blacks and whites understates the disadvantages of blacks.

The data displayed in Table 11 elaborate on the disadvantages of business ownership. The black receipt data were derived from the Commerce Department's Census of Black-Owned Businesses, and the total data were derived from income tax statistics as reported in the *Statistical Abstract of the United States.* The information, thus, shows the relative side of the black-owned business sector in comparison to American business in general. For example, in 1982, when all businesses generated receipts of 8.4 trillion dollars, all black businesses generated only 13.8 billion dollars—a little better than one-tenth of one percent of total receipts. As indicated by the figure in the top row of the third column, in comparison to their share of the population, blacks generated receipts of about 1.2 percent of what would have been expected if they had business ownership parity. In manufacturing, the black business sector accounted for only 1.16 billion out of a total of over 2.8 trillion dollars. The parity index again showed a glaring disparity with blacks generating only about three-tenths of one percent of the receipts that would be expected if they had parity of ownership in the manufacturing sector.

Review of the rest of the data in the first three columns of the table will show that this pattern was repeated for every sector. There is no sector in which black receipts reached even five percent of the level required for parity of ownership. Overall, as shown by the data in column four, the receipts generated by the black-owned business sector in 1982 fell about 1.16 trillion dollars short of what would have been required for business ownership parity. The reader can read the estimates of the shortfall by industry from the fourth column.

The final four columns of Table 11 show similar data for the number of firms owned by blacks and by the total population. Although the gaps by this

Table 11
Total Receipts (in Billions of 1987$) and Number of
Firms (1,000's) in 1982 by Industry

	BLK RCPT	WHT RCPT	B/W	RCPT GAP	BLK FIRM	WHT FIRM	B/W	FIRM GAP
Total	13.83	8,411.19	.012	1,155.92	301.43	14,315	.151	1,689.38
Construction	1.17	398.65	.021	54.27	23.06	1,551	.107	192.64
Manufacturing	1.16	2,804.56	.003	388.87	4.17	531	.056	69.68
Transportation and Public Utilities	.94	747.75	.009	103.06	24.40	585	.300	56.96
Wholesale Trade	1.01	1,308.24	.006	180.93	3.65	1,135	.022	59.76
Retail Trade	4.85	1,319.54	.026	178.66	84.05	2,949	.025	326.07
Finance, Insurance, and Real Estate	.88	1,209.60	.005	167.34	14.83	2,150	.050	284.18
Selected Services	3.82	622.87	.044	82.80	147.26	5,374	.197	600.11

Source: U.S. Department of Commerce, Bureau of the Census, *Surveys of Minority-Owned Businesses: Black*, 1972, 1977, 1982.

measure were not quite as large as the gaps by the receipts measure, they were still glaring. Overall, blacks owned 301,000 firms in 1982 out of a total of 14.3 million in the economy as a whole. Thus, blacks owned only about 15 percent of the number of firms required for parity in number of firms owned. The typical black firm was, understandably, significantly smaller than the typical white firm in view of the differences in the parity index by this measure and the parity index by the receipts measure.

Overall, blacks fell short in total number of firms owned by about 1.7 million businesses. The large shortfall in business ownership by blacks not only generated the lower earnings from self-employment and property but also caused blacks to be dependent on businesses owned by other groups for their economic opportunities.

Cause 2: Disadvantaged Labor Market Status. In addition to the disadvantage of limited ownership of businesses and wealth, blacks also had a disadvantaged status in the labor market. The underlying causes of this disadvantage were the human capital deficits that continued to limit the qualifications of black workers and unequal access to opportunities as a result of limited contracts and discrimination.

The labor market disadvantages may be divided into two components—employment and earnings. With respect to the employment component, blacks were disadvantaged by having lower employment rates and higher unemployment rates. The disavantageous earnings component emanates from less favorable occupational distributions and lower wage rates for employed blacks. During the 1980s, blacks were less likely to be employed; when they were employed, they were more likely to be employed in low wage, less desirable occupations.

The data in Tables 12 and 13 will provide an indication of the relative employment disadvantages experienced by the black population during the 1980s. Table 12 displays the employment population ratio for blacks and whites by sex and age. Throughout the 1980s, the proportion of the black population working was significantly below the proportion of the white population working. The range for the total employment proportion for blacks was between 49 and 57 percent, while the range for the white population was between 58 and 64 percent. It is interesting to note that there was no overlap between the two ranges. The low point for the decade occurred during the recession in 1982, when only 49.4 percent of the white population was employed. It is worth noting, however, that this proportion was still better than the best performance for blacks during the 1980s.

As shown in the bottom three panels of Table 12, the employment levels of black male adults and black teenagers of both sexes were consistently lower than those of their white counterparts throughout the 1980s, while the employment proportion for black females almost equaled the employment proportion

Table 12
Civilian Employment—Population Ratio
By Race, Sex, and Age
Selected Years

Total Population

	Black	White	Black/White
1989*	56.9	63.8	0.892
1988	56.3	63.1	0.892
1987	55.6	62.3	0.892
1985	53.4	61.0	0.875
1982	49.4	58.8	0.840
1980	52.3	60.0	0.872
1970	53.7	57.4	0.936
		Men (20 and Over)	
1989*	67.1	75.5	0.889
1988	67.0	75.1	0.892
1987	66.4	74.1	0.889
1985	64.6	74.3	0.870
1982	61.4	73.0	0.841
1980	65.8	75.6	0.870
1978	69.1	77.2	0.895
1972	73.0	79.0	0.924
		Women (20 and Over)	
1989*	54.8	54.9	0.998
1988	53.9	54.0	0.998
1987	53.0	53.1	0.998
1985	51.0	51.0	1.000
1982	47.5	48.4	0.981
1980	49.1	47.8	1.027
1978	49.3	46.1	1.069
1972	46.5	40.6	1.145
		Both Sexes (16 to 19)	
1989*	28.3	51.4	0.551
1988	27.5	51.0	0.539
1987	27.1	49.4	0.549
1985	24.6	48.5	0.507
1982	19.0	45.8	0.415
1980	23.9	50.7	0.471
1978	25.2	52.4	0.481
1972	25.2	46.4	0.543

*Average of first three quarters of 1989.

Source: Bureau of Labor Statistics, *Handbook of Labor Statistics,* June 1985, pp. 46, 47; *Employment and Earnings,* January 1989 and October 1989.

of white females during this period. The employment proportion for black males ranged from about 61 to 67 percent of adult black males compared to a range between 73 to 76 percent for white males. Throughout the 1980s, black males were employed at 84 to 89 percent the rate of white adult males. In their best years of the decade, adult black males had employment experiences that were substantially worse than the experiences of whites in their worst year.

The same is true for black teenagers, although the black-white gaps are more pronounced. Throughout the 1980s, fewer than 29 percent of black teenagers were employed, while typically about half of white teenagers were employed. Typically black teenagers were employed at about half the rate that white teenagers were employed.

Black women had employment rates that were only slightly lower than the employment rates of white women for most of the 1980s; for practical purposes, we can consider the employment rates of black and white women equal. During this decade, the employment proportions for women of both races ranged between 47 and 55 percent.

The recession of the early 1980s reduced the employment rate of all the demographic groups. As expected, all employment rates increased during the recovery. For males of both races the employment proportions at the end of the decade were still slightly lower than they were at the beginning of the decade. Racial inequality as measured by the ratio of black-to-white employment proportions was also higher for black adult males during the 1980s than during the 1970s. Employment proportions for black teenagers may have recovered to above their '70s level, while the ratio of black-to-white teenager employment-to-population ratios may have improved slightly. Employment proportions of women of both races continued to increase during the 1980s, excluding the recession years. The proportion of both adult female groups employed had reached all-time highs by the end of the '80s. However, the employment rate for black women became slightly less than that for white women during the 1980s; it had historically been larger than the white female rate.

The lower employment rates were costly. In the third quarter of 1989, this resulted in a loss of about 1.4 million jobs. These losses resulted from lower participation, higher unemployment rates, and fewer males in the black population. In 1989, for example, there were about 15 percent fewer black males than whites in comparison to the female population. Thus, there were about 1.3 million missing adult black males. This problem increased throughout the 1980s.

Table 13 contains data for unemployment rates for the 1980s. The pattern in this table reveals that blacks suffered from exceptionally high unemployment rates. For the population as a whole, even during 1989, the average unemployment rate was 11.3 percent, the lowest level obtained during the 1980s. Throughout the 1980s, black unemployment was at an elevated level in comparison to earlier post-war decades.

Table 13
Unemployment Rates
By Sex, Race, and Age
Selected Years

	Total Population		
	Black	White	Black/White
1989*	11.3	4.5	2.511
1988	11.7	4.7	2.489
1987	13.0	5.3	2.453
1985	15.1	6.2	2.435
1982	18.9	8.6	2.198
1980	14.3	6.3	2.270
1978	12.8	5.2	2.462
1972	10.4	5.1	2.039
	Men (20 Years Old and Over)		
1989*	9.8	3.9	2.513
1988	10.1	4.1	2.463
1987	11.1	4.8	2.313
1985	13.2	5.4	2.444
1982	17.8	7.8	2.282
1980	14.5	5.3	2.736
1978	9.3	3.7	2.514
1972	7.0	3.6	1.944
	Women (20 Years Old and Over)		
1989*	9.7	4.0	2.425
1988	10.4	4.1	2.537
1987	11.6	4.6	2.522
1985	13.1	5.1	2.298
1982	15.4	7.3	2.110
1980	14.0	5.6	2.500
1978	11.2	5.2	2.154
1972	9.0	4.9	1.837
	Both Sexes (16 to 19 Years Old)		
1989*	32.7	12.6	2.595
1988	32.5	13.1	2.481
1987	33.4	13.3	2.511
1985	40.2	15.7	2.561
1982	48.0	20.4	3,353
1980	38.5	15.5	2.484
1978	38.7	15.5	2.484
1972	35.4	14.2	2.493

*Average of first three quarters of 1989.

Source: Bureau of Labor Statistics, *Handbook of Labor Statistics,* June 1985, pp. 69, 71, 72, and 73; *Employment and Earnings,* January 1989 and October 1989.

Table 14
Occupational Distribution of Employed Workers 1988 and 1983

| | 1988 | | | | | |
| | Male | | | Female | | |
	Blk	Wht	B/W	Blk	Wht	B/W
Exec., Admin., & Managerial	6.6	14.4	0.46	7.0	11.4	0.61
Professional	6.8	12.2	0.56	10.5	14.9	0.70
Technicians & Related Support	2.3	2.9	0.79	3.4	3.2	1.60
Sales Occupations	5.3	11.7	0.45	9.1	13.5	0.67
Administrative Support	9.3	5.3	1.75	26.2	28.7	0.91
Private Households	0.1	0.05	2.00	3.4	1.5	2.27
Protective Service	4.4	2.5	1.76	1.12	0.5	2.20
Other Service	13.6	6.0	2.27	23.6	14.6	1.62
Precision Pro., Craft & Repair	15.5	20.3	0.76	3.2	2.3	0.96
Mach. Operators, Assem., & Insp.	11.2	6.6	1.70	1.2	0.8	1.50
Trans. and Material Movers	10.7	7.3	1.47	9.9	5.9	1.68
Handlers, Cleaners, Helpers, Labor	10.9	6.0	1.82	2.1	1.6	1.31
Farming, Forestry, & Fishing	3.5	4.7	0.74	0.4	1.2	0.33

| | 1983 | | | | | |
| | Male | | | Female | | |
	Blk	Wht	B/W	Blk	Wht	B/W
Exec., Admin., & Managerial	5.8	13.5	0.43	4.9	8.3	0.59
Professional	6.4	12.1	0.53	11.2	14.3	0.78
Technicians & Related Support	2.0	2.8	0.71	3.4	3.3	1.03
Sales Occupations	4.7	11.5	0.41	7.3	13.5	0.54
Administrative Support	8.2	5.6	1.46	25.6	30.5	0.84
Private Households	.2	.1	2.0	5.7	1.7	3.35
Protective Service	4.1	2.4	1.67	.7	.5	1.40
Other Service	14.3	6.3	2.27	24.2	15.3	1.58
Precision Pro., Craft & Repair	15.7	20.5	.77	2.1	2.2	.95
Mach. Operators, Assem., & Insp.	11.6	7.6	1.53	11.5	9.0	1.28
Trans. and Materials Movers	10.7	6.5	1.65	.9	.7	1.29
Handlers, Cleaners, Helpers, Labor	11.3	5.6	2.02	1.9	1.5	1.27
Farming, Forestry, & Fishing	5.2	5.5	.96	.6	1.4	.43

Source: U.S. Department of Labor, Bureau of Labor Statistics, *Employment and Earnings,* January 1989 and January 1984.

During the 1980s, all the black demographic groups experienced unemployment rates higher than the historical norms. Both male and female adults had unemployment rates above 10 percent each year except 1989. The teenage unemployment rate averaged over 40 percent during the first six years of the decade and remained at about one-third of labor force participants through the end of the decade.

Racial inequality in unemployment rates also increased for the population as a whole and the two adult groups. In 1989, the ratio of black-to-white unemployment rate for the population as a whole was 2.5 to one. This ratio was greater for the population as a whole and for both adult groups during the 1980s than it was during the 1970s. Black adults were typically about two-and-one-half times as likely to be unemployed during the 1980s versus about two times as likely during the 1970s. In the third quarter of 1989, the excess unemployment resulted in a loss of 905,000 jobs for the black population.

Tables 14 and 15 display data that reveal the second aspect of labor market disadvantage. Black earnings were lower because of less favorable occupational distributions and lower wage rates. The occupational data for 1988 are shown in Table 14. There were generally no noticeable trends in occupational standing during the 1980s. Both black males and females continued to be underrepresented in the best occupations and overrepresented in the worst occupations. Black males were less than half as likely to be in sales and managerial occupations, for example, and over twice as likely to be in other service worker occupations. Throughout this period, black males were significantly underrepresented as managers, salesmen, professionals, craftsmen, and technicians—all high-wage occupations, and significantly overrepresented as clerical workers, service workers, operatives, and laborers—all lower-wage occupations for males. Black females were underrepresented as white-collar workers and overrepresented as service workers, operatives, and laborers.

This unfavorable occupational distribution persisted throughout the 1980s. The disadvantages were actually greater than the differences in broad occupational distribution indicate since blacks tended also to have an unfavorable distribution across sub-occupations within each broad category. However, for the 1980s, as a whole, there may have been modest improvements in the proportion of both black males and females employed in the best white-collar occupations. Nonetheless, we estimated on the basis of the 1987 distribution that blacks had a good job parity gap of over 2.2 million jobs in 1988.

Data on the usual median weekly earnings of full-time wage and salary workers during the 1980s are displayed in Table 15. Wage rates for those blacks lucky enough to be employed full-time were generally about three-fifths of white wages. The relative wages of both black males and females in comparison to whites were generally slightly lower than their relative wage rates in comparison to those of whites in the previous decade. The median weekly earnings of black males ranged between 72.4 and 76.8 percent of white male earnings

Table 15
Median Weekly Earnings of Full-Time Wage and Salary Workers
By Race and Sex, 1979–1988

	Black	White	Black/White
1988	$314	$394	0.797
1987	301	383	0.786
1986	302	383	0.789
1985	292	374	0.781
1984	290	371	0.782
1983	291	363	0.802
1981	291	361	0.806
1980	282	361	0.784
1979	311	385	0.808
	Males		
1988	$347	$465	0.746
1987	326	450	0.724
1986	329	449	0.733
1985	322	441	0.730
1984	333	441	0.755
1983	338	448	0.754
1982	325	435	0.747
1981	326	435	0.749
1980	335	436	0.768
1979	351	467	0.752
	Females		
1988	$288	$318	0.906
1987	275	307	0.896
1986	272	305	0.892
1985	267	298	0.896
1984	265	289	0.917
1983	261	287	0.909
1982	249	283	0.880
1981	252	271	0.930
1980	250	277	0.903
1979	258	281	0.918

Source: Bureau of Labor Statistics, *Handbook of Labor Statistics,* June 1985, p. 94; *Employment and Earnings,* January 1986–89.

between 1980 and 1988. The relative wages of black females ranged between 88.0 and 93.0 percent of white female median weekly earnings.

Thus, the wage rate disadvantage continued and probably even worsened slightly during the 1980s. Our estimates for 1988 indicate that this inequality cost black male workers about $30.1 billion and black females about $7.3 billion.

CONCLUSION

The discussion in the preceding section indicates that, during the 1980s, no significant progress was made against the underlying economic conditions that continue to generate racial inequality in income and poverty rates. The basic problem is a failure to obtain equal labor market outcomes and a low rate of wealth and business ownership. We have suggested that the persistence of labor market inequality stems primarily from the fact that no significant progress was made in further reducing human capital inequality and providing blacks with increased equal opportunity. Similarly, the large gaps in wealth accumulation persisted because blacks were unable to acquire or generate enough wealth or business ownership to impact significantly the gaps resulting from a history of economic disadvantage.

During the 1980s, there was basically no public effort of significant magnitude to alter the underlying economic disadvantages experienced by blacks. Reliance on self-help made it possible for a small number of individual blacks to make personal gains but not enough to produce gains for the population as a whole. This is not a surprising outcome in view of the large magnitude of the basic disadvantages that prevent the achievement of equality. There are no ordinary circumstances under which one could expect self-help—reliant entirely on internal black community resources—to be able to produce sufficient increases in wealth, business ownership, human capital, and opportunity in the labor market to offset the historical legacy of inequality. Given the relative disparities in income and economic power, one would expect that internally generated resources under the best of circumstances would produce continuously increasing racial gaps.

Prospects for eliminating or significantly reducing racial inequality by the beginning of the next century will depend crucially on the magnitude of the influx of external resources to the black community. Equality cannot be obtained without reducing the gaps in wealth, business ownership, and human capital that resulted from discrimination and unequal opportunity. Attaining equality also requires the elimination of current unequal opportunities. However, current equality of opportunity will itself be promoted by the elimination of the differences in wealth, business ownership, and human capital. Eliminating this legacy of the past would break black dependency and would for the first time create the situation where black self-help would be able to bring about true equality of opportunity.

Put differently, equal opportunity for blacks within a reasonable time frame can only be made a realistic possibility by providing reparations to the black community. Nondiscrimination and *laissez faire* cannot bring about equality because much of current economic outcomes depends on the accumulation of wealth, business ownership, and human capital that is the legacy of the past to the present. Because blacks experienced such pervasive inequality in the past, they have not inherited the wealth, business ownership, and human capital that make it possible for them to obtain current equal outcomes. Moreover, since the rate of accumulation is tied directly to current economic results, the rate of accumulation for blacks must be expected to be lower than the rate of accumulation for whites. Without eliminating current differences in wealth, business ownership, and human capital, we cannot expect the elimination of inequality in the future.

The conclusion is simple and inescapable. Any realistic prospect for equality by the year 2000 will require reparations sufficient to eliminate the gaps in ownership of businesses, human, and nonhuman wealth. If society is not willing to recognize this reality and implement the necessary capital development programs at the magnitude required to eliminate the inherited gaps, society will simply be unable to attain economic equality between the races. This is at least true in a free market, largely *laissez faire* economy. Thus, those who advocate free markets and *laissez faire* and who also support the elimination of racial inequality in economic life must support reparations for the elimination of the inherited differences in wealth and ownership.

Budget and Tax Strategy: Implications for Blacks

Lenneal J. Henderson, Ph.D.

> The growth in domestic spending has been slowed, and the budget priorities have been shifted to those functions the federal government should provide, such as national defense, basic scientific research, and protecting the rights of all citizens.
>
> *The United States Budget in Brief, Fiscal Year 1990*

> A nation's values and concern for social and economic justice are measured by the fiscal priorities established in its national budget. Judged by these criteria, both the Executive Branch and a majority of the Congress failed the moral test of government in the decade of the 1980s.
>
> *The Congressional Black Caucus,*
> *Quality of Life, Fiscal Year 1990 Alternative Budget*

INTRODUCTION

To understand the relationship between budgetary and tax policy and the status of the African-American community is essential. The reason is simple: fiscal policy—the public financial transactions of government—determines the state of the overall economy and, consequently, the state of Black America. Simultaneously, at a micro-level, black Americans are in competition for public resources. Thus, whether the concern is about child care, the underclass, drug policy, AIDS, the homeless, teenage pregnancy, housing, health care, elder care, transportation, energy, or the environment, no concern of the national black community can escape the need to understand and address strategically fiscal policy.

Such a task is a complex one, for fiscal decisions are quite broad. Mikesell, for example, describes fiscal policy as inclusive of the budget cycle, taxes, charges and fees, administration of the government debt, bonds, procurement policy, public enterprise, and the creation and use of various trust accounts earmarked for specific purposes.[1]

In many respects, fiscal policy combines past, present, and future policy practices and issues. It asks how much the past allocation patterns should guide present (usually current fiscal year) allocation options. Simultaneously, it ponders and struggles over the short- and long-term consequences of selecting one financial option over the other. It debates one method of using budgets and taxes to respond to social priorities over another. Thus, historical, contemporary, and future policies toward blacks are reflected in the nature of fiscal policies adopted by government, whether blacks are explicitly or implicitly the focal point of such policies.[2] This process is further complicated by various

53

equity and equality issues, and the financial woes which undergird budgetary and tax decisions.

Such complications imply five essential points about the relationship between fiscal policies and black economic and political aspirations.

First, blacks continue to be disproportionately dependent upon public finance in order to advance their economic and political agenda. This fiscal dependence assumes three dimensions: (a) the generic or macroeconomic level of dependency; (b) the institutional level of dependency; and (c) the household level of dependency. These three interdependent levels are shared by other socioeconomically disadvantaged populations in the U.S.

Second, to grapple with and gain control over this dependency, blacks must consolidate their own financial expertise, particularly given the technocratic nature of many fiscal decisions.

Third, the stability of this dependency is threatened by the new emphasis in fiscal decision-making—the emergence of a "pay-as-you-go" and "pay-for-yourself" philosophy. This approach has led to a movement from direct, significant funding of a variety of social objectives to more circumscribed efficiency objectives driven by tax and expenditure limitations, deficits, balance of trade and balance of payments deficits, and adamant political conservatism.[3]

Fourth, given this new framework of fiscal decision-making and its associated fiscal strategies of self-financing, monetary efficiency incentives, and privatization, those involved in the development of the black community must update and revise their economic and political strategies. In particular, they must consider the roles public finance play in those strategies and the financial perpetuation of those strategies in an environment of budget reductions and hostile taxation policies.

Finally, fiscal control policies such as the Gramm-Rudman-Hollings Balanced Budget and Emergency Deficit Control Act of 1985, its 1987 amendments, and the Tax Reform Act of 1986, and the variety of state fiscal responses to tax reform provide the specific, limited context in which black economic and political development now struggle. While vigorously seeking to change national, state, and local fiscal priorities through such mechanisms as lobbying, the courts, and mass media exposure of presidential budget and tax postures, blacks should extend their use of fiscal impact assessments as part of their arsenal for addressing and transcending the new fiscal ethics.

Consequently, the Congressional Black Caucus, in its *Quality of Life, Fiscal 1990 Alternative Budget,* argues that "a nation's values and concern for social and economic justice are measured by the fiscal priorities established in its national budget."[4] And the League of United Latin American Citizens (LULAC) has repeatedly warned tax experts that failure to incorporate large numbers of unemployed and underemployed Hispanic citizens and aliens represents not only a fiscal failure but also a moral failure. The rapidly rising number of women entering the work force and subject to rising taxes without benefit of adequate child *and* elder care for those for whom they work makes a loud statement about value priorities and not just fiscal dynamics.[5]

The political economy of fiscal strategy is always more than a question of the econometrics of resource distribution and redistribution. It is even more than a question of *morally correct fiscal decisions* made by government. The issue is whether the fiscal decisions of government empower or enable citizens and groups of citizens, particularly with salient needs, to decide on the morality of their own resource exchange strategies. Thus, this maxim drives the consideration of each of the five propositions in this article.

THE CURRENT DEPENDENCY OF BLACKS ON FISCAL POLICIES

Paradoxically, blacks are simultaneously dependent on federal, state, and local governments for most of their household and institutional financial resources and regressively subjected to most taxing and revenue policies. It is essential to emphasize that "dependency" is not used pejoratively in this context. Many of America's largest corporate, nonprofit, and educational institutions are substantially, if not predominantly, dependent upon public budgets or tax breaks.[6]

However, of the more than 300,000 businesses owned and operated by black entrepreneurs, more than 90 percent of them supply or provide services to government. Less than 50 percent of all other enterprises are as dependent on the government dollar.[7] Black households are more than twice as dependent on some form of federal, state, or local transfer payment; subsidy; public assistance; or Aid to Families with Dependent Children as other households. A black student in any college or university is almost three times as likely to receive government support as the predominant support for tuition, room, and board as other students. And black men and women in the correctional institutions of the nation represent far more than their demographic representation in the population as a whole. Moreover, as Persons, Walton, and other experts on black elected officials point out, black elected officials usually serve the state or in jurisdictions containing large numbers of impoverished, poorly housed populations with health care, day care, education, employment, and infrastructural needs which severely strain city, county, or state budgetary resources.[8] Given advancing rates of poverty, homelessness, health care deficiencies, and other social maladies, the dependency of the needy on government will increase.

The Civil Rights, anti-poverty, feminist, and other movements in the '50s, '60s, and '70s thrust an ethic of social responsiveness upon fiscal decision-makers unprecedented even during the Great Depression. Through the Manpower Development and Training Act of 1962, the Economic Opportunity Act of 1964, the Cities Demonstration and Metropolitan Development Act of 1966, and other policies, the alleviation of poverty was placed higher on the public policy agenda than before. The result was a great redistributive impulse: a desire to reallocate the financial resources of the nation through fiscal policy. Walton has pointed out that federal outlays for civil rights regulatory activities increased from $900,000 in 1969 to $3.5 billion in 1976.[9] Also in 1976, the Small Business Act of 1958 was amended to create federal set-aside programs for minority businesses through what has become known as the 8(a) program.

Although it is common to be concerned primarily about those government programs earmarked specifically for blacks and other "target groups," the other levels of dependency must also be discussed. First, like all Americans, blacks are dependent upon government for "public goods." Support for national defense, the space program, research and development, law enforcement, parks and recreation, streets, highways, and bridges represent a generic or macroeconomic level of public goods and services depended upon by all Americans. Although blacks may receive inadequate quantities or qualities of these goods and services, they are *public* in the broadest sense of the term and are supported by a variety of public spending and revenue-generating schemes such as corporate and individual income taxes, property taxes, sales taxes, excise taxes, trust funds, and user fees.

Such generic spending, however, may affect black Americans in particular. This is because black Americans may depend disproportionately on key components of generic-level spending not evident in other groups of citizens. For example, when recommendations are made for across-the-board reductions in military installations, weapons systems, or research and development, blacks employed as civilians or enlisted in the armed services may suffer more than others because they are represented more in the employment at military installations than others.[10] When President Nixon decided to close or reduce 274 military installations in 1974, many blacks lost jobs or were transferred to lower-paying jobs in installations within or near cities like Philadelphia, Boston, and San Francisco-Oakland. Military spending does create jobs: each $1 billion reduction in Pentagon outlays affects 38,000 U.S. workers.[11]

Moreover, the combination of new military base reductions recommended by a presidential commission in 1989 and sweeping political change in Eastern Europe may trigger more substantial defense reductions than earlier anticipated. No one knows how deep or how far-ranging cutbacks in military spending are likely to be. Defense Secretary Richard Cheney has instructed the services to consider reductions of up to $180 billion for fiscal years 1992-94.[12] In addition, indirect macroeconomic effects from reduced military spending, such as decline in demand for electronic parts, vehicles, aircraft, and other goods and services produced for defense by the private sector can exacerbate economic conditions in metropolitan areas with substantial black populations.

A second point about the generic level of dependency is its intergovernmental nature. Federal defense, education, space, and infrastructural spending is so inextricably intertwined with fiscal decisions of states, cities, and counties, that any political or economic strategy involving public finance must consider its

Table 1
Department of Defense Share of Spending on Goods,
Services, and Research and Development (Excludes Military Payroll)

	Share of Total Spending	Share of R&D Spending
Los Angeles*-Long Beach	7.2%	19.7%
Washington, DC*-MD-VA	4.2	5.4
Norfolk-Virginia Beach-Newport News*	4.2	0.0
St. Louis-E. St. Louis, IL*	3.8	1.1
Nassau-Suffolk, NY	3.0	4.5
Boston	3.1	9.1
San Jose, CA	2.7	4.5
Philadelphia*-NJ	2.2	1.5
Fort Worth-Arlington, TX	2.1	2.4
Anaheim-Santa Ana, CA	2.1	3.7
Seattle*	1.7	3.9
Dallas	1.6	1.6
Denver*	1.5	7.8

Source: Adapted from the Bruton Center for Development Studies, The University of Texas at Dallas.
*Cities with black or Hispanic mayors

intergovernmental dimensions. Table 1 illustrates the impact of federal defense spending for goods, services, and research and development on selected metropolitan areas. Also, the federal interstate highway system is a critical point of interface for the thousands of miles of state and local roads.

A third point about the generic level of fiscal policy is its frequent lack of racial sensitivity. For example, the Tax Reform Act of 1986 is income-based rather than racially-based. The Earned Income Tax Credit (EITC) provides tax assistance to low-income working families to support their children. The assistance is provided without regard to family size, penalizing families like black and Hispanic families with larger family sizes.[13] Nor were Gramm-Rudman-Hollings sequesters sensitive to their adverse impacts on predominantly black institutions like the District of Columbia government.[14]

Consequently, an analysis of the generic level of fiscal dependency is essential to overall black economic and political development. It facilitates interface between black and other populations at the intersection of broad public use of public goods and services. Although its distributional effects on blacks vary, its objectives may be found in broad statements about national, state, or local public needs.

A third level of black fiscal dependency exists at the institutional level. Black schools, hospitals, churches, fraternal organizations, professional and occupational organizations, charitable and community-based organizations, and municipalities and counties depend disproportionately on public finance. This dependence reflects the ever-increasing needs of black individuals and households for goods and services beyond the reach of black incomes or inadequately provided by the marketplace.

This level of dependency includes "targeted" or "earmarked" public programs aimed at black institutional development. Black institutions are supported in order to generate more black educational, career, employment, or business opportunity. Several examples of these programs illustrate the point. The Small Business Administration's (SBA) Office of Minority and Small Business manages the 8(a) minority set-aside program. Of more than 400,000 minority-owned firms, just over 3,000 (Table 2) participate in the sheltered market reserved for them and consisting of work for various federal agencies. Through federal offices of "small and disadvantaged business utilization," the 8(a) program has generated millions of dollars for minority firms that could not have been generated in the competitive marketplace.

Another example of a targeted federal program is the U.S. Department of Energy's Office of Minority Economic Impact (OMEI). Created by Section 641 of the National Energy Act of 1978,[15] OMEI provides a comprehensive program of socioeconomic research on the impacts of energy prices, supplies, and policies on minorities; assistance to minority institutions of higher learning on research and development opportunities in the Department of Energy; a Minority Energy Information Clearinghouse, and a Comprehensive Business and Community Development Program.[16] Although small in both budget and staff (Table 3), OMEI is pivotal in both its monitoring of energy policies for minority impacts and its brokering of opportunities within DOE for a variety of non-white institutions. The monies reflected in these "minority programs" are minimal, but the impact on the financial well-being and development of the institutions they assist is substantial.

The last level of public financial dependency is quite direct. Black households are sensitive to minute changes in the financial disposition of either black institutions or generic fiscal policies. Taken together, Gramm-Rudman-Hollings, its 1987 amendments, and the Tax Reform Act of 1986 are fiscally regressive for black households. What minor benefits the Tax Reform Act provided to the poorest black households were eliminated by real-dollar budget-deficit reductions and changes in both generic and targeted federal programs.[17] Socioeconomic retrogression in inner-city and poor rural black communities are unfortunately correlated with declines in the levels of federal, state, and local spending *in black communities.*

Table 2
Number of Minority Firms Participating in SBA's 8(a) Program, 1985–1989

Year	Number of Participating Firms
1985	2,977
1986	3,188
1987	2,990
1988	2,946
1989	3,297

Source: Small Business Administration, Office of Minority and Small Business Files, 1989.

Table 3
Budget of the Office of Minority Economic Impact, U.S. Department of Energy, 1985–1989

Year	Budget (In Millions of Dollars)
1985	$2.4
1986	2.6
1987	2.8
1988	3.8
1989	4.1
1990	3.9*

Source: U.S. Department of Energy, Office of Minority Economic Impact.
*Reflects Gramm-Rudman-Hollings sequester.

THE ROLE OF FINANCIAL EXPERTISE

Efforts to arrest socioeconomic retrogression in black communities through fiscal policy face not only political obstacles but also technical obstacles. Econometricians, fiscal specialists, quantitative financial analysts, forecasting specialists, and social impact analysts dominate the fiscal policy arena. The expanding roles of the Congressional Budget Office, the Congressional Office of Technology Assessment, and the presidential Office of Management and Budget (OMB) have mobilized expertise to advance and support their budgetary priorities. The Council on Budget Priorities, OMB Watch, the Children's Defense Fund, the Joint Center for Political Studies, the Congressional Black Caucus, and the Urban Institute provide alternative conceptions of the priorities and analyses of budget and tax policy.

However, the '90s will require a more advanced level of analyses and expertise to assess fiscal impacts on blacks. Although moral persuasion should lead and define fiscal priorities, criteria for measuring, anticipating, and advancing such priorities need more development and thought, particularly as new fiscal strategies are advanced to meet current challenges.

In some respects, however, the federal government has adopted a philosophy antithetical to the fiscal needs of the black community.

THE CHANGING PHILOSOPHY OF FISCAL SUPPORT

The election of Ronald Reagan to the presidency set the tone for a radical departure from the responsiveness philosophy of the '60s and '70s. Before responsiveness could facilitate transition to greater self-determination among the needy, "the Reagan revolution" moved vigorously to reduce federal spending in many categories of social support while shifting primary responsibility for the poor to states and localities. The key components of Reagan's fiscal strategy were increases in defense spending, cuts in domestic spending, and cuts in taxes.[18] Although Reagan was unable to reduce entitlements, he did reduce discretionary social spending in both real-dollar terms and actual outlays. The Reagan strategy was accomplished by four principal administrative mechanisms:

1. The appointment to cabinet and subcabinet positions of loyalists to the president who had no independent standing and could be removed easily if they did not follow directions or "went native."
2. Budget impoundments, reductions, recisions, and deferrals to stop or curtail statutorily mandated income maintenance, housing, health, and other programs.
3. Reorganization and retrenchment.
4. Regulation writing. Rules were issued curtailing eligibility for entitlement programs. Programs were wholly or partially contracted out, and closer program monitoring was incorporated into regulations.[19]

However, the combination of tax cuts mandated by the Economic Recovery Tax Act of 1981, increases in social entitlements, and significant increases in defense spending resulted in $400 billion of accumulated deficits between 1981 and 1986. Policy retrenchment, driven by political and economic philosophy, soon gave way to deficit reductions, driven by fiscal necessity.

It is also imperative to emphasize the intergovernmental nature of the change in fiscal philosophy. Even before Reagan's election as president, many states and localities were imposing tax and expenditure limitations on government through initiative, constitutional amendment, legislative mandate, or even recall elections.[20] The famous Proposition 13 in the state of California best symbolized this backlash against taxation and in government spending. Property taxes were rolled back 57 percent, and property tax assessments were rolled back from 1978 to 1975-76 levels. California's cities, counties, and special districts experienced immediate and sharp revenue shortfalls. Discretionary spending, including many social initiatives, were reduced or forever eliminated.[21]

The ethical thrust resulting from most of these retrenchment initiatives was that government's fiscal burdens had become too heavy, that the beleaguered American taxpayer should not be expected to bear the cost of social change, and that citizens should become more vigilant about fiscal decision-making. Implicit in this thrust was a rejection of social transformation ideology apparent in the '60s. Neither an ethic of governmental responsiveness to the expensive needs of the impoverished nor a tolerance for the time and cost required for responsiveness to result in social transformation was evident in this ethic.

However, it is important to emphasize that government itself did not go away in this groundswell of dissatisfaction. Federal defense spending continued to escalate; states bailed out troubled localities, and states and localities invented or extended user fees, public enterprises, and consolidated financing to extend their operations in lieu of property taxes.

THE EMERGING FRAMEWORK OF FISCAL ETHICS

Given pervasive concerns about the nature and extent of government spending at the federal level; within the 50 states; 3,043 counties; 17,000 municipalities; 16,500 villages, hamlets, and townships; 15,500 independent school districts; and 31,000 special districts,[22] a new fiscal ethic has emerged with profound implications for racial and ethnic groups and the needy. This ethic is built on four salient foundations. First, deficit reduction, particularly at the federal level, must be taken seriously not just to balance the budget but also to facilitate the restoration of America's position as an international economic and trading force. Second, reduce government functions that are purely tax-supported. Replace these functions with those that are as self-financing as possible. The greater the degree of self-financing, the less fiscal burden on government. Third, provide monetary incentives to achieve administrative efficiencies. The objective is to reduce burdens on government bureaucracy without necessarily accomplishing social ends effectively. Fourth, give the problem of responding to the needs of the poor to states and localities and through states and localities, through a network of non-profit, church, and other benevolent organizations. All four principles minimize or subtract government from the fiscal equation. If government is present at all, it is as a seed funding source or the other part of a matching arrangement.

This philosophical orientation is further complicated by the fact that America has reached a level of obsession with its declining position in the world economy. Continuous and negative balance of trade and balance of payments; increasing foreign—particularly European and Japanese—investment in American states and cities; and persistent problems of petroleum, uranium, and other raw material dependencies jam daily newspaper headlines. The federal deficit and federal debt are frequently cited as major contributors to, if not sources of,

American economic decline.[23] Declining federal, state, and local tax and revenue yields have been associated with industrial and commercial decline.

To reduce tax burdens and to free up money for investment in U.S. enterprises, many have argued that new ways of financing government are needed. Some have suggested greater use of user fees so that those using government services pay at the time that they use such services.[24] Others suggest that public enterprises or government corporations be established or extended to thrust government more effectively into the marketplace as a producer of goods or services. Presumably, revenues from these enterprises would offset their costs of operation.

In addition to the two aforementioned proposals, experiments using monetary incentives to achieve government efficiencies have been utilized. These incentives or "shared savings" approaches reward government agencies attaining higher levels of efficiency with direct cash awards, or a share of the savings realized from the efficiency would go into the budget of the agency. For example, to alleviate overcrowding in pretrial detention facilities, the city of New York established a program offering substantial budgetary increments to those district attorneys' offices in the city that reduced the number of long-term detainee cases.[25] Frequently, effectiveness is sacrificed for efficiency in many of these experiments. The aim is often not quality of service but reduced quantity of burden.

THE RAVAGES OF FISCAL CONTROL POLICIES

This emerging fiscal ethic reflects obsession with the politics and economics of fiscal control. The deficit has insinuated itself into almost every debate and controversy over federal public policy. Every public policy proposal, regardless of its inherent value or ethical imperative, is subjected to the severe deficit addition test. Will it, and to what extent will it, exacerbate or alleviate the federal budget deficit?

Both the Balanced Budget and Emergency Deficit Control Act of 1985 (hereinafter referred to as Gramm-Rudman-Hollings or GRH and its 1987 amendments) and the Tax Reform Act of 1986 reflect impulsive fiscal control tendencies. GRH resulted from congressional frustration with its inability to reduce substantially the federal deficit. Since 1980, the deficit had grown from $60 billion to $220.5 billion at the end of 1985, increasing from 2.3 to 5.3 percent of the gross national product (GNP) of the U.S. Deeply concerned about the economic and political implications of continued deficits; about the failure of the National Economic Recovery Tax Act of 1981 and other measures designed to stimulate economic growth; and about the impact of these aggregate failures on upcoming 1986 and eventual 1988 elections, Congress assigned a high priority to deficit reduction in 1985.

Despite considerable efforts to reduce the budget, Congress and both Presidents Reagan and Bush have fallen far short of projected deficit-reduction targets. President Reagan's proposed Fiscal Year 1987 budget included a 5.9 percent real growth in defense, no tax increases, and massive domestic spending reductions, including termination of federal school lunch, Job Corps, Work Incentive Program (WIN), Urban Development Action Grants (UDAG), revenue sharing, and mass transit assistance programs. Congress, in its Omnibus Reconciliation package, found these cuts both economically and politically unacceptable. Both the economic and political resources of many political constituencies—both Republican and Democratic, regional, racial, gender, labor, and business—were jeopardized. Congress knew that these constituencies would use remaining economic and political resources against incumbents if the president's program was adopted.[26]

GRH sets a series of deficit ceilings designed to eliminate the budget deficit by Fiscal Year 1991 and provides a framework for across-the-board reductions (sequesters) in controllable domestic programs if the president and Congress cannot agree to a budget within the prescribed ceiling. GRH classifies federal programs into four categories: (1) Exempt; (2) Category I (indexed); (3) Health Services; and (4) Category II (controllable). The first category, entitled, "Exempt," does not allow mandatory reductions for: Social Security, interest on the federal debt, the earned income tax credit, prior-year obligations, and judicially ordered claims against the federal government, as well as anti-poverty programs such as Aid to Families with Dependent Children (AFDC), Food Stamps, child nutrition programs, WIC, community health centers, and Medicaid.

Category I designates a series of indexed programs and calls for up to half of all required savings to come from reductions in cost-of-living adjusted increases from these programs. Cuts in the base of these programs are prohibited. In essence, Category I froze programs at Fiscal Year 1985 levels. Of these programs, civil and military retirement and Special Milk programs, for example, would experience a direct reduction and real-dollar reductions due to inflation resulting from direct reductions.

In the Health Services category, GRH provided for reductions of up to one percent in Fiscal Year 1986 and two percent *per annum* thereafter in five health services programs, including Medicare. Given rapid increases in health care costs and failures in many health services areas to contain such costs, and given the emergency nature of health care inadequacies in poor and nonwhite communities, the real impact of these reductions will exceed the seven percent level through 1991.

Category II, the controllable category, subjects all other defense and domestic programs to across-the-board reductions if deficit targets specially identified in the statute are not met. The absolute size of these reductions is determined by the relationship of proposed budgets to budget targets established in the law. This process, known as "sequestration," automatically executes across-the-board spending reductions in Category II programs.

Under sequestering, the difference between the estimate and the target is automatically reduced, with one-half of the excess being cancelled from defense accounts and the other half from civilian accounts with numerous exceptions.[27] Thelwell estimates that in the Fiscal Year 1990 budget, 70 percent of the outlays are exempt from sequestering.[28]

In the original GRH, the sequestration-triggering decisions were left to the Congressional Budget Office (CBO), the Office of Management and Budget (OMB) and the General Accounting Office (GAO). CBO and OMB were to estimate jointly the size of the deficit for the upcoming fiscal year and to determine whether the deficit exceeded the specified limit by more than $10 billion. If so, CBO and OMB were required to calculate the two uniform percentages—one for defense and one for domestic programs—by which affected programs would have to be reduced in order to close the gap. This so-called "snapshot" of the federal budget situation was to take place on August 15 of every year. It would then be sent to the GAO for verification and transmitted to the president and Congress by August 25.

In pre-amended form, GRH set severe deficit reduction targets (Table 4) and all but eliminated the congressional budgetary role. However, the Supreme Court, in July, 1986, invalidated the automatic sequestration provision that required the Comptroller General, head of GAO, to perform an executive function assigned by the Constitution to the Congress in the case of *Bowsher v. Synar.*[29] The Act, however, contained an alternative which provided for presidential sequestration on enactment of a joint resolution—a procedure which, while not automatic, was constitutional.[30]

Table 4
Deficit Targets Under Gramm-Rudman-Hollings
Fiscal Years 1986–1991

Fiscal Year	Deficit Level
1986	$171.9 Billion
1987	144 Billion
1988	108 Billion
1989	72 Billion
1990	36 Billion
1991	$ 0 Billion

Source: Balanced Budget and Emergency Deficit Control Act of 1985 (PL 99-177).

The import of the Supreme Court's *Synar* decision for the black political economy is threefold. First, it restores congressional responsibility for deficit reduction. Congress remains the primary legal and political arena for difficult budgetary decisions, including both discretionary and nondiscretionary spending. Second, by reinforcing the constitutional role of Congress to make budgets, expertise about budgets and their socioeconomic impacts shifts from the GAO to the Congressional Budget Office (CBO). Blacks must not only follow the congressional debate in key Senate and House committees but also must track the analyses and proposals of the CBO, particularly those most likely to influence congressional thinking. Analyses become as critical for those supporting continued or increased levels of support for the needy as the ethical debate over spending priorities. And, three, because the mechanical role of the GAO was eliminated by the courts, direct conflicts between the Congress and the president over deficit priorities become sharper. Who prevails in such a conflict depends upon the strategies each party adopts and the constellations of interests each party is inclined to work with. However, neither Congress nor the president has taken a deficit policy stance that will take the federal budget deeply into social intervention or that sustains all discretionary social programming at current funding levels plus inflation. Hence, except in a few instances, the burden of responsive fiscal policies for blacks remains at the state and local levels.

FISCAL CONTROL STRATEGIES II: THE TAX REFORM ACT OF 1986

If the GRH was the major legislative initiative on deficit reduction, the Tax Reform Act of 1986 was the leading legislative action on revenue. The policy objectives of the Act included fairness; revenue growth simplification of tax regulations and forms; elimination of multiple tax shelters for those itemizing; increased taxes on capital gains from real estate sales; removal of more than six million poor households from the tax pools; a separate standard deduction for households headed by a single parent; low-income housing depreciation; retroactive repeal of the investment tax credit; and continued deductibility of state and local income taxes.

To reiterate, the 1986 Tax Reform Act illustrates the interconnection of budget and tax policies. Tax provisions were designed both to simplify tax compliance and, more importantly, to generate greater and more predictable revenues to address the budget deficit. And, as Lynn Burbridge rightly argues:

> . . . at the same time the tax law was encouraging more investment in low-income housing, the federal government was cutting its financial commitment to low-income housing in half. So whatever gain was made on one side was taken away on the other. Further, most tax economists agree that providing tax incentives for low-income housing is less efficient than directly subsidizing it.[31]

Furthermore, reduction of charitable expense deductions combined with real-dollar declines in a variety of income transfer programs tend to exacerbate poverty among blacks with income, employment, and occupational problems. As Darity and Myers indicate:

> Blacks unequivocally rely in disproportionate numbers on such programs for income. One-quarter of all blacks are enrolled in the Medicaid program, one-quarter receive food stamps, 20 percent receive support from the AFDC program, and one in seven blacks lives in federally subsidized housing. One-quarter of black households with school children five to 18 years old receives free or reduced-price school lunches.[32]

Income losses in any household translate into revenue losses for federal, state, and local governments. Revenue losses constrain policy responsiveness to blacks as reflected in public budgets, even when the will to be responsive is present.

Moreover, the psychological and administrative barrier created between tax-payer and government was severely exacerbated by the confusion over both tax provisions and tax forms following the enactment of the Tax Reform Act. Several versions of the 1040 Individual Tax Form were issued before the confusion abated. Phased-in elimination of the consumer interest provisions seemed complicated. And the backlog of cases at the Internal Revenue Service (IRS) involving the new tax law belied its policy objective to simplify the law. The result was a frustration of revenue generation and a smaller-than-anticipated contribution of the new tax provisions to deficit reduction.

Finally, it is also essential to understand the intergovernmental consequences of both federal budget and tax policy. "Tax conformity," the extent to which state income tax law reflected federal policy alternatives, became an immediate issue following enactment of the Tax Reform Act. States most intent on reflecting federal tax reform realized a revenue windfall at the expense of state taxpayers, particularly the poor. Those adopting a more gradualist approach displayed a sensitivity to voter intolerance of higher state taxes exhibited in most of the tax revolts of the '70s and '80s.

On the expenditure side, the elimination of state and local Revenue Sharing funds and reductions in most categories of block grant funding distributed from federal to state and local governments was both economically and politically expensive to nonwhites and advocates of the poor.[33] Need increased in cities, counties, school districts, and states where blacks, Hispanics, and women hold more than 90 percent of their elective offices. Consequently, both GRH and Tax Reform are having significant effects on the distribution and redistribution of economic and political resources among blacks, Hispanics, and the other needy and between the needy and other Americans. These impacts not only have quantitative impacts on the resource level of those who need but also qualitative impacts on both their standards of living and on the ethical orientation of American society as a whole. They imply an agenda for public officials, social service deliverers, advocates of the poor, and others with a strong fiscal component.

TOWARDS AN ETHICAL FISCAL STRATEGY

It is essential to maintain both the values implied in the struggle of nonwhite and poor Americans seeking fiscal alternatives and the related criteria for good fiscal policies. At a minimum, good fiscal policies include the principles of productivity, equity, and elasticity. A productive fiscal policy generates sufficient revenues to meet governmental needs on the tax side and makes investments in human needs, economic development, and defense on the spending side. If tax policies fail to generate adequate revenue, more public monies must be spent on borrowing with a subsequent effect on interest rates and economic growth. An equitable fiscal policy is fair to both taxpayers and to specific public constituencies benefitting from public expenditures. In tax policy, economists refer to two kinds of equity—horizontal and vertical. Horizontal equity means that taxpayers who have the same amounts of income should be taxed at the same rate. Vertical equity implies that wealthier people should pay more taxes than poorer people. A related principle is that tax policies should be progressive: taxes increase as income increases. Proportional principles of taxation increase taxes in exact and direct proportion to increases in income. Regressive taxes impose greater burdens on taxpayers least able to pay or taxes increase as income decreases.[34]

Although traditionally applied to taxes, notions of progressivity, proportionality, and regressivity also have a budgetary counterpart. Fiscal policies that tend to benefit the least needy and deprive the most needy are budgetarily regressive. Generally, GRH is regressive in its impacts on blacks and Hispanics because it utilizes budget bases that were already retrenched before 1985 as baselines for GRH-mandated cuts and because needs continue to rise as funding levels decline.

Finally, the principle of *elasticity* suggests that the fiscal system be flexible enough to address its revenue and spending needs regardless of macroeconomic changes in economic conditions. Taxes and spending make a contribution to the stabilization of the economy, as well as to the stability of socioeconomic components of society.

As the *Congressional Black Caucus Quality of Life, Alternative 1990 Budget* and work by organizations such as the Center for Budget Priorities point out, when GRH and Tax Reform are considered together, they are fiscally regressive for black and Hispanic households, individuals, and institutions. As Tables 5, 6, and 7 suggest, strict enforcement of Tax Reform objectives is generally progressive for low-income families and households; anticipated reductions in GRH Categories I and II, minuscule growth in exempted programs, and increased demands for both exempt and retrenched programs erode most of the benefits of tax reform for lowest-income households.

Moreover, in considering the ethics of good fiscal policy, it is also essential to consider the reciprocal relationship between households and institutions. Institutions like charitable organizations, businesses, advocacy organizations;

Table 5
Selected Tax Provisions Affecting Low-Income Households

	CURRENT LAW	NEW LAW*
TAX RATES		
Individual	14 brackets—11–50%	2 rates: 15% and 28% with phase-out for high income: 33% top rate
Corporate	15–40% on first $100,000; 46% thereafter	15–30% up to $75,000, 34% thereafter
Capital Gains	20% top rate	28% top rate
Minimum Tax	20% individuals, 15% corporate	21% with fewer loopholes
INCOME TAX THRESHOLD		
Standard Deduction Single	$2,480	$3,000
Joint	$3,670	$5,000
Head of Household	$2,480	$4,400
Exemption (per person)	$1,080	$2,000 (by 1989, phased out for high income)
Earned Income Tax Credit	$550 maximum	$800 maximum
LOW-INCOME HOUSING		
Depreciation	more favorable for low-income housing	same for all housing
Rental Loss Limitation	none	$25,000 in deductions or $7,000 in credits (phased out after $20,000 income)
Industrial Development Bonds (IDB)	volume cap excludes multi-family housing	volume cap includes multi-family housing
Low-Income Housing Credit	no credit	9% for rehabilitation and new construction, 4% if other subsidy
Criteria for IDB and Credit	For IDB: 20% of tenants below 80% of area median	For IDB and credit: 40% below 60% or 20% below 50% of area median

Source: Lynn Burbridge, Urban Institute, 1986.

*Some provisions are subject to transition rules and may not take full effect immediately.

Table 6
Median Income and Family Characteristics by Race, 1984

Characteristic	Number of Families				Median Income	
	White		Black		White	Black
	(millions)	(%)	(millions)	(%)		
All families	54,400	100	6,778	100	27,686	15,432
Type of family						
Married couple families	45,643	83	3,469	51	30,058	23,418
Wife in paid labor force	23,979	44	2,221	33	35,176	28,775
Wife not in paid labor force	21,664	40	1,248	18	24,246	14,502
Male householder no wife present	1,816	3	344	5	25,110	15,724
Female householder no husband present	6,941	13	2,964	44	15,134	8,648
Number of earners						
Total	53,777	100	6,671	100	27,752	15,337
No earners	7,674	14	1,376	21	12,941	5,277
One earner	15,219	28	2,312	35	22,050	11,809
Two earners	23,303	43	2,312	35	32,260	25,334
Three earners	5,317	10	527	8	40,374	32,984
Four or more earners	2,263	4	218	3	51,309	38,143

Source: U.S. Department of Commerce, Bureau of the Census, *Money Income and Poverty Status of Families and Persons in the United States: 1984,* Current Population Reports, Series P-60, No. 149 (Washington, DC: Government Printing Office, 1985).

municipal, county, and state governments; trade unions; and others provide essential services to their members and constituencies. Conversely, these institutions justify their existence and draw money and other resources from households. If fiscal policies adversely affect households, institutions are profoundly affected. Similarly, if fiscal policies damage institutions, households suffer.

Consequently, the ethical budget holds as its principal mission not only responsiveness to black economic and political needs in the United States,

Table 7
Family Income Distributions, 1984

Family Income Class	White		Black	
	Class (%)	Cumulative (%)	Class (%)	Cumulative (%)
Under $2,500	1.6	1.6	4.7	4.7
$2,500 to $4,999	2.2	3.8	10.1	14.8
$5,000 to $7,499	3.7	7.5	10.2	25.0
$7,500 to $9,999	4.4	11.9	9.0	34.0
$10,000 to $12,499	5.3	17.2	8.3	42.3
$12,500 to $14,499	5.0	22.2	6.6	48.9
$15,000 to $19,999	10.7	32.9	12.3	61.2
$20,000 to $24,999	11.0	43.9	9.4	70.6
$25,000 to $34,999	19.8	63.7	13.1	87.7
$35,000 to $49,999	19.4	83.1	10.5	94.2
$50,000 and over	16.9	100.0	5.8	100.0
Median income	27,686	—	15,432	—
Mean income	32,422	—	18,347	—

Source: U.S. Department of Commerce. Bureau of the Census, *Money Income and Poverty Status of Families and Persons in the United States: 1984,* Current Population Reports, Series P-60, No. 149 (Washington, DC: Government Printing Office, 1985).
— not applicable

but also economic and political empowerment. It is aimed at a redistribution of resources that only temporarily charges more affluent members for subsidies so that the less affluent eventually become more affluent. Human capital is as essential as physical capital. And long-term investments in human capital development are perceived as realizing multiple returns to society that will more than pay for themselves.

CONCLUSIONS AND RECOMMENDATIONS

What economic and political strategy implications do the new fiscal ethics have for blacks? How can blacks favorably influence the establishment of fiscal priorities at the federal, state, and local levels of government?

First, the moral struggle to attain equity and financial choice for blacks, Hispanics, women, and the poor should escalate. Majority Americans have as great, if not greater, a stake in the outcome of the moral struggle as do those that need. The ultimate financial and moral beneficiaries of this struggle are the majority businesses, educational institutions, and public agencies because the poor buy from them.

Second, local, state, and federal fiscal monitoring should continue to increase. Components of such monitoring include:

(a) Regular assessment of spending and taxing policies, proposals, and plans for the current potential impacts they have on the needy;

(b) Analysis of procurement and contracting practices to determine whether, and to what extent, small, minority, and women-owned business utilization plans are in place; and

(c) Where privatization occurs or is proposed, transitional plans include mandates to private owners to continue inclusion of the needy.

Third, expanded use of formal policy and impact assessments should be used by black organizations to advance the needs of the poor in legislative hearings, public rule-making, and regulatory processes and judicial proceedings.

All of these points underscore the need for black policy advocates to acquire, utilize, and work carefully with experts. Policy expertise comes from many disciplines and is the major weapon of interests whose ethical preferences prevail in policy. The new fiscal ethics is therefore best met by a new and more effective use of expertise.

Housing Opportunity:
A Dream Deferred

Phillip Clay, Ph.D.

INTRODUCTION

The 40th anniversary of the Housing Act of 1949 passed with hardly any acknowledgment. That historic legislation committed the nation to a policy that every American family should have ". . . a decent home . . . in a suitable environment." In 1990, the nation is far from this goal, although some real progress has been made. Just as in 1949, black Americans lagged behind their white counterparts in the extent of improvement.

Housing is a major component in the bundle of goods that defines social and economic well-being. It is an indicator of the social status of a family and of individuals. It is also the largest part of a household's budget and net worth. The lack of availability of housing forces families into serious crisis, and its great expense amounts to a burden which freezes out other important aspects of well-being such as proper nutrition.

After forty years, we have made substantial housing progress. Though we are well below the one-third of the population that President Roosevelt saw ill-housed during the Depression, we still have a long way to go with more than 10 million households still inadequately housed or, to an increasing extent, not housed at all. Black households have continued to be especially deprived, even though overall conditions have improved. The gap between blacks and whites continues.[1] More than three million of the inadequately housed households are black.

The steady progress which started after World War II, however, has been short-circuited in the last decade. For example, during the 1980s, for the first time, the rate of homeownership for the entire population and for blacks has declined as poverty and economic marginality have increased. Moreover, that black progress has been so substantial and that class concerns rather than racial concerns ought now to dominate is often voiced but not supported by the evidence.[2]

The purpose of this essay is to look at the housing status of blacks. This assessment is taken from several different points of view. We make the traditional assessment where measures of housing progress and deprivation are noted and compared. But we also take a more indirect view with the emphasis on the changes in policy and in the housing environment that affect opportunities for housing progress for all Americans and particularly their impact or blacks. The paper concludes with some recommendations for future approaches.

THE HOUSING PROBLEM OF BLACKS

Let me first put the housing problem of black households in some perspective.

- After a 20-year decline in the national poverty rate (from a rate of 20 percent), the nation experienced a major increase in the incidence of poverty among all households—from just under 12 percent in 1970 to as much as 15 percent in the early '80s to more than 13 percent in 1989. More than 30 percent of blacks were in poverty in 1989, and while the number was stable during the 1980s, the depth of poverty increased (that is, those who were poor were further behind).[3] In major cities, such as Cleveland, Newark, Detroit, and Oakland, the incidence of poverty was even higher—as much as 40 percent of black households.

  Federal programs that in the 1970s spared nearly 20 percent of families that would have otherwise been poor have been cut. For example, in public housing, where more than a third, of the beneficiaries are black, the cuts have been more than a third and HUD programs to produce affordable housing have been cut more than 80 percent since 1980.[4] There has been a large increase in the percentage of children who live in poor households, especially among blacks. In 1986, 15 percent of white children and 43 percent of black children lived in poor families.[5] Being part of such households gives the child a better than 50-50 chance of also being in a housing and neighborhood situation that put the child and the family at risk and denies them significant power over their lives. This higher incidence of poverty of families (mainly those headed by women) with children has remained steady despite five years of economic recovery.[6] When these numbers and trends are considered, there ought not to be surprise that there are one to three million persons homeless and that the biggest growth has been in the number who are in families (as opposed to single adults). The surprise is that it is not more pervasive.[7]

- During the 1980s, we witnessed a significant increase in the depth and concentration of poverty among blacks. While the increase in black poverty has followed the general pattern, the degree of poverty in inner city areas has deepened, and the number of such concentrations has increased sufficiently to prompt use of the term "underclass" to describe this persistently poor and deeply impoverished population concentrated in urban ghettoes.[8]

  All the difficulties of producing, conserving, and restoring housing in cities are compounded in these areas which are not only abandoned by whites, by merchants, and by investors, but also by working-class and middle-class blacks as well.[9]

  The emergence of the underclass really points to a larger phenomenon that has significant meaning for housing. The two fastest growing sectors of the black income distribution are those blacks earning more than $25,000 (the putative middle class) and those earning incomes below poverty level.

  Doing somewhat better are black married couples living outside the South whose earning gap with whites has narrowed considerably—from 71 percent of comparable whites' income to 78 percent. Female-headed households have lost ground during this period (61 percent to 57 percent of comparable white income).[10]

- All families with children (except those in the top fifth of the income distribution) lost income (in constant dollars) during the 1980s. For all families, this amounted to seven percent, but for families with incomes below the area median (which includes more than two-thirds of black households), this loss has been more serious. During the same period, housing prices, rents, interest rates, and other housing cost factors have leaped forward and remained at historic high levels.[11]

   The new development here is that housing is costly now not just to the blacks and the poor but also to a broad range of households as well. Blacks have the further disadvantage of being concentrated in areas where the effects of changes in the housing issue are exaggerated. Blacks are concentrated in coastal cities where there have been a run-up on reinvestment and economic revival and speculation. Blacks are also concentrated in still depressed heartland cities where there is too little basis for investment, leaving housing conditions and quality a problem even when prices are moderate.[12]

- About 12-14 million urban households are presently ill-housed, that is, they live in substandard units, are crowded, or pay more than 30 percent of their income for housing. According to the 1983 American Housing Survey, black households that constitute about 12 percent of total households are 31 percent of this number. Altogether, 52 percent of black households face one or another housing problem. The number approaches 75 percent for very low income blacks.[13]

- With this increasing poverty and growing evidence of a housing problem, we have, for the first time in recent history, no policy to address these needs. We presently produce fewer than 30,000 federally assisted units each year compared to an average of about 150,000 per year during the 1970s. Assisted units over the years served not only to fill the critical gaps of low income housing supply.[14] They also represented a major resource for minority households.[15]

- Homeownership is the single most important indicator of housing well-being. It is also the principal asset and medium of saving and financial security for many households. The decade of the 1980s marked the first time since the Depression and war years that the rate of homeownership for the nation as a whole did not increase. The ownership rate has actually declined from 66 to 64 percent after a steady 40-year climb. For young families (headed by persons aged 25-34), the rate decreased four percent between 1980 and 1985 alone, from 59 to 55 percent. This figure includes many middle-class as well as working-class families. The dream of ownership is hard to sustain, much less realize. For poor families, fewer than 20 percent can afford ownership. For blacks, the rate never exceeded 45 percent and like the rates for others, it, too, fell during the 1980s as prices rose, real incomes of black declined, and little was left in the way of substantive assistance.

We could go on with the statistics, but suffice it to say that not only have blacks found it more difficult to improve their housing status, but also the housing crisis broadened and deepened during the 1980s. More blacks became economically marginal and their isolation increased. In housing, this translates into or contributes to a host of problems for black housing consumers—fewer and poorer choices, continued segregation,[16] lack of private investment in black low-income neighborhoods, and complications in the housing development process brought on by problems of poverty and powerlessness.[17]

THE HOUSING PROBLEM IN NATIONAL PERSPECTIVE

The housing problems of blacks are best understood in the context of larger national trends. Given the progress that was made over the years, we might be tempted to view the nation's housing problem as just a "bump in the road" of progress and that some changes—reduction in interest rates, containment of speculation, reduction of regulation, a new federal initiative, etc.—will deal with our problems.

There are two ways of assessing whether we are dealing with a bump in the road or something more serious. First, after acknowledging that the poor have always been with us, we can ask why the old mechanisms that promoted progress despite poverty no longer seem to work.

Second, we can look at fair housing issues and see what is static and what is changing. Finally, we can look over national trends that shape where housing stands in the national economy and with our major institutions to assess the implications of these trends for blacks.

WHY CAN'T WE SOLVE THE HOUSING PROBLEMS
THE WAY WE USED TO?

The first part of the answer to this question is that policy has not been directed to addressing housing problems during the 1980s. It has been a long time since Congress took a look at housing and attempted to correct problems or update programs. A few demonstration and pilot efforts represent the only initiatives offered in recent years.[18]

This is in contrast to several decades when Congress directed housing policy in specific directions to address contemporary housing concerns. The 1980s is the longest period in 40 years when the most significant transaction affecting families has received so little support despite an acknowledged escalation of the problem.[19]

To put the nation's housing policy in perspective, we can identify three distinct phases to U.S. housing policy. In these phases—which go back to the 1940s—we constantly sought to remove roadblocks to improving the nation's housing supply. In the first phase, we instituted a public housing program and put a national mortgage system in place. We offered homeownership benefits to young families and veterans with FHA and VA programs. We created tax incentives and preferences to encourage housing development and consumption. The programs during this period did not help blacks very much. Indeed, the nature of the system was such that redlining was practiced officially ("redlining" refers to the practice in which lending institutions deny mortgage money to certain neighborhoods—typically black ones—based on presumed risk), and where black projects were built, they established or reinforced segregation that went unchallenged until the late 1960s, with new fair housing laws and court challenges.

In phase two, starting in the mid-1960s, we brought the private sector in—via programs such as Section 221 and Section 236—to produce assisted housing and to focus on housing for those whose income was just too low to afford decent private housing but too high for the public housing that (in segregated projects) was becoming increasingly housing of last resort for blacks. We also made a very modest effort at rebuilding urban communities with new housing on urban renewal land. While some blacks did benefit here, many more were victims of "Negro removal" (wholesale displacement of blacks to provide for more urban renewal). We initiated efforts to help poor families buy homes in the Section 235 program. Moreover, we expanded tax incentives and encouraged churches and other nonprofits to sponsor housing. The major point about this period—when almost 700,000 federally assisted units were built—is that many blacks did get better housing (albeit mainly segregated housing) and because of this progress and other efforts such as the anti-poverty programs, hope was alive and community institutions (whose loss we now mourn) were active.

In phase three, from 1975 to 1980, we built or rehabilitated a million units of housing with deep subsidies to serve the very poor. We also focused attention on rehabilitation and neighborhood conservation. The nation increased and enhanced tax preferences related to housing. We increased local discretion in program development with block grants programs and started the deregulation of financial institutions in the hope that it would bring more capital for investment in housing. New legal authority to challenge lending discrimination was instituted.[20] With the initiatives, the number of eligible households that received housing assistance went from 12 percent in 1970 to 25 percent by 1983.

These efforts in the various phases were never perfect, and discrimination was a constant companion for blacks who sought better housing.

We also need to examine what has changed in other ways, with reference to options available to families in the past, how these options worked, and where we stand with them today.

Traditionally, families have had four options to address their housing needs and goals: savings and family assistance, filtering down of older units, accepting public or assisted housing, or changing consumption goals and preferences. Blacks have always been at a disadvantage on all these dimensions.[21] These options, at different times and in different combinations over time, helped most families, including many black families, become better housed. The gap between blacks and whites did not shrink, however. That is how the system used to work. It doesn't work that way now. Why can't it work that way now?

First, saving is not a potential route for many households. Not only has the cost of housing gone up faster than income in recent years, but also families have had less real income from which to save. Moreover, the ability to finance home purchase with a low downpayment ran up against the realities of housing finance policy shifts and declining economic fortunes for poor and working-class families. In recent years, the metaphor for urban families has not been "building a nestegg to get the dream house," but "getting on the (housing) train before it leaves the station." Those who could play the game did, and those who could not have been left behind. Overconsumption and speculative behavior on the part of some to "get aboard" the housing train as an investment tend to inflate prices and make it difficult for others for whom inadequate shelter is the reason for being in the housing market. For all nonupper income households, this leads to declining ownership rates.

Second, families used to be able to improve their housing situation by taking units that were left by higher income people who moved into new housing. Over a number of moves, less well-off families would be able to improve their housing within limits of their income. Blacks, even under the worst situation (short of public housing), obtained units that were surplus to whites and those units which filtered down from upper income blacks.

The situation is quite different now. The demand for housing which used to be met, in net terms, by new construction, has been met recently to the extent of almost 20 percent—by older housing.[22] In other words, the poor have to compete with the nonpoor for older units that used to be both affordable and available.[23]

Third, families used to have access to a variety of new public and assisted housing opportunities. These programs were critical as temporary way stations and for many as a permanent subsidy. The units—greater than 150,000 a year in the '70s—not only were a direct response to need, but also indirectly helped to relieve pressure on the nonsubsidized stock. As Table 1 shows, these programs have made a declining contribution in the 1980s. This mechanism for relief is no longer available to a significant degree.

Finally, the households have been willing to change their preferences by aspiring for less, at least temporarily. Changing preferences is temporary and is only a viable option when progress is in view. It is now more an option for single individuals than for families. It is not appropriate for a family to choose bad housing in order to save, nor is crowding acceptable for a long time. Suffering is bearable when one sees redemption or reasonable hope thereof.

In short, the old tools for upward mobility in housing do not work effectively today. Families are not in a position to engage in self-help, and we have little at the

Table 1
New Budget Authority for Assisted Housing, HUD, FY 1977 to 1988
(billions of dollars)

Fiscal Year	New Budget Authority
1977	28.0
1978	31.5
1979	24.4
1980	26.7
1981	19.8
1982	13.3
1983	8.7
1984	9.9
1985	10.8
1986	10.0
1987	7.5
1988	7.0

Source: U.S. Department of Housing and Urban Development, Budget Authority for Fiscal Years 1977–1988 (Washington, DC: Government Printing Office).

federal level to help them. While some cities and states have been creative, only a small number of families in a limited number of places have benefited since state programs have been helpful to the poor, mainly by piggybacking onto federal programs. With the federal void firmly in place, "affordable housing" in many state programs is really housing for middle class families—those earning $35,000 to $40,000 per year.

FAIR HOUSING

No comprehensive assessment has been made of the exact status of housing desegregation since 1980. The 1980 census is the last date for which comprehensive microdata are available. The 1990 census will allow us to test how much progress we have made and what our continuing challenge is. We expect the challenge to be substantial and that progress made during the '80s to be limited and selective.[24] The 1990 census will show some additional shifts of Blacks from rural areas to metropolitan areas and to some modest degree, from central cities to the suburbs. The census will also show some continued high levels of segregation and perhaps in some cities an increasing level.[25] What bears careful monitoring are developments in the following areas where, if trends are as we fear, they have important meaning for the future.

1. Whether resegregation continues to be the pattern in black suburbanization;
2. Whether pockets of deep and persistent poverty, documented to exist in 1980 and suspected to exist during the '80s, in fact, do show up on a more massive scale than has been documented already, and whether the data indicate other signs of weakness (i.e., worse housing conditions, vacancies, etc., in these areas);
3. Whether blacks are part of the move to smaller cities and to major growth areas, especially job and economic growth areas; and whether in such moves their housing opportunities have matched the improved job opportunities in such areas;
4. Whether blacks have been disproportionately affected by the shrinkage of housing opportunities caused by a decade of rising rents and prices, historically high interest rates, and other features in the economy; and whether the contribution to net worth from higher housing values has been shared proportionately;
5. The 1990 census will give us a chance to test concerns about displacement and gentrification, about the achievement of the black middle class, and about the housing aspects of local issues (i.e., persistent economic stagnation in rustbelt cities, rapid growth in the South and West, and economic miracles in cities such as Seattle and Boston, etc.). The evidence suggests there is not much to be encouraged about in these areas.[26]

The issue of urban lending bears mention in connection with fair housing. Several studies recently have documented the continuing existence of credit discrimination in urban communities. This has been documented in detail in Detroit, Atlanta, and Boston, and in congressional hearings for the nation as a whole.[27] The discrimination seems to focus on minority areas and minority individuals and is not based on income. The denial of credit makes it difficult for housing development to proceed, for the market to function effectively in the sale and conservation of existing housing, and for the ability of families to be mobile. All of this restricts investment, which over time leads to a serious decline in neighborhood quality and housing value. For blacks who are able to escape low-income black areas do, this creates the "self-fulfilling prophecy" and massive disinvestment.

The nature of housing has changed such that the scope and nature of fair housing have to change as well. In particular, the historic attention to "open housing" has to be supplemented with attention to equal opportunity and affirmative efforts in the following areas:

- site selection for "affordable housing" (to assure that public initiatives expand choice and assure access to blacks);
- the nature of state and local housing programs;[28]
- local building and occupancy regulations and their enforcement;

- mortgage lending patterns of financial institutions;
- access to development and job opportunities for blacks and influence on stipulations that cities place on development in or near the core.

KEY HOUSING TRENDS FOR THE 1990s

A number of developments in housing and real estate have significant meaning for housing opportunity and status for our community.[29]

1. Increasingly, decisions about housing and real estate development in major cities will be made in the context of a national or even global real estate and capital market. While not every aspect of housing will be driven entirely by these sources, many by virtue of the capital market will be heavily influenced. As a result, the extent, nature, and the cost of housing are guided by these extra local concerns and not by community needs and resources.

2. Related to the point above will be the decline of small local lenders and the perspective that these institutions bring to the analysis of all the communities. This is especially true in the sense that it may be more difficult to exert local pressure on these institutions to address local credit needs or to be sensitive to complex investment judgments about local communities. To deal with this trend may require that the community development institutions that assist or act as intermediaries for local institutions and investors, likewise, go national.[30]

3. Because of the imminent reduction of the demand pressure caused by the end of the baby-boom cycle, development of new housing will be less significant in the 1990s. Improvement of existing housing and investment in second homes and housing for affluent middle-aged households will become more significant. A particular casualty of this and other developments will be housing production targeted toward first-time homebuyers who find it increasingly difficult to afford to purchase a home. The housing industry could well continue and accelerate its attention to upgraders and high income consumers rather than risk gambling with lower income groups whose ability to purchase a home is limited. Exceptions to this general proposition will be in the areas of the West and South, where significant population growth from immigration as well as the maturation of the children of previous immigrants will keep demand strong during the 1990s and where a broader spectrum of household consumers and price features continue to exist. Since blacks are a significant part of the southern market, guiding this development and assuring equal housing opportunity will be more important.

4. As federal deregulation continues, local regulations in the development area become increasingly more important, and because of local tax pressures, regulations will be increasingly used to support local fiscal goals.[31]

This has the effect of raising the cost of housing produced and in some communities may put upward pressure on local property tax. This pressure on local property tax might be one more reason to make homeownership more difficult to obtain.

5. There will be increasing pressure for the provision of low- and moderate-income housing, as we enter a second decade of declining incidence of homeownership, especially among young people, among people of color, and among low- and moderate-income households. Whether this pressure percolates to the national level remains to be seen as Congress continues to wrestle with the deficit and the still-unfolding HUD scandal.

6. Central cities will continue to be areas of gain or stability (not decline), especially in the downtown and especially in the dozen or so cities that continue to emerge as areas for tourism, retailing, office and service, and specialized activities. Foreign investment in these communities, as well as local and regional development, will continue during the '90s, albeit at a more deliberate pace. This activity poses both an opportunity and a risk for communities. The opportunity is that the momentum generated by invest-ment can make the development, of neighborhoods, as well as residential opportunity in the downtown, possible where it might not have been possible before. On the other hand, there is the risk that this development would take energy that might otherwise have been used to do neighborhood development or divert resources that might have been used for that purpose. This will be especially the case in cities that are not willing to somehow make links between development in the two areas.

NEW DIRECTIONS FOR NATIONAL HOUSING POLICY

It is not appropriate here to go into detail about housing programs. Part of the anguish in Washington and elsewhere in the country is that we have a list of problems and concerns but no way to address them. My view is that we need to develop a policy for the 1990s. In the section above, I outlined the three phases through which policy has gone in the past; we now need a comprehensive phase four. Where none of the other three was aggressive for the interest of blacks, a new policy has to take urban reality (political and otherwise) and justice in mind.

We cannot continue without a national housing policy if for no other reason than we will make negative progress. Taking account of all of the lessons we have learned from looking at the history of housing policy as well as the present situation, having a single grant program is not a good idea, even if it were likely. Nor should we assume that the federal government should take sole responsibil-ity. We need many initiatives which should be pursued in partnership with state and local governments, and with the nonprofit sector.

The major elements of a phase four policy might include the following:

• A housing production program for public and assisted housing that offers the prospect of permanent and affordable benefit. A production program of perhaps 100,000 units per year would be targeted to tight markets and to areas where new supply is needed.

- A continuation of vouchers for the poor and for families in markets where there are available units and to help close the gap of affordability in privately developed housing.

- Increased fair housing enforcement that prevents the kind of discrimination that is currently so widespread.

- An effective means to conserve the supply of public and assisted housing which will be at increasing risk over the next decade.

- Incentives and programs to encourage the private production of affordable private housing.

- Programs to develop greater capacity for nonprofit and community-based housing initiatives that can tap community spirit, promote self-help, and facilitate public-private partnerships.

Many of the policy suggestions above focus on shifts in national policy. State and local governments have as critical a role to play as well. The political power that blacks have mustered can be a powerful force in shaping local housing and development policy. This can result in policies that are more fair and could broaden the black community's stake in how cities take advantage of urban revitalization. While mayors may have little to do directly with unemployment rates or welfare levels, they have several powerful levers on the development process for housing and for other types of development as well.

Beyond what any level of government can do, we should also be mindful of the potential for self-help, both because of the likely void and paucity of ideas in public policy, but also because we need to use involvement in community development as a tool to empower individuals and community groups to take more responsibility for their own lives and thereby increase their personal confidence and control.

Such initiative and self-help are also important because good ideas for the community require that they be broadly accepted and initiated on the part of the people concerned. We have learned all too well that programs imposed from the outside are often insensitive to the internal issues in the communities, lack the involvement or the understanding on the part of the population they intend to serve, or fail to take into account the subtle dynamics of the neighborhood. Chances for success increase dramatically to the extent that initiatives can be undertaken jointly or initiated from within the community.

In order for this self-help role to be implemented effectively, there has to be significantly more attention paid to capacity building of institutions such as community development corporations and social agencies that operate in the community. While they have a demonstrated potential for making significant contributions,[32] there is very uneven progress in the extent to which that potential role has actually been realized from city to city.[33]

If we, in fact, take an approach where policies toward housing in communities are addressed from these four fronts: federal, state, local, and community based, we will have a chance to not only meet the housing needs of blacks but also build better communities as well. The 1990s offer the opportunity to make the most substantial progress we have made in this century.

CONCLUSION

The new, but still unfocused, recognition in the Congress that many of the problems from the '60s and '70s are still with us is a positive sign. In cities and communities across the country, there are ideas that, when given a fair hearing, will be compelling, budget constraints notwithstanding. Just as the Housing Act of 1949 ushered in a new era that spawned progress that lasted 30 years, our resolution in this new decade can restart the engine of progress and keep hope alive.

* * * *

The author gratefully acknowledges the research assistance of Angela Goode for her help in preparing this essay.

Understanding African-American Family Diversity*

Andrew Billingsley, Ph.D.

What the general public knows about African-American families can be loosely summed up by the following three concepts: single-parent families, poverty, and children in trouble. While these concepts call our attention to real, pervasive, and crippling problems in the black community, they do not capture the whole of African-American family life. Moreover, such overwhelming concentration on the problems of single-parent families, the poor, and young children gives two false impressions simultaneously. One is the impression that all these families are problem ridden and dysfunctional. The other equally false impression given is that black families who are not single parent, poor, or with young children do not have any problems that deserve special consideration. Both impressions grow out of the selective concentration by scholars and others on a limited range of the varied and complex African-American family diversity. The danger of such an approach is that in focusing so heavily on the 42 percent of single-parent families; the third of families that are poor; those with children in trouble; and failure to understand the full range of family situations is that we are likely to come up with false theories of black family life and inadequate solutions to the challenge of black family development in the 1990s.

Any serious effort to understand the many changes in African-American life which are likely to persist into the 1990s must be pursued within a framework which recognizes that the whole of African-American family life is greater than any of its parts. This proposition is "wholistic" in the sense that it encompasses African-American structure and functioning in all its variety.

In setting forth such a "wholistic perspective," we are reasserting a line of analysis established by the earliest and best of African-American scholarship on the family. W.E.B. DuBois, the pioneering African-American scholar, was eloquent in his insistence on taking a broad and inclusive approach to analyzing the African-American family.[1] In a paper before the American Academy of Political and Social Science in 1898,[2] DuBois argued that it is not possible to understand black life in America without systematically assessing the influence of historical, cultural, social, economic, and political forces. He specifically observed:

---

*This essay is taken from the author's new book, *Climbing Jacob's Ladder,* to be published by Simon and Schuster—Touchstone Books in fall 1990. It is a sequel to his widely read book, *Black Families in White America,* written with his wife Amy, first published in 1968 and recently reissued by Simon and Schuster-Touchstone Books in a 1988 Twentieth Anniversary edition.

. . . We should seek to know and measure carefully all the forces and conditions that go to make up these different problems, to trace the historical development of these conditions and discover as far as possible the probable trend of further development.[3]

It is this perspective that made DuBois such a pioneer among the early founders of sociology. We are also persuaded by a careful reading of E. Franklin Frazier that he, too, recognized and endeavored to reflect the multifaceted nature of the black family and the black experience.[4] By contrast, however, many contemporary scholars and policy analysts focus so exclusively on one dimension of family life such as single-parent families or the so-called underclass that they contribute more to stereotyping than to our understanding of the complex realities of the African-American family. This essay will discuss the diversity among these families including family-structural diversity, social-class diversity, as well as age and gender distinctions. In addition, we will show how the meaning of African-American family patterns must consider how these families are embedded in a network of community institutions and are subjected to the influence of the large-scale systems of the wider society.

DEFINITION OF AFRICAN-AMERICAN FAMILIES

What, then, do we mean by the African-American family? Essentially, it is an intimate association of persons of African descent living in America who are related to each other by a variety of means including blood, marriage, formal adoption, informal adoption, or by appropriation; sustained by a history of common residence; and are deeply imbedded in a network of social structures both internal to and external to themselves.

Blood ties or lineage constitutes the strongest element in the African-American kinship system. In the African heritage, families were defined more by blood ties than by marital ties. To some extent, this is still true among contemporary African-American families. This is particularly strong among black women, who are the primary culture bearers for the group. It often happens that if a choice must be made between allegiance to blood relatives, including siblings, parents, or children on the one hand, or to marital partners, the latter allegiance must give way. Black women will often go to extraordinary lengths to honor this ancient African principle of the primacy of consanguine relations (with blood relatives) over conjugal relations (with marriage partners). Wise and mature black men understand this and strive mightily to avoid such confrontations.

The primacy of blood ties, however, does not suggest that marriage ties are unimportant. Both relationships are highly valued, highly honored, and frequently expressed as elements of African-American family life. Indeed, at every time period since the end of slavery, a majority of African-American families have been married-couple families.

The value placed on marriage is still so strong that a majority of African-American youth and adults want to be married; and even when one marriage is dissolved, a majority seek still another. Many persons who are separated and divorced from an unsatisfactory marital experience continue to believe that marriage as an institution is preferable to their current status. Thus, we hold with Hylan Lewis, my first sociology teacher, that there is no need to focus on inculcating values of marriage and stability among African-American youth because they already exist. The need instead is to create the conditions which make it possible to consummate and sustain the marital bond which they value. And while marriage has experienced strong attack from a rapidly changing society, it is still an essential element of the family system among African-American people.

Moreover, marriage in the African tradition is not simply a union between two people but between groups of people. The kinship unit thus expands to embrace another whole set of kinfolk. Much of that tradition is still alive among contemporary African-American families. While marriage no longer requires the permission of parents, it is quite common to treat marriage as an event requiring the sanction and support of the two families. When that does not occur, an element of instability is introduced. Moreover, the relationship between members of the two families is often so close that even after divorce of a couple, one member will continue close relations with the family of the former spouse.

A third means of the formation and perpetuation of African-American families is formal adoption. This is the procedure by which black adults, married or single, go through legal procedures sanctioned by the courts to claim responsibility for a child not necessarily related to them by blood or marital ties. Formal adoption is highly valued and frequently practiced among African-American people. This is not always understood by the wider society or by social agencies. When in the 1960s and 1970s some social agencies began recruiting white adults to adopt black children, they were assured by some social scientists that African-American people had a cultural aversion to adopting these children, many of whom were born out of wedlock. It is, perhaps, the height of irony that while social scientists were describing black families as being characterized by a tendency toward female-headed families with children born out of wedlock, they also assured the public that blacks rejected these children for adoption. The truth is that at the very same time the transracial adoption movement was being championed as a solution to the problem of out of wedlock children, a majority of these children were accepted into the families of their blood relatives. This is still the case today.

While it is not generally reported, the fact is that middle-income African-American families adopt children at a higher rate than their white counterparts. This fact is often obscured by the practice of comparing black and white families from samples composed primarily of low-income black families and middle-income white families. Indeed, if we compare black married-couple families with similar white families, we find that the formal adoption rate is higher among the black couples. And since the evolution of black adoption agencies and programs, beginning with Sydney Duncan's Homes for Black Children in Detroit in the 1960s, the formal adoption rates for black married and single persons have increased. Formal adoption has a long and honorable tradition among African-American families.

It is in the realm of informal adoptions, however, where the black extended family has excelled. Thus, the overwhelming majority of black children born out of wedlock are cared for by extended families, generally their grandmothers, without the benefit of legal adoption.

Our definition of the African-American family includes the relationship of "appropriation." People can become part of a family unit or, indeed, form a family unit simply by deciding to live and act toward each other as family.

Reverend Otis Moss of Cleveland, OH, has illustrated this tendency in his family history. His mother died when he and the other children were young. His father worked hard to maintain and sustain the family unit. Then a few short years later, his father was killed in an auto accident. While young Otis was standing viewing the wreckage, a woman completely unrelated to him took him by the arm and said, "come home with me." It was from this lady's home and his new family that he was later graduated from high school, inducted into the Army, and went off to college. It was a very important form of African-American family life, even though there were neither blood ties, marriage ties, nor formal adoption.

The propensity to care for other people's children has led naturally into the foster care system where black families have distinguished themselves. Though the payments from the state for caring for these children are generally inadequate, many black families have raised these children for long periods of time. Often, they become the only families the children recognize.

There is an element in African-American family life which Carol Stack calls "fictive kin" and others call "play mother, brother or sister, aunt, uncle, or cousin." This can still be a strong basis for family unity in the African-American community. Indeed, our own children have so many "aunts," "uncles," and "cousins" unrelated to them by blood that they can hardly keep track of them. Whenever they are in need, however, or reach a particular transition in their lives, they can count on assistance from these "appropriated" family members.

Finally, in our definition of African-American family organization, people do not have to live in the same household in order to function as a family unit. They need only to share some history of common residence with some part of the family at some time in the past. Persons living in different households can function as members of the same intergenerational kinship unit.

Our definition of family allows for the tremendous diversity of family patterns which is the hallmark of the African-American family relationship. But it does not stop there. Indeed, such diversity is also reflected in the very structure of family life including who lives together, the nature of their relationship, as well as their numbers, gender, and ages. Thus, family structural diversity, age, and gender differences are all characteristics of African-American family life.

FAMILY STRUCTURAL DIVERSITY

The search for the meaning of recent transformation in the African-American community must take into consideration that no single family form characterizes the black community. Instead, a wide variety of structures have arisen. For the hundred-year period between the end of slavery and the aftermath of World War II, the structure of African-American family life was characterized by a remarkable degree of stability. Specifically, the core of the traditional African-American family system has been the nuclear family composed of husband and wife and their own children. Divorce was rare and couples stayed together till the death of a spouse. Children lived with their parents until maturity, then started their own families. A second element in the traditional African-American family system is the extended family, a carryover from the African heritage. Often, the nuclear core was joined by other relatives creating the extended family. A third element in this family tradition is the augmented family form. Sometimes the nuclear core and extended relatives were joined by nonrelatives, creating the augmented family. This, then, is the traditional African-American family system. It is not the same as the traditional American family system. Most black adults today are familiar with this traditional family system: the nuclear core, surrounded by extended relatives, and often augmented by nonrelatives as well. The stability of this family system is reflected by the fact that during the years between slavery and the 1960s, a majority of African-American families had married couples at their core, and a majority of children were reared by two parents plus other relatives. Indeed, it has been pointed out that the net decline in black married-couple families between 1890 and 1960 was less than 10 percentage points through the entire period. Among all black men, the proportion married declined from 67 percent in 1890 to 64 percent in 1960. Among women, it ranged from 56 percent to 58 percent over this period. After World War II, however, the decline became phenomenal, and this traditional African-American family structure began to give way to a wide variety of alternative forms.

As late as 1960, when uneducated black men could still hold good paying blue-collar jobs in the industrial sector, fully 78 percent of all black families with children were headed by married couples. By 1970, only 64 percent of African-American families with children were headed by married couples. This declined steadily to 54 percent by 1975; to 48 percent by 1980; and to a minority of 40 percent by 1985. This trend is likely to continue into the future. Meanwhile, one of the alternatives to the traditional family, the single-parent family—particularly the female-headed family, has escalated enormously over the past generation. Consisting of a minority of 22 percent of families with children in 1960, this family form had increased to 33 percent by 1970, to 44 percent by 1975, to 49 percent by 1980, and to a whopping 57 percent by 1985.[5]

Thus, beginning in 1980 for the first time in history, female-headed families with children outnumbered married-couple families with children. It also means that for the first time since slavery, a majority of black children lived in single-parent families. This, too, will continue to expand into the future. While black married-couple families are projected to increase by 11 percent between now and the year 2000, the number of female-headed families will increase by 25 percent.[6] Thus, the nuclear, extended, and augmented family forms which were adopted after slavery and which were to serve the African-American people well for 125 years are all in a rapid state of decline.

The decline in the marriage relation which stands at the center of the African-American family crisis has been so sharp and sustained in recent years that a number of observers have begun to talk of the "vanishing black family." Indeed, a national forum at UCLA in 1989 brought together a group of leading black and white students of the black family to examine the future of marriage among African Americans.

The abandonment of the marriage relation is severe among both black males and females. The decline has been greater, however, among females. Thus, among adult black males, 18 and over, the proportion married declined dramatically from an overwhelming majority of 67 percent in 1970 to a bare majority of 51 percent by 1985. Meanwhile, the proportion of black women who were married plunged from a similar majority of 63 percent in 1970 to a minority of 43 percent by 1985 (see Table 1).

These trends do not support the commonly held view that black men have a weaker attachment or commitment to marriage than black women. Indeed, it may suggest just the opposite. The fact that the proportion married is higher and the proportion divorced is lower and the proportion remarried is also high among men may suggest that black men have a greater attachment to and dependence on marriage than black women. In any event, however, the major observation here is that both black men and women have been avoiding or abandoning the marital status in record numbers during recent years. This behavior constitutes the leading edge of the contemporary African-American family crisis. But this is more a crisis in the marriage relation than in the family. Marriage, as we have pointed out above, is one of several bases for family formation and endurance. The allegiance to family is still so strong that on any given day, fully 75 percent of African-American people will be found living in families of one kind or another. Contrary to popular belief, this is about the

Table 1
African-American Family Structure 1960-1990 (in percentages)

	1960	1970	1975	1980	1985	1990*
Families with children:						
Two parents	78	64	54	48	40	37
Mother only	20	33	44	49	57	60
Father only	2	3	3	3	3	3

*1990 estimated by author

Source: U.S. Bureau of the Census, *Household and Family Characteristics,* March 1985 (Current Population Reports, Population Characteristics, Series P-20, No. 411), p. 9.

same as the proportion of whites who live in families, though among Hispanic persons, a phenomenal 84 percent still live in family households.

What, then, has taken the place of the traditional family system? At least nine alternative family structures have arisen in post-Industrial America to characterize the contemporary pattern of African-American family diversity.

1. Single-Person Households

First, increasing numbers of African-American adults are living in single-person households. They are single, either because they have never been married or have been married and separated, widowed, or divorced. Young persons are delaying marriage longer than in former years. Many are deciding to forego marriage altogether. The norms of society no longer require that persons be married in order to live respectable, healthy, and happy lives.

The world of black adult singles has expanded enormously in recent years. As late as 1975, only 11 percent of black men, ages 35 to 44, were still single. These figures had not changed appreciably since 1890. The proportion of black adult single women was slightly lower and also steady at about eight percent over this period.

After 1980, however, the population of adult black singles would rise dramatically. Not only were large numbers remaining unmarried but also substantial proportions of those were choosing to live apart from their families in single-person households.

In 1983, of the 8.9 million black households in the nation, a total of 2,056,000 were single-person households with adults living alone. This represented 23 percent of all black households. Women outnumbered men slightly at 1,120,000 to 934,000.

By 1986, these numbers had increased to 2,500,000, constituting 26 percent of the 9l8 million black households in that year. Single females living alone continued to outnumber single men.

This does not mean, of course, that they are absent family relationships. As we have observed above, they may have quite strong family ties, relationships, and responsibilities without living in the same household.

2. Cohabitation

A second alternative to the traditional family is cohabitation. Small but expanding numbers of adults are choosing to live with another person of the opposite sex and sometimes of the same sex in a marriage-like relationship without benefit of legal marriage. While fewer than five percent of black adults live in cohabitation relationships, the numbers also are expanding rapidly. Some do so as a prelude to marriage. Others do so in the aftermath of marriage. Still others pursue cohabitation as an alternative to marriage. Social norms have changed so drastically in recent years that, even in the black community, cohabitation—which has a long history, referred to as "shacking up"—has come to be quite acceptable and almost respectable. These arrangements tend, however, to be short lived and less stable than conventional marriages.

The number of cohabiting couples is difficult to know. In addition to the unmarried persons above living in single-person households, large numbers live in two-person households with persons to whom they are not married and not related. In 1983, there were 266,000 such couples representing 2.9 percent of all black households.

By 1986, these numbers had increased to 297,000, accounting for 3.2 percent of all living arrangements. This is the most likely pool from where cohabiting couples may be found.

3. Children, No Marriage

Among the most rapidly expanding family structures are those where there are children without marriage. In 1983, there were 3,043,000 black single-parent households (as compared with 3,486,000 married-couple households and 2,386,000 nonfamily households). Of these, 1,989,000 were single parents with children under 18. Of these, 127,000 were male-headed families and 1,864,000 were female headed. The 872,000 black female-headed families, all of whose children are 18 and over, must surely be distinguished from the 1.8 million who have children under 18.

What is the source of their single-parent status? Among men 98,000 were never married, 79,000 were divorced, 68,000 were widowed, and 64,000 were married with absent spouses due to incarceration, long-term illness, or desertion.

Among women the same pattern obtained. The largest number was never married, comprising 899,000. Next were divorced mothers at 655,000, followed by those married with absent spouses, 646,000, and 534,000 widows with children.

By 1986, single-parent families from all sources had expanded. Overall, the number had increased to 3,242,000, representing 33 percent of the 9.8 million black households.

4. Marriage, No Children

A further deviation from traditional families is married couples without children. This, too, has been expanding among African-American families.

In 1983, there were 1,585,000 black married couples without children. This represented 18 percent of all 8.9 million black households. By 1986, this had increased to 1,683,000, representing a similar proportion of the 9.8 million households.

Who are these couples without children? They are generally the more highly educated, higher income, two-earner families.

Not only is this an expanding family form but also a highly satisfactory one. Our studies show that married partners without children exhibit the highest level of personal satisfaction, family satisfaction, and satisfaction with life in general, with higher self-esteem than that found in persons in any other type of family structure.

5. Marriage and Children

Finally, we come to a family pattern that approaches the traditional. These are married couples with children. In 1983, there were 1,901,000 such families, exceeding slightly the number of couples without children. Altogether, they accounted for 21 percent of the 8.9 million black households.

By 1986, despite population growth, there were still only 1,997,000 black married-couple families with children. This amounted to a declining 20 percent of the 9.8 million black households.

6. Children and Relatives

Parents are not the only persons to head families. Grandparents still play an important role in extended families. Altogether there were 548,000 black extended families in 1983, accounting for six percent of the 8.9 million households. By 1986, this had expanded to 607,000 extended families, representing a similar proportion of the 9.8 million households. These families with other relatives living with them are shown in Table 2.

By 1986, the mix had changed somewhat, with a substantial increase in the number of single-parent families taking in other relatives and a slight decline in the number of married couples doing so.

Table 2
Families with Extended Relatives

	1983	1986
Female-headed families	120,000	132,000
Married-couple families	50,000	47,000
Male-headed families, no spouse	48,000	53,000

Still another arrangement increasingly common in the black community is a type of extended family where children live with relatives, usually grandparents, quite apart from their parents altogether.

7. Blended Families

A seventh family structure is composed of a married couple, one or both of whom have been married previously and often with children from a prior relationship. Sometimes referred to as blended families, or reconstituted families, these constitute a part of the whole of African-American family patterns. The escalating divorce rate and the increasing remarriage rate are the sources of this family form. In addition, unmarried mothers with children often get married later to men who are not the children's fathers. Sometimes these men are divorced with their own children. Thus, it is not uncommon for children to have two sets of grandparents and one or more sets of step-grandparents. Moreover, sometimes the step-grandparents take a greater interest in the children than some natural grandparents.

8. Dual-Earner Families

Married-couple families increasingly depart from the traditional relationship where the husband works in the labor force and the wife is a full-time homemaker. Among African-American families, dual-earner families have a long history but their numbers have accelerated in recent years. Moreover, since dual-earner families have such higher earnings than single-earner ones, it is understandable why the latter, more traditional pattern is vanishing. Indeed, black dual-earner families under 35 years old and who live outside the South constitute the only category of black family whose earnings have reached parity with their white counterparts. Even this is due, in part, to the fact that black wives have a longer and more consistent history of full-time work than do white wives. Often, however, this arrangement places extra strains on the wife who must work both in the labor force and at home. Husbands do not share equitably the responsibility of child care and housework, even when wives work outside the home. This, in turn, often puts extra strains on the marriage.

9. Commuter-Couple Family

Another alternative to tradition is the commuter-couple family. Under this structural arrangement, the husband works and lives for the workweek in one city while the wife and the children live in a different city, usually where the wife has a career.

All these diverse family structures, now common and growing, constitute the essence of contemporary African-American family life. Some are involuntary, some temporary and transitional. Some are filled with pain and suffering. All, however, have arisen to fill some need and function.

It is clear, moreover, that neither of the types of structures that have evolved is exclusive to African-American people. Because they are driven by larger forces which affect the entire population, they appear in other groups as well. If the pattern is different among African Americans than among other American families, it is because of the reality of the American experience.

The key to understanding African-American family structure is to see the whole picture with its many variations and to note its flexibility. Almost no one remains throughout life in any one of these structures. Most adults pass through several family structures in the course of their lives. All single adults do not remain single. Cohabiting couples do not stay permanently. All single mothers do not stay single, all married couples do not stay married, and all divorced persons do not remain divorced.

These structures represent, in part, the fallout from the decimation of the traditional family forms. They also represent, however, the remarkable capacity of these people to hold on to the spirit and the experience of family even in the face of this vanishing tradition. Such flexibility, adaptability, and diversity are among the often under-appreciated strengths of African-American families. This is why on any given day three-quarters of all African-American people will be found living in families of one form or another in the same proportion as in the nation-at-large.

SOCIAL-CLASS DIVERSITY

If the African-American people are characterized by diverse and rapidly changing patterns of family structure—rather than by any one family structure—this diversity is equally true with respect to social class. As important and troubling as is the celebrated "underclass," it represents only a small fraction of all African-American families who range across the entire spectrum of social classes. There are a number of reasons why it is important to take a wholistic view of the social-class structure encompassing the entire range of social classes in the African-American community.

First, it helps to avoid stereotypes. A focus on only one stratum tends to suggest that it is characteristic of black families. Second, a view of the entire class structure helps to show that there is upward and downward mobility in operation. It shows, for example, that one class may be expanding at the expense of another or that one class may be the source of expansion in other classes. Additionally, a view of the entire class structure shows the dynamism in the African-American community. It helps to avoid the often repeated suggestion that the underclass is permanent, or that there are only two classes—underclass and middle class, or that there is no black upper class, all of which are part of today's fashionable but false conventional wisdom.

More importantly, a view of the entire class spectrum will reveal that it is none of the above classes but the black blue-collar working class that is the backbone of the black community. Finally, it will show that it is precisely this working class that is being decimated by changing technological, economic, and social conditions which, in turn, constitute the major reason for the demise of traditional African-American family patterns. From the perspective of social change and reform, then, an appreciation of the entire social-class structure of the black community is important.

The concept social class suggests that some families have greater resources, higher status, and more options than others in managing their lives. The three most common indexes for measuring social class are the amount of family income, the educational level, or the occupational prestige of the family head. Each index has advantages and limitations. The family income measure is superior to the others as a measure of economic and social well-being.

Five Social Classes

In our own work, we have identified five distinct social class strata in the African-American community. Based primarily on level of family income, complemented by education, occupation, and style of life, these five strata include: (1) The underclass, consisting of poor families where no member has a permanent attachment to the work force; (2) The working poor, where despite working for low wages, they are not able to earn above the poverty line; (3) The nonpoor working class, composed of unskilled and semi-skilled blue-collar workers with earnings above the poverty line; (4) the middle class, comprised primarily of white-collar skilled and professional workers with family income above the median for all families; and (5) a small black upper class of families with high incomes and substantial wealth as well as social and economic influence.[7] Relying primarily on median combined family incomes converted into 1983 dollars, we have identified these five social-class strata at three points in time: 1969, 1983, and 1986. These data are shown in Table 3.

This table reveals, in part, that as important and troubling as is the celebrated black underclass, it comprises only one of the five social-class strata and includes not more than one-fifth of all African-American families.

One of the most striking features of the entire social-class structure is that while the underclass has been expanding over this period, the nonpoor working class was declining by almost the exact same magnitude, from 44 percent in 1969 to 36 percent in 1983 and to 34 percent of all African-American families by 1986.

Table 3
Social-Class Structure of African-American Families, 1969-1986

	1969		1983		1986	
	Families	%	Families	%	Families	%
Upper Class	143,000	3	267,000	4	624,000	9
Middle Class	1,100,000	25	1,500,000	25	1,910,000	27
Working Class Nonpoor	2,100,000	44	2,400,000	36	2,420,000	34
Working Class Poor	688,000	14	963,000	14		
Underclass Nonworking Poor	716,000	14	1,500,000	23	2,142,000	30

Source: U.S. Bureau of the Census.

This shows with dramatic clarity that the underclass is expanding at the expense of the nonpoor working class. In turn, this removes a considerable amount of the mystery as to why the underclass is growing and from where this growth is coming.

The underclass, then, those families where no member has a secure and productive niche in the work force, is at the bottom of the social structure. With increases in the poverty level, they were overwhelmingly single-parent families with fully 75 percent single-parent and only 25 percent husband-wife families. Where did they come from? Some families in this stratum expanded by persons leaving one family and creating another underclass family without bettering their conditions. The birth of children to persons who moved out of their parents' home forming new families is another. But just as surely, large numbers of these families were downwardly mobile from the working poor and the nonpoor working class as the rapid march of technological change has thrown millions of unskilled, uneducated, and inexperienced workers out of work.[8]

Moving up the socioeconomic ladder, just above the underclass, we find a second stratum. These are families of the working poor. If we combine the nonworking poor with the working poor, we note that African-American families in poverty after declining dramatically in the 1960s expanded from 28 percent of the total in 1969 to 37 percent by 1983 before declining slightly to 30 percent by 1986. Consequently, poor black families nearly doubled, increasing from 1.4 million families in 1969 to more than 2.4 million by 1983. Even though the poverty rate had declined further to 30 percent by 1986, this means that there were still some 2.1 million poor black families in 1986; somewhat more than the 1.9 million in 1959 who constituted 46 percent of black families at that time. It is also important to note that poverty is not so permanent or intractable as some commentators suggest. Starting with a high of 46 percent of all black families in 1959, poverty was dramatically reduced to 26 percent by 1969 after a decade of reform. It remained steady through the 1970s and escalated sharply again during the 1980s. This analysis shows distinctly that some families are poor because they do not have work while others are poor despite work at low-wage jobs in the labor force.

The working poor are those families where at least one member is employed. They have median incomes below the poverty line due to low wages, including a minimum wage which has not kept pace with inflation. Even the rise in the minimum wage passed by Congress in 1988 is so far below inflation that it will lift few families out of poverty.

Only one-third of these working poor families are husband-wife families and as many have working husbands and wives. This stratum remained steady at 14 percent of all African-American families between 1969 and 1983. Because of the expanding population, the actual numbers of African-American families in the working poor stratum increased from 688,000 in 1969 to 963,000 by 1983. Thus, there were more working poor black families in 1983 than there had been in 1969.

If we combine the working nonpoor and the working poor, we note that the working class continues to comprise the largest sector of the African-American community, ranging downward from 58 percent of all African-American families in 1969 to 50 percent by 1983 and declining further by 1986. Where did they go? Some moved up to the expanding middle and upper classes. More, however, moved down to the expanding underclass.

Above the working poor in the socioeconomic structure is a sector we call the nonpoor working class. The nonpoor (or near poor) working class is composed of those families with combined family incomes ranging from just above the poverty line of $10,000 in 1983 dollars to just under $25,000. Composed largely of blue-collar, skilled, and unskilled workers, these families are less dependent on dual earners than the middle and upper classes. Only 45 percent have working wives and husbands. Most have a high school education.

This largely blue-collar nonpoor working class has declined dramatically since 1969. That year some 44 percent of African-American families were in this class comprising some 2.1 million families. This was and still is the largest single stratum serving as the economic, social, and political backbone of the black community. By 1983, this stratum had declined to 36 percent of all African-

American families. Because of the expanding population, however, this still represented an actual increase to 2.4 million families. The strength of this social class is reflected in the fact that fully 60 percent were husband-wife families as late as 1983. In our view, this is at once the most important and vulnerable of all sectors of the class structure. It is not the underclass nor the middle class but the stable blue-collar working class. A fortification and growth of this stratum would have two effects simultaneously. It would help to stem the downward flow into the underclass and resume the upward flow into the middle and upper classes.

A modicum of public attention is now being given to the black middle class. It is as though this is another discovery of "the new Negro." Middle-class families are those with family incomes between $25,000 and $50,000 in 1983 dollars. They also tend to be highly educated, with a majority having education beyond high school, and to occupy professional, technical, and managerial occupations. They also tend to be dual-earner families.

Indeed, as Harriette McAdoo has pointed out, black middle-class husbands often maintain their level not only by using a second working person in the family but a second job as well, generally on a part-time basis.[9]

While the proportion of middle-class families doubled during the decade of the 1960s from 12 percent to 25 percent, reaching an all-time high of 29 percent in 1978, there has been a decline in recent years. While the percentages have been declining, the actual number of middle-class families has expanded from 1.1 million families in 1969 to 1.5 million by 1983. And, by 1986, there were 1.9 million black families in this sector.

The black middle class also tends to have a high proportion of husband-wife family structures. Thus, an overwhelming majority of 83 percent of families in this sector were husband-wife families. Further, working wives and mothers are the keys to the viability of the black middle class. Fully 78 percent of these families have working wives, more than any of the other four socioeconomic sectors. Moreover, the financial contribution they make to the family income is increasing and is substantially higher than that in white families.

Finally, at the peak of the African-American social-class structure is a small and growing black upper class. This sector is completely overlooked in most studies of black families, in part because it is so small. Still, an accurate understanding of African-American family life requires a recognition that this stratum has significance far beyond its numbers.

Upper-class families are those with median family incomes ranging upward from $50,000 to above $200,000 and who possess substantial wealth and economic power. It is not the absolute income, however, but the accumulated wealth which distinguishes the black upper class. Wealth or net worth is measured as total assets owned minus total debts owed. Overall, the average black-family wealth is less than 10 percent of average white-family wealth, nearly $4,000 for black families and $40,000 for whites. Even among middle-class black families, it is $18,000, constituting only a third of similar white families. However, among a few black families, the accumulated wealth rises distinctly above the white median.[10] Thus, some 12 percent of black families have accumulated wealth above $50,000. Moreover, some four percent of all black families have accumulated wealth above $100,000, a position they share with 24 percent of white American families. These families tend to be headed by highly educated parents in middle- and high-status occupations and to involve a high proportion of two working partners in the labor force.

For those African-American families who have been able to accumulate substantial financial assets, the principal instruments are home ownership, real estate, automobiles, and savings accounts. Relatively little has been invested in business ownership, stocks, and bonds. The eight major categories of investment in order of the percentage of black families participating are listed below. The second column shows the average value of the investment held.

For black parents, teachers, professional counselors, and others in a position to socialize with and advise black children and families, this pattern of successful investment and wealth accumulation provides important guidance not generally found in studies of black families.

Still further support for the socialization of black children with pioneering role models is provided by the small group of black families who have moved to the top of the socioeconomic structure by the ownership and management of their own business enterprises. Each year *Black Enterprise* magazine profiles the black families owning the largest 100 black businesses. Few more inspiring role models of upper-class blacks can be found than the John H. Johnson family of Chicago, the George A. Russell family of Atlanta, or the Earl Graves family of New York.

These families are not likely to be as well-known as some other upper-class families such as the Jesse Jackson family, which made such a positive impression at the 1988 Democratic National Convention, or the Bill Cosby family, whose example, achievement, and philanthropy make us all proud. But they are important role models, nevertheless, especially in a society which places such high values on private enterprise and in areas where blacks need a great deal of encouragement.

Table 4
Sources of Wealth Among African-American Families

Instrument	Percentage of Families	Mean Value of Assets
1. Automobiles	91	$ 4,275
2. Savings Accounts	70	1,143
3. Home Ownership	59	32,146
4. Real Estate	11	2,288
5. IRA & Keogh	11	2,288
6. Stocks & Mutual Funds	9	3,157
7. Business Ownership	4	6,578
8. Money Market Funds/Bonds	3	953

These families at the top of the socioeconomic structure are few in number, but the important point is that their tribes are increasing. In 1969, there were some 143,000 families in this black upper-class stratum comprising a tiny three percent of all African-American families in the nation. Half of all these families had working wives, and the other half were more traditional with husbands in the work force while wives and mothers were full-time homemakers. By 1983, this stratum had expanded to embrace some 267,000 families comprising four percent of all African-American families in the nation. This small sector of African-American families had expanded so rapidly during the 1980s that by 1986, they comprised nine percent of the total and included some 624,000 families.

One reason for looking at social-class stratification is that it helps to show diversity in other dimensions of life including family structure. Thus, among the black upper class, an overwhelming 96 percent are husband-wife families. At a time when it was commonly asserted that 42 percent of all African-American families were female-headed families, it is of some consequence to note that only four percent of the black upper class, 17 percent of the middle class, and 40 percent of nonpoor working-class families consisted of single parents. Only among the two poor sectors did single-parent families constitute the majority.

Briefly, the impact of social class on family status is suggested by Table 5 below.

In sum, socioeconomic class stratification is an important, if often over-looked, dimension of African-American family life. A wholistic approach which understands the full range of socioeconomic statuses in the black community can teach all of us the following lessons crucial to the well-being of black families.

First, it can teach all of us and our black children and youth that there is, indeed, room at the top and all along the socioeconomic ladder in legitimate enterprises to challenge and channel all their talents and interests and abilities.

Table 5
African-American Social Class and Family Structure

	Family Structure		
Class	Married-Couple	Single-Parent	Working-Wife
Upper Class	96%	04%	50%
Middle Class	83%	17%	78%
Working Class (Nonpoor)	60%	40%	45%
Working Class (Poor)	33%	67%	33%
Underclass (Nonworking Poor)	25%	75%	25%

Source: U.S. Bureau of the Census

They can achieve their aspirations in a wide variety of fields and be rewarded for them if they have the talent, the interest, and the help that they need.

Second, a view of the entire socioeconomic structure can teach us that individual achievement is not incompatible with stable family development, but, instead, they often go hand-in-hand.

Third, we learn from reflecting on these successful families that a remarkable concomitant to financial, occupational, and educational success is the ability to make a contribution to others.

Finally, we learn that even those with socioeconomic success, who have escaped the worst features of the underclass, still have to face and fight to overcome injustices and other obstacles unknown to their white counterparts. For those who believe that middle- and upper-class black families have no problems with racism, a recent study by *Money* magazine should be most instructive.

> A four-month investigation by *Money* shows in dollars and cents that racial discrimination still prevents middle-class (and upper-class) black families from earning as much as whites; lowers their access to mortgages, business loans, and other financial services; retards their homes' rate of appreciation; prevents them from increasing their wealth effectively; and deprives them of the economic well-being enjoyed by their white middle-class counterparts.[11]

These, then, are insights we gain from understanding African-American family diversity that we would never appreciate from a concentration of the black underclass alone.

AGE STRUCTURE

After noting the diversity of family forms and social classes in the African-American community, it is important to recognize the diverse and changing age structure and its impact on both the needs and the resources of these families. Traditionally, very young members and very old members are dependents whose care is a major responsibility for family members in the middle adult years who increasingly constitute a "sandwich" generation.

While the aged population will continue to expand through the year 2000, the declining birth rate will produce a steady decline in persons at the younger end of the life cycle.

Infants and Toddlers

If we view the totality of the life span, we note that each age range presents its own special challenges to African-American families. There were some 3.1 million infants and toddlers in the nation in 1985, evenly divided between males and females. These numbers will expand to 3.2 million in 1990 before declining to 3.1 million again in the year 2000. A major challenge for their families at this stage is infant mortality, where despite the substantial changes over the last half century, the rate is still twice as high as for children in the nation as a whole. A second challenge is to avoid the crippling, preventable illnesses that inflict children not regularly exposed to high quality prenatal and postnatal care. The third major challenge is to provide the type of socialization experiences, protection, and guidance that will enable them to develop strong self-esteem as well as positive individual and group identities. Finally, parents are challenged to prepare infants and toddlers for the progressive learning and mastery experiences required for successful integration into the world of childhood.

The challenges are so great and the rewards so increasingly small that many young couples are deciding to postpone having children and others avoid having them altogether. The resources to help with the rearing of these infants and toddlers are steadily dwindling. The extended family, older siblings, and neighbors are not nearly as available as in previous years. Quality child care at affordable prices presents a major obstacle. And the economic costs of rearing children are staggering. Still, it must be noted that despite these challenges, most black parents manage to get their infants and toddlers through this stage with remarkable physical and mental health, and with an eagerness to learn and to grow that continues to baffle the experts. Buoyed by the African heritage of child centeredness, mutual aid, willingness to suffer for the sake of the children, flexibility of family roles, and strong determination to succeed, most African-American families guide their infants safely into childhood.

Childhood

When children reach the age range five to nine, they become school children, and they have different needs. In the nation as a whole, there were some 2.5 million black children in this age range in 1985, again one-half male and one-half female. By 1990, these numbers will increase to 3.1 million and to 3.2 million by the year 2000. Most of these children have working mothers. This means extraordinary efforts are needed to provide adult supervision after school. It is a problem black working parents have long faced. In years past, they could count on a great deal of support from the extended families. Now these, mostly grandmothers, are themselves in the work force. Thus, the latchkey children—those who come home after school with no adults present and who have recently drawn special attention in the white community—have a long history among African-American parents. We need to know more about the arrangements these parents have made and the quality of care provided. Recent studies suggest a great need for high quality and affordable after-school programs.

Early Adolescence

It is the next age group in the life cycle which has been grossly neglected in social policy and programs. These are the 2.5 million black early adolescents between the ages of 10 and 14. This group, too, is expected to expand to 3.2 million by the year 2000. A recent comprehensive study by the Carnegie Corporation shows that parents, schools, and other community institutions are failing these children severely in almost every one of their developmental needs. The report focused on the need to restructure the junior high schools to make them more compatible to the developmental and learning needs and styles of this age group. At the same time, it called on parents and other community agencies for more cooperation in focusing on the needs of this age, which has often been neglected in our concern for teen pregnancy, juvenile delinquency, and other behaviors associated with the older adolescents.

While the bodies, minds, and psyches of these 10-to-14-year-old youth are developing more rapidly and sometimes erratically than they ever will again, society seems to try to look the other way. The raging hormones produce both explosive growth and mass confusion. Because they are not as likely to act out in antisocial ways as older adolescents, they, nevertheless, are harboring the seedbeds of all this behavior. Seventh grade seems to be a turning point for black children to move into the mainstream or to begin the path toward school dropout and other antisocial behavior. The 2.5 million black youth in this early adolescent stage of the life cycle will grow to 3.2 million, half male and half female, by the year 2000. Their families, their communities, and their society are largely unprepared for them.

Children are not only problems to society and to themselves but also often to these families as well. For example, they may seek to separate themselves from their families and particularly their mothers in order to establish their own identity and to establish relations with the outside world. They may no longer need or desire the constant attention from mother. Many mothers have difficulty making the adjustment and experience a sense of loss or rejection or abandonment.[12]

Late Adolescence

The late adolescent years between 15 to 19 are the most challenging years for African-American parents. Their physical maturation provides parents with the triple challenge of keeping them in clothes, keeping them in food, and keeping them in school. The challenge is most severe for low-income families and somewhat less taxing for upper-income families. It is, however, a challenge that faces all parents of adolescents. If parents have been successful in instilling a set of personal values about bodily care and correct conduct, adolescents will have a stronger set of armor with which to fight the efforts of the peer groups, the streets, and the mass media to reduce their appetites and conduct to the lowest common denominator. If families have nurtured a set of skills and high aspirations, they will have even more protection. If the family and the youth are tied into social, economic, and political institutions in the community, additional protection will provide for their growth and development. The key for adolescents, however, is whether they have developed by then a love for learning and whether they are placed in a supportive and demanding learning environment.

The hazards of adolescent years for the youth, their parents, and society are as severe as they will ever get. The high school dropout rate, teen pregnancy, drug abuse, accidents, homicide, and suicide are all crippling afflictions for this age. On the other hand, the level of altruism, the capacity for firm commitment, will never be higher. Adolescents are at once suspended between childhood and adulthood. They can be the most loving, helpful, humanitarian, and reformist of any age group. They can also alternate between those lofty ideals and crass individualistic narcissism. No parents—whether single, double, or triple—can cope alone with the bursting energy, strong will, and may-care attitudes let loose without moral, physical, and social constraints that the young people themselves can understand and accept.

It is at this stage that young people desert their family traditions with seeming reckless abandon. Religion, personal conduct codes, sexual codes, dress codes and language codes all become brittle and are often toppled by the popular culture, popular media, and the power of commercial exploitation. Youth will spend as much for the right type of jeans or sweater as their fathers paid for an entire suit of clothes.

It is also during the tender teenage years that the drug culture can be attractive and gang life stands poised to replace home life and church life.

Both the joys and the agonies of parents of adolescents are likely to become even more keenly arrayed against each other in the years ahead. There will be at first a slight decline and then a sharp growth in late adolescents from 2.7 million in 1985 to 2.5 million in 1990 and then to an upswing to 3.1 million by the year 2000. Altogether the early and late adolescents, between the ages of 10 and 19, will expand from 5.2 million in 1985 to some 6.3 million by the year 2000. Thus, both the joys and the problems of adolescence offer long-term challenges to African-American families, their community, and their society.

Young Adulthood

If young people can pass successfully through the challenges of adolescence, with a high school education, positive skills, and positive attitudes and if they can face an opportunity structure which beckons and welcomes them, they move into the years of young adulthood, ages 20 to 24, full of promise. The numbers in this age group will decline steadily from three million in 1985 to 2.7 million in 1990 and to 2.6 million by 2000.

If they can look forward confidently to college, trade school, the military, or a meaningful entry-level job, they can become the best and most productive of citizens. Postponing marriage, living the life of adult singles, often in cohabitation relationships with other youth, they can prepare for the transition into adulthood with all flags flying. Unfortunately, all too many of these young adults face the consequences of failure to make the transition from adolescence. Many will be convicted of crimes and serve long jail sentences. Others will spend years of unemployment and drifting from one situation to another. Often, they will find that they cannot be self-supporting and will seek to return to live with their parents. Young, unmarried mothers will inevitably seek the protection of their mothers' and grandmothers' homes. The extended family will be taxed often beyond its limits.

The upside and the downside of young adulthood cause many parents to extend their parental role and concern well beyond the age of majority of their offspring. We have come to witness a type of reverse empty-nest phenomenon as many young adults find it more comfortable to return to their parents' home.

The Middle Years

Those who survive with their persons, values, and opportunity structure in tact move into middle adulthood (ages 25 to 39) ready to tackle the challenges of completing their higher education, achieving occupational stability, and entering the realm of marriage and child rearing. This group will expand from 7.1 million in 1985 to 8.2 million in 1990 and 8.3 million by 2000. If their first priority is establishing their occupational and economic stability, their second priority is socializing their children along the lines indicated above and protecting them from the hazards of life and racism. Whatever their social class, they face enormous challenges in the area of housing, health care, and education for their children.

They share these challenges with the mature group aged 40 to 64, which will expand from 5.8 million in 1985 to 6.5 million in 1990 and to 9.2 by the year 2000, where they will constitute the largest and most stable segment of the black community. They will constitute the classic sandwich generation with concern for both their children and their parents.

Seniors

Family members are living longer and creating a larger old age group of dependents. The number of African-American persons over 65 years is projected to expand from 2.4 million in 1985 to over three million by the year 2000. The numbers over 85 will expand even more rapidly, from 189,000 to more than 412,000. Finally, blacks 100 and over will expand from 6,000 in 1985 to over 10,000 in the year 2000.

At the same time, many of the elderly are less dependent economically because of improved social security and pension benefits. Because of improved health care, many of the elderly are not physically dependent until they reach advanced years. The black elderly, as a number of scholars have pointed out, are not only a source of dependency to their families but also a source of assistance to them. Grandmothers are the most characteristic family supports in that they provide a great deal of the child care, particularly for the increasing numbers of working mothers.

One of the most striking changes in the African-American population during this century has been in the age structure, represented especially by the aging of the black population. In 1900, the average life expectancy of black males was 32.5 years, and for females it was 35. By 1985, this had expanded to over 65 years for black men and to over 70 years for black women, with black women living substantially longer than men.

The diversity and trends across the entire African-American age structure are portrayed in Table 6.

Table 6
Table 6
African-American Age Structure Through the Life Span 1985 to 2000 (in millions)

AGE RANGE	1985		1990		2000	
	Number	Percent	Number	Percent	Number	Percent
All Ages	29.1	100	31.4	100	35.8	100
Male	13.8		14.9		17.0	
Female	15.3		16.5		18.7	
Infants/Toddlers						
Under 5	3.1	11	3.2	10	3.1	9
Male	1.5		1.6		1.6	
Female	1.5		1.6		1.5	
Childhood						
5–9 years	2.5	8	3.1	10	3.2	9
Male	1.3		1.6		1.6	
Female	1.2		1.5		1.6	
Early Adolescence						
10–14 years	2.5	8	2.5	8	3.2	9
Male	1.3		1.3		1.6	
Female	1.2		1.2		1.6	
Late Adolescence						
15–19 years	2.7	9	2.5	8	3.1	9
Male	1.4		1.3		1.6	
Female	1.3		1.3		1.5	
Young Adulthood						
20–24 years	3.0	10	2.7	9	2.6	7
Male	1.5		1.4		1.3	
Female	1.5		1.4		1.3	
Adulthood						
25–39 years	7.1	24	8.2	26	8.3	23
Male	3.4		3.9		4.1	
Female	3.8		4.3		4.2	
Middle Years						
40–64	5.8	20	6.5	21	9.2	26
Male	2.7		2.8		4.2	
Female	3.1		3.7		5.0	
Seniors						
65–84 years	2.2	8	2.2	7	2.6	7
Male	1.0		.8		.9	
Female	1.3		1.4		1.7	
Elders						
85–over	189*	1	257*	1	412*	1
Male	60*		77*		110*	
Female	129*		180*		302*	
Median	26.2		27.7		30.2	

*thousands

Source: Bureau of the Census, Current Population Reports Series P-25, No. 952, *Projections of Population of the U.S. By Sex, 1983–2080.*

CONCLUSION

In sum, then, generalizations about African-American family patterns often degenerate into stereotypes because they fail to put these families in a wholistic perspective. They fail to understand the complexity and diversity of these families. In their legitimate concern with single-parent families, they fail to appreciate the extent of black family structural diversity. In their focus on the underclass at the bottom of the socioeconomic scale, they ignore the working class, middle class, and upper class. In their focus on adolescent behavior, including school failure and teen parenting, they ignore important dimensions of the life cycle at younger and older age ranges. Finally, in an often myopic focus on the family as an institution, they ignore its interdependence with the institutional structure of the black community and with the systems of the larger society.

There is an urgent need in African-American family studies for a broader view as urged by DuBois a hundred years ago. Such an approach will help us understand these families better. It will help us to see more clearly their connection with other families. More importantly, it will help us to fashion sounder theories and sounder policies to enhance the structure and the functioning of these families.

The Rewards of Daring and the Ambiguity of Power: Perspectives on the Wilder Election of 1989

Matthew Holden, Jr., Ph.D.

THE ATTAINMENT OF POWER

For a long time now, many African-American intellectuals and others have been talking about "empowerment," when the real objective is the attainment of power. There is a difference. "Empowerment" is an idea that comes from social work. It involves the caseworker attitude toward the client whom the caseworker very much wants to help. It "refers to a process whereby persons who belong to a stigmatized social category throughout their lives can be assisted to develop and increase skills in the exercise of interpersonal influence and the performance of valued social roles."[1] Power, however, consists in getting others to do what they would not do if you did not intervene. Power is not something to which people are "assisted," but which they themselves attain.

There is a tendency to expect the attainment of power to be in relation to the number of positions held, especially in black majority areas. State government has seemed an improbable arena. The last black-majority state was Mississippi, as shown in the 1940 census. Present demographic trends do not lead us to expect another attainment of high office where blacks are a distinct minority—a more subtle problem about which we have given less than desirable periods of thought.

THE VIRGINIA BASELINE

Yet, in a sudden way, the Virginia election of 1989 gives us a new reason to think carefully. Ten years ago, no one gave public voice to the expectation of a black governor in the Confederacy's capital city than to that of the collapse of communist rule in Eastern Europe. There is, of course, a natural tendency to discuss Virginia by discussing the personality of L. Douglas Wilder. But most of that is necessarily speculative, no matter how close those who claim to interpret him say they are. Public evidence is better, at least when it is consistent with the actions that take place. Wilder is, so it is said, a cook. One author even says he is virtually a gourmet chef. He says that he cooks merely for relaxation. In any event, he has given public voice to ideas about cookery that may be taken as a clue to his political style. During the campaign, one paper, the *Richmond Times-Dispatch,* printed a "personality" interview in which he offered some comments about his attitude toward cooking. Hidden in the cookery interview were at least three decision rules that the outside observer may impose on the public career of Wilder as politician. (1) Consider the consequences. ". . . Keep your cholesterol down. Don't eat a lot of egg dishes. But I like seafood . . . I like a nice trout or some nice Norwegian salmon, if you can grill it nice and succulent and keep your cholesterol down. Don't put butter on it." (2) Follow your own intuition. "I use three and four different recipes by mixing them all together. I measure by my hands and fingers rather than by dishes and spoons and cups." (3) Keep your privacy, and do not let others see too much. "I like to cook totally by myself. I don't like anyone peeping over my shoulder."

It is remarkable how much this reminds one of the political style of Franklin Delano Roosevelt, of whom *all* intimates commented, and sometimes complained, that they were really not in his confidence, that he would not take the chances they wanted him to take, and that his actions seemed incomplete or inconsistent.

Governor-Elect Wilder is an African American, and he, thus, is a member of a group that has been stigmatized. His election shows the development and increase in "skills in the exercise of interpersonal influence and the performance of valued social roles." Wilder's election is, at the very least, an extraordinary personal attainment: it is a sign that the individual's identification as African American no longer constitutes automatic rejection. In Wilder's election as Governor of Virginia, what one perceives is the rewards of daring and what one forecasts in the governorship to come is the ambiguity of "power." What is not true is that he was "assisted" to do so, but that he forced his way through the complex realities of Virginia politics to become accepted as such.

Doug Wilder is different from most establishment African-American politicians in that his career has oscillated among severe pressure upon those in control, accession to a new level of power, accommodation and defense of pragmatism, and new pressure upon those in control. Late in the gubernatorial campaign, two political journalists described Wilder as "the master of political chutzpah, relying on the sheer force of his personality to work his will; . . . an outsider—even a rebel—with a flair for populist rhetoric; someone who will humiliate supposed friends, then deny it; a self-made millionaire who pleads poverty in his campaigns; . . . also the insider, the cocky and cagey veteran of the legislative warren; someone who can bloody his enemies without being soiled himself."[2] Daring has been an essential feature.

This achievement is framed in a recent report by Larry J. Sabato. Professor of government and foreign affairs at the University of Virginia, Sabato is the premier commentator on election politics in Virginia. His coverage of elections is so thorough and his reputation for knowledge of election history so deep and detailed that he is rather analogous to Henry Kaufman on the stock market. No matter how hard he may try to deny it, any statement of what he believes is fact, or any reported projection is taken seriously by players in Virginia politics. Sabato's *Virginia Votes* is biblical. Just before Christmas 1989, he published an update analyzing "Virginia's National Election for Governor—1989."[3]

The play on words is patent and valid. The Virginia election of 1989 *is* nationally significant. The culture of Virginia is more civil, more restrained in tone than one normally associates with the Deep South. But Virginia's role in African-American history is as tough—coercion masked over with civility. Judge Leon Higginbotham's studies of the legal history of slavery are in point. So was the suppression of African-American citizenship in the late 19th century and the 20th century creation and maintenance of the Byrd machine. So was the politics of school segregation known as "massive resistance." There are, in the black community, persons in their sixties who recall very well the denial of jobs and credit as penalties for opposing the racial status quo.

The residues of segregation still show themselves. There is an occasional roadside cafe that says it will not serve blacks. There are rural neighborhoods—and even cities—where people may be coerced physically into removing themselves from residences they had intended to occupy. Richmond was one of the cities that attempted to adopt formal segregation ordinances, "municipal apartheid," about 1930—years after the Supreme Court held that such could not be done constitutionally. The Prince Edward Educational Foundation, in the area known as Southside, was one of the private academy systems affected by the question of whether income tax deductions could be taken for contributions to support segregated private schools.

There is no need to recite the history in further detail, except to mark the baseline against which L. Douglas Wilder was elected to the state senate 20 years ago, the first black state senator since Reconstruction. Wilder has come to be the personification of *realpolitik*.

While Wilder has been described as a "liberal," a term he does not now seem to cultivate, his senate career was probably helped by the fact that Virginia was not a place where liberal Democratic politics was strong. He had to deal with rural whites—some of whom might have been called "rednecks" and old-time conservatives—on the basis of purely expedient alliances. In that isolated situation, inter-*personal* politics depended on mutual liking or mutual distrust and on convenience.

> Although he was one of the state senate's two members from Richmond, Wilder said he found himself ignored by the city's Main Street business establishment which, in tandem with the old Byrd Democratic machine (later to transfer its loyalty to the GOP), had ruled Virginia for 50 years.
>
> "They were as nice as they could be," Wilder recalled of the Richmond money men, "but they ignored me."[4]

In the senate, he entered into an offensive and defensive alliance with others who were not yet members of the "club," thus developing a power to veto, if not to pass, legislation. In the same way, he managed to develop a working understanding with a conservative Richmond senator who chaired the finance committee. The chairman soon discovered that Wilder, however tempestuous his original reputation, did not go off the reservation casually. In a sense, he learned the same lesson that Senator Daniel P. Moynihan (D-NY) learned when Russell Long (D-LA) was chairman of the Senate Finance Committee. "I would like to know," he once asked, "how the Chairman is going to vote. I don't intend to waste mine."

"With tenure and seniority, however, Wilder found a way to get their attention—by aligning himself with other lesser legislative lights to kill their legislation. By the mid-1970s, Wilder had begun to acquire friends in the senate and found even the standoffish Richmond business community coming to him."[5]

THE REWARDS OF DARING

Lieutenant Governor

When Wilder was but a "black state senator" from Richmond, dramatic politics on his part was both explainable and practical. Once he began to be a member of the legislative "club," such politics was more debatable. Yet, he suddenly shifted course most dramatically in 1982. Robb, as Governor, sought to exercise leadership in the Democratic party by securing quiet consent to the U.S. Senate nomination of Owen Pickett, now a Congressman and then a state legislator from the Virginia Beach area. Pickett had been identified in the past with the Byrd machine, the symbol of which—"massive resistance"—is indeed phobic to African Americans in Virginia. Wilder's threat was to run himself as an independent candidate for the U.S. Senate, thus crystallizing the split and drawing off the black vote that is essential to the victory of Democrats statewide. Robb and others capitulated, nominating a more acceptable candidate, Lieutenant Governor Richard J. Davis, who lost the election to Paul Trible.

The idea that a legislator could threaten to bolt, embarrass his governor-party leader, arguably contribute to the loss of a U.S. Senate seat, and still run successfully for lieutenant governor in the same party but three years later might seem mind-boggling.

Yet, this is precisely what did occur. Senator Wilder was evidently a major behind-the-scenes player in the Robb administration. The question was what would occur when he sought to become a statewide candidate himself. The common supposition was that a black candidate would drag the state ticket down to defeat. Thus, the first problem approaching 1985 was to secure the Democratic nomination for governor.

At some point during the Robb administration, Wilder began to take seriously the concept of himself being nominated as the Democratic candidate for lieutenant governor. He was not taken seriously by others. The principal impediment to others, however, appears to have been the fear that running against Wilder would be taken as "racist" politics. This would obviously have

112

been disadvantageous since black voters were an essential part of the Democratic base.

The anxiety of Democrats about the candidacy was acute. Early in the campaign, the governor's press secretary spoke of the need to be realistic, saying that "Virginia is still Virginia." Many people spoke of their anxiety that a Wilder candidacy would cause the whole ticket to lose, but no one seemed determined to run directly against Wilder.

Governor Robb issued an open invitation, saying that it was neither "sexist" for others to consider running for Attorney General—the other candidate for that was Mary Sue Terry—nor "racist" to consider running against Wilder. Robb has always maintained that he gave Wilder credibility by framing the issue that way. Wilder has emphatically disagreed. Robb's role in the 1985 campaign has remained a subject of controversy. He and Wilder later had an unpleasant exchange of letters on the subject.

Wilder and his advisers skillfully maneuvered to keep the tension level high so that other candidates would not enter against him. He also adopted the strategy of bargaining with the two main contenders for governor in 1985. One was then-Lieutenant Governor Richard J. Davis, the other was Attorney General Gerald L. Baliles. The point was to get each to commit his support from other areas in exchange for Wilder's support in Richmond. In the end, the more "conservative" Baliles made the stronger commitment.[6]

In any event, the desire to run for lieutenant governor forced upon Wilder the clear need to adapt to a broader constituency. The black population of Virginia, then providing 12 or 13 percent of the electorate, was not to provide the necessary numbers for statewide victory. But he evidently took his candidacy seriously.

"I am not running to prick any consciences," Wilder once said. "I'm running to get elected."[7] In 1985, and again in 1989, this strategy led to avoidance of the Jackson identification or anything that would automatically separate him from white voters.

With the nomination in hand, the problem was to secure the election. The basic strategy that Wilder adopted was to play for the rural and conservative Democrats first, taking more or less for granted support of blacks and urban liberals. The strategy worked, though at some risk of losing black support for resentment or lack of motivation.

Why Wilder Won the Governorship

About seven weeks before the 1989 election, Senator Charles S. Robb (D-VA) campaigned in Northern Virginia in behalf of Wilder. Robb said that an earlier exchange of letters with Wilder reflected his feelings then and no longer apply. "Those letters reflected the situation then. That's one year out of 14," Robb said, referring to letters he wrote Wilder shortly after the 1985 election in which he questioned Wilder's honesty and whether he was a team player. "We have a 14-year history of cooperation and personal relationship."

Asked if he would take back anything he said, the former governor said, "You'll never see me try," but he believes the episode is over.[8]

The dispute had been about Wilder's 1985 campaign, and about how much Robb had helped or not. Robb's role in the 1989 campaign reveals a different element: the necessary adjustment—the adoption of Wilder's victory as a preferred outcome for the Virginia Democratic establishment.

There is a lady of my acquaintance, a true Virginian whose vowels are charmingly as broad as the James in flood. For five years, she has been convinced that Wilder is "a good ole boy," black or not—and convinced ever since the talk began that he could win the governorship. Once I suggested that Wilder would be a sure-thing candidate if there were a citizens committee headed by Mills Godwin. (Godwin, a legend in his own time, was the last pure-Byrd Democratic governor. He returned to office in 1973 as a Republican, rolling back the "moderate" approach to Republicanism that Linwood Holton had adopted in 1969. Holton was one of the first of the southern governors to adopt an overt acceptance of blacks as a normal part of the polity. Godwin, who could show great flexibility on some matters, remained the leader of the old guard in these matters. He has since remained as a looming presence for the Virginia conservatives.)

Five days into the new year of 1989, she sent me a clipping from the *Richmond Times-Dispatch* reporting that Douglas Wilder would hold a $1,000 per person fund-raiser at the Jefferson Sheraton on January 24, announce his candidacy at the state capitol on January 26, and hold a $100 per person "fund-raising gala" at the Richmond Omni on January 28. Deep in the story was a single-sentence paragraph: "Last month, Wilder generated at least $55,000 at a cocktail party organized by S. Buford Scott, Jr., the Richmond financier and top fund-raiser for Gov. Gerald L. Baliles."[9]

My friend's note was unusually forthright. The paragraph referring to Mr. Scott was encircled, and the typed message said: "This is not a citizens committee with Mills Godwin at its head, but it's damn close." In any event, he permitted himself to be identified with the Wilder campaign. The first of the official campaign financial reports showed "Sidney Buford Scott" with a contribution of $10,200 in January 1989.[10] The required report (eight days before the November general election) also showed Scott with an aggregate contribution of $25,200. Scott, a devout Episcopalian, devoted University of Virginia alumnus, and head of the Scott & Stringfellow stock brokerage firm, is a critical person.

Other contributors are reported publicly with vastly greater sums—a Northern Virginia entrepreneur at well over $100,000 and John W. Kluge at $200,000. The relevance of the Scott contributions is that a pillar of the Virginia establishment could so openly support the Wilder candidacy.

We should not underestimate the importance of the small donors. About 15 percent of the $7,000,000 reported by Wilder came from donors who gave $100 or less.[11] But the key feature to consider is the adoption of the Wilder candidacy as a part of establishment Democratic politics.

Perhaps some Theodore White will give the 1989 campaign the subtle analysis and extensive scrutiny that it deserves. Its organization and relationship to the social structure of the state, to the political structure of Black America, to the Democratic party, and to the ways of the business and labor communities warrant closer attention than we can now give, based upon press reports.

The doctrine was widely circulated that the campaign had "no organization." "In political circles, Lt. Gov. L. Douglas Wilder . . . is not known for an ability easily to reach out to others . . . [and] some Democrats say that his campaign seems chaotic and preoccupied with secrecy."[12] This report continued: "After weeks on the defensive, Wilder has learned the hard way that his campaign desperately needs structure and that he must regularly consult with a range of Democratic leaders or their subalterns."[13] Such a story can only reflect the guerrilla warfare that afflicts political campaigns, when even supposed allies try to influence each other through media signals and when subordinates similarly try to influence their superiors.

It is plausible, or course, that a man who does not adhere too much to formulae and who prefers not to have others look over his shoulder would operate in that manner. The story does reflect that, on the public record, Wilder and his immediate colleagues—Senator Robb and Governor Baliles—have not always been able to coordinate closely.

There is another dimension of the Wilder campaign organization that may return as we foresee the governorship. Wilder has some unexplained appeal to children of the establishment.

Whatever is to be said of that, Wilder chose overtly to identify himself with the political styles of Robb and Baliles. He spoke of "a new mainstream," of fiscal prudence, of carrying Virginia forward without being immersed in old issues. The Republican campaign attempted, persistently, to disturb this style. It almost succeeded. The campaign involved a series of personal problems that his opponents attempted to display as a failure of "character." These involved his handling of some real estate held for investment and a problem with a dissatisfied client whose complaint led to a reprimand from the state supreme court.

In the end, the votes that sustained Wilder came from two crucial sources.

There was a six-point gender gap, to which the unexpected emergence of abortion as a state political issue contributed something. Women favored Wilder by 53 percent; men picked Coleman by 53 percent. More women than men voted, giving Wilder his winning plurality.

As the Sabato report showed in extraordinary detail, abortion's influence (as well as race) may have showed up again in the preferences of younger voters.

Those aged 18-44 gave Wilder 56 percent, those age 60 and over only 38 percent. Coleman lost more of the normal Republican constituency than Wilder did of the normal Democratic constituency. One-third of Wilder's voters had voted for Bush Bush in 1988.

The Wilder camp came to regard the abortion issue as their "magic bullet,"[14] although press coverage of the campaign shows that it took some while for Wilder to discover how he would best approach the issue. The public discussion of abortion had a crystallizing effect, but is more complex than we now understand. Actually, slightly more voters expressed support for more restrictions or complete restrictions on abortion rather than freely available abortions. Coleman got the votes of about a third of those who had pure pro-choice views, and Wilder got the votes of about a fifth of those who wanted abortion prohibited entirely.[15] "Of course," as Sabato says, "elections are won or lost at the margins, and Wilder used abortion to squeeze out just enough votes— mainly from Republican-leaning, white suburban women—to [win the gubernatorial] prize."[16]

Wilder captured a quarter of the votes of conservatives. He captured virtually all of the liberals' votes but also a 55 percent landslide among the swing moderates. Wilder lost most among white blue-collar workers.

At least a third of the voters ticket-split, a substantial increase from 1985.

Wilder's victory was built on a massive majority (69 percent) in central cities, where turnout was exceptionally high (22 percent of the total vote, far above normal). Coleman won the suburbs with 53 percent, but the suburban vote was down as a proportion of the total.

Wilder won 96 percent of the black vote. Black turnout skyrocketed—73 percent of those registered, about seven percentage points higher than white turnout. Blacks comprised 17 percent of election day turnout, an exceptionally high proportion.

The Wilder proportion of the black vote in 1989 was about the same as the proportion in 1985. The difference was that more people voted. In the last three elections—contrary to some mythology—blacks had shown a slightly higher turnout rate (in percentages) than whites. In 1977, the overall rate was 61.9, and the black rate was 62.8. In 1981, the overall rate was 64.9, and the black rate was 67.5. In 1985, the overall rate was 53.0, and the black rate was 53.9. In 1989, the Wilder turnout rate in the same sample precincts was 72.6 percent in contrast to the overall turnout rate of 66.6 percent. "The turnout of blacks," said Sabato, "startled even the Wilder campaign."[17] There doubtless will be much debate about whether the turnout was due to the get-out-the-vote organization by the Wilder campaign, to Wilder's own campaigning in the black community, or to the sheer fact of intensive television reportage that activated the black part of the electorate.

Coleman won 59 percent of whites . . . Wilder's 41 percent of whites was down three percent from 1985 but far above Dinkin's 30 percent in New York. Two-thirds of Wilder's total votes came from whites.

Coleman's voters were far less committed to his candidacy than were Wilder's. Moreover, the electorate as a whole was far more inclined to say that Coleman had spent his time attacking his opponent rather than talking issues. On the other hand, the evidence from the election results is that the attacks had substantial impact.

THE AMBIGUITY OF POWER

If the Wilder election is the reward of daring, and if it is further sustained by the adoption of the Democratic establishment, there is a further question. What will the *governor* face? "Power" is something that we talk about in common sense language all the time. It is hard, in reality, to be sure what it is.[18]

There will be, with Governor-Elect Wilder as with any new chief executive, much speculation on the basis of real or presumed "inside sources." This may have its value, but I find it preferable to focus upon the *logic* of observable situations. What realities are present and what options should those realities be expected to present?

Virginia governors are, inherently, powerful people, perhaps a good deal more so than most governors. "Formal powers and political tradition," says one author, "have made the office of governor of Virginia one of the strongest in the land."[19] This is partly because of the governor's official authority over budget preparation and personnel choices, and doubtless because it developed at a time when one consolidated political machine controlled both state government and the local governments. That power, of course, is shared with the legislature, which is still regarded as one of the more traditional and quietly managed legislatures in the country.

The question, in due course, must come as to the relationship of Governor Wilder who, on one hand, was an extremely sophisticated legislator when functioning for himself alone, but who—unlike his two predecessors—comes without the background of a deep set of organizational and factional networks supporting him. Inevitably, there will be some ambiguity about the power of the governor until that power is tested in exercise. Ambiguity will also present itself in the executive-administrative arena and its overlap with the legislature.

One of the most significant powers is the appointment power. Steven Johnson, a young scholar-reporter who has recently written about the Robb administration, says the governor appoints top agency heads and "the 3,000 members of boards and commissions that help to oversee a range of the state's activities."[20]

As a practical matter, the governor has the opportunity to convey some degree of prestige or power on one in every 2,000 citizens of the state. Johnson reports that Robb used his appointment powers quite purposefully:

> In all, Robb appointed 540 women and 300 blacks to the state's boards and commissions, about one-third of all appointments. The appointments followed a strategy of open hiring practices further down the secretarial levels. In the transportation office, there were 92 blacks and 124 women appointed among 336 appointments in fiscal year 1983.[21]

The "top agency heads" just cited include, at the very top, seven "cabinet" secretaries—Administration, Economic Development, Education, Finance, Human Resources, Natural Resources, and Transportation and Public Safety. The secretaries, coordinated by the "chief of staff," are the governor's overseers for some 60 or more agencies and entities within the state governments. The agencies—ordinarily called "departments"—are coordinated by a "chief of staff" who has a close political and administrative relationship to the governor. In the next administration, this relationship presumably will be maintained at the outset, for Governor-Elect Wilder has announced the designation of J.T. Shropshire as his chief of staff. If biographers are to be believed, Wilder and Shropshire have provided a good conduit to the conservative, rural legislators who have provided most of the Virginia legislative leadership.

These seven cabinet secretaries are the main places where the actual administrative decision-making and work of state government take place. Here is where the state employs more than 80,000 full-time salaried employees and spends more than $20 billion. The administrative tasks can be formidable, and some governors appear to find them unwelcome.

The governor's responsibilities for the budgetary process will come rapidly to rest on the new administration. In December, 1989, shortly after the election, Governor Gerald Baliles announced that it was now clear that there would be a revenue shortfall sufficient to call for spending cuts of about two percent in agency budgets. While two percent spending cuts may not be catastrophic, they would impose an impediment to Governor-Elect Wilder's pursuit of some tax reduction about which he has talked.

Economic conservatism has been a central element of Virginia politics. State law has been generally unfavorable toward unionization, and some conflict on this issue has appeared, even as of the time of the 1989 election campaign. The center of the issue lay in the coal fields of southwestern Virginia, an area that was very important to the initiation of Wilder's successful lieutenant gubernatorial campaign in 1985. The fight was between Pittston Coal Company and the United Mine Workers over the ability of the company to reduce worker benefits in the interest of what management deemed prudent action.

Wilder had become identified in the coal fields as having some sympathy with the miners, and the charge came late in the campaign that he actually promised them something that threatened Virginia's long-standing "right to work" law. It is plausible that this issue will come again, but it is hard to imagine one more difficult for a governor with support in both the business and labor sectors.

Within the first 18 months, more or less, the Wilder administration may have to cope with reapportionment as a racial issue. There is no black member of the Virginia congressional delegation. In 1990, however, it is predicted that the census will show Virginia is entitled to an additional congressional seat. The legislature and governor will have to decide how to apportion the seats, or how to draw the lines to reflect the realities of the 1990 census. Political observers expect the issue to be presented as to whether the new district lines will maximize the chances for a black candidate to be elected (which means a seat in the Tidewater region) or whether it will maximize the chances for a Democrat in suburban northern Virginia. In a sense, then, Governor-Elect Wilder will face the choice of a seat in northern Virginia, where his support in 1989 was very strong, or a seat in the black region, which was the natural base from which he started in 1985.

The very fact of the Wilder victory may also raise new issues as to the basis on which the courts will look at local government apportionment issues. The usual range of state government issues will always be present. Higher education is always expensive, and it is also entangled with the fate of the historically black institutions. Wilder made a strong attempt to identify himself with a tough anti-crime and anti-drug posture and appears to have said he wants to retain close control over the prison system through an aide in his own office. That seems surprising, as prison management has generally not been a winning political issue, whether the governor is "conservative" or "liberal."

In such matters, the authority of the governor to make legal decisions will not be in question. What may come into question is the ability of a governor to make decisions that will be politically sustainable.

Finally, the pressure of state politics, in which the governor is expected to take a leading role, and of national politics will be part of the picture. The pressure of national politics will be especially acute, if one follows out the logic of underlying relationships.

The obvious fact is that the Democratic party will have, at its 1992 national convention, the most visible black political figure ever to have appeared. The equally obvious fact is that the Democratic party needs a political figure who cannot only help to paper over the racial schism within the party, but also one who has no doctrinaire adherence to themes that have been thought by some to dominate the party's action in conventions since 1968 or 1972. Equally obvious is that the Democratic party needs a political figure that can appeal to the black part of its constituency and that does not have a record of reciprocal discomfort with the Jewish part of its constituency.

On that logic, the Democratic leadership cannot fail to find whites an alternative to Jesse Jackson. This is not a matter of Doug Wilder's wish or Jesse Jackson's wish; it is the logic of the situation.

Therefore, the obvious question is what *role* can the Democratic leadership assume for a Governor Wilder?

Among other things, Wilder becomes a self-evident subject of discussion about a place on a national ticket. At the least, he will be no less credible in such a role than Jesse Jackson. Once the politics takes that form, it may be that he will not be obviously less credible than Senator Robb. It is not a question of whether he would entertain such a thought, but whether other national Democrats will not be driven automatically to such a thought.

In 1928, Governor Alfred E. Smith (New York) not only wanted to run for president, but also personally handpicked Franklin Delano Roosevelt to run for governor. Roosevelt did not then desire to run, and much persuasion—including some from his wife—was necessary to secure his agreement. Neither contemplated that Roosevelt would stand in Smith's path, nor that Smith would become Roosevelt's bitter enemy. But Roosevelt, as governor, and Smith fell into dispute, and they did become antagonists. The logic is relatively basic. When people approach the executive pinnacle, whether in churches, universities, corporations, or government, competition between those who may be presumed allies otherwise is intense. On the basis of the existing track record from 1969 until 1989, Governor-Elect Wilder has displayed an extraordinary ability at following a rational politics of self-interest, without assuming that alliances are permanent.

Health Status of Black Americans

LaSalle D. Leffall, Jr., M.D.

It is vital that as a nation we do everything in our power to ensure equal access to the best health care possible for all Americans, for without good health nothing in life has meaning. Striving to extend high quality health care to all of our citizens is a process which also grants them hope. Granting people HOPE is one of the greatest of all human joys—the joy of anticipation that perhaps there is something that can be done for them.

In spite of a century of overall improvement in the health of Americans, statistics show a persistent negative disparity between the health status of blacks and other minorities and that of the population as a whole. The alarming decline in black life expectancy over the last several years emphasizes the fact that life expectancy at birth for the nation's black population stands now at a level achieved by whites over 30 years ago.

Black Americans experience complex health disadvantages, which are exacerbated by a combination of poverty, racial bias, ignorance, and lack of access to quality health care. Of these factors, poverty may be the most devastating and the factor most easy to isolate.

It is an irrefutable fact that people of the lowest socioeconomic status have higher death rates. This was a finding of the 1973 study by Kitagawa and Hauser. Commenting on this finding recently in *A Common Destiny: Blacks and American Society*, the National Research Council said that this ". . . classic study. . . found that there was a gradient of mortality rates with steady increases from the highest to the lowest social classes. Mortality rates were higher as socioeconomic status declined for both whites and blacks, whether that status was measured by family income, educational level, or occupation . . . . In addition to increased mortality, almost every form of disease and disability is more prevalent among the poor."

Writing in the January 13, 1989 edition of the *Journal of the American Medical Association*, Dr. Robert E. Windom, Assistant Secretary for Health, recounted the origins of the Secretary's Task Force on Black and Minority Health, appointed in 1984 by Margaret Heckler, then Secretary of Health and Human Services. The purpose of this task force was to investigate the health problems of black and minority populations, analyze resources, and make recommendations to close the gap in health status between these populations and whites. Among the results of the task force's work was the establishment of

---

Author's Note: Analyzing the health status of Black America requires comprehensive and extensive research. Two excellent sources of current information were relied upon and—in some instances excerpted—by the author in preparing this chapter and are singled out here as well as in the bibliography found in the back of this volume. They are the *Journal of the American Medical Association* [referred to as *JAMA* throughout the text], 261(2), January 13, 1989, which focuses on black and minority health in several key areas, and G.D. Jaynes and J.R.M. Williams (eds.), *A Common Destiny: Blacks and American Society* (Washington: National Academy Press, 1989). The author commends these two sources to anyone wishing a more detailed and statistical overview of the current state of health care for African Americans.

the Office of Minority Health (OMH) to coordinate departmental efforts to "reduce excess mortality and morbidity among blacks and other minorities." Another result of the task force was a study which revealed that there were 60,000 more minority deaths per year, based upon an expectation of equal death rates for blacks and whites.

The study also found that more than 80 percent of those "excess" deaths—or the difference between the actual number of deaths among blacks and the number that would have occurred if blacks had died at the same rate, for each age and sex as whites, could be attributed to the following causes:

- cancer
- cardiovascular disease and stroke
- chemical dependency
- diabetes
- infant mortality
- homicide and injuries

(Since the 1985 report, blacks and Hispanics also show a disproportionately higher rate of acquired immunodeficiency syndrome (AIDS) related deaths.)

The mortality rates for these six conditions do not give a complete picture of the personal and societal costs of death from other causes and of chronic or acute illness. Also not addressed by this methodology are the health problems of black children. Two excellent sources of information on children are *The Health of America's Children*, published in 1989 by the Children's Defense Fund, and "Black Children in America," by CDF president Marian Wright Edelman in *The State of Black America 1989.*

In general, black Americans have a death rate one and one-half times that of whites, and black life expectancy is declining – from 69.7 years in 1984 to 69.4 years in 1986. During that period, life expectancy for the entire population remained constant at 75 years.

Lastly, the OMH established a nationwide hot line to sources of information on minority health issues. The hot-line number is 1-800-444-6472. The hot-line staff uses a data base of organizations and 2,000 volunteers nationwide to provide information, locate speakers, and assist in local minority health programs.

LACK OF ACCESS TO MEDICAL CARE

JAMA reports that "[a] 1986 survey of use of health services shows a significant deficit in access to health care among black compared with white Americans. This gap was experienced by all levels of black Americans. In addition, the study points to significant underuse by blacks of needed medical care. Moreover, blacks compared with whites are less likely to be satisfied with qualitative ways their physicians treat them when they are ill, more dissatisfied with the care they receive when hospitalized, and more likely to believe that the duration of their hospitalizations is too short."

Blendon and his associates found blacks worse off than whites in terms of access to physician care, with blacks having "a significantly higher rate than whites of not seeing a physician within a one-year period." They further reported that the average annual number of physician visits among blacks compared with whites also is considerably lower, 3.4 compared with 4.4. They make the point that "the lower rate of visits to physicians by blacks than whites clearly is of major concern, given the evidence that serious illness is much more common among blacks than whites."

Other reasons for the disparity in health care include the undersupply of black and other physicians in minority communities; blacks have less insurance coverage; and ignorance in the black community about the role of the medical profession in determining, solving, and preventing problems.

As shown in Table 1, one of 11 blacks reported not receiving health care for economic reasons compared with one in 20 whites. One in four blacks who reported that they had one of 10 chronic illnesses about which they were specifically questioned did not have an ambulatory visit in the year preceding the survey, compared with one in six white persons surveyed (Tables 2 and 3). Among persons reporting they had hypertension, 30 percent of blacks have not had an annual blood-pressure check compared with 19 percent of whites.

Regarding dental care, 50 percent of blacks, compared with 36 percent of whites, received no dental care in the year prior to the survey.

To understand the black-white differences in access to care, over and above the direct effects of poverty, the *Journal* also reports a number of measures that reflect differences in health care arrangements were examined. It said that "the

Table 1
Indicators of Inequities in Medical Care by Race

Indicator	White, %	Black, %	p<
Not receiving health care for economic reasons	5.0	9.1	.01
Individuals with a chronic or serious illness not having an ambulatory visit in last year	16.6	25.1	.01
People with hypertension without an annual blood-pressure check	19.0	30.0	.01
No dental visit in a year	36.1	50.3	.01

Source: *Journal of the American Medical Association,* 261:279, Table 4, January 13, 1989.

Table 2
Physician Visits, According to Source or Place of Care
and Selected Patient Characteristics
United States: 1964, 1975, and 1980

Selected Characteristic	All sources or places			Doctor's office or clinic or group practice			Physician visits Hospital outpatient department			Telephone		
	1964	1975	1980	1964	1975	1980	1964	1975	1980	1964	1975	1980
	Number per person			Percent of visits								
RACE												
White	4.7	5.1	4.8	71.0	68.1	68.4	10.2	11.9	11.3	11.7	14.0	13.8
Black	3.6	4.9	4.6	56.2	58.5	57.0	32.7	23.5	26.2	4.2	7.0	5.5

Source: NCHS: Data from the NHIS, Division of Health Interview Statistics. In Health United States, 1982. DHHS Pub. No. (PHS) 83-1232

Table 3
Physician Visits, by Source or Place of Care
and Selected Patient Characteristics
United States, 1983

Selected Characteristic	Doctor's Office	Source or place of care Hospital Outpatient[1] Department	Telephone
		Percent of visits	
Total	55.9	14.9	15.5
RACE			
White	57.4	13.4	16.2
Black	44.1	26.5	9.7
FAMILY INCOME			
Under $10,000	49.8	18.4	12.3
$10,000–14,999	52.2	17.7	13.2
$15,000–19,999	54.2	16.7	16.3
$20,000–34,999	59.0	13.2	16.1
$35,000 or more	59.6	11.5	18.8

[1]Includes hospital outpatient clinic, emergency room, and other hospital visits.

Source: Division of Health Interview Statistics, NCHS: Data from the National Health Interview Survey.

Table 4
Percent under age 65
With No Health Insurance Coverage

• Blacks	22.6%
• Whites	14.0%
• Families with income under $10,000	37.0%
• Families with income over $35,000	3.9%

Source: NCHS, 1986.

black-white differences on these measures reflect the indirect consequences of the economic level of living," suggesting, therefore, more general, ethnic-related differences in health care arrangements and lifestyle.

Such differences include lack of private coverage—85.1 percent compared to 72.5 percent (Table 4). Blacks, too, are significantly more likely to reside in states with the least generous Medicaid programs, which tend to be in the South and Southwest.

Reduced opportunities for medical care are also a result of the undersupply of black physicians and of physicians in general in minority communities. The Public Health Service has reported that many counties with dense minority populations have substantially lower ratios of health professionals than similar communities with primarily white populations.

CARDIOVASCULAR DISEASE AND STROKE

In 1986, age-adjusted rates from disease of the heart and cardiovascular system for blacks were 1.4 and 1.8 times those for whites, respectively, according to the Office of Minority Health. For example, the death rate from heart disease for middle-aged minority men was 29 percent higher than that for white men in the same age group. For minority women, the death rate was nearly double that of white women.

Twenty-eight percent of adult blacks suffer from hypertension, compared with 17 percent of adult whites, with blacks developing high blood pressure at a younger age than whites. Severe hypertension is five times more common in blacks, according to the *JAMA*.

The morbidity and mortality of hypertension in blacks is well-known. The *JAMA* refers to a "stroke belt" running roughly from the eastern border of Texas to the Georgia coast, south of the Mason-Dixon line, where overall stroke mortality is higher than anywhere else. This high mortality rate is directly tied to the black populations.

JAMA further cites a National Heart, Lung, and Blood Institute report that shows blacks have a stroke mortality rate 65 percent higher than whites. Ischemic heart disease, caused by blockage of the arteries of the heart, is also more common in blacks. It appears that black persons with hypertension may be more susceptible than white hypertensives to the disease's related complications.

Dr. Michael Alderman of New York's Albert Einstein College of Medicine at Yeshiva University studied 1,700 whites and 1,200 blacks in all, followed for an average of four years.

According to the *JAMA*, Alderman says that whites and blacks responded to antihypertension therapy very similarly and were able to achieve control in about the same numbers. However, the whites in the program fared worse overall.

This was despite the fact that more black patients smoked and more had enlarged hearts. While the incidence rates of stroke were essentially the same for both groups, the white group had more myocardial infarction (heart attacks). Alderman attributes the equivalent stroke rate to medication. The black stroke rate closely approximated the white group's rate because stroke is related to blood pressure, although heart attacks can be caused by many factors. Researchers say the environment, diet, stress, and genetics predisposition contributed to blacks' tendency toward hypertension. Salt-sensitive hypertension also appears to be more common in blacks.

Despite improvements in education and awareness in the black community, black people in this country are still not receiving treatment for hypertension at the same rate as whites.

Although one study from Evans County, GA, noted a higher incidence of coronary heart disease among white men compared with black men, the bulk of available evidence suggests that blacks may have equivalent, if not greater rates of coronary disease. Blacks have a high prevalence of cardiac risk factors, such as hypertension and diabetes. Overall, mortality rates for ischemic heart disease also appear to be greater for blacks than whites. In 1985, the national age and sex-adjusted rates for coronary heart disease mortality were 10 percent higher among black men than white men, and 50 percent higher among black women than white women.

To examine interracial differences in the utilization of coronary angiography, coronary artery bypass grafting, and coronary angioplasty for white and black patients, Wenneker and Epstein examined all admissions in 1985 to Massachusetts hospitals for circulatory diseases or chest pain. After controlling for age, sex, payer, income, primary diagnoses, and the number of secondary diagnoses, whites underwent significantly more angiography and coronary artery bypass grafting procedures. Whites also underwent more angioplasty procedures, but the difference was not statistically significant. Although utilization differences may reflect patient preference, different levels of disease severity, or socioeconomic status not adequately accounted for, this study suggests that substantial racial inequalities exist in the use of procedures for patients hospitalized with coronary heart disease.

Over a 12-month period, Cooper and his associates studied a consecutive series of 111 black patients admitted to a municipal hospital in Chicago. The two-week mortality rate for the entire group was 19 percent (95 percent confidence intervals, 11.7 to 26.3), and the rate was twice as high for women as for men. A history of systemic hypertension was encountered in 75 percent of the patients, and diabetes mellitus was present in 33 percent, although they were not significant predictors of mortality within this group. The delay time from onset of symptoms to arrival at the hospital was markedly prolonged compared with studies of predominantly white populations—twice as long at the median, and three times as long at the mean. Preventive campaigns aimed at this population should include educating patients on the symptoms of coronary artery disease, encouraging them to seek prompt medical care, and eliminating obstacles to access to care.

CANCER

National attention is being focused on the increasing cancer incidence and mortality among black Americans.

As a result, the American Cancer Society and many black American organizations are beginning a creative coalition to control and prevent the disease. Initiatives reflect the Society's balanced programs of research, education, patient service, and rehabilitation.

Progress against cancer cannot be defined in quick and easy catch phrases like "encouraging" or "disappointing." We cannot afford illusions about cancer. Neither can we fail to herald the solid, steady progress in controlling this disease. Thus, we know that cancer is many diseases and that dramatic gains have been made against some cancers and less against others.

We express cures in terms of years of survival—five years, 10 years, 20 years—so, as today's statistics measure the effectiveness of the therapies of the 1950s, 1960s, and early 1970s, today's progress may not be measured precisely for several more years.

A study of cancer rates over several decades shows that the cancer incidence rate for blacks is higher than for whites, and the death rate is also higher. Over a 30-year period, black male cancer death rates rose by 77 percent compared to a 10 percent increase in black females. Incidence rates in blacks also have increased in both males and females.

The overall cancer incidence rate for blacks went up 27 percent, while for whites it increased 12 percent. Cancer mortality has increased in both races, but the rate for blacks is greater than for whites. The rates were virtually the same 30 years ago. Since then, cancer death rates in whites have increased 10 percent, while black rates have increased almost 50 percent.

Cancer sites where blacks had significantly higher increases in incidence and mortality rates included the lung, colon-rectum, prostate, and esophagus. Esophageal cancer, long considered mainly a disease of males, remained about the same in whites and rose rapidly in blacks of both sexes.

The incidence of invasive cancer of the uterine cervix dropped in both black and white women, although the incidence in blacks is still double that in whites. However, the rate for endometrial cancer—cancer of the body of the uterus—for white women is almost double that of black women.

According to data from the National Cancer Institute's SEER (Surveillance, Epidemiology, and End Results) program—a population-based tumor registry reporting system, blacks have the highest age-adjusted incidence rate for all cancers combined of any ethnic group studied. Compared with whites, blacks have statistically significantly higher age-adjusted incidence and mortality rates for

Table 5
Black/White Ratios of the Age-Adjusted Cancer Incidence and Mortality Rates, Both Sexes, 1985

Site	Ratio: black/white Incidence*	Mortality†
All sites	1.1	1.3
Oral cavity	1.2	1.8
Esophagus	3.5	3.0
Stomach	1.8	1.9
Pancreas	1.6	1.4
Lung	1.4	1.2
Female breast		
Ages under 40	1.5	1.7
Ages 40 and over	0.8	1.0
Cervix uteri	2.2	2.7
Corpus uteri	0.7	1.7
Prostate gland	1.5	2.2
Bladder	0.6	1.0
Multiple myeloma	2.1	
Leukemia	0.9	0.9

†Mortality data is for the total United States
*National Cancer Institute's SEER program.

several cancers (Table 5). Blacks have poorer five-year relative survival rates for a number of cancers, including bladder, breast, corpus uteri, oral, prostate, and rectal cancers.

Factors thought to contribute to the excessive cancer rates in blacks include cigarette or smokeless tobacco use; tobacco combined with heavy alcohol use; exposure to occupational hazards; poorer nutrition; more limited access to medical resources; less patient knowledge about diagnosis, treatment, and prevention; and greater vulnerability to histologically aggressive tumors (e.g., of the uterus and bladder).

To date, there is no known genetic basis to explain the major racial differences in cancer incidence and outcome. According to numerous studies, such differences appear to be largely attributable to *environmental* factors, including socioeconomic status. There are two notable exceptions in which there may be racial disparities unaccounted for by known environmental and/or socioeconomic factors—namely, cancer of the body of the uterus and cancer of the urinary bladder. In both diseases, the survival rates for blacks are markedly lower. Differences in histologic type between blacks and whites have also been noted for these two sites. Further research is required to elucidate these findings.

Dr. Harold P. Freeman, Director of Surgery at Harlem Hospital and President of the American Cancer Society, has written on cancer and the socioeconomically disadvantaged.

> Black Americans and native Hawaiians have a higher overall incidence of cancer compared with whites. With respect to some selected sites:
> - Black males have the highest incidence of prostate cancer in the nation.
> - The incidence of breast cancer is higher in white than in black females. Breast cancer also has a very high incidence in native Hawaiians.
> - Cervical cancer has a high incidence in blacks and in Native Americans.
> - Blacks have a higher incidence of lung cancer than do whites. This is related to the fact that black males smoke more than any other sex-race group in this country.
> - Black Americans have a relatively high incidence of stomach cancer and a much higher incidence of esophageal cancer compared with whites.
>
> It is noteworthy that blacks have a higher incidence of several of the cancers that are highly lethal, irrespective of race (lung, esophageal, and stomach), a factor that increases the relative mortality rate in blacks. White females have the lowest cancer mortality and the highest survival rates. Black males have the highest cancer mortality and lowest survival rates. In between are white males, who have a higher mortality rate than do black females.

In 1985, the Centers for Disease Control reported on the rates of cancer-attributable years of potential life lost; these were age-adjusted by race-gender groups. The highest rate occurred for black males (1208.1 per 100,000), followed by white males (949.4), black females (876.7), and white females (840.5). The rates in all four major race-gender groups also declined differentially. The average annual decline between 1968 and 1985 was approximately twice as great for black females (a decline of 18.9 per 100,000 per year) as for black males (9.4), white females (9.6), or white males (9.9).

The American Cancer Society's July 19, 1989 "Report to the Nation" found that poor Americans are forced to accept substandard health care services and to endure assaults on their personal dignity when seeking treatment for cancer. The Society estimates that the survival rate of poor people with cancer is 10 to 15 percent lower than that of other Americans.

There are 39 million poor Americans. Two-thirds of the poor are white, and nearly one-third is black, even though blacks comprise only 12 percent of our country's population. Black Americans have a five-year survival rate 12 percent lower than that of whites: 50 percent for whites and 38 percent for blacks. Racial disparities in cancer results are due primarily to differences in economic status. The relatively poor cancer results in black Americans are an indication of the health consequences that befall a group that represents one-third of the poor and one-fourth of the unemployed, but slightly over one-tenth of the population.

In 1983, the National Cancer Institute set a goal to diminish the mortality from cancer by 50 percent by the year 2000. While epidemiologists seek clues to explain the disproportionate cancer burden in blacks, intervention efforts are underway. The National Cancer Institute's Cancer Prevention Awareness Program for blacks, for example, represents a major intervention by the Institute to increase cancer prevention behavior in the black population and to promote the lifestyle changes that can lower cancer risk. Now in its third year, the program has expanded its network of national black organizations, health and medical groups, business and industry, mass media, and community groups.

An increasingly individualized approach characterizes cancer management today in both diagnostic procedures and treatment. Early detection, precise staging of the disease, and the use of more than one type of therapy, often in combination, are getting increasingly better results.

INFANT MORTALITY AND LOW BIRTH WEIGHT

Infant mortality, the rate at which children die before their first birthday and which is determined by the number of deaths per 1,000 live births, serves as the chief indicator of the overall status of health of a country. Despite significant progress in reducing the U.S. infant mortality rate, the rate for blacks remains twice as high as that for whites. In 1986, the infant mortality rate was 8.9 for white infants, 15.7 for nonwhite infants, and 18.0 for black infants. The excess mortality among blacks is attributed largely to a greater number of low birth weight infants.

Analyzing low birth weight (2500 grams) in terms of moderately low birth weight (1500-2500g) and very low birth weight (below 1500g) sheds light on the complexity of the problem. Very low birth weight infants have the highest risk of death and serious morbidity. Moderately low birth weight infants are at lower risks of death and serious morbidity but still are substantially higher risk than infants who weigh more than 2500g.

Between 1970 and 1985, rates for very low birth weight infants showed the least improvement. During that 15-year period, the incidence of babies with low birth weight declined from 68.4 to 56.4 per 1,000 live births among whites, from 138.3 to 124.2 among blacks. Yet, the incidence of babies with very low birth weight decreased only slightly among whites—from 9.5 to 9.4 per 1,000 live births—and increased among blacks—from 23.9 to 26.5. Thus, the overall decline in babies with low birth weight occurred as a result of the decline in the birth of infants with moderately low birth weight.

Kleinman and Kessel examined the effects of four traditional maternal sociodemographic characteristics (age, parity, marital status, and education) on rates of very low birth weight among whites and blacks. *JAMA* reports that 15 percent of the decline in the rate of babies with moderately low birth weight among whites was attributed to favorable changes in maternal characteristics, primarily an increase in educational level. Among blacks, 35 percent of the increase in very low birth weight infants was accounted for primarily by an increase in births among unmarried women. The study noted the persistence of large racial differences in birth weight even among mothers at low risk.

These statistics provide the basis for making efforts to reduce infant mortality one of our highest priorities. Perhaps the most striking statistic is years of potential life lost (YPLL), that is, the sum of the differences between average life spans and actual years lived. Between 1983 and 1985, infant mortality accounted for 5,444,417 YPLL for white Americans and 2,156,758 YPLL for black Americans, a total of 7,601,175 years. Calculated per 1,000 live births, YPLL were 617 for whites and 1,107 for blacks, a 490-year excess.

Programs to improve prenatal care, thus decreasing the number of low birth weight babies, are critical. Compared with normal birth weight infants, low birth weight infants are almost 40 times more likely to die in the neonatal period. The role of good diet and nutrition and avoidance of alcohol and tobacco have been documented in reported studies. The threat of AIDS is an increasing hazard for black infants. More than twice as many black babies as whites are born weighing 2500g or less (12.5 percent vs. 5.7 percent, respectively). The National Institute of Child Health and Human Development (NICHD) is supporting a clinical trial of 600 pregnant women in Washington, DC, to study this problem. It seeks to identify those nutritional, medical, and psychosocial factors that contribute most significantly to the incidence of low birth weight in urban black populations. Preliminary data show that 25 percent of the women are getting less than 70 percent of the recommended daily allowance for protein, ascorbic acid, thiamine, riboflavin, and niacin; about 35 percent are getting less than 70 percent of the recommended daily allowance for vitamins A, B^6, and B^2 and for calcium and iron.

The NICHD is involved also in the Better Babies Project, aimed at reducing the rate of low birth weight infants in a target area in Washington, DC. Outreach workers are identifying as many pregnant women as possible within the target area and encouraging them to begin prenatal care; to improve their adherence to medical advice; to participate in specific programs designed to reduce smoking, alcohol consumption, and drug abuse; and to provide social support. This project will continue through 1990.

The U.S. Department of Health and Human Services (DHHS) has been conducting a substantial infant mortality reduction effort for some years and recently stepped up its activities. Under the Maternal and Child Health Services Block Grant, which exceeds $500 million a year, funds are allocated to states and territories to provide a broad range of health services to mothers and children. The services include primary care, lead-based paint poisoning prevention, genetics education, sudden infant death syndrome prevention, adolescent pregnancy care, and rehabilitation. About 15 percent of the block grant funds are awarded for special projects, including some that focus on inner-city minority residents and rural blacks in the South.

CHEMICAL DEPENDENCY

It is not an exaggeration to say that the growing threat of chemical dependency, particularly the use of illegal drugs such as crack, marijuana, and PCP, is tearing at the very fiber of the African-American community. Its dramatic impact is evidenced by increased crime, wanton violence, mental disorders, family disruptions, and social problems in school and on the job. A previous edition of *The State of Black America* has called attention to this growing problem. Noted expert Beny Primm has called drug abuse "the most serious and perplexing problem facing Black America."

Most experts agree with this assessment in *A Common Destiny*:

> The true dimensions of drug use for blacks may be underreported. This hypothesis is supported by a 1979 survey that found mortality from drug-related deaths increased steeply in nine major metropolitan areas, and about one-third of those fatalities occurred among black youth in the 15 to 24 age group (National Institute on Drug Abuse, 1980). Currently, cocaine and its potent derivative "crack" show increased use among all youth. In 1986, the first national data report of high school seniors found that 4.1 percent had used crack in the past year, and 17 percent had tried cocaine (Johnston et al., 1987). By any measure, drug problems have greatly increased over the past 40 years, and although that increase may now have slowed, a majority of adolescent blacks and whites have experimented with illicit drugs. The drug problem is potentially far more serious now because of the AIDS risk associated with the sharing of needles or "drug works." Although heroin use is minimal among adolescents, there is an increasing trend toward intravenous injection of cocaine. Cocaine injection poses a higher risk of HIV infection because cocaine's effects are of short duration, and so users inject far more frequently than do heroin users.

Smoking cocaine is a very different drug experience than snorting, or using cocaine intranasally. When smoked, the onset of intoxication is more rapid, almost instantaneous, though the effects last only half as long as when snorted. After the "high" from each dose dissipates, users experience an often crushing depression, feel irritable or agitated, and have a "drug hunger" that demands more cocaine. Not only is smoking cocaine a different experience, but it is also by far the most compulsive cocaine behavior, accelerating the progression from first use to addiction. By contrast, the usual pattern of addiction for snorting may take several years. When cocaine is smoked, the progression may take just several months.

A recent series by Marcia Slocum-Greene in the *Washington Post* painted a chilling scenario of the impact of the cocaine epidemic on our children:

> An increase of crack-cocaine addiction in Washington has brought an unprecedented surge in the number of children being abused, neglected, and mistreated.

Parents seeking the next crack fix have abandoned their young children in the streets and in hospitals. They have sold food stamps and their children's clothes for drug money. A few have sold their children as prostitutes.

Like children of war, the neglected youngsters wipe their tears, eat what they can find, and spend hours—sometimes days—at home alone. Authorities have found six-year-olds taking care of two- and three-year-olds, and preschoolers begging neighbors and strangers for food. Some children have been beaten, burned, or sexually abused. A few have died.

These damaged children are among the newest and most helpless victims of crack cocaine, which has created more profound changes in human behavior than any other illegal drug in recent history, including heroin, PCP, and the more traditional form of cocaine powder. It alters the brain chemistry to such an extent that it makes addiction almost a certainty, usually in a matter of months.

Moreso than with other drugs, crack addicts are found among young mothers, with small children, few child-rearing skills, and no spouse to share their load. In their extended families, even some of the grandparents are addicted.

The rate of infant mortality, sudden infant death syndrome, child abuse and neglect, as well as HIV infection are significantly linked to maternal substance abuse—caused most often today by crack-cocaine use but also by other illicit drugs and alcohol.

Chasnoff and his associates reported on 75 cocaine-using women enrolled in a comprehensive perinatal care program. They were divided into two groups: those who used cocaine in only the first trimester of pregnancy (group 1, n = 23) and those who used cocaine throughout pregnancy (group 2, n = 52). Both groups of cocaine-exposed infants demonstrated significant impairment of orientation and motor behavior on the Neonatal Behavioral Assessment Scale.

Another major problem produced by the drug crisis is that of infants who are abandoned by their mothers shortly after birth and become long-term hospital residents.

In 1987, Primm wrote about the 140 "boarder babies" in New York hospitals. Since then, other cities such as Washington, DC, have experienced this growing phenomenon. "Boarder babies are essentially permanent residents of their hospitals and have no access to the outside world. Their world is the pediatric ward, with multiple nurse-surrogate mothers changing every shift. The mothers of these children are intravenous drug users, alcoholics, and other substance abusers. Boarder babies have little hope of adoption because would-be foster parents and relatives fear the onset of fetal alcohol syndrome (FAS), the fetal marijuana syndrome, cocaine (crack) and opioid protracted-abstinence effects, and—most of all—AIDS-related complex (ARC) and full-blown AIDS leading to eventual death. This problem, one of immense proportions with few solutions, is yet another major by-product of drug abuse."

Beyond the human toll on the babies and on the limited nursing staffs, the *Washington Post* estimates the financial costs at $100,000 a year or more for each child. For each of the boarder babies, "there is a tragic story in which the main character is a mother whose crack-cocaine addiction has stripped her of the desire or the ability to care for her child."

We must remember that the hospital environment, no matter how sophisticated and benign, is not established for the nurturing and long-term care of otherwise healthy infants.

Ghostbuster, space blaster, and bazooka refer to a new drug combination: crack mixed with PCP. This combination of a stimulant with a hallucinogenic drug has accounted for increases in violent crime wherever the use has been high.

Methamphetamine, like cocaine, is a stimulant. Its use has been known to cause a state of arousal, wakefulness, mood elevation, insomnia, mental confusion, depression, aggressiveness, and death. Yet, its desired effects and long duration of action make it attractive to abusers. As a result, it can be very addictive in a relatively short time.

Particularly disturbing is the sudden popularity of "ice," a new crystalline, smokeable form of methamphetamine. Ice differs from the old methamphetamine, "speed," popular in the '60s and '70s, in that it can be smoked. Ice can intoxicate its users for 12 to 20 hours (crack for only 15 minutes), and preliminary studies show that continued use of ice can produce serious psychological and physical disorders.

Criminologist and scholar Lee P. Brown has written that "combatting the drug problem is complicated because drugs are big business in America. . . . Thus, for many, there is a strong economic incentive to see drugs consumed in the community."

The seduction of so-called "designer drugs," the relatively easy access to drugs, and a reluctant tolerance on the part of many in the black community add to a situation that is explosive in terms of its ravages on our present generation and our community's future. This state of emergency demands a highly visible and coordinated strategy to fight this scourge.

HOMICIDE AND INJURIES

An Institute of Medicine study in 1985 on "Injury in America" [*JAMA*] emphasized the public health importance of injuries in the U.S. and indicated that the injury burden rests disproportionately among the poor, many of whom belong to minority groups. The report described four causes of injuries with the largest disparities in black-white deaths in 1984 and discussed opportunities for intervention. It focused on deaths from homicides, residential fires, drowning, and pedestrian mishaps—each of which accounted for over 1,000 deaths and showed a ratio of mortality rates between blacks and whites that exceeded 1.5. Other injuries, such as those caused by motor vehicles, accounted for many deaths but did not show statistically significant black-white differences in death rates.

In 1984, although blacks represented 12.0 percent of the U.S. population, they accounted for 15.3 percent of all deaths due to injury. Among the four causes studied for both blacks and whites, homicides accounted for the most deaths from injury. For blacks, homicides were followed by pedestrian mishaps, residential fires, and drowning. For whites, homicides were followed by pedestrian mishaps, drowning, and residential fires. The rate ratios of black-white deaths were highest for homicides (5.2:1), followed by residential fires (3.2:1), drowning (1.8:1), and pedestrian mishaps (1.6:1). Among the four race-sex groups, black males had the highest death rates from these causes; white females had the lowest death rates. Black females had death rates similar to those of white females except for homicides and residential fires; in those two categories, black females had higher death rates than both white females and white males.

Homicides accounted for the greatest disparity in injury mortality rates between blacks and whites. In 1984, the homicide rate for blacks was 29.0 per 100,000. This rate was just over five times higher than the homicide rate for whites of 5.5 per 100,000. For both blacks and whites, the age-specific homicide rates decreased from infancy to ages five to nine years and then began to increase. For blacks, the rates peaked at ages 25 to 29 years, declined markedly to ages 65 to 69, and then declined slightly. In contrast, the rates for whites peaked at ages 20-24, declined gradually to ages 65-69, and then slightly increased.

For both males and females in 1984, homicide rates were highest among young adults ages 20 to 39. Rates for black males peaked at 99.6 for the 25- through 29-year-old age group. Although rates were higher for black males than for any other race-sex group, black females also were at high risk of homicide. Their rate also peaked in the 25- through 29-year-old age group at 21.9. Rates for black males were four to five times greater than those for black females in all age groups above 15 years of age. A similar pattern was seen among whites—that is, young adults were at highest risk, and males had consistently higher rates than females in each age group. The ratio of male-to-female rates, however, was less for whites, with the rate for white males generally ranging from two to three times higher than that for white females. Among blacks, 67 percent of homicides were committed with firearms, compared with 58.6 percent among whites.

Fatal injuries exact a disproportionate burden on blacks compared with whites. Homicides, residential fires, drowning, and pedestrian mishaps account for most of this difference. To reduce the higher death rates due to injury among blacks, investigators must define the race- and cause-specific risk factors that can be used to guide intervention strategies. These findings then must be integrated into public health programs designed to reduce the injury burden on blacks in this country.

AIDS

Acquired immunodeficiency syndrome (AIDS) is an area that was not addressed by the Secretary's Task Force on Black and Minority Health. However, it is clearly one of the most crucial health problems affecting the black community today. While blacks constitute about 12 percent of the U.S. population, they

136

make up 27 percent of all Americans with AIDS. Fully 53 percent of AIDS cases among children under 13 years old in the United States have occurred among blacks.

It is important to note that the patterns of human immunodeficiency virus (HIV) transmission differ between black and white Americans. While only one percent of reported AIDS cases in whites has resulted from heterosexual contact, that figure is 11 percent for blacks.

Since January, 1988, minorities have comprised about 46 percent of reported AIDS cases. The number of AIDS cases in white homosexual men is declining, while the number of new cases among intravenous drug users—many of whom are black or Hispanic—is rising.

Homosexual or bisexual men constitute 78 percent of the reported AIDS cases among white Americans, while the comparable figure for blacks is 37 percent. While only seven percent of whites with AIDS have been heterosexual intravenous drug users, that figure rises to 38 percent for blacks—a fact reflected in the overwhelming proportion of black children with AIDS transmitted by mothers who were intravenous drug users or the sexual partners of drug users.

Of the 66,464 cases of acquired immunodeficiency syndrome (AIDS) reported to the Centers for Disease Control (CDC) in the period June 1, 1981-July 4, 1988, most (60 percent) occurred among non-Hispanic whites; however, blacks and Hispanics accounted for 70 percent of the cases in heterosexual men, 70 percent of those in women, and 75 percent of those in children. To study the association between AIDS and racial/ethnic groups, the AIDS Program, Center for Infectious Diseases, analyzed the presumed means by which each patient became infected with human immunodeficiency virus (HIV), i.e., exposure category. The analysis revealed that AIDS patients are disproportionately black and Hispanic and that the proportion of AIDS cases associated with IVDA (intravenous drug abuse) is substantially greater in U.S. blacks and Hispanics than in U.S. whites.

The disproportionate numbers of blacks and Hispanics treated for heroin abuse suggest that they may have a higher prevalence of IVDA than whites. Black and Hispanic communities in the United States and Puerto Rico should be especially targeted for measures to prevent HIV transmission by treating drug abusers and by counseling drug abusers and their sex partners on the risk of HIV infection. Recommendations for preventing HIV transmission to intravenous drug abusers, their sex partners, and their children have been published.

DIABETES MELLITUS

At a conference in 1988 sponsored by the National Institute of Diabetes and Digestive and Kidney Diseases, scientists were of the opinion that obesity and heredity probably account for the higher rate of diabetes in blacks as compared to whites. Rates of diagnosed diabetes are 50 percent higher in black males, and 100 percent higher in black females, compared with their white counterparts. With the exception of hypertension, blacks with diabetes also experience higher rates of complications. For example, rates of severe visual impairment are 40 percent higher, amputation rates more than double, and end-stage renal disease (ESRD) is four times higher.

One reason for this racial disparity may be the high level of obesity in blacks, one of the most important risk factors for non-insulin dependent diabetes. Obesity is defined as 20 percent above ideal weight matched for age, height, and sex. For example, according to the National Health and Nutrition Survey, 83 percent of diabetic black women, ages 20 to 74 years, are obese, compared with 62 percent of white women of similar age.

But obesity is not a sufficient explanation. At each level of obesity, the rate of diabetes is higher in blacks than whites. Therefore, other factors must be involved, and most likely these include unexplained genetic factors.

According to the most recent data, the age-adjusted death rate from diabetes for blacks is 2.4 times that for whites. More than 30 departmental programs dealing with diabetes prevention and control in minorities were reported by the Office of Minority Health (OMH), including those of the diabetes research centers and the National Diabetes Information Clearinghouse supported by the National Institutes of Health. Additionally, the Centers for Disease Control's Diabetes Control Program has had a minority focus since 1984.

KIDNEY DISEASE AND TRANSPLANTATION

Blacks experience a disproportionate risk of end stage renal disease (ESRD) compared with whites. The increased prevalence of hypertension in blacks has been suggested as an explanation for this increased risk. McClellan et al. were able to examine this possibility using hypertensive ESRD incidence rates in a population with well-characterized prevalence of hypertension and rate of its control. After adjusting rates of hypertensive ESRD for age, sex, and differences in the prevalence of hypertension by race, they found the relative risk in blacks compared with whites still to be increased. Differences in the control of hypertension between the two race groups are of insufficient magnitude to explain the increase in adjusted relative risk. This observation suggests either that there are racial differences in the susceptibility to renal damage and elevated blood pressure, which may explain increased risk for hypertensive ESRD in blacks, or that hypertension is being erroneously diagnosed as the cause of the ESRD in blacks when another cause is present.

Fifty to 70 percent of all dialysis patients listed with the Southeastern Organ Procurement Foundation were black, yet fewer than 10 percent of the organ donors in that group were black. Callender looked at the reasons that blacks were such infrequent organ donors. The most common reasons for blacks not wanting to donate organs were identified as follows: (a) lack of awareness about transplantation; (b) religious myths and misperceptions (superstitions); (c) distrust of the medical community; (d) fear of premature death; and (e) racism. Another factor was the lack of trust and confidence among physicians, hospitals, and especially black organ and tissue donors.

Blacks with untreated hypertension have more kidney failure than any other ethnic group (17 times that in whites). Black kidney recipients rarely receive organs from black donors. Only 20 percent of the kidneys received by the transplant recipients at Howard University Hospital were from blacks. Graft survival rates were 10 to 20 percent lower for black kidney recipients than for any other ethnic group. Of whites, 20 percent of those who could be transplanted are transplanted, whereas only 10 percent of blacks who could be transplanted are transplanted.

Callender concludes the following: (1) statistically significant differences in transplant outcome exist between black and white transplant recipients relative to graft failure one to five years after kidney transplantation; (2) persistently poorer graft survival rates occur in blacks with living related donor transplants at two years: blacks had a graft survival rate of 75 percent, whereas whites had a rate of 89 percent; (3) the poorer outcome of blacks after kidney transplantation may be part of a larger problem reflecting the second-class status of black health care in America; and (4) a national stratagem to related scientific and educational efforts must be developed to answer the questions posed by the results of the investigation.

GLAUCOMA

Glaucoma is the leading cause of blindness among blacks in the United States. As Wilson has pointed out, the prevalence of blindness from glaucoma in the U.S. black population is sevenfold that of the white population, and this differential becomes 15:1 for those aged 45 to 64 years. This difference is not explained by socioeconomic factors or by restricted access to health care. Instead, it seems that glaucoma is both more common and more aggressive in blacks. Recent studies by Mason et al. and Leske et al. of the black West Indian population of St. Lucia and Barbados, West Indies, reveal inordinately high prevalence rates of 12.2 percent and 13.0 percent, respectively. Results from the Baltimore (MD) Eye Survey also suggest an increased prevalence of glaucoma among blacks. In addition, blacks present at an earlier age with more advanced optic nerve and visual field changes, and progression of these parameters occurs at a faster rate than in whites despite similar intraocular pressures. Responses to medical, laser, and surgical therapy also seem to be influenced by race.

The American Academy of Ophthalmology, acknowledging that these disparities could have an adverse impact on optimal patient care, issued a special announcement at its 1984 annual meeting urging clinicians to recognize glaucoma as a major health issue for the American black population. At the most recent annual meeting of the National Medical Association, an entire scientific session was devoted to an exploration of "Special Considerations of Glaucoma in Blacks."

SICKLE CELL ANEMIA

Dr. Roland Scott, a leading advocate for sickle cell research and treatment, has contributed the following information for inclusion with this section.

Prior to 1970, sickle cell disease (SCD) was regarded as a malady of low national profile that mainly affected blacks in Africa and the United States. In his message to Congress in 1971, President Nixon stated that SCD was a neglected health condition and that something should be done to benefit the victims of the disease. As a result of his efforts, the National Sickle Cell Anemia Control Act was passed by Congress in 1972. This legislation set in motion the development of the National Sickle Cell Disease Program, which comprised the inauguration of comprehensive sickle cell research centers, education and demonstration programs, and proficient hemoglobinopathy testing. This action stimulated considerable research efforts that have now resulted in a new outlook. This earlier pessimistic attitude in reference to SCD has changed to one of hopeful optimism. Victims of the disease can look to such positive achievements as better-informed physicians, availability of early diagnosis (prenatal and neonatal), development of newer methods of treatment, and improvement in educational and counseling programs.

Support from the National Sickle Cell Disease Program in the United States is resulting in significant advances in health care. Ten regional comprehensive sickle cell centers provide a variety of management strategies. An example is the inauguration of neonatal diagnosis for sickle hemoglobinopathies, with parental education and the utilization of special follow-up clinics for affected infants. The administration of prophylactic antibiotics and improved vaccines for control of life-threatening infection is enhancing survival in infants and children. A number of antisickling agents are under preliminary clinical investigations in adult patients. Bone marrow transplantation represents another potential method for management of selected types of sickle cell disease. The results of a national cooperative study on the clinical course of the disease, which was inaugurated in 1978, is providing new information that will be helpful to clinicians and health planners. The federally funded sickle cell centers have effectively utilized interdisciplinary personnel to provide comprehensive medical care, psychosocial support, and patient education. These centers serve as models or bridges whereby the fruits of research activity can be more readily applied to the care of patients. This comprehensive approach, no doubt, can contribute to improvement in the survival of and quality of life for patients. There is, however, a need to continue national support for research efforts to attain a definitive cure for this serious, painful, and disabling illness, which affects about 50,000 people in the United States and many more in other countries. Currently, many families of affected patients are unable to cope personally with socioeconomic problems imposed by the long-term nature of this illness: insufficient income, inadequate insurance coverage, and escalating cost of health care. Clearly, there is a need for additional state and/or federal programs to provide supplements for the medical expenses incurred by persons with long-term handicapping diseases of genetic origin. (*Excerpted with permission from the American Journal of Diseases of Children 139:1219-1222, 1985.*)

HEALTH CARE TRAINING

The training of minority health care professionals is essential to increase the number of qualified persons who will render care to the minority population of our country. The Association of Minority Health Professions Schools is commended for its sterling efforts in fostering the interest of young minorities in the biomedical and biobehavioral sciences. Members of the Association are Charles R. Drew University of Medicine and Science, Los Angeles; Meharry Medical College Schools of Medicine and Dentistry, Nashville; Morehouse School of Medicine, Atlanta; School of Pharmacy and Pharmacology at Florida A&M University, Tallahassee, and at Texas Southern University, Houston; School of Veterinary Medicine at Tuskegee Institute; and Xavier University, Cincinnati. Although not a member of the Association, Howard University College of Medicine plays a major role in the training of minorities in the health sciences. All of the above-named institutions provide much needed health manpower to meet the ever-increasing health needs of our minority population.

SUMMARY

A review of the facts presented in this report on studies of health for African Americans reveals that major problems remain. Local, state, and federal programs are needed to bring parity in health care for all Americans. Major initiatives are required to ensure that adequate measures are undertaken to correct the inequities that exist in the current health care delivery system.

The following recommendations are made:

- Develop educational programs to inform the black population about the importance of the special health problems they confront and what measures can be taken to improve their health.
- Ask local, state, and federal governments to consider mechanisms for funding health care systems for the socioeconomically disadvantaged that eliminate obstacles to access for this group.
- Emphasize prevention of disease, combined with a healthy lifestyle as a major health strategy.
- Develop cost-effective screening programs for common cancers and hypertension.
- Develop special programs emphasizing the critical problems of drug abuse and AIDS in the black community and offer counseling and treatment.

- Identify intervention techniques (medical and psychosocial) for drug abuse victims.

- Develop clinical programs for newborns to detect sickle cell disease and to detect drug withdrawal symptoms and to provide long-term management for them.

- Develop programs to ensure adequate prenatal care and counseling, thus, decreasing the incidence of low birth weight and infant mortality.

Preventing Black Homicide

Carl C. Bell, M.D.
with
Esther J. Jenkins, Ph.D.

Homicide is the leading cause of death for black males and females, ages 15–34 (Secretary's Task Force on Black and Minority Health, 1985). In 1986, the last year for which complete figures are available, blacks accounted for 44 percent of all murder victims, but only 12 percent of the nation's population (FBI, 1987). Furthermore, after a 15-year decline, homicide among blacks is increasing. The number of homicides increased nine percent in the general population between 1985 and 1986, but increased 16 percent among blacks; among black males, ages 25–29, there was a 29 percent increase in homicides during that year. In 1986, black men were six times more likely to be a homicide victim than a white male, and black women were four times more likely to be a homicide victim than white women (Griffith and Bell, 1989).

According to media reports, black homicide has increased even more within the last two years, as many cities with large minority populations have reported a record number of homicides ("Tide of Drug Killing," 1989). Even in cities that have noted an overall decline in homicides, there have been record numbers of killings of young black males. For example, Chicago reported a four percent decline in the number of murders from 1987 to 1988, but witnessed a five percent increase in violent deaths of youth ages 11–20 (Recktenwald and Blau, 1989). Furthermore, it has been estimated that for every completed homicide, there are 100 assaults (Rosenberg and Mercy, 1986), with blacks being over-represented among serious assault victims (Dietz, 1987).

The emotional and economic costs of this violence to the black community are staggering. The most obvious and immediate impact is the emotional pain of the survivor's family. However, there are other, more insidious effects which have long-term consequences for the entire black community. The loss of so many men prior to or just entering into their prime years of work and family development has a direct impact on the declining male-female ratio in the black community and the very structure and economic health of the black family (Guttentag and Secord, 1983; Wilson, 1987). In addition to the loss of the victim, there is the loss of the perpetrator, who, though probably receiving less punishment for killing another black man than had the victim been white (Hawkins, 1986), nonetheless, will have some kind of police record (prison time or probation). This ex-offender status lowers his/her marketability and increases his/her chances of continued criminal activity.

This violence may also impact on the survivors. Families and friends of victims often carry emotional scars which, if unaddressed, will negatively shape their lives (Masters, Friedman, Getzel, 1988). A distressing number of children actually witness this violence against family and friends, frequently suffering post-traumatic stress symptoms of emotional and behavioral disturbances (Pynoos and Eth, 1985). To the extent that much of this violence occurs in the home, it is a major contributor to family breakups and to the socialization of children who will perpetuate the cycle of family violence (Kalmus, 1984; Jaffe, Wolfe, Wilson, and Zak, 1986).

Clearly, the issue of preventing black homicide needs addressing. However, any preventive effort must be grounded in an understanding of the dynamics of black homicide, which vary across time and locale.

DYNAMICS OF BLACK HOMICIDE

There are several misconceptions around the perpetrator, victim, and circumstances of black homicide. One such "myth" in the black community is that blacks are killed by whites, often, it is assumed, in police shootings or other racially motivated situations. However, the reality is that 95 percent of black homicides are committed by black perpetrators (FBI, 1987). Thus, black homicide is quite accurately referred to as "black-on-black homicide."

Contrary to the misconception that individuals are killed by criminals, the killings typically occur between individuals who know one another as a result of a disagreement. From 1976 to 1983, black homicide victims knew their assailants in 59.8 percent of the homicides which occurred during those years. Among black males, homicide victims knew their assailants in 58.3 percent of the cases and over three-fourths of those men who knew their assailants knew them as friends or acquaintances. Black female victims knew their assailants in 65.8 percent of the cases, and in 43.8 percent of those homicides, the assailant was a family member (Centers for Disease Control, 1986). Such killings, marked by anger and impulsivity, are referred to as primary homicides and differ markedly from secondary homicides, which take place during the commission of a felony and are typically perpetrated by strangers.

The circumstances of homicide for blacks are different from those of other racial and ethnic groups. Complicating the matter even further, these circumstances often vary from year to year and by locale. (The dramatic increase in homicide among the young suggests that these dynamics may be currently in a state of flux.) A review of homicide trends from 1965 to 1981 (Block, 1985) found that blacks, in comparison to Hispanics and whites, were more likely to be killed in the home with a handgun during a verbal argument (primary homicide). Male victims were typically killed by a friend or acquaintance, while female victims were most often killed by their spouses. (Hispanic males were most likely killed in the street by a friend or acquaintance; killing of Hispanic women and children and killings in the home were extremely rare. Whites were most likely killed in the home with a handgun during a criminal activity committed by friends, acquaintances, and strangers.)

Furthermore, the contribution of gang and drug activity to the black homicide rate varies over time and location and, at least until recently, was not as much a factor in black homicides as was commonly thought. For example, prior to 1981, gang-related homicides accounted for approximately one percent of the nation's homicides. In Chicago, gangs accounted for five percent of the total murders; however, they were responsible for 25 percent of youth homicides and 50 percent of Hispanic youth homicides (Block, 1985). Drug-related homicides (which typically occur around the business of selling drugs) also varied considerably from area to area. For example, Chicago, which actually reported a decline in overall homicide deaths in 1988, reported that fewer than 10 percent of those deaths were drug-related (Recktenwald and Blau, 1989). Although that number is an increase from previous years and is a conservative figure, it is in sharp contrast to Washington, DC, which recorded a 65 percent increase in homicides in 1988 and reported that 80 percent of those killings were drug-related (Office of Criminal Justice Plans and Analysis, 1988).

The fact that about three out of five murder victims are related to or acquainted with their assailants has led to the conclusion that "murder is a societal problem over which law enforcement has little or no control" (FBI, 1987, p. 11). The argument is that such homicides, given their pervasiveness and circumstances, must be addressed as a public health problem by a number of agencies and with a number of interventions. The findings that the characteristics of black homicide vary across time and from place to place suggest the need for community-specific homicide interventions based on an awareness of homicides in that area. For example, if most homicides are a consequence of expressive violence between family and friends, crime-prevention activities directed at criminals/strangers will have little impact on the homicide rate. Block (1985) noted that if all of the robberies, rapes, and burglaries that occurred in Chicago between 1965 and 1981 had been prevented, over 70 percent of the homicides during that period would still have occurred. Similarly, if gang and drug activities are major contributors to the homicide rate, monies and programs should be directed into this area. However, one should not make a prior assumption about the predominant cause and thus the appropriate treatment of homicides in a particular community based on the most dramatic and sensationalized events.

OBSTACLES TO SOLVING THE PROBLEM

In addition to the misconceptions concerning the epidemiology and circumstances of black homicides, biases and fears on the part of both black and white Americans pose obstacles to the formulation and implementation of effective programs to reduce their occurrence. Among blacks, racial consciousness—ironically, both the presence and lack of it—can operate to decrease blacks' ownership of the problem. At one end of the continuum, blacks low in racial identity—with highly individualistic explanations for blacks' success and failure—may see black homicide as characteristic of a criminal element in the community and, therefore, a personal issue for the victims and perpetrators. At the other extreme is a concern that the homicide figures will reflect negatively on blacks as a whole, reinforcing whites' stereotypes of blacks as violent, fueling white fears and racism. Such fears lead to a reluctance to endorse large-scale public campaigns with their attendant publicity around black homicide figures and/or a situation in which more energy is put into defending, apologizing for, or explaining away the statistics than is invested in trying to change the reality of the situation.

Blacks also may be reluctant to take ownership of the problem because they are aware that poverty is a primary contributor to homicide and that when income is held constant, racial/ethnic differences in homicide are greatly reduced or disappear (Flango and Sherbinou, 1976; Loftin and Hill, 1974; Williams, 1984). As a result, blacks blame whites for the problem of black-on-black murder: they feel that until the racism that generates the disproportionate numbers of impoverished blacks stops, there is little that the black community can do about the problem.

As homicide does not affect whites at the rate that it affects blacks, there is simply less concern about it in the white community. Of much greater concern to whites is the issue of suicide, which affects them in a disproportionate manner similar to homicide among blacks. For example, looking at head injury-associated deaths (Sosin, Sacks, and Smith, 1989), white suicides accounted for 72 percent of the firearm head injury-associated deaths (HIADs); for blacks, homicides accounted for 72 percent of HIADs. When the numbers are combined, the black-white difference is obliterated, and since whites outnumber blacks, 63 percent of all firearm-related HIADs are directed at suicide rather than homicide prevention, thereby leaving out the "black problem."

Among whites who are aware of the black-on-black homicide figures, there may be a reluctance to address the issue for various reasons. Some well-intentioned whites are no doubt reluctant to raise the issue for fear of being attacked as racists; less well-intentioned whites may be rather relieved that it is occurring. In addition, some whites actually believe that if blacks stop killing each other, they will begin to kill whites. The result, for any number of reasons, is often a lack of support in the white community for state- and local-level homicide initiatives.

The lack of basic empirical research on issues relevant to black homicide is a major obstacle to intervention. For example, detailed information on the characteristics of victims and perpetrators, their relationship, and the circumstances under which the killings occurred is not kept by many police or public health departments, although such information is critical to designing community-specific interventions. In addition, there has been little systematic research on black domestic violence (although there is some indication that it may operate somewhat differently for blacks than for whites (Block, 1985) and even less on black females who kill, even though black females have the second-highest offender rate (Mann, 1986).

There is also a paucity of research on the impact of acquired biologic factors on aggression in blacks. Recent reviews of the literature noted the relationship between acquired central nervous system damage (which usually results from head injury) and violent behavior (Bell, 1986; 1987). And although head injury is much more prevalent among blacks than whites (Rivara and Mueller, 1986), most of the research on head injury and violence has used white subjects. Similarly, most of the research on the use of propranolol, an anti-hypertensive medication that reduces explosive behavior that results from biologic conditions, has been done on whites, although blacks seem to be more likely candidates for its use.

CONSCIOUSNESS RAISING

Prior to implementing specific strategies for the prevention of black-on-black homicides, considerable education is needed to raise the consciousness of various segments of society regarding the issue. This awareness and education must focus on destroying certain "myths" of black homicide while creating an understanding of its actual dynamics, developing black community ownership of the problem, stimulating self-help initiatives, and developing a commitment for policy and action. Primary target groups are the black community, which is eventually responsible for implementing strategies, and policymakers who can stimulate activity in an area mainly through their appropriation of funds.

A primary goal of an education and awareness campaign will be to increase the black community's understanding of the problem and increase black ownership of it. First of all, many black Americans are simply not aware of the extent of the problem. While most black people "feel" that blacks are more likely than whites to die violently, they are genuinely shocked at the magnitude of the difference. These numbers need to be publicized in a meaningful and impactful manner, i.e., in comparison to whites, in relationship to the black population, as they compare to the number of blacks who die from other causes such as AIDS and sickle-cell anemia. Community-based organizations and conferences (e.g., Black-on-Black Love Campaign in Chicago, Save Our Sons and Daughters in Detroit, Blacks Mobilized Against Crime in Richmond, and the New Orleans Association of Black Social Workers Anti-Violence Program) have started the process of educating the public. Black-oriented radio stations are ideally situated to help raise consciousness around this issue. Recently, a number of newspapers have run articles on the exposure of inner-city children to violence (Kotlowitz, 1987; Ogintz, 1989; Timnick, 1989). Such stories bring a human face to the statistics and allow individuals to connect emotionally to the issue.

As blacks are made aware of the extent of the problem, they must also be educated about the characteristics of the victims, offenders, and circumstances of the homicides. The misconception that most blacks are killed by whites or gangs or by strangers in the commission of a crime needs to be replaced with the knowledge that most blacks are killed by someone that they know, in the home, as a result of an argument, with a handgun that was bought to protect them from criminals. This knowledge focuses prevention in the right direction, and may serve as a prevention function in its own right as knowledge of the circumstances may decrease the likelihood of their occurrence. Furthermore, this knowledge may increase black ownership of the problem of black-on-black homicides.

PRIMARY PREVENTION

Primary prevention refers to those actions that stop a problem from occurring and can be contrasted with secondary and tertiary prevention, which are remediations that occur in the early and late stages of the illness, respectively. Primary prevention strategies are tied to the causes of homicides and cover a number of approaches, including provision of conflict-resolution skills, improvement of family systems, provision of productive outlets for youth, reduction in acquired biologic contributors to violence, education regarding the responsible use of handguns, and improved racial identity.

Conflict-Resolution Skills

As noted previously, most homicides occur as a result of altercations among acquaintances, fueled by emotion and anger. Violence erupts as individuals get locked into an escalating situation from which it is difficult to extricate oneself without loss of face, and for which they lack skills, other than violence, for defusing. Some individuals apparently have a propensity for this, as homicide victims and perpetrators have a higher frequency of involvement in physical altercations than others (Dennis et al., 1981; Rose, 1981).

More structured conflict-resolution training teaches individuals how to negotiate difficult situations and identify and implement solutions that are acceptable to both parties—the "win-win" situation. At a less structured level, simple techniques can be used to defuse potentially dangerous situations. For example, the use of humor in such situations (if it's not at one's adversary's expense) can be effective; pretending not to hear the person and asking him or her to repeat the insult can be quite effective, as the repeated insult will be less venomous. With a little assistance, students can generate additional such techniques.

Programs that reduce violence through knowledge and skill-building are currently in place with some apparent success (National Committee for Injury Prevention and Control and Educational Development Center, 1989; Prothrow-Stith, 1986). For example, the Violence Prevention Curriculum for Adolescents, in place in Boston high schools, teaches kids how to deal constructively with anger and potentially violent situations.

The placement of such curricula in primary and secondary schools is critical. School-based programs, particularly in the early grades, ensure that all students are exposed to the information (many of the most troubled students may have left the system by high school). In addition, a classroom approach can establish norms for the group, which members then use as a standard for evaluating each other's behavior. Ideally, norms of competitiveness and face-saving through aggression can be replaced with a norm of nonviolence that is reinforced by the group. Group members no longer expect and urge each other to fight, as this has ceased to be the appropriate behavior.

Community-Based Programs for Youth

Community-based programs that provide a sense of direction for youth can be quite successful in altering attitudes and lifestyles that predispose them to involvement in gangs, drugs, and violence. For example, Sister Fattah's House of Umoja in Philadelphia offers vocational training, in an atmosphere of "faith and love," that provides young males with a legitimate means of making money, replacing their involvement in less legitimate and more dangerous enterprises. Similar programs exist throughout the country (Sulton, 1987) and are typically aimed at reducing youth's involvement in gangs, drugs, and violence by enhancing their self-esteem, improving conflict-resolution skills, and encouraging and/ or providing education and job training in a supportive, yet disciplined, environment.

Support for Families

Some families, when under stress, particularly if isolated and without support, experience considerable domestic violence (Gelles, 1987). Such stress may manifest itself as child abuse (the murder of young children, which was the second-leading cause of death for black kids ages one to four, typically starts as physical abuse), elderly abuse, and/or domestic violence. Social supports that reduce the isolation and tension of these families greatly diminish the potential for abuse and violence. Drop-in day care programs for children and the elderly, as well as elderly respite-care programs, reduce some of the stress resulting from intense involvement with a dependent family member.

Parenting classes, particularly for young, single mothers who are often the most stressed-out, can prevent both the injury of the child and the socialization of an aggressive child. Such classes can also provide specific information on how to produce less aggressive children, such as the simple act of rocking the infant, which stimulates brain development and improves impulse control (Prescott, 1975). Whatever "nurturing" services are available for families— parenting classes, respite care, family counseling, and therapy—must be publicized to the community, with the understanding that families most in need, because of their isolation and stress, may be the most difficult to reach.

149

Reduce Acquired Biologic Factors

Research indicates a strong link between head injury and violent behavior (Bell, 1987; 1988). One study that outlined the biopsychosocial characteristics of teens who murdered found that head injury was present in two-thirds of the sample (Lewis, Moy, and Jackson, 1985). A similar study of 15 death-row inmates found that all of them had extensive histories of head injury (Lewis, Pincus, and Feldman, 1986). Poor people suffer more head injury than the less poor (Jennett and Teasdale, 1981), men more than women (Sosin, Sacks, and Smith, 1989), and blacks more than whites, mainly attributed to racial differences in income (Frankowski, Annegers, and Whitman, 1985). Head injury among blacks results from accidents, assaults (Whitman et al., 1984; Cooper et al., 1983) and free falls from heights, particularly for children (Ramos and Delany, 1986) for whom early head trauma may cause central nervous system damage that is manifested as an aggressive personality disorder. Thus, disproportionately high levels of black-on-black homicides may, in part, be accounted for by acquired biological factors, which should not be confused with genetic predispositions.

In addition to head trauma and the accompanying central nervous system damage, alcohol abuse has been linked to aggression through its impact on central nervous system functioning. Specifically, abuse of alcohol has been shown to deplete the brain's level of serotonin, an important neurotransmitter that plays a role in the regulation of aggression (Linnoila et al., 1983). At the least, alcohol serves as a situational determinant of aggression as it lowers inhibitions against aggression. Efforts to reduce head injury and alcohol consumption in the black community should result in lower levels of black-on-black homicides.

Control Firearms

In 1986, 58 percent of all murders were committed with a firearm (FBI, 1987). From 1984 to 1986, firearm fatalities among black males, ages 15–24, increased by 20 percent (U.S. House of Representatives Fact Sheet, May, 1989). While most individuals have firearms in the home to protect themselves and their families from intruders, the harsh reality is that a handgun in the home is 21 times more likely to be used to shoot a family member than an intruder (Kellerman and Reay, 1986). Although the use of a gun is often a matter of accessibility, some social psychological research has shown that the mere presence of a weapon, through its association with violence, may produce a stronger aggressive reaction than would have occurred in the absence of the weapon (Berkowitz and LePage, 1967).

The issue of gun control is a controversial one; however, individuals who own guns need to be encouraged, at the least, to unload and store them properly and securely. Obviously, attempts must be made to keep guns out of the hands of criminal offenders (who usually "acquire" them from the homes of law-abiding citizens) and off the person of individuals where they are easily accessible.

Enhance Racial Identity

There is some evidence that strong ethnic identity may decrease involvement in self-destructive behaviors (Gary and Berry, 1985). At the least, a sense of ethnic pride and respect should lead to a greater value being attached to blackness and black life, decreasing involvement in activities that destroy that life and increasing involvement in activities and institutions that support and enhance that life. This racial identity is manifested most clearly when black professionals and business people sponsor programs geared towards helping the least fortunate and most vulnerable in the black community. For example, several years ago, the president of a black hair care company in Chicago established the "Black-on-Black Love Campaign," which was aimed at creating love, discipline, and self-respect. As part of the campaign, the company adopted a building in a public housing development and invested in a library, computer lab, ceramics shop, and an outdoor mural exhibiting black pride. Since this program has been in place, there have been decreased gang activity, fewer fights, and less graffiti on the walls of this building (Griffith and Bell, 1989), which is in the midst of the police district with the highest homicide rate in the city (Chicago Police Department, 1988).

All of the aforementioned primary-prevention strategies appear to be synergistic in that ethnic pride, community-based programs for youth, increasing conflict-resolution skills, and a safer environment in which to live all work together to strengthen the black community and to prevent violence before it gets started.

SECONDARY PREVENTION

Secondary prevention refers to measures that can be taken before the problem does damage that is irreversible. In terms of homicides, this means intervening in the violence process before it results in a death by identifying and treating victims and perpetrators of nonlethal violence. Fortunately, from a prevention perspective, most of these individuals engage in "pre-homicidal behaviors" that bring them to the attention of law-enforcement officials and other public agencies and private professionals (Hawkins, 1986).

Research indicates that spouse abuse is a frequent occurrence in this society. One national survey estimated that 15 to 30 percent of American couples annually experience marital violence (Straus, Steinmetz, and Gelles, 1980). Contrary to the notion of these incidents as relatively harmless domestic "spats," it has been estimated that 20 percent of all visits to an emergency room by a woman resulted from abuse by a mate (Stark and Flitcraft, 1982). As CDC's Dr. Mark Rosenberg noted, "car accidents, rapes, and muggings cause fewer injuries requiring medical treatment than husbands cause their wives" fewer injuries requiring medical treatment than husbands cause their wives" ("Violence: Public Health Enemy," 1985, p. 1). Thirty percent of the women murdered in this country in 1986 were killed by their husbands or boyfriends (FBI, 1987).

There is evidence that domestic violence may be even more of a problem among blacks. Straus et al. (1980) found that black husbands were four times more likely than white husbands to have assaulted their wives and that black women were twice as likely to have assaulted their husbands. Interestingly, however, black husbands are more likely than black women or white men or women to be killed by a spouse (Block, 1985) acting in self-defense (Okun, 1986).

In many instances of domestic homicide, the couple has come to the attention of the police prior to the murder. For example, a police foundation study of domestic homicide in Kansas City in 1977 found that in 85 percent of the cases, the police had been called to the residence at least once prior to the murder and five times or more in 50 percent of the cases (Police Foundation, 1977). Similar patterns of previous assaultive behavior are believed to characterize other types of acquaintance homicides (Hawkins, 1986).

The notion that homicide is a public health issue, not a criminal justice one, does not mean that the police do not have a role in its reduction. Indeed, the police are often the first to become aware of assault victims/perpetrators and are ideally situated for identifying and referring for treatment those individuals at risk for homicide. Hospital emergency rooms are also a prime source of identification and referral of persons at risk. Furthermore, it is suggested that physicians, clinics, and health care facilities routinely screen for patients' involvement in violence (Bell, Taylor-Crawford, Jenkins, Chalmers, 1988; Bell, Hildreth, Jenkins, Carter, 1988) and make referrals where appropriate. Protocols for identifying, as well as treating, victims of interpersonal violence are available and have been shown to work in emergency rooms where such patients are frequently found (Surgeon General's Workshop on Violence and Public Health, 1986). Gynecologists can routinely inquire about their patients' involvement in domestic violence and, at the least, make available handbooks on domestic violence. Victimization screening of the mentally ill is especially encouraged, as this group is at increased risk for assault (Bell, Taylor-Crawford, Jenkins, Chalmers, 1988) and homicide (Hillard et al., 1985); their victimization has important implications for their treatment. The need for routine screenings is important, as research indicates that individuals often will not give unsolicited information regarding an incident but will respond honestly if asked directly (Jacobson, Koehler, Jones-Brown, 1987). Also, routine screening for violence exposure along with other physical and mental health problems legitimizes it as a health problem that can be treated.

In addition to victim identification, perpetrators of repetitive sub-lethal violence can be identified and treated. Many of these individuals will show up in emergency rooms as victims. Others can be identified in correctional institutions by health care professionals, provided there is support from institutional policies such as those recommended by the National Commission on Correctional Health Care (1987).

Once individuals at high risk for being victims and/or perpetrators have been identified, a variety of treatments can be offered, depending on the exact nature of the problem. For individuals prone to impulsive violence, a number of medications can be prescribed (e.g., propranolol, lithium, trazadone, carbanazepine) which, along with psychotherapy, can aid these offenders (Bell, 1987a, 1987b). The recognition that a blow to the head that renders a person unconscious can have serious consequences for the individual should lead to medical treatment and follow-up to determine whether or not central nervous system damage has occurred. If so, referrals to appropriate rehabilitation services should be made. Families in crisis with patterns of domestic violence need to be referred to therapy at their local mental health centers before, as everyone in the neighborhood recognizes, "something happens."

More effective police responses to domestic violence, particularly to repeat cases, can serve as a deterrent to future violence. The police oftentimes do not treat domestic violence as a serious offense and intervene by having a spouse batterer walk around the block to "cool off." A much more effective strategy would be to detain the batterer and give him or her the choice of going to jail or to counseling to address his or her problem. Also having the police, rather than the battered, press charges is reported to be more effective in bringing the batterer to trial (Attorney General's Task Force on Family Violence, 1984; Lystad, 1986); and a trial for assault could be an extremely effective deterrent to spouse battering.

Finally, there is a lack of coordination among professional groups around solving the problem of black-on-black violence, which often leads to black-on-black murders. Liaisons are needed among black community groups, black police associations, black nurses, etc., so that multidisciplinary coalitions can get together to do basic empirical research and test interventions derived from this study. Such coalitions need to convince the black church—one of the most viable and influential institutions in the black community—to take a greater role in responding to the issue of black-on-black murders. Ministers can survey their congregations to see if there is a need for victims' services among their membership. Services such as home-based "sofa bed" shelters can be begun, using existing church resources. Black professional mental health groups can train black clergy in family therapy techniques designed to reduce family violence; these services can be offered by the church.

TERTIARY PREVENTION

Tertiary prevention occurs after considerable damage has been done. Unfortunately, in the case of homicides, it refers to interventions that occur after the murder has been committed. While the death cannot be reversed, the morbidity of family and friends of homicide victims and perpetrators may be significant and demand that these co-victims be serviced by health professionals and social support systems. Being a family member or friend of a homicide victim who was murdered, particularly in a grisly manner, predisposes those individuals to cope with feelings of grief, stress, and depression, which may lead to post-traumatic stress disorders and major depressions (Rynearson, 1986).

As one would expect from the high homicide rate, exposure to violence—as a witness and/or having a friend or relative killed—is extensive. In a Community Mental Health Council, Inc. (CMHC) survey of its clients, 25 percent reported that someone close to them had been murdered (Bell, Taylor-Crawford, Jenkins, Chalmers, 1988); 29 percent of a medical outpatient group had a "significant other" murdered (Bell, Hildreth, Jenkins, Carter, 1988). Distressingly, this knowledge and exposure are not limited to adults. In Los Angeles and Detroit, it has been estimated that between 10 to 20 percent of all murders are witnessed by a dependent youngster (Pynoos and Eth, 1985; Batchelor and Wicks, 1985). A CMHC survey of 536 elementary school children found that one-quarter had seen someone shot (Jenkins and Thompson, 1986); a survey of 1,000 high school students found that 23 percent had seen someone killed, and 40 percent of those victims were family, friends, classmates, or neighbors (Shakoor and Chalmers, in press). Exposure to, and especially witnessing, such violence can lead to a number of emotional problems associated with post-traumatic disorder, including depression and anxiety, impaired cognitive functioning (with direct implications for learning and achievement), and an increase in aggression and behavioral problems (Pynoos and Eth, 1985). A school social worker in Chicago reported that of six black males individually referred from the same classroom for behavior problems and poor academic performance, all of them had an extensive history of family violence resulting in the murder of at least one family member (Dyson, in press). She noted that unresolved grief around these major losses was a major factor in the boys acting out an aggressive behavior. One elementary school in South-Central Los Angeles has so many students experiencing violence and death of significant others that a regular class is in place to address issues of grief and loss (Timnick, 1989).

It is essential that we recognize the psychological aftermath of homicides for witnesses and survivors and put appropriate services in place. It is equally essential that we come to grips with the reality that many black people, particularly inner-city children, exist in what can only be described as war zones, experiencing chronic threat, which (assuming they physically survive) will seriously diminish their life chances by impacting on their cognitive and emotional development. Given the pervasiveness of the problem, children in high risk areas should be routinely screened for exposure to violence by school personnel and that appropriate services (e.g., Pynoos and Nader, 1988) be put into place in the schools (Shakoor and Chalmers, in press).

Although service providers may be reluctant to deal with this group because of negative transference, individuals who commit murder and are released back into the community (usually through parole) need treatment, particularly if they are suffering from neuropsychiatric impairment. Often these individuals need aid in coping with their impulsive act of homicide, in readjusting to the community, or in managing a chronic mental illness.

CONCLUSIONS

To paraphrase a National Urban League statement (Mendez, 1989), "fratricide is not a part of our heritage." Blacks must come to recognize the terrible toll that black-on-black homicide is having on the entire black community—not just the "underclass"—and must take ownership of the problem. Given the seriousness and pervasiveness of the problem, the entire community must work together to mount a multifaceted public health approach to the problem. Health care professionals, social service providers, criminal justice professionals, school officials, public policymakers, grass roots community organizations, the black church, and others must coordinate their efforts to reduce black-on-black homicides.

Television Advertising And Its Impact on Black America

Gene S. Robinson, Ph.D.

THE "GOLDEN AGE" OF TV COMMERCIALS

In the '60s, then FCC chairman Newton Minow described television programming in a way that would influence television and what audiences would see throughout the decade. His characterization of television as a "vast wasteland" was a major factor in changes in television programming. The networks were forced to take a long, hard look at what American audiences were seeing and the quality of the programming offered. Throughout the changes made in TV programming, one facet of network operations and practices remained the same—TV programs continued to be funded by sponsors who wanted their products presented to the American consumer in the most effective way possible.

Commercial television in America is sponsored television, and sponsors pay for the privilege of having their products presented to potential consumers during commercial breaks between program segments. If a program is not successful, the sponsors will not buy time. Thus, in an indirect way, Minow's characterization was a slap at sponsors. If, in fact, they, the sponsors, demanded higher-caliber programming, American audiences would have a better choice of TV fare.

However, TV programming did not undergo any rapid and dramatic change. Minority segments of the American population were still invisible or seen only as "visual ambience," a way to compose a scene or establish characterization along narrative lines. Blacks in particular, while pushing for change and demanding inclusion into mainstream American society, saw the fruits of their efforts realized only as very slow gains in TV portrayals. TV commercials in the '60s seemingly preferred dancing cigarettes, singing bottle caps, and most admired people (white) to black; so their presence or economic viability was not reflected there either. Madison Avenue, responsible for a major role in how Americans view themselves, reflected a white America in its product, the TV commercial. The 30- and 60-second narratives, while deflecting attention away from programming, presented blacks as menials, characters to fill out a scene if they were to appear at all. Ignoring blacks was a long-established practice continued by '60s TV spots.

TV advertising in the '60s has been called the Golden Age of TV commercials. This period saw advertising agencies giving great latitude to creative people to produce the most innovative commercials regardless of cost. Unfortunately, such innovations did not include widespread flattering portrayals of blacks. In fact, commercials in the '60s borrowed from European films and filmmakers' techniques and portrayals that focused on such elements as "the unspoken word," borrowed from Federico Fellini and Luis Buñuel's surrealistic visions of starkness in black and white. Among those contributing to American influences were film directors John Ford, who had captured the quintessential White Anglo-Saxon Protestant at the frontier bringing civilization, and Frank Capra, with his episodic style that reflected great American moments. While it may be argued that what was being presented to American audiences in TV commercials was more of that to which they had become accustomed, the fact remains that blacks continued to be taken for granted insofar as their choices of products to purchase were concerned.

THE CULT OF PERSONALITY: SLICE OF LIFE

While offering new products and so-called new images, a media cult of personality that extends well into the '70s developed. Such characters as Auntie Bluebell, Mr. Whipple, the Pillsbury Doughboy, Speedy (the Alka Seltzer Kid), and Josephine, the plumber, were added to the body of American popular culture.

Not everyone saw the '60s as the Golden Age of TV commercials. A blanket assessment of all commercials of the decade as exceptional ignores the reality that they were barely responsive to black demands. In an overall critique, Bob Garfield, advertising critic for the magazine *Advertising Age,* observes that "The '60s Golden Age of Advertising, momentous as it was, didn't have a material effect . . . . What made the era so heady wasn't the proliferation of advertising creativity across all categories, but rather the reverberation of an inspired few campaigns in the utter commercial wasteland of the period."[1] Advertising creativity did not spread across all categories; in those situations in TV commercials where and when blacks could have had significant visual impact, those opportunities went largely undeveloped. The cult of personality contained few black personalities, but blacks continued watching TV commercials, perhaps with the hope that a black presence would verify for them the strength of their economic ability to purchase the products of the American Dream, and to give certainty to positive black interests.

As an outgrowth of the cult of personality, TV advertising introduced what has become the most popular genre in TV commercials, the Slice of Life. This genre owes its endurance and popularity to the fact that it focuses on a cross section of American life. This cross section is most easily identifiable because it reflects those values that define and form the national character. Hermann Bausinger refers to the slice of life as the culture of the everyday.[2] Moreover, he warns:

. . . the everyday is seen as a sphere which, though masquerading behind 'common sense,' often blocks rational action and which doesn't easily question what lies behind itself. Everyday: this is the stuff of inertia which is soft on the surface, but in effect hardly movable—a blocking against any far-reaching change.

The message for blacks in what Bausinger writes is that they should not be deluded by the seductive qualities of the slice of life. For, as he notes, "it inhibits human beings from changing their situations and their thoughts."[4] Bausinger's specific semantic of everyday life as translated in the American Slice of Life genre is based on values that are white, suburban, and middle class. These values represent what advertisers acknowledge as major components of the *general market,* a market segment that excludes both blacks and Hispanics.

THE AGE OF EXCESS

TV advertising in the '80s is ineluctably tied to the election of Ronald Reagan as president and his years in the White House. The Reagan presidency brought with it a major change not just in the American character, but also in the American image. Ultimately, that image would come to be a most frustrating and difficult one for American blacks who across the social and class spectrum had made significant gains in the '60s and '70s. The symbols and the symbolism of the new telegenic America gave new impetus to the pursuit of that old enduring aspect of America, the American Dream. Nowhere else could the millions of blacks in America find better examples of their plight than in the TV commercials of the '80s. Here, advertising and American economic policies merged to play a major role in shaping the decade.

While the Reagan administration sought to expand the political base of the Republican Party by making attractive appeals and advancing policies that favored the Hispanic community, it tended to ignore the black community. Further, as a result of the economic policies of the Reagan administration and the president's exhortations to buy American, the definition of middle-class America was changed to reflect the new patriotic zeal and made more inclusive to sell more products. This expansion coincided with America's move to the right ideologically and politically, a move that provided the decade with the designation, the Age of Excess.

To expand the middle class, Americans had to believe they were in the mainstream. While mainstream had heretofore been relatively narrowly defined and structured, Americans had to be convinced that first, it was possible to change the definition that had prevailed, and second, that means were available to effect such change.

The president and his minions exhorted Americans to buy American products. To do otherwise, it was implied, would place them outside the mainstream. Not surprisingly, those Americans who followed or headed the president's exhortations in the mainstream tended to be white.

Black Americans exhibited no such fealty to Reagan or his policies; an examination of black voting records reveals no great support for the Reagan-Bush ticket in either presidential election of the '80s. Moreover, they did not trust Reagan and were inclined to disbelieve anything he said because they did not share his vision of America. Thus, for most of the decade, blacks remained outside Reagan's expanding mainstream America.

The story of TV advertising in the '80s was *contradictory*. Initially, the message of TV advertising championed the vision and change of direction of America as articulated by the president, who came to be called the "Great Communicator." It hawked products at a rate that exceeded the consumer's ability to purchase them. "New and improved" became the operative phrase. As the president's popularity soared, products and their commercial presentation climbed. Consumption flourished.

Leo Shapiro and Dwight Bohmbach examined the link between consumer spending and the way people feel about the U.S. president.[5] In a poll conducted during 1987,[6] a link was established between how people feel about finances, the nation, personal spending, and the president. In addition, it was found that those pleased with the president's performance were more likely to be optimistic about the country and the economy, more hopeful for their own future, and more inclined to go out and buy all kinds of consumer goods.[7] What this suggests is that these are the folks who will believe the president when he expresses confidence in the economy; if he links feeling good about one's station in life with the acquisition of products, these same Americans will seek out those products that are perceived to enhance their status. Thus, the president used consumption as a means to build support for his economic policies.

TV advertising, which takes great pride in having its finger on the pulse of the nation, sensed changes in the attitude of the American consumer. These attitudinal changes reflected the economic schizophrenia that was enveloping the country. American business enjoyed unprecedented growth and profits in the '80s. As the decade drew to a close, U.S. growth income for the top 500 advertisers experienced a 9.8 percent gain—to 6.8 billion;[8] consumers were not saving—in fact, they were spending at an even more frenetic pace; the national debt had bloated to unheard-of proportions; and economists across the political spectrum were squabbling with each other, supply-siders, and the Federal Reserve Board.

Even in the wake of the stock market plunge of October, 1987, American consumers continued to purchase products at a frantic rate. One of the best examples of *carpe diem* advertising was the new series of TV spots by AT&T that almost immediately followed Black Monday. These spots, featuring swish-pan camera techniques, grainy texture, and sepia tones, reflect economic uncertainty and anxiety. By commercials' end AT&T, presenting itself as the corporate savior, resolves the created tension. These spots introduced a whole new genre of TV commercials called, ironically, Slice of Death—a term coined by *Advertising Age*'s Barbara Lippert. These commercials relied on a frenetic, jarring style to shift attention away from symbolism to anxiety; interestingly, they had almost no effect on the consuming public. That anxiety did affect corporate America though, with some of its leading members becoming ensnared in ever-widening scandals involving insider trading and underfinanced leveraged buyouts.

American advertisers, in the wake of a shaky stock market, began looking about for new markets. They turned to previously unexploited markets, blacks and Hispanics. Where in the decade this change in direction began is difficult to trace. It would be difficult to explain by suggesting that advertisers were attempting to treat blacks fairer in the TV commercials by favorable representations. No, the change was propelled by two economic realities:[9]

1) black purchasing power, estimated at somewhere between 157 billion and 187 billion dollars a year; and

2) blacks are more brand-name loyal than any other consumer group.

TV advertising's initial attempts to attract black dollars followed that old practice of placing black faces in white situations. Blacks outright rejected that practice because it represented both a total lack of awareness and any understanding of black life. While TV advertisers felt that they were pursuing an aggressive strategy to attract the black consumer, they were, in effect, missing their target. Marshall Johnson, President of Malmo/Johnson, Inc., a black advertising agency, in 1985 commented on these efforts: "Marketing to blacks is a minstrel show. It's white marketing in blackface."[10]

While slow in recognizing black sensitivity, TV advertisers were, at least, well ahead of the Reagan administration. They uncovered some salient facts which were then factored into their commercial messages to the black community.

William O'Hare noted that though blacks and whites both work—and earn most of their money, blacks are significantly more dependent on wage and salary earnings.[11]

Lawrence Bowen, in a monograph, *Advertising and the Poor,* observed that blacks are part of an economically attractive audience reached efficiently by the mass media. They spend almost twice as much time with electronic media as do their middle-class counterparts, and are stimulated to desire products portrayed by advertisers, whether or not they are able to evaluate material desires against economic resources.[12]

In addition, O'Hare noted that blacks in America are major consumers of electronic equipment, accounting for 10 percent of most expenditures in the television, radio, and sound equipment category.[13]

Relying on Census Bureau reports, TV advertisers discovered that in 1984 almost three million of the 20.5 million black adults were single parents, the overwhelming majority of them women.[14] They also learned that while blacks believe in advertising, they have to feel it is talking to them. They are astute enough to see and be offended by the blatant placement of a black model in a white ad. Moreover, creative execution must step into areas that relate to black history, culture, and emotional needs.[15]

161

This is the kind of information that would be reflected in TV advertising to the black community in the '80s, in every commercial from electronics equipment to food and apparel.

URBAN SCHIZOPHRENIA

The economic schizophrenia that gripped America in the '80s became urban schizophrenia with regard to the black market. The black community, beset by fatalism, alienation, isolation, and deprivation, saw its conceptual styles affected and its limited attempts to cope, mediated.[16] The urban environment was at once a haven, offering security, and a purgatory, offering hopelessness. Television commercials merely served as a constant reminder of the social and economic gaps between both classes[17] and color.

In scene after scene, in 30- and 60-second formats, the smiling faces of a happy, contented America were seen by millions of blacks in urban environments. Bill Cosby became the most recognizable black in America in a time when American music came to be dominated by Michael Jackson. The portrait of Black America became a Cosby-Jackson composite while the rest of Black America in reality was having a difficult time defining itself and barely recognizing the popular and safe portrayals offered by TV advertisers in their initial efforts at crossover marketing.

Imagine for a moment a situation in which on the one hand you are invisible, and on the other, you are told you are recognized and valued. This is the situation in which blacks found themselves in the America of the '80s. The American Dream was actualized in the TV commercial. All things were possible and attainable. The problem? In reality they had to be paid for. The American Dream could be purchased but, as mentioned earlier, blacks lived and purchased products with income derived from wages and salary. No job meant no money. While whites obtained a larger proportion of their income from sources other than earnings, no other established source was available to blacks.[18]

In fact, the black community in its long history since the end of slavery in America has had no broad or deep, and certainly no intergenerational, financial, or educational bases on which to build. The aspirations of blacks were limited by the realities of the white world rather than their own.[19] Blacks were stripped of economic resources as soon as they were taken from Africa as slaves. Those resources have *never* been restored. There was almost no base on which anything solid could be built.[20]

Thus, without a solid economic base and surviving the economic changes in Black America in the '60s and '70s, blacks remained poised through much of the '80s for an economic breakthrough that would never arrive. While some small numbers of blacks were allowed into the mainstream, large numbers remained far outside it. Additionally, as they perceived the expansion of the middle class (even though illusory), they found themselves further entrenched in America's swollen underbelly, the underclass.

In response to this, Bowen poses pertinent questions.[21] Are poor blacks particularly sensitive to product advertising that capitalizes on status appeal? *And,* because advertisers rely more on emotional manipulation than reasoned appeals, do black Americans who are constantly bombarded by TV and radio commercials develop a skewed, dysfunctional interpretation of reality?

The answers to these questions are found in an examination of the black community prior to the '80s. In the '50s, for example, Black America was continuing to look to black institutions for guidance and nurturing. Blacks, though historically under siege, had by some dynamic managed to survive. Instilled in the black community was that factor common to all Americans— the work ethic. No matter the job, black husbands and fathers worked side by side with black wives and mothers, somehow managing to pass on values to their children. Another black institution also was a major contributor—the black church. The church provided moral values, leadership, and role models. Though suffering mightily from neglect and dwindling resources, black colleges and universities continued to offer education to those who sought it, even when they could little afford it. Although these black institutions were modeled after white institutions, theirs was a distinctly different product based on black culture, history, and tradition. Blacks absorbed these institutional assumptions of black space, black time, black sexuality, and black moral behavior—thoroughly incorporating them into black reality. These factors, recognized and characterized as cultural myths,[22] are so deeply embedded in the black psyche that they are highly resistant to change.[23]

Into the fray moved the TV advertisers. With their messages of status consumerism; that is, not whether you buy, but that you are what you buy, one could detect mounting frustration in the black community. Moreover, with the rise in single-parent households, with women as heads of such households, the black urban community fell victim to another social dynamic of the '80s: more children having children than at any other time in black American history.

These young mothers, many with more than one child, and many who had children who became teenagers in the '80s, found themselves isolated, lonely, sometimes homeless, often dependent on a governmental bureaucracy for sustenance, and living in substandard urban housing.

The TV commercial then offers up the symbols of the good life, of the benefits of the middle class. The young, black mother and her teenage sons and daughters, watching their favorite TV program, see the TV commercial and believe the message. If we believe, as Bowen contends, that the poor black tends to live in the present and seeks immediate gratification, then the voice of authority of the TV commercial becomes the source for decisions.[24] The avenues to achievement that existed before and already mentioned as possible sources of support for blacks then become irrelevant. Immediate gratification becomes the way out, and the way out is by whatever means available. To these children and their children, the getaway car of the '80s—crack cocaine—has been the scourge of the black community, leaving in its wake ruined lives and unfulfilled expectations. This drug has become the quick fix, the key to economic stability, the path to prosperity, and the urban painkiller.

If one were to examine the symbols of prosperity and well-being in middle-class America touted in the TV commercial, and then travel the streets of black urban ghettos, one would be struck by the bastardization of those symbols into real products. An almost surrealistic urban landscape—littered with Milky Way wrappers and styrofoam Mickey D hamburger containers, crowded cheek-to-jowl with Reebok-shod black youths, noisy with the sounds of rap music, and parked curbside with end-to-end stretch limos—can be found in major American cities where black populations are densest. Add to this scene the sound of gunshots and the discovery of a young black teenager lying in a pool of blood, and the American Dream becomes a nightmare. The powers that be will argue that TV commercials and TV advertisers are not responsible for the crack-cocaine epidemic that is rampant in America today, an epidemic that has, in fact, dominated the entire decade.

Nevertheless, the land-of-plenty motif, with all the products that identify who one is, was not lost on blacks living in the urban ghettos at or near poverty levels. A defensive argument also will be made that TV advertising acts merely as a marketplace wherein people can examine all the products of a modern middle-class society and then make informed decisions at point of purchase. The TV commercials and TV advertisers in pressing such arguments really are shaping the debate. What they are doing is focusing attention to their commercials on an overt level, ignoring the ramifications of the covert signals to which urban blacks are responding. These covert signals are rooted in the cultural consumption of the '80s that is intertwined with and embedded in the fundamentalism of the far right and the silently advocated image-class conflict of the Reagan years.

CULTURAL CONSUMERISM

Black Americans are as susceptible to cultural consumerism as white Americans. The ability to buy the products of America and concomitantly to be in support of the system was and remains a continuing source of comfort for those Americans, white and black, who are considered as having made it. Advertising sells labels and these labels are then used to define American character. A person's advertising orientation is a set of interrelationships among elements of the advertising process, each possession salience and pertinence, components that are normally expressed in terms of gross negative or positive evaluation.[25] Each of us, black and white, brings some knowledge of our culture, some facet of cultural myth, to the advertising experience. We draw from that experience information that informs, constructs that structure and guide, and warnings of a life that does not subscribe to the products of a benevolent society. The upper and middle classes are presented as ideals, or rather the images of upper- and middle-class life patterns are presented in classical narrative form. As Cedric Watts observes, "life has both overt and covert plots, some inherent in nature and some generated by man's pattern-making abilities."[26] Man's pattern-making abilities can be seen in every TV commercial, and those commercials of the '80s fit perfectly the gross indulgences of the decade that form the Age of Excess. By examining the text of the '80s TV commercials, and by observing the conditions and circumstances of black urban life in the decade, it may be concluded that black Americans bought into the American Dream, but their Dream of America was patterned in a way that accorded with their economic realities.

The black class structure of the '80s evolved from the anti-discrimination legislation, affirmative action, and equal opportunity programs of the '60s and '70s. Those blacks who could afford it purchased their way up. In so doing, they distanced themselves from the black underclass, and as Alexander Alland has noted, they were forced to operate as a part-time white in the business community, but remain black socially and culturally after hours.[27]

All these changes were observed by TV advertisers. Some of them turned to black advertising agencies to learn how to communicate with blacks. Others took what they believed to be popular fads, mannerisms, dances, and black speech and created TV spots targeting the black market. Wrapping their messages in cultural signifiers; that is, cultural myths recognizable by blacks, the advertising messages of "buy now" contributed greatly to black economic displacement in the '80s. Black youth remained unemployed. The black middle class reinforced its entrenchment by purchasing as many of those products as possible. In addition to the automobile ads (one of which has a jingle with the lyrics: "This is not your father's Oldsmobile"—truly bewildering in light of present-day black realities which, as already noted, showed that single black women in increasingly large numbers were heads of households), the products of the new technology were included: VCR's, remote color TV's, and the genie of the decade, the personal computer.

In one sense, this sparked the acquisitorial materialism of the '80s that was practiced by both the black middle class and young whites. They were not shopping the American marketplace out of need, but for self-esteem and gratification. Those few blacks allowed entrance to the upscale, yuppie, DINK, buppie lifestyle found it to be vastly different from the portrayals of the TV commercial. Once allowed in, they, too, were then ignored. The reality of a black middle class suggests black solidarity. To the extent that black solidarity exists, it is seen as a product of social conditions which, if changed, could provide new social cleavages.[28]

Indeed, the decade of the '80s saw social conditions changed and new social cleavages that were especially remarkable for their devastating effect on the black underclass. At the same time as the avenue out of the ghetto became longer, TV commercials continued celebrating and reveling in the new feel-good

America of Ronald Reagan. As they had done between 1950 and 1960, the cultural-aesthetic values of blacks changed[29] again in the '80s due largely to TV advertising, and by examining the commercial text, black middle-class values and aspirations and black underclass frustrations became apparent.

Before examining the commercial text, it is important to consider the neo-sanctions and ideological-cultural mergers which were highlighted in TV commercials of the '80s.

In TV advertising, the market must be segmented to obtain a structure in which information is gained regarding customs, traditions, rituals, relationships, and identities of people who are potential consumers.[30] As already mentioned, contemporary TV advertising had divided the market into general, black, and Hispanic. This reflects an awareness that consuming, while apparently diverse, i.e., different cultural groups have different cultural preferences, actually expresses a way of thinking or living. Further, it expresses a cultural viewpoint on how to accomplish certain goals.[31] For the advertiser then, benefits must be offered for buying an advertised product. On the other hand, if one does not purchase an advertised product, then one must be subject to censure. What this does is to establish immediately an "in group" and an "out group." The "in group" fosters feelings of security in belonging, in knowing the "right" things to do and how to do them; the "out group" is threatening since it is hard to understand and might try to destroy the "right" ways.[32]

In the '80s, TV advertising redefined the "in group," allowing it images of unhappiness and isolation in life. If you were unhappy and alone, then the TV commercial would introduce to the viewer all the rewards of economic well-being.

But the black underclass, in this case, the "out group," provided the richest resource for advertisers in the '80s.

The "out group" represents adventure, a way of rebelling, of resisting conformity,[33] and radical departure from usual patterns of communication. In 1985, Burger King was the first to use breakdancing in a TV spot.[34] This reflects the view by some that popular culture is really black in origin.[35] In another example, Burger King uses a "great balls of fire" commercial in which a flaming piano (certainly a dangerous assault on conservative careful mores) illustrates the fast food chain's flame-broiled difference.[36] California "raisins" made wholesale raids on the Motown archives in "Heard it Through the Grapevine" to gain instant recognition using claymation starring black-featured raisins. The implications are enormous. TV advertising was showing that black culture had worth! More importantly, what the commercials also indicated was that art forms and art expressions emanating from the black underclass could be used to sell products.

But the greater significance of this borrowing from black underclass culture was the major ramification in the ideological-cultural merger that occurred in TV commercials for every product from soap to skinless franks. As the decade progressed, more and more commercials were accompanied by more and more black music, music sung by black artists that reflected black-on-black relationships, black culture, and black life. Aretha Franklin's "Natural Woman" was used to sell cosmetics to primarily white female audiences, and Ray Charles' "Hit the Road, Jack," to sell Kentucky Fried Chicken to a fast-moving white middle-class audience already well-informed about the dangers of high cholesterol, high-fat foods. These are but two of the thousands of examples of black life used to make significant crossover gains. Perhaps, as some have suggested, even though blacks themselves were not in real terms moving into the mainstream, a perception of vertical ascent was created. However, this conclusion was missed by some urban researchers. For example, George Sternlieb, director of the Center for Urban Policy Research at Rutgers University, was quoted by *Washington Post* columnist Henry Allen as follows: "Successful blacks are the most forgotten group of Americans there are."[37] In fact, they were not forgotten nor ignored by TV advertisers. As their movement up the economic ladder and into the middle class was targeted in TV spots, their journey was not ever the focus of a TV spot in the '80s. They were portrayed in white situations exhibiting white behavior. Their only contribution in the TV spot was their appearance. But significantly for TV commercials, it was considered good strategy to employ these black types because it would gain the sponsor access to black dollars. Hence, they were not forgotten, at least by one major player in America's economic mix, but rather exploited.

In a *Washington Post* article, "How Life Went On in the '80s," Henry Allen directs attention to a recent *Washington Post*-ABC News poll which showed that white intolerance to blacks declined from about half to about a third during the '80s.[38] The poll also suggested an increase in the black middle class. The significance of these developments is that it made blatant appeals to black consumers less risky. Products could be positioned in messages to blacks without alienating white consumers.

The fast-food industry led the way in reaching out to the black community. After a long history of aiming its messages at white women ("You Deserve a Break Today" and "You, You're The One") and their families, after launching campaigns at white retired senior citizens, and even going after the deaf market, this industry suddenly realized that blacks were the largest consumers of fast food. As already noted, Burger King used black music; Wendy's used black spokespersons. But it was left to McDonald's to herald the arrival of the black middle class. In commercial after commercial, McDonald's redefined the black middle class. Blacks were shown as having households where both parents worked—the husband at night, the wife in the day. The presumed conclusions are that the black grip on middle-class status is tenuous at best, that black middle-class families are fragmented, that there is little opportunity for intimacy, and that black children suffer because of their parents' demand for middle-classhood. McDonald's carried the drama even further. Blacks sang out their orders at the McDonald's counter, they gathered at McDonald's for lunch in their business attire, and Africans in tribal attire were seen in McDonald's spots commenting on the wondrous cuisine. But most recently, the new McDonald's spot features a black comedian offering up the newest in inanities, the "McRib." There is really no doubt as to the audience for this entree to the "table."

There is another promise of the message of the McDonald's campaign: Through the Golden Arches is the path to the mainstream, but more importantly, the path to assimilation.

The argument can be made that McDonald's and the other fast-food restaurants are portraying positive black role models, and that black men—long the target of social indictment with regard to parenting—were being depicted in loving, caring, and responsible relationships. But this argument ignores the fact that black underclass families, with black women as the heads of households, are victimized by an artificial TV reality that has suddenly created archetypal, responsible, loving, and caring black men out of the thousands of black men who have vanished after the act of creation. This brutal reality, the truer one, is due in large part to mass, intergenerational emasculation caused by white fear. What heightens the absurdity of this constructed reality is the counterpoint of present-day white males (whose familial fealty and strength are emulated by black males in the commercials) who are fleeing their families in droves. As Allen so aptly describes:[39]

> In other words, white males did the political equivalent of uttering the great American exit line, "Honey, I'm going out for a pack of cigarettes." They stopped by the polls to vote for Reagan and never came back.

For those urban underclass blacks, their most common role models for success are those who have made it in sports, music (entertainment), or crime.[40] TV commercials (other than the food commercials) reinforce sports and music as the two most acceptable areas of black achievement in America. The message is not lost on black youth of the underclass who see success as excelling in sports or music. However, the reality has been such that, once again, in the TV commercials of the '80s, few examples of "acceptable" black sports or music heroes reached back, down, and out to those less fortunate. In the fantasyland of TV advertising, black compassion is out, black selfishness is in. People like those involved in the Mentors program (a group of young black professionals who advise, counsel, and act as positive role models for inner-city groups) in Washington, DC, are not the stuff dreams are made of, at least not in the TV spot. But the glass and glitz of the form of TV advertising with its message of immediate packaged solutions opts for the safety of pleasant environments and black families patterned after the Cosby-Huxtable model. "Be something" was more important than "do something," as Allen notes.[41] Be famous, be rich, be successful, the commercials urged. They spent little time instructing "*how* to be," and perhaps because of that omission (and others as well), black urban youth who could not get a job and who found themselves mired even deeper in poverty, turned in some instances to the "hero" who was ignored in the TV spot, the black criminal. This essay will not examine in-depth the black criminal here. Suffice it to say that in black urban life, the role and impact of the black criminal have been great. While blacks and crime were used by the Republicans in the presidential campaign of George Bush, specifically, the Willie Horton issue, blacks saw it as merely another effort to instill fear in a white electorate still reeling in the aftermath of Jesse Jackson's unsuccessful attempt for the Democratic nomination. But of more immediate concern for the black unemployed youths, the black criminal in their communities represented an untold American success story. After all, appearances indicated that for the black criminal, the Dream had become a reality.

BLACK DEMANDS FOR THE '90s

The closing of the decade has seen blacks as more media-conscious than ever. As noted by Alland, blacks have a culturally derived love of music, presumably borne out of the need by white plantation society to discourage oratory.[42] That love of music was acknowledged by TV advertisers in the decade as the volume of commercials using black music increased. For example, the Levi Strauss 501 jeans commercials with their bluesy, jazzy feeling speak directly to the black consumer.[43] Studies have shown that black consumers respond more readily to advertising[44] because they see consuming as the way into the mainstream; it also affords them an outlet to build self-esteem. These factors support the awareness of blacks not only to media, but also particularly to TV advertising. They also reflect an acute awareness of how black stratification became more skewed in the '80s as advertisers aggressively pursued black consumers. Many blacks, unable to make that enormous leap into the mainstream, found themselves in much the same situation as those described by Katherine Newman:[45]

> People who lived through downward mobility are often secretive and cloistered or so bewildered by their fate that they find it hard to explain to themselves. They are a very special tribe. Some are heroes who find ways to rise above their circumstances; others are lost souls, wandering the social landscape without direction.

Perhaps the decade shouldn't be characterized in such stark terms as done by Newman, because her view is rather horrific by what it implies. But it enhances her later conclusions that "We carry the formative influences of our lives with us, and they shape our responses to downward mobility just as they define our attitudes toward success."[46] Those formative influences and attitude shapers did not spring from nowhere. In the total media surround of Black America, TV advertising's message was loudest.

From Newton Minow's vast wasteland description of the '60s to the Land of the Bountiful of the '80s, America has undergone a radical restructuring of its national values, image, character, and national goals. Nowhere has this been reflected more acutely than in the black urban community. The images and values of the '80s were translated into effective and dramatic narratives called TV commercials and offered up as signs of the new conservatism built on the economic policies of Adam Smith and forged with emphasis on individual over community and *laissez-faire* over social compassion.[47] It seemed blacks in this decade witnessed an America no longer willing to right those wrongs of its historical past by addressing black aspirations for economic justice. Instead, as the message of the TV commercial announced, in feel-good America, social problems no longer existed. The Promised Land had been reached, and now was the time to enjoy the opportunities available and awaiting those desiring to join the Reagan Revolution.

Cast adrift, left to solve their own problems, blacks turned to the media that, differing from the movies, served more as a socializing function than one of escape. While the movies offered an escape from reality, the TV commercial created a new reality, and the price of admission was merely a switch or a button away. As the decade wore on, the price became increasingly high. Urban blacks saw their dreams of a better life portrayed by characters who bore little resemblance to them. The frustration mounted as blacks moved farther and farther away from those values that had sustained them historically. Children having children changed as the children became providers for the mother-children, hawking the only commodity in plentiful supply in the ghetto—drugs. With the income derived from drug sales, they purchased the symbols of the American Dream that paraded across their TV sets to the accompaniment of songs and dance performed by black sports heroes and entertainers. Gold-chain tagged BMW's (with and without tinted windows); Ford Escorts with kits; wearing apparel and shoes by Skids and BK; real gold earrings, chains, and bracelets; leather or fur coats—the march of status products never slowed throughout the decade, and blacks, emulating the acquisitorial materialism practiced by whites, joined this parade, although, once again, at the end of the line.

The power of advertising is such that it can shape and reshape entire cultural structures. However, the fact that it is such an integral part of the structure it defines forces it to celebrate those practices and values that sustain such a structure.

TV is a powerful medium without the necessity of any enhancements. But TV and advertising together comprise a level of seduction and manipulation unsurpassed by any of the products of the new technology touted therein. In fact, TV advertising is used to sell the new technology, representing it as man's inexorable march to the new age.

In this environment, blacks need to resort to new survival skills. Closer attention must be paid to those spots purporting to be cast in black images and celebrating black life. Every TV commercial has two agendas: one overt, the other covert. These agendas can be compared to hard-sell, i.e., buy now, and soft-sell, i.e., buy later. The covert agenda with its soft-sell message works psychologically to have the consumer perform (at some later date) according to certain visual cues. Those cues are designed to touch certain cultural chords. As the black level of consumer sophistication increases, TV advertisers will be forced to change the way they attempt to address their message to the black consumer. However, by demanding that black consumers subscribe to white products, white values, and white culture by purchasing products that define white attitudes, blacks will of necessity continue to feel the frustration of trying to assimilate into a society whose mainstream widens, shrinks, or is redirected by "a word from our sponsor."

By understanding the signification of the "word," black consumers will and must understand the emptiness of that sign. In the metalanguage of Roland Barthes,[48] that sign, the word, is devoid of meaning. It is merely a means to further the assault on black dollars and direct them to the vaults of the sponsor.

As the decade ends, the landscape continues to be marked by the fallout from the throwaway society America became in the '80s. Affordable housing and the myth of disposable cash insofar as the black community is concerned have gone the way of affirmative action. Black definitions in terms of identity, life, and behavior, must be left for blacks to determine. Television advertising must be aware and be made aware that for blacks to be a part of its reality requires more than 30 or 60 seconds. In other words, black history and life are of epic proportions and that while ignored or distorted in the '80s, black dollars and black purchasing power will demand more.

Toward An African-American Agenda: An Inward Look

Ramona Hoage Edelin, Ph.D.

> This the American black man knows: his fight here is a fight to the finish. Either he dies or wins. If he wins it will be by no subterfuge or evasion of amalgamation. He will enter modern civilization here in America a black man on terms of perfect and unlimited equality with any white man, or he will enter not at all. Either extermination root and branch, or absolute equality. There can be no compromise. This is the last great battle of the West.
>
> W.E.B. DuBois,
> *Black Reconstruction*, p. 703

OVERVIEW AND DEFINITIONS

Standing at the threshold of the new millennium, African Americans have the responsibility and opportunity to unify around decisions and plans which address directly the problem of racism in the United States. In solving the problem of the color line, we must fully redevelop our culture, reclaim our children, renew our ancient mastery in learning, build a solid economic infrastructure, and empower ourselves in policy and political arenas by developing and implementing achievable agendas in this decade—*if we are willing, finally, to understand the truth of who we are as a people and launch a serious and systematic cultural offensive, together.*

A historic confluence of factors comes together in the 1990s which, if we do our part, will make racism, as we have experienced it over four centuries, a luxury far too expensive to be continued in America. Economic opportunity and a stable standard of living, and the orderly functioning of the democratic society—the twin pillars on which America as the leader of the free world stands—are both jeopardized at their very core by the domestic demographics and global realities now at hand. When President Bush says, "We must leave that old, tired baggage of racial bigotry and discrimination behind,"[1] it is because—whatever his personal convictions on this matter—he understands well that not only the work force of the immediate future but also the leadership and national security of this nation *depend* upon America's ending racism in this decade.

While domestic demographic projections differ,[2] there is no question about the facts that the number of workers available to the U.S. work force is in sharp decline—that is to say, we already know there will be a labor shortage in the next century; that the need for higher educational and technological expertise of that work force has increased dramatically at the same time that the preparation in mathematics and science of *all* American high school graduates has declined alarmingly, relative to other students in the global economy; that children of color have been underprepared at an unconscionable level and to a totally unacceptable degree, particularly in the technological fields; and that, when we add women, who are also underprepared in the technical fields, to the pool of available workers, the percentage of potential workers requiring great investment in their talent and knowledge approaches 85 percent. Racism, classism, and sexism must not continue to prevent the development of a solid American work force, if economic opportunity and a stable standard of living are to remain all-important to Americans.

With respect to global realities, speculation that the movement toward democracy in Eastern Europe will result in the wholesale importation of these workers to replace people of color in the U.S. workplace has begun. This very real option, coupled with the prospect of the U.S. joining the European Economic Community (Common Market) in 1992, would solidify a unification of people of European lineage for the first time in their history.[3] In this way, the group that is the world's distinct minority, in terms of population, would seek to hold on to its global cultural, economic, and political dominance despite the emergence of the Pacific Rim nations and the inevitable victories of liberation movements in Southern Africa. Ending the Cold War may reduce the level of Eastern assistance to these liberation movements.[4]

However, "free enterprise" will no longer mean what it means today if mature communist and socialist expatriates from Eastern Europe become part of the American mainstream. Despite what the American media would like to have us believe, Eastern Europeans may not be so seduced by the glitter of the consumer paradise that they will relinquish their beliefs that poverty, hunger, joblessness, homelessness, and ill health must never be tolerated while profits continue to be made at unparalleled rates. In fact, the U.S. is the only industrialized nation that does not accept state responsibility for certain levels of employment, education, health care, and nutrition for its people—Asians, Western Europeans, and Canadians have long since provided for these basic citizenship rights. The look-alike, two-party political system in America will be strongly challenged by populist, progressive, socialist, and communist candidates whose agendas will certainly include economic planning and a major shift in the distribution of wealth. These challenges, combined with the unfathomable consequences of imprisoning, warehousing, and otherwise continuing to underdevelop larger and larger numbers of indigenous U.S. people of color, pose a definite if not terminal threat to the leadership and national security of our nation.

We define racism not in personal but in systemic terms,[5] hoping and believing that the dismantling of institutional racism will result in the sharp curtailment of acts of individual racism such as the tragic death of Yusef Hawkins in 1989, the rise of hateful and racist acts toward fellow students on elite college campuses, and the new phenomenon of white voters lying to exit pollsters out

174

of shame for their inability to vote for the candidate they think is best because of race. We know that policy-makers, at least, fully understand the issue of ending systemic racial discrimination.[6] And while we understand the cultural nature of politicians not always acting reasonably upon what they know,[7] in view of what has been interpreted as voter preferences, still we press for the light of reason.

Despite the range of personal feelings and opinions in matters of race, there have been substantial changes in the status of African Americans over the past 50 years—due to *systemic* public and private responses to the need to develop America's human capital.[8] We want to press such changes much further, to their conclusion: to the perfect and unlimited equality of the African American, and of other people of color.

THE ROLE AND FUNCTION OF THE AFRICAN-AMERICAN GROUP IN THE ERADICATION OF SYSTEMIC RACISM IN THE UNITED STATES

Whatever we may correctly say about the need for European cultural corrections in the areas of the need to feel racially superior, materialism, and bellicosity, a case at least equally as strong can and should be made with respect to the cultural inadequacies of the African group at this time. In fact, if we were to heed the biblical admonition not to worry about the speck in our neighbor's eye until we have removed the log from our own, we would say nothing more about Europeans until we have answered the haunting challenge: If everyone of European descent were to disappear from the face of the earth tomorrow, *what would we do?*

As a frontline proponent of the African-American cultural offensive now underway,[9] this writer joins many of our scholars, artists, and activists in asserting that we will never sit at the table of cultures as equals with the rest of the world's people until we *redevelop our culture* based upon the truth of who we are and the unlimited possibilities that agenda-setting, educational mastery, community and economic development, and political empowerment in a cultural context will open up to us.

A fully developed African-American culture and agenda will ensure that racism is too costly to continue in the years ahead, and the systematic building of impervious bonds throughout the African diaspora will ensure new respect for global interdependence.

What Is Culture?

Culture is the vehicle which moves all human groups forward. It is the intentions, decisions, inclinations, and adjustments to life of a people who are identified as one group by blood and lineage, history, and circumstance. To quote DuBois:

... the history of the world is the history not of individuals but of groups, not of nations, but of races, and he who ignores or seeks to override the race idea in human history ignores and overrides the central thought of all history. What, then, is a race? It is a vast family of human beings, generally of common blood and language, always of common history, traditions, and impulses, who are both voluntarily and involuntarily striving together for the accomplishment of certain more or less vividly conceived ideals of life. Turning to real history, there can be no doubt, first, as to the widespread, nay universal, prevalence of the race idea, the race spirit, the race ideal, and as to its efficiency as the vastest and most ingenious invention for human progress.[10]

In order to achieve its purpose as the vehicle for human progress, a certain *integrity* must inhere in and guide the culture, uniting correctness and wholeness. It is precisely such cultural integrity which must be redeveloped in our people because of the heinous African slave trade that spanned 250 years, and the subsequent colonialism and underdevelopment which leave us in virtually a feudal state throughout the world yet today. The African-American cultural offensive begins again the process of self-correction and consensus-building for the explicit purpose of regaining that cultural integrity which precedes group development. It seeks agreement among us to vitally important questions such as "Who are we?", "What do we believe in?", "How do we raise and educate our children?", "What behavior is acceptable, what honored, and what punished—both internal and external to our group?", and "What do we do best, which can be strategically utilized to support and sustain us, so that we can provide for our needs and live as we choose and decide to live?" Answering these questions together, and setting and implementing our agendas accordingly, will produce a quantum leap in our advance *as a group* into the new millennium.

Absolutely central to the process of cultural renewal is the issue of *identity*. What is the truth of who we are? We must begin at the beginning; and we *are* the beginning;

Ancient Egypt was a Negro civilization. The history of Black Africa will remain suspended in air and cannot be written correctly until African historians dare to connect it with the history of Egypt. In particular, the study of languages, institutions, and so forth, cannot be treated properly; in a word, it will be impossible to build African humanities, a body of African human sciences, so long as that relationship does not appear legitimate. The African historian who evades the problem of Egypt is neither modest nor objective, nor unruffled; he is ignorant, cowardly, and neurotic. Imagine, if you can, the history of Europe without referring to Greco-Latin Antiquity and try to pass that off as a scientific approach.

The ancient Egyptians were Negroes. The moral fruit of their civilization is to be counted among the assets of the Black world. Instead of presenting itself to history as an insolvent debtor, that Black world is the very initiator of the "western" civilization flaunted before our eyes today. Pythagorean mathematics, the theory of our four elements of Thales of Miletus, Epicurean materialism, Platonic idealism, Judaism, Islam, and modern science are rooted in Egyptian cosmogony and science. One needs only to meditate on Osiris, the redeemer-god, who sacrifices himself, dies, and is resurrected to save mankind, a figure essentially identifiable with Christ.[11]

The movement of our people from ancient Kemet (Egypt) into western Africa and throughout the diaspora over a period of more than 12,000 years[12] has been closely investigated by such scholars as Diop, John Henrik Clarke, Asa Hilliard, Ivan Van Sertima, Richard King, Charles Finch, Beatrice Lumpkin, Maulana Karenga, and Yosef Ben-Jochannan. In order to achieve the level of certainty, confidence, and detail we need about the basic question of identity, we must *study the work of our scholars*—many of whom have traveled throughout the world to retrieve personally the important texts, oral histories and linguistic comparisons, artifacts, art, and photographs which are needed to untangle the lies, distortions, and stolen legacies of our past. Not only were African people the first earth creatures to will themselves human, they established the scholarly disciplines; engaged in a level of technological and scientific prowess which is still mysterious today; and established prosperous and *peaceful* societies that spanned not generations or centuries but millennia. When we, and our children, know who we are, then we know that our *possibilities* as a people are infinite.

In West Africa, where most African Americans lived before the commencement of the slave trade, effective organization of government and commerce, the blossoming of intellectual centers, and the amassing of great wealth characterized the three African states of Ghana, Mali, and Songhay.[13] Of them, Lerone Bennett says:

Ghana, which was old when the Arabs first mentioned it in A.D. 800, dominated the Sudan for almost three hundred years, flourishing in the ninth and tenth centuries and reaching the peak of its power in the early part of the eleventh century.

(Mansa) Musa . . . came to power in 1307 (in Mali) and put together one of the greatest countries of the medieval world. Musa was best known for a pilgrimage he made to Mecca in 1324. He went in regal splendor with an entourage of sixty thousand persons, including twelve thousand servants. Five hundred servants, each of whom carried a staff of pure gold weighing some six pounds, marched on before him. Eighty camels bore twenty-four thousand pounds of gold, which the black monarch distributed as alms and gifts. Musa returned to his kingdom with an architect who designed imposing buildings in Timbuktu and other cities of the Sudan.

Mali declined in importance in the fifteenth century and its place was taken by Songhay, whose greatest king was Askia Mohammed. Askia, a general who had served as prime minister, seized power in 1493. . . . He reigned for nineteen years and built the largest and most powerful of all the Sudan states. His realm was larger than all of Europe and included most of West Africa. . . . A brilliant administrator and an enlightened legislator, Askia reorganized the army, improved the banking and credit systems, and made Gao, Walata, Timbuktu and Jenne intellectual centers (*Before the Mayflower*, pp. 15-17).

The decline of great African kingdoms has been attributed to a combination of Christian-Muslim conflict; to decadence and the loss of spiritual fortitude as a result of easy living; and, most of all, to the advent of the unparalleled holocaust of the African slave trade and the European conversion of fireworks into gunpowder.

The 250-year slave trade—"justified" by manufactured myths meant to dehumanize fellow human beings and rewrite their history to rationalize utter barbarity and unspeakable cruelties—created the identity crisis which still plagues African Americans and other African people throughout the diaspora and on the mother continent. Slaves were torn from their motherland; separated from their kin; denied and forbidden their names, customs, and religion; and stringently prohibited from securing formal education or marriage. To the extent that it was possible, they were forced to face enslavement in a new land singly, one by one, alone, and without even the understanding and promise which their families had infused into their highly personal *names*.[14] Isolation and loss of identity were systematically continued by means of the establishment of an American apartheid which accompanied the defeat of Reconstruction. We can argue today whether apartheid-U.S. ended with the passage of civil-rights and voting-rights laws in the 1960s—or whether economic segregation and the perpetuation of our essentially feudal status amount to its continuation, in fact, if not in law. Correcting the conditions of isolation and loss of identity is necessary to correct the condition of economic segregation as one whole, indivisible, people. "Rugged individualism" is a fatal trap, a lie, and an egocentered seduction. As DuBois illuminates, the history of the world is the history not of individuals, but of *groups*. We are proud of the spectacular successes of a few African-American entrepreneurs and stars; but we understand that their success not only does not equate with the advance of our whole group, it actually widens the gap between our own "haves" and "have-nots." We will not prevail one-by-one—but together, in unity.

Thus, the role and function of the African-American group itself, in the eradication of systemic racism in the United States, are to effect a serious cultural offensive which will finally and definitely resolve our problems of cultural integrity, identity, and isolation, and provide the fertile soil for united agenda-setting and development.

UNIFICATION AND THE FORGING OF A GROUP DEVELOPMENT AGENDA FOR THE 1990s

One of the perfect and most exquisite, albeit cruel, ironies of the African experience in America has been and is the *stereotyping* of members of this group. We, of *all* the world's peoples, defy stereotyping: others may look alike—we come in every complexion and texture known to humankind; others may dress alike—we have translated all of nature itself into the colors and layers of fashion; others may think alike—we make a point of distinguishing our unique points of view and perspectives; others may act alike—we personify the creative impulse.

Add to our natural diversity, religious preferences, socioeconomic classes, political affiliations, regional ethos, and membership in organizations, lodges, and clubs—and add to this the realities of enslavement, segregation, desegregation,[15] and European cultural hegemony—and we see that *unification* itself is the biggest single challenge facing the African-American group. The quintessential paradox facing us is that we will only advance as a group; yet we will have to make the *decision* to unify personally, one by one. Perhaps it will help us to realize that in our historic cultures, personality or individual talents and gifts were seen as tools given to us or shared with us by our Creator for the purpose of making our unique contribution to the harmony and good of the whole. Our power resides in precisely this diversity, so long as we choose to use it for the co-creation of harmony, uplift, and the good of all.

Unification will be a matter of decision on the part of "enough" members of our group. (How many *are "enough"* remains to be seen; we recall that during the 1960s, as few as 10 percent actively took part in demonstrations and direct action.)

Nevertheless, over the years a more or less tentative African-American identity has been formed which, though hardly monolithic and not free of the tensions and treasons which are endemic to the process of overcoming oppression and exploitation, can be seen in certain behaviors and preferences of the vast masses of this group. There is an identity, but it entails a built-in dilemma of intense proportions. Again, DuBois puts it best:

> It is a peculiar sensation, this double consciousness, this sense of always looking at one's self through the eyes of others, of measuring one's soul by the tape of the world that looks on in amused contempt and pity. One ever feels his two-ness, an American, a Negro, two souls, two thoughts, two unreconciled strivings: two warring ideals in one dark body, whose dogged strength alone keeps it from being torn asunder.

> This, then, is the end of his striving: to be a coworker in the kingdom of culture, to escape both death and isolation, to husband and use his best powers and his latent genius.

> This waste of double aims, this seeking to satisfy two unreconciled ideals, has wrought sad havoc with the courage and faith and deeds of ten thousand people—has sent them often wooing false gods and invoking false means of salvation and at times even seemed about to make them ashamed of themselves (*Souls of Black Folk*, pp. 16-17).

As the African-American group looks at its condition and its future, DuBois' two-ness still has a searing reality which only our own *choices and decisions* can relieve. Before cultural renewal can unfold, before education can lead our group back to its ancestral mastery in learning, before the development of a self-sustaining economic infrastructure can be realized, we must *want and decide* to make the most of being African in America. This key decision can be a compelling creative challenge resulting in perfect equality if we properly under-stand our possibilities and work together toward achieving them.

The best way to start our cultural engine and engage our collective will in cultural renewal is to *do* something together. Remember that the real magic of the Movement years was that we set goals, never doubted or feared that we would not reach them, and worked toward them together. Our success and our motivation were one and the same. Today, as we forge agendas for the new decade and new millennium, let us never forget to make them *action* agendas.

Agendas that address what we need or should have from the external or larger society include impacting public policy at the state and local as well as federal levels, particularly in areas related to ending our segregation from capital, and ending discrimination in housing, employment, education, and the criminal justice system. Renewed demands for reparations and resistance with respect to Reagan Court roll-backs in affirmative action affecting employment opportunity and economic development are the clear priorities. The private sector, expected by Ronald Reagan to "take up the slack" left by massive federal budget cutbacks in social programs, is inundated with proposals and requests for support of organizational and community-based efforts to alleviate deepening problems of poverty, disease, addiction, homelessness, and work-force preparedness. Some corporate and private philanthropic representatives are also moving in to fill a policy void created by federal disinterest in these matters so crucial to the stability and productivity of American society.

This paper will continue to focus primarily on the inward-looking agenda of our group: what we ourselves can and must do.

Let us build a new model for our development, in every city and community where we comprise the numerical majority, for a start. The new model would build upon our ancient and traditional values and customs of respect and independence, love and protection of children and family, cooperation and accountability in building institutions for the common good, justice and fair play, mastery in learning and creative genius, and deep spirituality. The new model would tightly coordinate, or merge, the work of our organizations, businesses, and institutions into one effective, whole, cultural engine that would drive our personal and group development. Understanding that our freedom and development as African people is indivisible—that so long as any are in bondage or underdeveloped, all are—we would set goals and timetables for the advance of the whole group in implementing the new model, considering implications for the entire African world.

What is the ideal site for policy development and the delivery of direct services to our group?

I submit that it is essentially a campus, a learning environment around which comprehensive services; developmental programs; a cluster of businesses that provide products and services; retail shops; subsidized artists' enclaves; residen-tial and recreational areas; spiritual centers; and an amphitheater and cultural center are integrated into one whole physical and cultural entity. The new model is the recreation of that *place* where we all come together; it is the *way* we carry out our beliefs and decisions; it is *why* we need to develop resources together; it is what we do best and what we enjoy.

All the research corroborates our experience, that isolation of parts of our group, such as "drop-outs," "unwed teens," "learning disabled" children, or "senile" senior citizens only increases their inability to function productively in society. The middle class wants a structured way to share talent and advantage with those less fortunate who are of their families and group, and to reverse the brain-drain that depletes our still-segregated cities. Children and young adults often do not have the benefit of an extended family, with seniors or elders who can share wisdom and practical counsel with them. Far too many women, who are not inherently unable to raise families by any means, lack the support network of male and female family and friends who are *always* needed to help in the raising of children as part of a social or cultural group. Our leadership often goes for extended periods of time without personally relating to the children and families the leaders sincerely seek to represent. And the need for *learning* and cultural renewal could not be greater. The new model—the 21st Century model—seeks to prove once again that the whole truly is greater than the sum of its parts, by bonding them all together.

We would like to see the national prototype of the model established in Washington, DC, with variations on the theme established in every other city and community where we reside in significant numbers. Following are suggested facilities of the campus models:

- *Businesses* large and small, offering all of the products and services needed by our group, including low- and high-technology, communications and information, manufacturing, entertainment, retail, hospitality, personal grooming, and educational and social-service delivery supports. Hundreds of jobs could be created by hiring staff for these businesses, and to help in running the other campus components to follow.

- *Family Learning Center* large enough and fully equipped to run programs for early childhood; enrichment and research through all grade levels; mathematics and science programs; intergenerational activities; strategy clubs for teens; parenting and home management courses; comprehensive social-services counseling and health care; entrepreneurship training; aptitude testing, literacy and skills-building for adults; library and laboratory; and the state-of-the-art in technology. A 6:00 a.m.–12:00 midnight family development center, ultimately, a laboratory school, could be founded.

- An *administrative office building* to house several of our organizations and institutions who will tightly coordinate their work and services, including conference rooms; training and leadership development institutes; computer center and satellite communications connected nationally (and eventually globally) to other model campuses, schools, colleges and universities, businesses, and governmental agencies.

- *Residential development* ranging from one-room apartments and day rooms to private homes. Our dignitaries and celebrities—here and throughout the diaspora—should be contacted and asked to stay with us when they are in town, in private accommodations in keeping with their needs and preferences. And we should board the city's foster children and potential dropouts in small clusters with adult leaders. Perhaps we are talking about a hotel-sized facility in addition to single-family and smaller multi-family dwellings.

- A residential plant of that size would support *cafeteria and restaurant* services. We could make these dining facilities attractive to the progressive community, city-wide. A small nightclub and private dining rooms—for national and international, behind closed-doors business and political dealings—would be in order.

- *Athletic fields* for team play and recreational amenities such as courts, swimming areas, and golf course would be needed for strategic purposes, as well as for having fun together. Nothing sets in motion the personal discipline and team spirit that youngsters need better than a strong, positive, athletic-team experience led by good coaches. And nothing alleviates stress and fosters fitness and companionship better than recreational sports and games for adults.

- An active *cultural center,* complete with amphitheater, where some type of activity will occur each evening (talent shows, plays, musical and dance performance, cameo appearances by visiting scholars, athletes, and entertainers, children's theater, etc.). Artist studios; recording rooms; writers' workshops; radio, television, and newspaper labs; graphic arts; debating and oratory societies; historical societies; and performance should be part of the cultural center.

By uniting our leadership and building together such a future-oriented model life campus, we acknowledge and celebrate the unlimited possibilities that agenda-setting in a cultural context offers us, for the purposes of business and economic development, educational mastery, and empowerment in the policy and political arenas. Right now, we can and do and must work together where we are and with what we have, to come closer each hour and each day to the future we envision for ourselves.

CLOSING THOUGHTS

Will we make the personal decision to be part of a cultural movement with infinite potential? Will we pool and invest our resources in cooperative business and learning environments? Will we see our freedom and advancement as indivisible, recognize all African people as our kin, and support and protect our families and children together? Will we turn negatives into positives and challenges into opportunities in our inner cities and other still largely segregated residential areas where we are in the majority? Will we convert our potential power into actual group empowerment in policy and political arenas?

The choices are ours to make; but we must not make them half-heartedly, in fear or doubt, or with the cynicism that so often lies behind our feigned sophistication. We must truly respect and appreciate the *power of our expectations for ourselves*

Just as we absolutely *must stop using and permitting the use of negative, pathology definitions of our children and families* such as "permanent underclass," "at risk," and "disadvantaged," which are powerful, negative self-fulfilling prophesies, so we must set in motion powerful, *positive* self-fulfilling prophesies for ourselves. If we genuinely see ourselves in the progressive cultural contexts and processes that we describe, it will not be possible for us to continue to talk to each other and our children as disparagingly as we too often do; to believe what we believe that is negative and self-defeating; and to disbelieve the enormous positive potential which is right here for us. Even accountability—which is immeasurably more achievable in a clear cultural context where we know what is expected of us—is best achieved in positive, constructive ways.

We do not want to, and will not, stand by as our children become the human sacrifices of American society and our communities become graveyards. We have reached the time and place to which Dr. DuBois refers in our opening quote, where we must choose perfect and unlimited equality over the literal and symbolic death that racism is to us. If we match our faith with deeds and bring into active focus all that it means to be an African people in America, we will realize our goals!

Will the Cold War among Europeans end, only to be replaced brutally by an arctic freeze directed against peoples of color?

How can we ensure that systemic racism will be too costly to be continued in the 1990s? When we understand what it means to be equal, to make ourselves the perfect and unlimited equals of any group, to regain control and power over our lives and destinies and those of our children—when we have chosen to redevelop ourselves and our culture, then the costs of institutionalized discrimination against us will be too high in America. A successful cultural offensive— which would unite us and coordinate and focus our leadership; create markets, businesses and jobs; reestablish mastery in learning; and materially change the lives of our poor, near-poor, and middle classes so that our group substantially enhances the productivity and competitiveness of this nation—will ensure that the "old, tired baggage of racial discrimination and bigotry" must be discarded on the way from the 1980s to the new millennium. As we look together at ways to work together more effectively; to lay a solid economic infrastructure for our group advancement; and to be a vital part of the policy and political processes of this nation, we should remember well that systemic racism was unknown to the earth before 1830, and that its rise is directly related to the economic interests of the Europeans who invented it.[16]

We can—and would argue *must*—make it clear first to ourselves and then to all humankind that our development and the full flowering of our culture are at least as central to continued stability and prosperity of the planet Earth as was our enslavement. Together, we *can* do what we *will* do.

CONCLUSIONS AND
RECOMMENDATIONS

Conclusions

It is not just a new year that we are entering, but a fresh decade—a truly pivotal one in our history. America's future place in the world will be decided by how it meets the challenges of the 1990s.

One such challenge is the economic challenge of building an infrastructure for an economy capable of competing in the world's markets. While Japan is consolidating its hold on the technologies of the future, Europe is moving toward becoming a single economic entity, with more people and a larger gross national product than either the United States or Japan.

Both Europe and Japan either have in place or are building an infrastructure for the new world economy, with high speed trains and road systems to carry cargo and people and first-rate schools that train their future work force in tomorrow's technology.

The United States is clearly lagging behind. Our roads and bridges are deteriorating rapidly and our schools are not educating our children.

That is the legacy of the 1980s, which put private greed above public investments in the physical and human infrastructure. The 1990s will have to be a time of playing catch-up, and doing what our global competitors did while we were partying.

A second challenge of the 1990s will be to construct a global framework for peace. The end of the Cold War and the imminent democratization of vast areas that have been in the grip of dictatorships offer tremendous opportunities. The most obvious one is the opportunity to redirect our energies from preparing for war to winning the peace. With the Soviet Union calling an armistice in the Cold War, we are without a powerful, active enemy for the first time in a half century.

Without an enemy to fight, we can no longer justify a massive defense establishment draining the civilian economy. Experts say that the end of the Cold War means the United States could have an adequate national security system for about half of what we currently spend on the Pentagon. That means $150 billion a year—or some $1.5 trillion over the decade—could be diverted to cut the deficit and investing in the human resources we need to make our economy strong. Part of those savings could be used to meet the third challenge of the 1990s—ending poverty and racial disadvantage in America.

We reiterate our national goal of parity between the races by the year 2000. To accomplish parity means not only dismantling the remaining discriminatory barriers in our society, but also investing in programs that help make people independent earners and that contribute to a high-tech economy. Such programs would range from better schools to job programs to meeting the health and housing needs of the poor.

More than four out of five new workers in the 1990s will be African Americans, other minorities, and women—the groups traditionally left out in the past. They will be counted on to help support an aging population, and they cannot do that without good jobs at good wages.

There is a vital economic interest for America to institute policies that close the black-white gap. But there is also a moral imperative as well.

During the demonstrations that led to the recent change in Czechoslovakia, the American Declaration of Independence was read aloud—the words "all men are created equal" helped inspire the revolution that swept through Eastern Europe.

The American civil rights anthem, "We Shall Overcome," has become the world's anthem, being sung around the globe—in Africa, China, Europe, and South and Central America.

As the leader of the free world, America must put its own house in order and give to its own people the rights that it supports for others. We must make the 1990s the decade in which we finally eradicate racism and end the terrible gap that keeps African Americans from parity.

To that end, the National Urban League presents the following recommendations.

Recommendations

RACE RELATIONS

As America moves toward the twenty-first century, we remain steadfast in calling on our national leadership—public and private—to make the improvement of race relations a national priority. The waves of racial incidents have escalated within the last years. Not only must racism be eliminated, but also equality and racial harmony must be national goals.

CIVIL RIGHTS

The spring of 1989 will go down in history as one of the most devastating and anti-civil rights periods in this nation's history. The United States Supreme Court reversed critical civil rights laws in minority set-aside programs and employment discrimination. The damage that this court has inflicted has left minorities and women more vulnerable to discrimination than before the historic protection of the Civil Rights Act of 1964.

The Congress and the president have authority to reverse the Supreme Court's damage. Therefore, we urge total support from the Congress and the president to pass legislation to correct the Supreme Court's decision in limiting minority set-aside programs in local government participation. Legislation to correct this deficiency should be passed and signed into law before the end of the 101st session of Congress. Additionally, the Congress and the president should pass and sign into law the "Civil Rights Act of 1990." Discrimination in the workplace must end *now.*

Failure to act in an expedient and productive manner will scar race relations and further threaten the many gains made in previous decades toward bringing this nation together.

FEDERAL BUDGET

The 1990s must be the decade when this country reignites the stalled engine of racial progress. We can begin by rearranging our national priorities from excessive defense spending to a rebuilding of America's human and physical capital. The bottom line of public policy priorities must be reflected in our national budget plan. The budget is where the goal of a fair America is reconciled with the resources to achieve it. The shift from excessive defense spending to a wise investment in our human infrastructure must begin immediately with the FY1991 budget plan if we are to compete effectively in the global marketplace.

EMPLOYMENT

The disparity between African-American and white unemployment rates has been widening. Consequently, racial parity in the incidence of unemployment will not occur if the observed trend continues.

African Americans need jobs and the business community needs a trained work force. Continued efforts among government, business, and community-based organizations to develop productive training and employment programs for African Americans are imperative. Where legislative solutions are needed, we encourage the Congress and the president to provide adequate resources to implement successful employment programs. The proposed revisions to the Job Training Partnership Act currently in the 101st Congress should be passed and signed into law.

CHILD CARE

Racial disparity in poverty rates has been declining slowly. However, at the observed pace of relative progress, the proportion of African-American families in poverty would not match that of whites until the year 2154. One critical component towards moving out of poverty is economic self-sufficiency through employment. For many African American the availability of affordable, quality child care represents an essential link to a job.

Therefore, the second session of the 101st Congress must immediately proceed to complete its work on comprehensive child care legislation. Members of Congress must enact the Dodd-Hawkins agreement with improved tax credits for low-income families, with or without a Title XX increase. Congress must fund this legislation at not less than $1.75 billion and must provide for the guarantee of improvements in the protection of children in child care.

EDUCATION

In general, the evidence indicates that African Americans have made great strides in educational achievement over time. However, it is also clear that racial parity in this area is a considerable distance away.

In education, African Americans are on a pace that would bring parity in high school completion rates by the year 2001. Thus, improvement on this measure has been exceptionally impressive.

The president and the nation's governors convened a major education summit to address education as a number-one priority for the nation.

We are encouraged by their efforts; however, as leaders in the efforts to ensure quality education to African-American school children, the National Urban League has stressed and will continue to stress the importance of our role in achieving parity in education for the disadvantaged.

The League has recommended the following goals to the federal and state governments' Task Force on Education:

- To provide all students with the academic knowledge and skills needed to be successful and to become lifelong learners.

- To provide opportunities for all students to acquire an understanding of the knowledge and skills required to develop workplace literacy.

- To recognize from a national perspective the centrality of community and parent involvement to the educational process. To advocate forcefully for a national program addressing the issue.

ECONOMIC DEVELOPMENT

The difference between the average income of African American and white families has been steadily growing, raising the prospect that the attainment of parity in this area will not happen. The observed change in the per capita income ratio suggests that racial parity on this measure will not occur until the year 2151. The observed rate of relative progress will have to increase by more than eleven times to reach parity by the year 2000.

While full employment will help ultimately in closing the wage gap, we continue to urge a national program of African-American economic development supported by the federal government and the private sectors that assists in creating jobs for the African-American community. There must be a combined effort on both the part of the private and public sector if African Americans are to achieve parity by the year 2000.

HOUSING

The housing crisis continues to be a national problem requiring a comprehensive national solution. This problem is evidenced by the increasing numbers of the homeless, including families with children. The crisis is also evident in the shrinking supply of affordable housing and in the mounting number of foreclosures against families who have lost their tenuous grip on the American Dream.

We urge immediate intervention to help the homeless and to develop housing in the African-American community.

The attainment of parity in both the rental and ownership of housing will not be realized unless the federal government makes a serious commitment to bring housing within the financial reach of African Americans. Research indicates that in terms of homeownership for African Americans, the projection is that the parity goal would not be attained until the year 3148.

Without a comprehensive national housing policy directed at low-income families, the outlook is bleak. We call upon the administration and Congress to pass comprehensive housing legislation with full funding and to commit the necessary human resources to solve the complex housing problem. We also call upon local governments to recognize and give financial support to the hard work of community-based organizations who have created effective model housing development programs.

DRUGS

The intermingling of drug trafficking, drug pushing and drug abuse in communities where there is a high representation of African-Americans exacerbates existing disparities in the African-American community in such critical areas as life expectancy, poverty, school dropout rates, and unemployment. In its comprehensive report on drug trafficking, the National Urban League has outlined strategies to eradicate the drug epidemic. Key strategies include: Presidential declaration of the drug crisis as a national emergency; full implementation of federal anti-drug efforts passed by Congress; treatment on demand; mandatory school curriculums on the danger of drug abuse; and institutionalization of Afrocentric development, socialization, and enculturation.

HEALTH

At the present rate of progress, it will take until the year 2025 for the average life expectancy of African Americans to be equivalent to that of whites (2017 for females and 2038 for males). On the critical health indicator of infant mortality, "parity" would never eventuate if the current trend (widening racial gap) continues. The persistent disparity in health status among African Americans and other minorities has yet to be reflected in national health policy. The decade of the 1990s must therefore be the decade when this nation finally commits itself to affordable, quality health care access for *all* its citizens through the development of a universal health care plan that is reflective of the needs of unserved and underserved populations.

INTERNATIONAL AFFAIRS

While we celebrate freedom movements throughout Europe and the world, we must not only remember South Africa, but we also must actively work toward ending apartheid, which is the most brutal, dehumanizing form of official state-sanctioned oppression in the world.

We therefore urge that our national government make the liberation of the people of South Africa a public policy national goal, that we pursue economic sanctions, diplomatic isolation, and other means to aid in the struggle of the South African black majority for freedom and democracy through the legislative process and enacted public law.

We look forward to the day when black South Africans are free and are rightfully running their government. Post-apartheid South Africa will require intensive educational, financial, and other support so that the black South Africans are prepared to govern effectively a country where their participation has been systematically denied. We urge public and private agencies to be prepared to assist in what we hope will be South Africa's transition from an outlaw country to a country that is an integral part of the civilized and moral world.

APPENDICES

Those of Broader Vision:
An African-American Perspective on Teenage Pregnancy and Parenting

Georgia L. McMurray

Teenage pregnancy is one of those social problems that just won't go away. Despite recent efforts of community agencies and government to reduce the incidence of pregnancy among teens, far too many adolescent girls give birth each year, many of them unmarried and without the father intimately involved in the care of his child.

The U.S. has the highest teen pregnancy rate among Westernized nations, and the problem, with its societal implications, is growing. Contrary to media presentations, teen pregnancy occurs among all racial and ethnic groups, and in all classes of this society. Nevertheless, its most devastating impact is undoubtedly being felt among African Americans because of the disproportionate number of adolescent unmarried females in this community who get pregnant and give birth each year.

Moreover, although low in actual numbers, the incidence of pregnancy and parenting among African-American youth is pervasive enough to threaten the quality of life in many poor communities and may be even the very survival of family life as it has now evolved among Americans of African descent.

The problem of teenage pregnancy and parenting is aggravated by the lack of viable training and job opportunities for adolescents as alternatives to college education and by the paucity of resources now available through the government to enhance child and youth development.

This diminishing public interest in the young reflects a growing conservatism in the U.S., which was culminated during the 1980s by the radical-right policy shifts of the Reagan administration. Fueled by a proliferation of research by neo-conservative scholars such as Charles Murray and George Gilder, the administration directly contested and frequently cut back government outlays for health and social services programs. These reductions remain.

Like the rest of the nation, during the past decade, the African-American community turned increasingly inward, preoccupied with personal satisfaction or survival, and less active in confronting social issues. Even more critical, many African-American youth, like their white counterparts, seem to be cultivating new and perhaps libertarian views towards sexual activity and personal responsibility that do not augur well for the future development of black families. These trends continue.

Today, according to the National Commission to Prevent Infant Mortality, a black infant born in the U.S. is twice as likely to die before his or her first

195

birthday than a white infant. Many of these babies are born to poor teen mothers[1] who are becoming an increasingly high percentage of all new mothers.

Because of these dismal figures, community-based programs have developed over the past few years to help teenagers struggling to control their sexual behavior and its negative consequences. Many of these programs are rooted in the African-American community itself in the true tradition of mutual support.

The National Urban League, particularly through its affiliate system, has been instrumental in developing and supporting community-based programs to serve young parents and to reduce the incidence of teenage pregnancy. This effort has been one of its top priorities with a major focus on male responsibility.

Generally, though, the notion that some people bear children "too early" is reflective of how a society perceives the appropriate age for marriage and for the development of a family. It also denotes sharp conflict over how societal resources should be allocated to children and families. As Dr. Robert Hill states, "Public concern [about teen parenting] is generated by the belief that young black fathers totally neglect their children who must then be supported by welfare."[2]

AFRICAN-AMERICAN FAMILIES VIEWED FROM THE PAST

The extent that chattel slavery has had a negative effect on the development of African-American family life remains controversial even today among scholars and lay people alike. Some, black and white, argue that slavery almost totally destroyed kinship bonds among imported Africans and their descendants, tearing the familial traditions of West Africa asunder, and precipitating the evolution of a dysfunctional family structure particularly devastating for participation in the urbanized society of the 20th century.

Yet, the historian Herbert Gutman contends that the slave culture was adaptive, a cross-fertilization of West African, European, and even Native American civilizations, with many African customs and values surviving in spite of the economic and social degradation slavery represented. Also, using information found in plantation records documenting marital and kinship ties among slave populations, he presents cogent arguments to support this contention.

Gutman suggests that many West African customs carried over into child-rearing practices during slavery. For instance, West Africans placed prime value on caring for their young, usually breast feeding infants until two or three years old. Mothers frequently abstained from intercourse until the child was weaned, and child-bearing was spaced as evidenced by fewer children per family. As a result, the bonding of an infant and mother occurred over a longer period of time. In contrast, European families tended to bear children more frequently and, presumably, bonding between mother and child may have been more tenuous.

Considering this cultural backdrop, the physical and emotional brutality associated with the separation of slave mother and child had to be heart-rending. The strong mother derivative of African culture driven at all costs to protect her young became a towering figure, even, as Toni Morrison depicts in her brilliant, prize-winning novel, *Beloved,* to the point of child murder rather than child slavery.[3]

Any number of scholars speak of the communal life which characterized traditional West African villages. It is believed that this experience carried over into slavery and has had a lasting effect on the development of African-American family life with its commitment to extended family relationships and its expressed close and intimate ties, particularly in rural black communities and the church.

For example, it is interesting to note that, in the first third of the 20th century, just a few generations from slavery, the African-American family, both mother and father in the home, seemed stable and enduring, despite the harsh deprivation and overt racism present in the American culture. Gutman documents that, in New York City's Central Harlem—the classic symbol of urban black life—six out of seven households had a husband or father present in 1925, up from five out of six 10 years before. We can assume that most child births occurred inside marriage regardless of the circumstances of conception.

Northern migration after World War II is often cited as a probable cause for destabilizing African-American families, severing the deep family and community roots of the rural South. But a look further back in time may be more appropriate.

The migration of southern blacks has a long history, tracing back to the Underground Railroad through Reconstruction. World War I was a major impetus with the promise of jobs and freedom in the North, and black communities, such as Harlem, thrived.

Then came the Great Depression of the 1930s, devastating the social and economic status of most Americans, but those of African descent most severely, because their hold on the economic ladder was more attenuated. Recovery during World War II was only marginal for most black families and communities despite the increase in jobs because of the war.

During the 1950s, while most Americans settled into peacetime prosperity, blacks began to migrate again from the South, this time not only to escape oppression but also because of the loss of farm employment due to mechanization. But the North proved to be no promised land. Jobs requiring unskilled labor began to be in short supply.

Amid the deliberations about rising rates of teen pregnancy and probable causes, scant attention has been paid to the impact of northern migration and subsequent urbanization after World War II on black family life. Like immigrants the world over, from rural to urban areas, from one nation to another, African Americans migrated in wave after wave, seeking the better life—good jobs, a future for their children, freedom from oppression. And they settled mostly in cities where over 70 percent of them now reside. And they settled in localities on the brink of the post-industrial society.

What blacks found in northern cities has been the harsh reality of de facto segregation in housing, in education, and in employment, and a public tolerance of exploitation, violence, and crime which subsumes any marginal gains that they could have made. These northern cities have evolved into hostile places where black folk are subservient to institutions which regulate their lives. What they left behind in the South were the remnants of a feudal system with a loosening of communal ties, probably contributing to high rates of teenage pregnancy and parenting in this region even today.

In the communities, North and South, where most blacks now cluster, they do not manage or even influence the schools. The few health or social service programs present are run by government or voluntary agencies mostly directed by whites. In the past three decades, particularly in the North, these private agencies have deserted black neighborhoods, leaving the residents who remain with few or no services at all. And the recreation centers have left, along with movie houses, and even the supermarkets.

Through these years, many black parents have increasingly lost control over their children's behavior, becoming helpless in the face of the deterioration spreading around them. Who can doubt that premature sexual activity would prosper in such places?

Too many young women now seek to establish their independence from parents whose values they view as irrelevant or impotent, energized by the dominant culture's championing of reproductive freedom and youth emancipation—both noble causes, but dynamite in the hands of teenagers too young, too inexperienced, and too ignorant to handle them. And too many young men believe that fatherhood and violence are the ritual steps to manhood, viewing their parents as failures. Now children are bearing babies, while parents, communities, and the dominant culture wring their collective hands.

Changes in sexual mores and parental responsibilities are affecting white and more affluent black communities too, but those in the middle class can minimize the negative consequences of teen sexuality because they have resources and access to services, as always. The tragedy was and is that poor blacks do not.

THE STIRRINGS OF A SOCIAL PROBLEM

Until the 1960s, services for pregnant unmarried adolescents were as racially and socially segregated as other parts of American society. A white female pregnant out of wedlock, particularly if middle class, was offered the comfort of maternity shelters, where hidden from community view, she could wait out the arrival of her child, who would usually be put up for adoption. After delivery, the young mother could return to her parental home and resume her normal life with only herself, her parents, and the social worker knowing the ordeal and pain she had experienced.

During the period of confinement, the young mother-to-be had available a broad range of health, educational, and social services to assist in maintaining her development. Because pregnancy out of wedlock was considered a social disaster, young, middle-class women who "made mistakes" were felt to be under psychological stress, not sexually permissive. After all, why did they get pregnant unless they were acting out some emotional trauma? Social work intervention was predicated upon separating the young mother from her self-induced social ostracism; adoption was encouraged.

For most teenage African-American females, the situation was different. Rarely did they seek admission to maternity shelters, and, if they did, rarely were they admitted once they indicated they planned to keep their child. That these pregnant teenagers wanted to keep their babies was not an indication that pregnancy out of wedlock was more acceptable among African Americans, although the white dominant culture thought so and perpetuated myths of black sexual proclivity. Young girls getting pregnant was just one in a myriad of troubles African Americans faced; besides, the community was used to caring for its own offspring or taking in other children, despite the circumstances of their birth. So these pregnant teens remained at home or in the community. Many times, they married. But regardless, motherhood meant a change in status. School was now closed to them because pregnant and married students were legally barred from the classroom in public education systems around the U.S. Moreover, unless their parents, husbands, or fathers of their children could provide financial support, these young mothers, unskilled and uneducated, inevitably found their way to welfare. There, they would most likely remain, perhaps with more children coming, but certainly living on the edge of life, poor and frequently lonely.

Thus it was, two very different responses to a common human occurrence, forged by historical circumstances and by how human sexuality and childbirth were viewed among the races. Thus it remained until the 1960s, when, in the thrust of the Civil Rights movement and the embryonic push for women's rights, community activists began to organize health, education, and social services for poor, young, pregnant minority women.

The story of these activists has yet to be told fully. They fought against the prejudices of their day and the legal barriers to education and child care, which condemned poor, minority, and young parents to a lifetime of poverty. They established services right in the communities where these young mothers lived, demanding education on a par with the programs in maternity shelters. Later, they would argue successfully for the right of pregnant students to remain in their regular classroom and to continue their education after giving birth with proper child care and other help available. They would also advocate for legalized abortion services.

Their programs were born of local initiative, not government planning. They were born as a response to a clear and compelling human need. They came alive because someone cared. They also symbolized profound societal changes in how sexuality, not only among adolescents but also among women generally, was being viewed.

Newspaper accounts during the 1960s indicate that the public, while confused by these value changes, was nevertheless sympathetic to the plight of unmarried adolescent parenthood, even among minorities. In this atmosphere, services for teen parents flourished. By 1970, over 350 programs for teen parents were operating. Soon after, federal legislation was enacted to provide a modicum of support; barriers to public education highlighted by Title IX amendments to the Civil Rights Act began to fall.

And then, something happened. As the 1970s wore on—with rising youth unemployment among minorities of color, particularly males; with cutbacks in social spending at all levels of government; with articulated views that poor and minority people had gotten too fat at the public trough—resentment in the dominant culture began to fester and then bubble over against poor, African-American women having babies, perpetuating old tales about the fecundity of black women and the shiftless irresponsibility of their men.

But teenage pregnancy is much more complicated. How teenagers, both black and white, assume adulthood in this society needs to be confronted. Teenage pregnancy has yet to be defined as the result of titanic social changes requiring broad public solutions. There have been relatively small shifts in conceptualizing adolescent pregnancy since it was first deemed "a social problem" in the 1960s. Moreover, services for teen parents or to prevent teen pregnancy continue to be minimally available.

TEENAGE PREGNANCY AND PARENTING TODAY

Despite the heightened public interest in teen pregnancy, a review of historical data will show that, though the number of births among adolescent women has increased in the past few decades—reflecting their sizable age group, birth rates among this group have not risen as sharply. What has changed, however, is society's views about teen child-bearing, married or unmarried.

Early family formation is now considered to be dysfunctional in a world increasingly technology-based and urbanized and requiring a skilled and committed paid work force, male and female. Today, poor and young people are expected to complete schooling and become wage earners before they become parents.

This is a far cry from the past, when the primary role of women was parenting, and the sooner the better! Although African-American women often worked outside the home as an economic necessity, their mothering responsibility was central to their lives and to their families. Their men worked the farms or as unskilled labor in factories, jobs they assumed while in their teens or younger.

These functions have become vestiges in today's society where women of the dominant culture question traditional roles, and men and women need education and training if they are to command decent-paying jobs. Consequently, most young African Americans today are increasingly caught in a cultural bind not of their own making and with few institutional supports to aid them in the transition to this "new society" where they only marginally belong, or so they believe.[4]

In 1985, according to the Children's Defense Fund's analysis of federal government health data, of nine million teenage girls living in the U.S., almost

900,000 became pregnant; about half of them—477,000—gave birth; and of that number, 58.7 percent were unmarried at the time. For nearly 50 percent of these pregnant teenagers, abortion was the alternative.

Almost two-thirds of these births, 62.7 percent, occurred among young women, ages 18 to 19, and about half of them were married when they gave birth. About 2.1 percent of births occurred among teenage girls younger than fifteen. Of the total number of teen girls who gave birth in 1985, about 110,000 had already given birth once.

Although blacks constitute almost 15 percent of teen girls, they make up 29.3 percent of the births to teens under 20, 35.2 percent births to teens under 18, and 57.3 percent to teens under 15. Even more critical, they also are the majority, 57.5 percent, among teens 14 and under who have repeat births.

White teenagers actually gave birth more often, (322,826 births in 1985 compared to 140,138 among blacks). Moreover, between 1970 to 1985, the percentage of white teens giving birth out of wedlock declined at a slower rate, 25 percent or 57.4 to 42.8 percent per 1,000 births, compared to black teens whose birth rates actually fell from 140.7 to 79.4 percent per 1,000 births or 31 percent during this period.

Not surprisingly, most teen births occur in urban and suburban areas, for the U.S. is a highly urbanized society. Nationally, 90 percent of black teens giving birth are unmarried. Moreover, the younger the mother, the less likely she is to be married.

Unmarried frequently means a lack of stable support coupled with emotional distress. Teen parenting is believed to be a leading cause of poverty among African Americans. CDF notes, for instance, that in 1986, the poverty rate among children younger than three in households headed by 15- to 21-year-olds was 81.6 percent for blacks, and around 60 percent for whites and Hispanics.

Teenage pregnancy affects more than the pregnant teenager if she decides to go to term. Her plight spreads to encompass others as well: the grandparents, maternal and paternal, who are sometimes left with the infant; and the baby's father, whether he provides support or not. Some teen mothers marry, albeit a declining proportion; others leave home to live with the baby's father or friends (male or female). And some live by themselves, even becoming part of the homeless population. Also, as mentioned previously, many African-American teens, like others who find themselves pregnant, opt for abortion. Very few choose formal adoption of the baby as an alternative.

Few studies have documented the long-term effect of teen parenting. The most widely influential of those have dwelt on welfare dependency. However, one report on a group of Baltimore, MD, teens who became mothers (some as young as 13) in the mid-'60s and who received services from a special program indicates that, with direct intervention, teen parenting does not have to be a dead end. Very few of the mothers tracked had become part of the so-called underclass 17 years later. Most completed high school and supported their families by working rather than receiving welfare. Few had large families. And one-fourth of the group "became a part of the middle class, with family incomes of more than $25,000, mostly because of the presence of a husband in the home.[5]

Some of the concern about teenage pregnancy reflects a general uneasiness among adults about the liberated behavior of youth—liberated without a sense of responsibility, some adults believe. Despite this perception, the fact remains that most young women are not getting pregnant and even fewer are giving birth. The issue is which teenagers are really at risk; techniques must be developed to identify and help those adolescents prone to premature sexual activity and who may subsequently become pregnant and parents.

Based upon several studies on teen parenting, certain at-risk groups among adolescents can be pinpointed. For example, girls who have school problems—poor achievement, poor discipline, truancy—and whose families receive public assistance tend to be at highest-risk of pregnancy. This seems to hold true for males as well.[6]

However, as an April, 1989 article in *Harper's* reminds us, poor adolescent girls are not the only ones vulnerable to pregnancy. Describing the situations of young mothers in a community program located in the Bronx, Elizabeth Marek finds that they came from working and middle-class families. Their pregnancies tended to be the result of sexual naivete, failed love affairs, or emotional difficulties with parents.[7]

Most intriguing, the extensive research study reported by RAND found that girls willing to entertain the idea of pregnancy were two to three times more likely to bear a child. Moreover, black females were at the highest risk of single child-bearing, but a "conscious rejection of this works better for blacks than for other groups." For instance, young black women who aspired for a college education had "dramatically" lower nonmarital birth rates than their peers with no college aspirations. And again, low family socioeconomic status was determined to increase young parenting risks for blacks, though, interestingly, less so for Hispanics, and not so for whites.[8]

Conversely, close parental supervision seemed to have an inhibiting effect on pregnancy among black teenagers in the study; for Hispanics, it was religion; and for whites, a high-quality relationship with their parents. Black and Hispanic girls were also found to be at high risk if they came from single-parent families.

What behavior should be encouraged then to prevent teen pregnancy? Most critically, parental involvement in the lives of their teenagers. In the Baltimore study mentioned earlier, the mothers reported that 78 percent of their children, who are now adolescents, were sexually active. Yet, only one percent of the boys had fathered a child, and nine percent of the girls had become pregnant, many choosing to abort. Seventy-two percent of the parents reported that their teenagers used contraceptives, and 93 percent stated they discussed birth control with their children.

Clearly, teens who can turn to their parents for psychological support and guidance may avoid the pregnancy trap. Most important too is adolescent awareness of what is really at risk by becoming pregnant and bearing a child. Adolescence is a time of turbulence, the space between childhood and maturity, when life decisions made frivolously can have lifetime consequences.

Becoming a parent, either when a teen or an adult, means restricting activities in behalf of the child's interests. Teenagers unwilling to do so may become a source of escalating tension in their parents' home. Adolescent parenting can place whole families economically, socially, and emotionally at risk.

It appears that families who can heighten and broaden their teens' awareness about future opportunities lower the risk of teen pregnancy. Moreover, those families in which parents have gotten at least halfway through high school provide motivation and role models compared to those where parents dropped out of school.[9]

What many families need and seek is support. Some can find this through their churches or neighbors. Others are isolated in this highly mobile society from relatives and friends who could lend a helping hand.

For teens who may be emotionally isolated from their families, special attention from a caring staff in a community-based program can have an immediate payoff—returning to school, using contraceptives, and developing parenting skills. Most of all, studies documenting the efforts of such programs validate that building the self-esteem of teens, whether pregnant or parents, is central to making a positive difference in their lives.

Despite these exemplary efforts, the problems confronting teenagers today seem to set young people apart from earlier generations. The Ford Foundation, in its recent study on social welfare issues, states that, "compared to 20 years ago, pregnant teens and parents are more troubled, are experiencing multiple problems, are without family supports, and are often caught up in drugs."[10]

Even more illuminating, the mothers in the Baltimore study described their teenagers' lives as problematic. Many of their offspring were failing in school or having discipline problems. They reported their children as runaways or using drugs and alcohol. And boys were viewed as more troubled than girls.[11]

YOUNG MALES: A SPECIAL DILEMMA

Despite all the discussion about adolescent pregnancy, very little attention was given to the sexual behavior of males and their role and responsibility for the burgeoning teen pregnancy problem until recently. Part of this neglect was undoubtedly due to a general and legitimate public concern for the young female's more immediate problem; that is, preventing pregnancy, traditionally viewed as the female's responsibility, or assuring proper care for the beginning family.

However, there is a growing body of literature on males who father children born to adolescent girls; much of this information regrettably is anecdotal, based on individual contact rather than large-scale research which could under-gird improved social policies that would reduce teen pregnancy. Because of the limitations in existing data, generalizations about the male part of the teenage pregnancy equation should be greeted of necessity with some skepticism.

Nevertheless, let us look at what is generally known. Contrary to conventional wisdom, men who father children born to adolescent mothers tend not to be teenagers themselves. According to national health statistics, 35 percent of the fathers recorded for 62 percent of teen mothers reporting were in their early twenties. This should not be surprising since the majority of adolescent mothers are in their late teens when they first give birth. Most women tend to mate with males older than themselves.

The reaction of males to fatherhood is quite varied, again not surprising given the complexities of human behavior. Some avoid parental responsibility; others become quite involved, visiting regularly and providing financial support.

What else can we surmise about males who father children born to adolescent mothers when compared racially? According to a project assessing what has been found about young unwed fathers, black fathers tend to be like their peers, unlike white fathers who tend to have histories of socially deviant behavior (drug use, crime, etc.), suggesting that fathering without marriage may become normative behavior among African-American males. [12]

Moreover, an analysis of the National Longitudinal Study of Labor Force Behavior 1979 to 1986 by Lerman revealed that, of 6400 youth, ages 14 to 24, 27 percent of black males reported that they had been unwed fathers at least once compared to 10 percent of Hispanic males and three percent of whites. In addition, almost twice the percentage of whites and Hispanics had married by 1984 compared to blacks. Black fathers more than whites, on the other hand, were more likely to be living with a parent. Regardless of race, young men with incomes above the three-person poverty line tended to be married over three times more than men with less earnings. [13]

Without a doubt, economics play a major role in making a decision about marriage in these modern times, but not totally. True, young minority males and females without job skills are less competitive in the labor market as evidenced by the high unemployment rates among this population since the 1970s. [14]

But among African Americans, "hard times" is not a new phenomenon. What is new is the change in expectations for personal responsibility, not only in black culture, but also in U.S. society as a whole. Moreover, the destigmatization of premarital sex and bearing children without marriage may have as equally devastating an effect as the lack of a good job on whether to marry, even to be responsible for the consequences of sexual activity.

Because of countervailing values about male responsibility, many teen mothers fail to establish legal paternity for their children. Their families may also insist upon no contact with the babies' fathers. In any event, CDF reports that, in 1985, fewer than 18 percent of unwed mothers 18 and under had court-ordered child support payments.

The niche of African-American males in this society poses a special dilemma when discussing paternal responsibility. As males, they have historically been viewed as a threat to white male dominance and thus have been denied opportunities to be "men," to be viable heads of household. This maleness viewed as natural assertiveness and, believed by many to be innate, seems to be turned inward now.

Self-destructive behavior, as evidenced by high rates of substance abuse and suicide, and pervasive acts of homicide and crime among young black men are disproportionate to other racial and ethnic groups. Accordingly, Julia Hale, a noted urban sociologist, and many others surmise that, "The destruction of the black male is the biggest problem facing the black family today."[15]

Because of the pervasive forces aligned against black male development, the early childhood years reinforced by strong parental guidance is crucial. Yet, schools, for the most part, have been unable to meet that challenge. To some researchers, the educational system is very much the problem. Quoting Dr. Willian Lyle, an African-American psychologist, "Urban schools are particularly cold and unforgiving (hostile) to black males. Their behavior is viewed as a nuisance and they are labeled hyperactive, slow learner."[16] Increasingly, black scholars are documenting how young Americans of African descent are sent to special education and tracked for school dropout.[17]

Tragically, the distorted upbringing of black males can bear "bitter fruit." The news media project an image of physical rather than intellectual prowess, promoting violence rather than peaceful behavior. Absent fathers in the home, some black mothers seeking to transcend their own youthful experiences or wanting to guard their young males against the outside world may inadvertently be over-protective or place them in the role of "man in the house" without teaching or demanding that they perform as such.

Whatever the rationale, the street smarts so evident among young black males, especially from poor families, reinforce a culture of male bravado, strengthened among peers, that is, in all practicality, dysfunctional in today's world. Moreover, this male bonding is becoming more destructive of intimate male and female relationships which are the basis of family life.

The development of black males is an ever-unfolding issue for African Americans and the broader U.S. society. Robbed of their birthright to become self-sufficient adults and parents, particularly if poor, their anger and frustration are turning against themselves, their families, and their communities. It is an issue raised with alarm at two recent conferences sponsored by the National Urban League.

ATTITUDES TOWARDS FAMILY PLANNING

In the 1960s, black activists were openly hostile to family planning, arguing that the use of birth control was genocidal and, indeed, they believed that the promotion of family planning methods was a conspiratorial move by the dominant culture to limit the population growth of African Americans, then as now a higher rate than that of whites. Although the cries of these activists did not represent black views generally, their resonance is still heard when discussing the use of birth control, particularly by unmarried adolescents.

Regardless of ideology, information about the availability of contraception, even sex education in some localities, remains sparse in the U.S. As a consequence, for many teenagers, pregnancy occurs because of the lack of knowledge about birth control, or because of magical thinking about sex and its relation to pregnancy, or due to shyness about seeking contraceptive help. Moreover, some adolescents may be embarrassed or uncertain about engaging in sexual activities and therefore take no responsibility in exercising control over their reproductive processes. The issue though is not only to know about preventing pregnancy, but also to use methods that will achieve that end. For that to happen, young people have to believe they can exercise control over their lives.

The idea that sex education in the schools could curb teenage sexuality and pregnancy gained some currency during the past two decades, along with the expansion of family planning services. Yet, at the local school board level, resistance exists today to teaching about sex, both about the age or grade level such instruction should begin and the content of the material.

Much of the opposition came from religious and conservative groups who fear loss of parental control over the child's value formation or who believe that family planning, if taught, will be contrary to religious proscriptions against controlling reproduction. Although most school districts in the U.S. now provide sex education, the quality of instruction and curriculum varies greatly. In areas like New Orleans, sex education in schools has been voted down continuously, so no instruction is available at all.

Black parents, many of whom are deeply religious, carry similar views about sex education and family planning, often shying away from telling their young, male and female, about sexual responsibility until it is too late.

Despite the observed inadequacies of sex education, teenagers seem to be using birth control increasingly. However, teens 15 and under are relatively less able to prevent pregnancy if sexually active, probably for the reasons stated above. And the increasing use of abortion as a birth control method among older teens seems to be clear evidence that better sex education and increased access to contraception are called for.[18]

How to engage teenagers in pregnancy prevention is a program and policy issue of concern to all involved in maternal and child health, and in providing services which strengthen the capacity of African-American families to survive and prosper. It is within this context that many African Americans believe the abortion debate should take place.

206

WHAT THE FUTURE HOLDS

It should be evident by now that, for African Americans, unlike other groups in this society, poverty and its destructive impact on family life may be a leading factor in persistent high rates of teen pregnancy and parenting. Poverty is also the single major contributor to infant mortality, despite the fact that teen pregnancy and poor maternal health are statistically associated with premature birth.

Can anyone doubt that poor housing, frequent moving, and overcrowding affect child-bearing and rearing? Studies show that such conditions harm laboratory animals. Why then not humans? The lack of help while pregnant—assistance in shopping and household tasks—and unavailable emergency child care have equally devastating effect.

Moreover, the use of crack and cocaine and the AIDS epidemic among black women and children because of direct association with intravenous drug users are now spreading, compounding the burden of teenage parenting and deepening family poverty. These apocalyptic forces may be achieving what 400 years of slavery and oppression failed to do; namely, the destruction of the African-American family.

In contemplating the impact of poverty, drugs, and other social afflictions, their erosive effect on the human spirit needs to be of major concern. Without a doubt, many young unmarried people, caught in the throes of teen parenting aggravated by poverty or worse, feel separated from family, friends, and community. Their capacity for intimacy, to trust someone, is thwarted. They anticipate that relationships won't last. But, after all, to trust depends upon sound early childhood experiences and positive relationships with parents, something many young parents today have never had.

In a thought-provoking presentation, Dr. Alvin Pouissant, the noted Harvard psychiatrist, argued that "the concept of family may be too narrow for our purposes. We need to think children first." He goes on to say that we need to "create alternative institutions for helping to raise our children."[19]

RECOMMENDATIONS

Building self-esteem then should be a key theme in providing services for adolescents and most particularly for those from economically and emotionally impoverished circumstances. Other services are also basic: information and access to contraception, concrete help to pursue education and career goals, options for experiencing success in school and in the workplace, and the steadfast support of caring adults. Each can be instrumental in preventing a first pregnancy. Together, they have been proven to be effective within the context of a well-planned, coordinated community service program.

For young parents, these services and more are needed, including maternal and child health services, child care, access to financial support, and, most assuredly, parent training in sound child development practices. They also need employment and training.

Education is fundamental to dealing with teen pregnancy and parenting. Staying in school can be a measure of motivation, as the study reported by RAND indicates. Family life education, including well-defined instruction on sexuality and the meaning of parenting, should be an integral part of schooling like reading, writing, and counting. The schools where youngsters spend most of their day then must be a focal point of any policy strategies.

Underlying these must be a frontal, concerted attack on poverty and an articulation of values which promote individual growth and responsibility within the framework of community survival. As African Americans, we need again to cultivate communal child-rearing.

GOVERNMENT ACTIONS NEEDED

Government at each level bears some responsibility for ameliorating the social and economic distress caused by teen pregnancy and parenting. Certainly, the immediate need for health care, education, jobs, and training can best be handled by governmental intervention. The underlying poverty many young African Americans face each day also requires governmental solution.

The recommendations for governmental action which follow address not only the specific needs of teen parents, they also call for policies which open opportunities for African-American youth generally. In the long run, this is the most viable way to reduce the incidence of teenage pregnancy and its consequences.

In Health Care:

Universal access to full time maternal health care services, including family planning and abortion, if desired. Ability to pay should be deemed secondary and based on policies which would entitle the working poor to fully subsidized services. Aggressive outreach and treatment retention techniques should be developed as a top priority for young, drug-addicted pregnant women.

Universal access and entitlement of all children to pediatric services until age five.[20] The full implementation of the federally-mandated early intervention systems by each state for children developmentally at-risk and their families. The care and treatment of children with AIDS or drug addiction should be given top priority with emphasis on home or community-based services.

Universal home visiting by trained community workers on a regular basis once a pregnancy is determined through the first three years of a child's life.

The provision of adolescent health services, preferably integrated within the school system, to assure appropriate pregnancy prevention, substance abuse education and treatment, routine screening and diagnosis, and other medical attention.

Federal reimbursement for nutrition and health education, and expanded community coordinated health services linked to a viable social services system.

In Child Care:

Quality, affordable child care at hours and locations favorable to parental needs and interests. These services should be available for infants, toddlers, school-age children—as well as preschoolers. Community-based services owned and managed by local residents should be the preferred form of delivery.

Current federal legislation to expand child care should be supported with appropriate standard-setting to assure sound child and youth development. Child-care tax credits, while notable as an income-support measure, should not be confused with the need to expand quality child care.

Child care viewed as a continuum of services for the young child and linked to primary education services which build upon preschool learning experiences. A significant increase in Head Start to cover all eligible children is called for. So is a monitored pattern of cooperation between public and private, including proprietary, agencies, which are involved in child care and preschool education.

In Social Services:

Again, community-based services, small and intimate in style, but linked into an effective, one-point entry network, are of top priority. These services should be integrated across service boundaries to assure the comprehensive intervention needed in many deteriorating black communities. The basic goal of such services should be prevention, not remediation. Of particular concern is the development of minority-specific children and family services agencies. Currently, few African-American child welfare agencies exist in the U.S.

After-school services, available as well during summer vacation and holidays, should be established to fill the highly recognized gap that exists in African-American communities for youth development activities. Such programs could offer tutoring, recreation, creative arts, and other activities provided by churches and other community institutions, and would assure opportunities for adults, particularly males, to become involved.

In Welfare Reform:

A truly federalized welfare reform system with unified standards is called for. Funds should also be allocated for child care to avoid competition with working poor families over limited public subsidies available through Title XX. In 1988, the U.S. passed major welfare reform legislation, the first in many years. While calling for employment, training, and education to be available routinely to welfare recipients, no specific provisions are made for child care. That is left to the states. Moreover, no national standards for welfare benefits have been set, again leaving to states the option for determining need and level of payment.

This legislation also seeks to deal with the relationship between teen parenting and welfare dependency by restricting teen mothers' eligibility to Aid to

Families with Dependent Children. These provisions should be strictly monitored state by state because of their probable impact on family development.

Other income-support measures are needed as well, including increased Earned Income Tax Credits and state liberalization of nonfederally reimbursed public assistance as a strategy for involving single male adults in structured employment and training programs. Also, improvements in child support programs are needed, beyond current federal mandates, which would increase paternity establishment and better consider the father's short- and long-term economic prospects.

In Employment and Training:

Full employment and a decent minimum wage require congressional action NOW. Any veto by the president should not be sustained.

Young fathers should be given priority for employment and training programs as a strategy for promoting their parenting responsibilities.[21]

In Education:

Programs designed to reduce school dropout should be instituted in the early grades. Students who are presenting disciplinary and learning problems can be identified, and they, along with their parents, should receive immediate help.

The African-American community should become more directly involved in school management by promoting local school involvement, pressing for increases in minority staff, and supporting proposals which would permit non-educationally credentialed people to teach.

Universal preschool education should be promoted but within the context of a total system of child care and development.

Special education in school districts around the country needs major overhauling. Minority children with disabilities do not get the services they need. African Americans, particularly males, are routinely dumped into these programs and labeled learning disabled or emotionally disturbed, thus tracking them for school dropout and failure.

The provision of a family life curriculum, including education about parenthood, developed in concert with parents, should be instituted in the primary grades.

For the long term, the feasibility of educational allowances for youth to serve as incentives for staying in school should be explored. Other Western nations provide youth allowances and extended higher education benefits as well.

THE RESPONSIBILITY OF AFRICAN AMERICANS

These proposals for government action are indeed broad. But remember, family life among African Americans is in crisis. As an immediate strategy, African Americans need to develop sizable niches in human services, including child care and education. Both of these are growth industries and have a direct bearing on how black children grow and develop. Through agencies such as the National Urban League, technical assistance and training to sustain minority service providers are available.

Maintaining support for affirmative action policies by advocating for congressional action to limit the reach of recent U.S. Supreme Court decisions should be pursued. African-American youth need strong role models, adults who are achieving. And the community needs a middle class. Despite the dire accounts of poverty, African Americans have benefited from affirmative action and other government policies since the 1960s. We cannot turn our backs on these now.

Fundamentally though, African Americans need to initiate a value clarification process, involving parents, religious and civic leaders, and scholars. Such a process would establish a mindset around the need for helping black children and aid parents who need all the support they can get. Black youth should participate. A continuing exchange about values and responsibility between all members of the community can only have positive payoffs. But the adults must lead. Moreover, as Dr. Poussaint recommends, we need to develop institutions to sustain our children's development, building upon the extended family and concepts of interdependence.[22] Right now, value formation is being left to other institutions. It is time for African Americans to recapture this for their children.

The propulsion for demographics is upon us. By 2020, the U.S. Census Bureau projects that minorities will constitute over one-third of the nation's population, a steady increase from the estimated 22 percent now. The changes in the economic, social, and political landscape occasioned by such population shifts can only be imagined. We can deduce though that minorities of color will be a dominant force in the labor market, as evidenced by their relatively larger birth rates compared to whites, and their younger age cohorts overall.

Whether African Americans will be able to exploit this increasing demographic advantage is a challenge confronting this community. Certainly, this advantage challenges them to exert greater control and direction over the development of their children.

GEORGIA L. McMURRAY is president and owner of The Georgia L. McMurray Group, a New York consulting firm. She is nationally recognized for her leadership in promoting improved social and economic policies for children, women, and families and was a pioneer in developing education and community services for teenage parents and their children. She was recently appointed a distinguished visiting professor in social policy at Fordham University.

The Unemployment Experience of African Americans: Some Important Correlates and Consequences

Billy J. Tidwell, Ph.D.

INTRODUCTION

As we enter a new decade, counting down to the year 2000, the decline in the level of African-American unemployment observed over the past several years has been a noteworthy development. In 1983, for example, the official jobless rate among African Americans was a towering 19.5 percent. In 1988, the rate was 11.7 percent. And through the first three quarters of 1989, African-American unemployment averaged 11.3 percent, and the figure for the full year is likely to be comparable. Of course, these changes reflect improved conditions for American workers in general, as the national unemployment rate declined by 4.1 percentage points between 1983 and 1988.[1]

As welcome as the rate reductions have been, however, there continues to be cause for concern. Specifically, the incidence of unemployment among African Americans remains greatly disproportionate relative to its incidence among whites. The racial unemployment gap has actually widened over time. In 1983, African Americans were 2.3 times as likely as whites to be jobless. In 1988, the figure had climbed to 2.5. An additional concern relates to the adversities that accompany unemployment and the extent to which such conditions are more prevalent or pronounced among African Americans.

While differences in the *incidence* of unemployment between the races have been a prominent focus in public discussions, less attention has been given to racial differences in the nature and consequences of the unemployment experience itself. This is unfortunate, as such differences in experience could have important policy implications in their own right.

A higher likelihood of unemployment in combination with a higher probability of facing severe hardships when a jobless episode does occur constitutes a peculiar "double bind" that puts the well-being of African-American families at serious risk. This paper seeks to broaden understanding of this predicament and the African-American unemployment problem by examining differences in the unemployment experiences of African Americans and whites. The emphasis is on correlates and consequences of the unemployment experience that might limit the family's ability to subsist and maintain its quality of life. The issues

213

include duration of unemployment, income loss, receipt of unemployment compensation benefits, and health insurance coverage. In addition, racial differences in the end result of joblessness are considered.

It is worth mentioning at the outset that adverse impacts are less likely to the extent that a family has reserve financial resources that can be called upon during a jobless episode. More generally, a family's wealth status or net worth (i.e., assets less liabilities) is a crucial determinant of how well it fares when unemployment occurs. In this regard, African Americans are profoundly disadvantaged. Thus, African-American families average just nine percent of the wealth of white families. They are much less likely than white families to own liquid assets or assets that are easily converted into cash, and those they do own tend to have a much lower dollar value. Regardless of income level, the racial disparities are sizable.[2] The magnitude of the wealth problem greatly intensifies concern about the unemployment experience among African Americans and the double bind predicament they face.

UNEMPLOYMENT DURATION

Length of unemployment is a basic measure of its potential severity. In general, the cumulative research indicates that the longer the jobless spell, the greater the chances of economic hardship and the more severe the effects will be.[3] Also, studies have consistently found that African Americans experience longer jobless episodes than do whites. The disparity has been observed in favorable economic conditions as well as during recessionary periods.[4] The data in Table 1 replicate the usual findings.

Table 1
Percentage Comparison of African American and
White Unemployment by Duration, 1988

Weeks Unemployed	African-American			White		
	Total	Male	Female	Total	Male	Female
less than 5	42.4	38.4	46.5	47.2	42.2	53.6
5–14	30.8	31.8	29.9	29.7	30.4	28.8
15–26	12.1	13.1	11.1	11.9	13.3	10.1
27 or more	14.7	16.7	12.5	11.2	14.1	7.6
Average wks	15.4	16.9	14.0	12.9	15.2	10.0

Source: Bureau of Labor Statistics, *Employment and Earnings,* January 1989, Table 15, p. 176.

In 1988, African Americans were less likely than whites to experience short-term unemployment (defined as being out of work for less than five weeks) and correspondingly more likely to be jobless for an extended period. Overall, 42 percent of African-American workers who experienced unemployment were unemployed for less than five weeks, compared to 47 percent of their white counterparts. Conversely, almost 15 percent of the African-American unemployed were jobless for 27 weeks or longer, as against 11.2 percent of whites. On average, African Americans were unemployed some two-and-half weeks longer.

The racial differences tend to be larger among female workers than among males. Thus, the difference in average duration among females is a full four weeks, compared to a difference of 1.7 weeks among males. As we will see below, the unemployment experience is also relatively more problematic for African-American females in other significant respects.

INCOME

The degree of adversity of the unemployment experience is appreciated primarily in terms of its impact on family income. Although the magnitude of the effect depends on a number of factors, including the length of unemployment, a disrupted income stream might require difficult adjustments in lifestyle and aspirations. In extreme cases, a family might face the frightening prospect of repossession of goods, mortgage foreclosure, or bankruptcy. The growing number of homeless families in part attests to the devastation that joblessness and income loss can bring.[5] We examine the income issue from several perspectives.

A general but useful way to investigate the income effect is to compare the family income of persons who experienced unemployment in a given year with the family income of persons who did not. Table 2 provides such comparative data for 1985. For both African Americans and whites, there are differences in the family income of persons with and without unemployment. However, unemployment has a sharper impact on the income of African-American families. Overall, the average family income of African-American individuals who experienced unemployment is about 46 percent lower than that of unaffected workers. By contrast, this difference is only 37 percent among whites.

Taking into account the family relationship of the unemployed person, we observe that the smallest racial disparity occurs in cases where the husband was jobless. Among African Americans, the family income of husbands who were unemployed was 46 percent less than the family income of husbands who were not affected by unemployment. The impact of unemployment was about four percentage points greater for African-American husbands than for whites, as the degree of income loss for white families in which the husband encountered unemployment was about 42 percent. The income loss for African Americans was less (36 percent) when the wife was the unemployed person. Nevertheless, it was almost eight percent greater than the loss to white family income when the wife was unemployed.

Table 2
Comparison of African American and White Family
Income by Occurrence of Unemployment, 1985

	No Unemployment	African-American Some Unemployment	Percent Difference
Total	$24,883	$13,553	–45.5
Husbands	30,759	16,757	–45.5
Wives	32,635	2,894	–36.0
Female heads	15,971	5,204	–67.4
		White	
Total	$33,465	$21,175	–36.7
Husbands	37,092	21,175	–41.5
Wives	37,587	26,998	–28.2
Female heads	20,679	8,567	–58.6

Source: Bureau of Labor Statistics, *Linking Employment Problems to Economic Status,* August 1987, Table 4, p. 11.

The most compelling comparison involves female family heads. Consistent with more general concerns about the well-being of female-headed families, the impact of unemployment in this case is by far the most acute. The family income of African-American female heads who encountered unemployment was more than two-thirds less than the family income of female heads who were free of unemployment during the year. The income difference between white female heads, while also large, was about nine percent less than the difference for African Americans.

A related measurement of the income effect is the occurrence of poverty among families in which someone becomes unemployed. Again, the overall difference between African Americans and whites is pronounced (Table 3). Some 37 percent of African-American workers who became unemployed during the year had their family slip below the poverty level, compared to 18 percent of white workers, a 19 percent difference. If the worker was a husband, the incidence of poverty drops sharply for African Americans, while it stays about the same for whites. As might be expected, if the wife was the jobless person, the proportion of families in poverty was lower in both racial groups. In either case, however, the proportion of families in poverty is higher among African Americans. Since future job growth is expected to be slower in manufacturing industries where African Americans have largely been concentrated, the prospect of unemployment-triggered poverty could be even larger by the year 2000.

Mirroring the pattern observed with income, the impact of joblessness increases dramatically among African-American female family heads. More than three-quarters of African-American female heads who encountered unemployment had their family drop into poverty. This condition occurred among only 49 percent of white female heads.

Table 3
Incidence of Poverty Among African American
and White Families with Unemployment Worker

	African American	White
Total below poverty level	36.9	18.2
Husband unemployed	24.3	18.8
Wife unemployed	17.5	9.1
Female head unemployed	76.6	49.1

Source: Bureau of Labor Statistics, *Linking Employment Problems to Economic Status,* August 1987, Table 3, p. 10.

The longer the unemployment episode lasts, of course, the greater the likelihood of slipping into poverty. (Table not shown.) Thus, when the duration was 15–26 weeks, the poverty incidence for African Americans was 39 percent versus 19 percent for whites. Similarly, when the duration was 27–52 weeks, the incidence of poverty was 48 percent and 34 percent for African Americans and whites, respectively. For any given duration of unemployment, however, African-American families were more likely to suffer economic decline.

The economic effects of unemployment may be cushioned by the presence of multiple earners in a family. As Table 4 shows, African-American families that are hit by unemployment are less likely to have this advantage. About 41 percent of African-American families that experienced unemployment during 1988 had no employed person in the family as a result, as opposed to just 25 percent of white families that encountered unemployment. Similarly, African-American families were distinctly less likely to have at least one person employed full time.

The overall patterns vary greatly, however, by family type. Indeed, the racial differences disappear in the case of married-couple families. African-American and white married-couple families are equally likely to have at least one

Table 4
Percentage Comparison of African American and
White Families Affected by Unemployment
by Presence of Other Employed Members, 1988

	African American	White
	All Families	
No employed person	40.7	25.0
At least one employed person	59.3	75.0
At least one full time employed person	50.1	65.7
	Married-Couple Families	
No employed person	18.5	18.3
At least one employed person	81.5	81.7
At least one full time employed person	71.7	72.6
	Female-Headed Families	
No employed person	57.7	48.7
At least one employed person	42.3	51.3
At least one full time employed person	33.3	41.2

Source: Bureau of Labor Statistics, *Employment and Earnings,* January 1989, Table 49, p. 214.

employed person and at least one person employed full time when a member becomes unemployed. Once again, however, African-American female-headed families fare much worse than their white counterparts. When unemployment occurs, 58 percent of them are left with no employed person, and only 33 percent have someone employed on a full-time basis. By comparison, only 49 percent of white female-headed families are left with no wage earner, while 41 percent have at least one full-time worker.

Just as the type of family is a key factor, the position in the family of the person who becomes jobless is also a major influence. Considering all persons with unemployment, 41 percent of African Americans had no employed member of the family as a result of the jobless experience, compared to 27 percent of whites (Table 5). On the other hand, when the husband is the person with unemployment, the racial difference is erased. In fact, African-American families are somewhat more likely than whites to have other employed persons when the husband becomes unemployed. When the wife or female head encounters a jobless episode, African-American families are less likely than their white counterparts to have other employed members or someone working full time.

Table 5
Percentage Comparison of African American and
White Unemployed by Family Relationship and
Presence of Other Employed Family Members, 1988

	African American		White
		Total in Families	
No employed person	40.9		27.3
At least one employed person	59.1		72.7
At least one full time employed person	49.8		63.5
		Husbands	
No employed person	35.6		37.6
At least one employed person	64.4		62.4
At least one full time employed person	52.5		47.6
		Wives	
No employed person	22.2		15.6
At least one employed person	77.8		84.4
At least one full time employed person	67.8		77.9
		Female Heads	
No employed person	88.1		80.0
At least one employed person	11.9		20.0
At least one full time employed person	6.5		12.6

Source: Bureau of Labor Statistics, *Employment and Earnings,* January 1989, Table 50, p. 215.

In summary, the income condition of African-American families is more likely to be impacted adversely by the occurrence of unemployment than is that of white families. However, the evidence illuminates important differences by family type and by the family relationship of the unemployed person. In key respects, African-American female-headed families are especially vulnerable to economic hardship as it relates to unemployment. As the 21st century approaches, concern about the disproportionate number of such families is well justified by the data reviewed here.

UNEMPLOYMENT COMPENSATION AND HEALTH COVERAGE

The receipt of unemployment compensation benefits during the jobless episode may alleviate the degree of economic adversity the worker and his or her family might otherwise endure. Similarly, whether or not there is health insurance coverage during an unemployment spell has serious implications for the physical well-being of family members. The unemployment experience can be a painful ordeal in the absence of either resource. Therefore, it is instructive to examine how well African Americans fare in these two respects. Longitudinal data that track the same individuals over time are available for this purpose. The data cover workers who began and completed a jobless spell between 1984 and 1986.[6]

The data in Table 6 show unemployment insurance coverage for African Americans and whites, both by total and by length of the unemployment spell. Overall, 9.3 percent of the spells involving African-American workers had some coverage, while 6.2 percent were covered for the duration of the spell. By contrast, 18.2 percent of the spells of white workers had some coverage, and 13 percent were covered throughout. Thus, African Americans were only about half as likely as whites to receive unemployment insurance benefits while unemployed.

Table 6
Percentage Comparison of African Americans
and Whites with Unemployment Insurance
Coverage by Duration of Unemployment*

	Tot	1 mth	2 mths	3 mths	4 mths	5 +
			Length of Spell African American			
Some coverage	9.2	—	7.8	16.0	10.1	18.3
all mths	6.2	—	7.8	12.5	8.0	8.6
			White			
Some coverage	18.2	—	17.7	27.4	21.4	40.9
All mths	13.0	—	17.7	22.6	15.1	22.8

*Spells beginning and ending between 1984 and 1986

Source: U.S. Bureau of the Census, *Current Population Reports,* "Spells of Job Search and Layoff . . . and Their Outcomes," July 1989, Table H, p. 9.

For both African Americans and whites, the likelihood of receiving benefits increased with the length of the unemployment spell. Nonetheless, African Americans were consistently less likely to have coverage. For example, for spells lasting only two months, the likelihood of some coverage among African Americans was slightly less than eight percent, as against almost 18 percent for whites. For spells lasting five months or longer, the coverage rates were 18.3 percent and 40.9 percent for African Americans and whites, respectively.

Of course, in order to receive unemployment benefits, one must have worked in a covered industry and long enough to qualify. African Americans may not meet these requirements to the same extent as white workers. Whatever the explanation, the unemployment experience of African Americans is more problematic because of their limited receipt of unemployment compensation benefits. There is need to reexamine the adequacy of current coverage provisions.[7]

In general, the pattern for health insurance coverage parallels that for unemployment insurance: African Americans are less likely to have coverage (Table 7). Only 33 percent of African-American workers had health insurance during the entire period of their unemployment, while 54 percent were not covered at any time during the spell. By contrast, 57 percent of white workers were covered throughout, while only 34 percent were not covered at any time.

The coverage differences decline substantially when the focus is on workers who had health insurance in the month before their unemployment began. In this case, we find that 70 percent of African Americans were covered throughout the spell. However, this is still an 11 percent lower coverage rate than existed among their white counterparts. Conversely, 13 percent of the African Americans in this group were not covered at all while unemployed, compared to about nine percent of white workers. Among workers who were covered in their own name before unemployment, African Americans remained considerably less likely to be covered throughout the spell and more likely to not be covered at all.

Table 7
Percentage Comparison of Health Insurance Coverage
Among African American and White Unemployed*

	All Months	Coverage During Spell Some Months	No Months
		African American	
All workers	33.0	12.9	54.1
Covered before unemployment	70.1	17.2	12.6
In own name	62.3	21.6	16.2
Not covered before	2.7	9.4	87.8
		White	
All workers	56.6	9.5	33.9
Covered before unemployment	80.9	10.5	8.6
In own name	72.0	15.4	12.6
Not covered before	5.5	7.3	87.2

*Spells beginning and ending between 1984 and 1986

Source: U.S. Bureau of the Census, *Current Population Reports,* "Spells of Job Search and Layoff . . . and Their Outcomes," July 1989, Table F, p. 8.

The fact that African Americans experienced longer periods of unemployment undoubtedly account for much of the disparity in coverage for the entire period. In any event, a disproportionate number of African-American families are placed in a precarious position because they lack health insurance coverage during all or part of the unemployment spell. Existing public programs, such as Medicaid, do not fully address this problem.

END RESULT OF UNEMPLOYMENT

A jobless episode ends at some point, as the unemployed person either finds a job or leaves the labor force. It is important to compare African-American and white workers in terms of this ultimate outcome of the unemployment experience. The longitudinal data are particularly well-suited for this purpose.

The unemployment spells of African Americans were much less likely to end with a job and more likely to end with the worker dropping out of the labor force (Table 8). Some 53 percent of the spells of African Americans ended as a result of finding or returning to a job, nearly a 20 percent lower rate than the corresponding rate for whites (71 percent). In general, African-American males fared somewhat better relative to their white counterparts than did African-American females. A notable exception occurs among the 20–24 year-old group. In this case, African-American male workers were 28 percent less likely than their white counterparts to end the unemployment spell with a job, while

Table 8
Comparison of Unemployment Outcomes Among
African American and White Workers*

| | African American | | White | |
	Found Job	Withdrew	Found Job	Withdrew
Both Sexes	52.7	47.3	71.0	29.0
Male	64.7	35.3	80.1	19.8
16–19	44.9	55.1	70.2	29.8
20–24	58.2	41.8	86.7	13.3
25–54	84.2	15.8	85.0	15.0
Female	44.6	55.4	62.8	37.2
16–19	40.8	59.2	62.9	37.1
20–24	42.7	57.3	66.2	33.8
25–54	46.9	53.1	62.1	37.9

*Spells beginning and ending between 1984 and 1986

Source: U.S. Bureau of the Census, *Current Population Reports,* "Spells of Job Search and Layoff . . . and Their Outcomes," July 1989, Table I, p. 10.

African-American females were about 24 percent less likely to do so than white females. In any event, the data indicate that young adult African-American workers, of either sex, are especially hardpressed to end the unemployment experience with a job.

CONCLUSION

This paper has reviewed some important correlates and consequences of unemployment and how the unemployment experience differs between African Americans and whites. More awareness of these differences is important to achieve a better understanding of the African-American unemployment problem in its totality. Of course, unemployment can be a problematic experience for any family. Based on the above assessment, however, it is clear that African-American families are particularly susceptible to its hardships. This conclusion underscores the need to eliminate racial disparities in the incidence of joblessness itself as we move toward the year 2000.

Dr. BILLY J. TIDWELL is Director of Research, National Urban League, Inc.

School Power:
A Model for Improving Black
Student Achievement

James P. Comer, M.D.
Norris M. Haynes, Ph.D.
and
Muriel Hamilton-Lee, Ed.D.

During recent years, the status of public education in America has been severely criticized. The Coleman Report[1] stated that Catholic schools had significantly higher achievement levels than public schools and that private schools were better able than public institutions to narrow achievement gaps that exist among children of different socioeconomic backgrounds. This report attributed the superiority of Catholic schools to higher academic demands and greater discipline. The National Commission on Excellence in Education[2] also issued a scathing report on American schools, finding that 13 percent of all 17-year-olds and 40 percent of minority youth were functionally illiterate. This latter point is crucial because it underscores the serious underachievement and other school-related problems facing black children in public schools.

West[3] reported on the results of a 1982 Gallup poll in which a national sample of citizens were asked their opinions on the state of public schools. Whereas in 1974, 48 percent of individuals interviewed rated public schools "A" or "B," in 1982 only 37 percent gave public schools an A or B rating. Further, seven out of ten individuals indicated that discipline was a serious problem in schools. West also cited data from the U.S. Law Enforcement Administration's national crime survey of public schools, which indicated that 68 percent of robberies and 50 percent of assaults against young people occur in schools. A National Institute of Education report[4] indicated that students in public schools had a fairly high probability of being robbed and attacked.

Thus, within the past 10 years, a lack of discipline and the presence of both vandalism and violence have been identified as serious problems that plague public schools. These problems appear to exist at a disproportionately high level in urban inner-city public schools where black and minority children often comprise the majority of the total student population.

Parker[5] presented rebuttals to these beliefs made by several distinguished educators who criticized the negative reports of American schools as being too pessimistic and unbalanced. Ernest Boyer, president of the Carnegie Foundation for the Advancement of Teaching, faulted the National Commission on Excellence in Education for not reporting that reading and math scores had improved since the 1970s. Boyer accused the commission of oversimplifying the data and presenting too grim a picture. Ben J. Wattenberg of the American Enterprise Institute chastised the commission for omitting significant information. He indicated that preschool attendance rose from 37 percent to 57 percent between 1970 and 1983; the high school dropout rate fell from 39 percent to 14 percent between 1960 and 1983; and the percentage of young people graduating from college doubled in 20 years. Patricia Graham, Dean of the Harvard University School of Education, attributed the reported declines in American schools to the fact that educators were being asked to perform too many nonacademic tasks. Myron Atkin, Dean of the Stanford University School of Education, reminded critics of the considerable amount of improvement that has taken place in American education.

SCHOOL REFORM MOVEMENTS

Despite the recognized gains made by American schools in recent years, there is general agreement that public schools still need considerable improvement, both in terms of academic achievement and social climate. In fact, the insidious and perfidious threat to the well-being of children posed by widespread drug use and the escalating incidence of adolescent pregnancy, especially in inner-city schools, have created a new urgency for school reform. School reform movements of both past and present have failed to deal with the root causes of school failure and disaffection with education among black youth; such reform movements have made only cosmetic educational changes with limited beneficial effect. Following is a brief chronology of school reform movements identified by Bruce:[6]

- Academic Reform Movement (early 1960s). This movement gained impetus after the Russians' success with Sputnik in space. Concerned citizens wanted to know "why Johnny could not read" while "Ivan" could. The result was the development of new curricula such as new physics and new math.

- School Reorganization Movement (early 1960s). Concurrent with academic reform was an attempt at school reorganization. Schools were regarded as centers of inquiry. Teachers were encouraged to try new methods of teaching. In-service education was stressed and team teaching was popular.

- New School Designs Movement (mid-1960s). The architectural design of schools was based on specific teaching philosophies. For example, Bruce noted that "some schools were built around concepts of multimedia storage and retrieval systems with flexible learning spaces built throughout their environments. Other school designs stressed the learning center concept which could be reoriented as philosophies changed." The open classroom structure was a good example of this movement.

- Social Reform Movement (mid-1960s to early 1970s). Multi-cultural education was emphasized. The major purpose was to help expose students to diverse cultures and promote respect for and tolerance of cultural differences.

Two other important school reform movements that Bruce did not identify, the Compensatory Education Movement and the Effective Schools movement, are discussed below.

Compensatory Education

Compensatory education strategies were based on specific assumptions regarding the causes of chronic underachievement among minority children. Three of the most significant and well-known programs initiated were Head Start, Follow Through, and ESEA Title 1. The basic thrust of compensatory education was the identification of deficiencies in basic skills such as reading and writing and the provision of remedial assistance to slower children.

Many educators and psychologists felt that compensatory education programs were not responsive to the demand for successful and meaningful education of large numbers of schoolchildren. Programs for enrichment, remedial reading, ungraded classrooms, team teaching, and special education teachers were found to have no relationship to the management of the educational system and thus had limited impact. Their effectiveness was usually dependent upon the ethos of the school community into which they were introduced. Preschool programs, while perhaps themselves useful, frequently had debatable longitudinal effects. Insofar as they had only limited parental involvement, while such programs may have reduced parental alienation from their childrens' educational experience, they did not involve parents in school management and operations in a meaningful way. Additionally, too many participants in such programs were unfamiliar with the communities in which they served. It has become increasingly evident that too few parents of black children are intimately involved in their children's educational experience and that ways must be found to involve them.

Effective Schools Movement

The most recent thrust in school reform is the growing call for effective schools. Proponents of effective schools identify exemplary schools that they believe are effective based on criteria they establish, and describe the characteristics of these schools that make them effective.

Edmonds[7] defined effective schools as those which are "sufficiently powerful to raise otherwise mediocre pupils to levels of instructional effectiveness they might not ordinarily have, though they could aspire to." In his study of 1,300 public schools in New York, this author classified those schools as effective if they demonstrated the ability to deliver basic school skills to all students, regardless of race or socioeconomic status for at least three consecutive years. A needs assessment was done for each school to identify its strengths and weaknesses with respect to five characteristics, and technical assistance was offered to make schools effective. The five characteristics of effective schools identified by Edmonds are:

- Style of leadership.
- Instructional emphasis.
- Climate.
- Implied expectations derived from teachers.
- Presence, use of, and response to standardized instruments for increasing pupil progress.

Bossert et al.[8] identified essentially the same characteristics of effective schools as did Edmonds. Bossert listed the following:

- School climate conducive to learning, free of disciplinary problems and vandalism.
- A school-wide emphasis on basic skills instruction.
- Expectations among teachers that all students can achieve.
- Clear instructional objectives for monitoring and assessing students' performance.

For both Edmonds and Bossert, a positive school climate, an emphasis on the achievement of basic skills, high expectations for students, and clear instructional objectives with efficient mechanisms for monitoring students' progress distinguish effective schools from other schools. Coleman[9] noted that a consensus appears to be emerging that effective schools differ from other schools in significant ways that can be reliably associated with student achievement. One of the key differences between effective and ineffective schools is the instructional climate discussed in the literature, Rutter et al.,[10] McDill, Rigsby and Meyers,[11] and Brookover et al.[12] Effective schools are seen as having environments that foster academic success on the part of students.

A significant flaw of the effective school movement is the limited value given to parental involvement. For this movement, school administrators and teachers are primarily responsible for creating the environment conducive to achievement, while the role of parents is minimized. However, in the model presented by the present authors, parental involvement is a key component. It is viewed as particularly essential to the improvement of school climate and the enhancement of academic achievement among black children, who may perceive home and school as being separate entities more than do other students.

Achilles[13] provided a thorough review and summary of the effective school literature. He identified school climate and administrator and teacher behaviors that correlated significantly with school outcomes. These climate and behavior variables include: coordinated instructional programs, emphasis on basic skills achievement, frequent evaluations of pupil progress, orderly learning environments, specific instructional strategies, high expectations of students, task-oriented classrooms, structured direct instruction, use of a variety of reward systems, involvement of administrators and teachers in curriculum planning, and preventive rather than punitive discipline discussed by Weber,[14] Edmonds,[15] Goodlad,[16] Clark et al.,[17] and Venezky et al.[18]

Critique of the Effective Schools Movement

Proponents of effective schools have developed, as it were, a laundry list of positive characteristics that make schools "effective." Their approach has been to establish certain effectiveness criteria, to identify schools that meet these criteria, and then observe the processes within these schools to demonstrate the operation of an effective school in a qualitative manner. The consideration given to climate is really only superficial, in the sense that only such surface operations as discipline and rules are emphasized. Deeper and more basic concerns, such as school organization, decision sharing, and parental involvement are not highlighted.

Purkey and Smith[19] faulted the effective schools literature on the following grounds: (1) research on effective schools utilized small and narrow samples that severely limited their generalizability; (2) only one study was longitudinal, presenting conclusions being drawn concerning the staying power of effective schools over time; (3) the studies are mostly correlational, thus begging the question on cause and effect, a problem exacerbated by their lack of a theoretical model; (4) the definition of effective schools masks the fact that most of the inner-city schools identified as effective still have lower mean scores than do more affluent schools within the same district; and (5) there is a tendency for studies in effective schools to compare exceptionally bad schools (negative outliers) with exceptionally good schools (positive outliers); this approach risks missing those characteristics that differentiate the majority of average schools from both extremes.

Thus, Purkey and Smith viewed research on effective schools as being weak and simplistic. They suggested that research into educational innovation should look more at school organization and school culture, as did studies by Berman McLaughlin,[20] Meyer and Rowan,[21] Miles,[22] Sarason,[23] and Weick.[24] Indeed, the work of O'Toole[25] on workplace culture is seen as having provided a useful framework for examining the effectiveness of schools. Selby[26] noted that the "ethos" of a school or any learning environment has a significant influence on the quality and quantity of learning that takes place in that school or learning environment. The School Development Program described below reflects the sentiments and ideas of those who support systemic organizational changes in schools to meet the unique needs of black and other disadvantaged children.

THE SCHOOL DEVELOPMENT PROGRAM (SDP): A MODEL FOR MEANINGFUL CHANGE

The School Development Program (SDP) model is not new. It was initiated by Dr. James P. Comer, the senior author, and his colleagues, in collaboration with the New Haven (Connecticut) Public Schools System in 1968. The model was refined from 1973 to 1975. Since 1975, the effectiveness of the model in this school system has been evaluated and documented.[27] This documentation has led to adoption of the model by several other school systems around the country.

The School Development Program (SDP) was not derived from a specific theory, but is based on a theoretical formulation that combines elements from several models. These include the population adjustment model by Beck, Wyland, and McCourt,[28] and Harman,[29] and the social action model by Reiff.[30] The SDP contains components of the adjustment model that apply intervention strategies to groups identified as having psycho-educational problems. Further, it seeks the best possible adaptation of children (particularly those of minority groups) to the school environment through the implementation of child development and systems management principles.

The SDP resembles a social action model in that it attempts to serve children through social change. More specifically, it seeks to open social structures to a variety of inputs, build parent involvement, and empower the community. While the intervention resembles the adjustment and social action models, it is best conceptualized as an example of the ecological approach to prevention as discussed by Kelly.[31] The intervention is designed to change the human interactions—ecology—within the social system of a school. The improved interaction promotes the development of an ethos or social climate which, in turn, facilitates desirable management, teaching, and student learning and behavior. In this regard, it contains elements of Lewin's[32] social psychology: The adoption of the ecological approach in intervention and research programs has been urged by many mental health professionals, such as Weinstein and Frankel[33] and Wilkinson and O'Connor.[34]

School Planning and Management Team

An essential characteristic of the model is to move the school from a bureaucratic method of management to a system of democratic participation in which parents play a key role. The purpose of this team is to establish a representative body within each school to address the governance and management issues of the school.

The Governance and Management Team is comprised of 12 to 15 individuals and is representative of all adults involved in the school. It is led by the school principal, and also includes two teachers selected by their colleagues at each grade level, three or four parents selected by the parent organization, and a

Mental Health Team member from the school (as described below). This group meets on a weekly basis.

The function of the governance and management group is to: (1) establish policy guidelines to address the curriculum, social climate, and staff development aspects of the school program; (2) carry out systematic school planning, resource assessment and mobilization, program implementation, and evaluation and modification in the curriculum, social climate, and staff development areas; (3) coordinate the activities of all individuals, groups, and programs in the school; and (4) work with the parent group to plan an annual social (activity) calendar. The governance and management group systematically structures and coordinates these activities to improve the climate of the school.

Mental Health Team

The team is usually composed of the school principal, assistant principals, school psychologist, social worker, special education teacher, guidance counselors, nurse and other pupil personnel staff within the school.

The team provides input to the work of the governance and management body, integrating mental health principles with the functioning of all school activities. The team also serves individual teachers by suggesting in-classroom ways to manage early and potential problem behaviors. It trains school personnel in providing a variety of child development and mental health-sensitive services.

The Mental Health Team meets on a weekly basis to respond to referrals from classroom teachers. The referrals are presented and managed like a clinical case conference. The Mental Health Team's responses to the referrals include a variety of services including immediate consultation with the classroom teacher, observations and extensive consultations, and direct counseling for students. An alternative in some cases is that children are referred to the Discovery Room (described below).

The activities of the Mental Health Team sometimes suggest school policy and practice changes that are then communicated to the governance and management group and reviewed and implemented if approved (e.g., the Discovery Room).

The Mental Health Team differs from the usual pupil personnel teams in that it serves both a preventive as well as a treatment function in schools. In its preventive role, it identifies potential problem situations and acts to prevent them from developing into full-blown crises. Further, it brings together the mental health professionals in the school in a unique way that affects the entire school climate. In its treatment function, it works with individual teachers to address specific classroom problems and deals directly with individual student problems. The concept of the discovery room and the transfer orientation program are examples of activities instituted by Mental Health Teams in some schools as prevention and intervention measures.

The discovery room program was designed and directed by a resource teacher/research assistant and was created to meet the needs of children who have difficulty adjusting to school. Such adjustment difficulties frequently stem from shyness, withdrawal, acting out, or low self-esteem. These children tend to be of normal intelligence and exhibit no serious learning problems, yet they are not able to cope with the demands of the classroom.

Children are referred to the discovery room teacher by both the mental health team and the classroom teacher: The standard referral procedure is through the classroom teacher, while referrals are made by other members of the core mental health team via the school's internal Pupil Personnel Services. Groups of three or four children spend two or three hours a week in the discovery room throughout the academic year.

The discovery room was designed to be an attractive setting that draws children out of their defensive postures of negative ways of handling fears and anxieties. The materials and teaching methods are individualized to help children establish more positive ways of thinking about themselves as learners and behaving in school. Activities are structured to allow the discovery room teacher and the children to discover their interests and strengths. Within the small groups, the children's behavior is directed toward positive social interaction and their attitudes are influenced in the direction of learning.

The transfer orientation program was designed to decrease the anxiety and acting-out behavior often associated with transfer. All students transferring out of the intervention school were prepared by their teachers and the mental health team members. Students transferring into the school were assigned a guide who took the student around the school. The guide introduced the transfer student to every aspect of the school and instructed him or her on what to do if the new student had an academic or social problem. Placement testing was conducted in mathematics and reading so that children were not frustrated or understimulated in the classroom. Teachers developed a classroom introduction. New students were assigned to one of the most successful students in the class for guidance during the initial weeks.

Parent Participation Program

This component of the model consists of three sequential levels of parent participation. The first level is concerned with structuring broad-based activities for a large number of parents. At the second level, approximately one parent per professional staff member works in the school as a classroom assistant, tutor, or aide. At the third level, highly-involved parents participate in school governance. The project provides consultation and material resources to operationalize parent participation at all three levels.

Level I: Broad-Based Participation. This level of broad-based participation is designed to include most or all of the parent body. The school builds a cultural bridge into the community through the formation of a parent-staff organization. Activities include general meetings, potluck suppers, gospel music nights, children's pageants, report card conferences, school newsletters, fundraising events, and other functions culturally compatible with the community.

Level II: Parent Participation in Day-to-Day School Affairs—The Parent Stipend Program. At the second level of participation, parents become active in the ongoing life of school and classroom. A range of parent education activities are offered that focus both on parenting skills and teaching methods. The key component at this level is the parent stipend program. About 15 parents from each school are employed as classroom assistants, tutors, and clerical and cafeteria aides. Parents are paid the equivalent of minimum wage for about 15 hours a week. In addition, parents function as unpaid volunteers for an average of five hours per parent per month.

Level III: Parents in School Governance. The third or most sophisticated level of the parent program is the participation of parents in school governance. In this intervention model, parent-staff collaboration is stressed and, therefore, parents tend to participate in the school's regular governing body rather than in a separate parent advisory group. Training in participatory skills is provided by the intervention staff, principal, and parent coordinator on an issue-by-issue basis. Techniques for letter-writing, telephoning, follow-up with the central office, and mobilizing the larger parent-staff community are taught as needed to solve specific problems. For example, in 1979, in the Brennan New Haven elementary school, parents were assisted in completing a community survey that formed the basis of their recommendations to the Superintendent of Schools for a change in the physical plan. Similarly, they documented a high level of community and school support for the parent stipend program, which was reflected in a successful application to the school system to utilize Title I funds to continue the stipend program after the project ended. Finally, Brennan parents joined with staff to initiate a selection procedure for a new building principal.

Curriculum and Staff Development

This component provides instruction, direction, and support to teachers to enhance the quality of education received by children. The aims of this component are carried out in curriculum planning, which integrates a mental health approach into curriculum activities, and in the provision of resources to teachers to enhance their effectiveness in the classroom. Teachers review achievement data, determine needs for each grade level, and bring in curriculum specialists on a consulting basis.

Monthly seminars are based on building level objective. Consultants are selected by the teachers and instructed to address areas where they feel they need skill development. This approach differs from traditional in-service education, in which central office curriculum specialists impose district staff development activities on school staff, whether or not they are relevant for the school.

Curriculum development takes two forms. First, teachers are expected to plan and organize basic skills instruction. Second, they are encouraged to submit individual or group "social skills curriculum" proposals. Social skills projects incorporate both social and academic skills in a series of "units" designed to improve students' self-concepts and enable children to more successfully negotiate mainstream American society.

Basic Skill Instruction. Skill instruction is usually undertaken in response to teacher requests for help with learning-disabled students. A reading-learning disabilities consultant works with teachers around these specific requests, and he or she is increasingly utilized to assist staff with the organization of the reading program for all students.

Intervention staff and consultants meet to prepare individual programs for each child classified as "high risk" based on the results of diagnostic tests. Areas of strengths and weaknesses in both reading and math are identified, and individualized programs are prepared. In order to facilitate administration of individual programs, subgroups (by domain areas) of the high risk children are formed. These groups include Verbal Ability, Perceptual Performance, Quantitative Ability, and Motor Coordination. "Stations" or centers are set up around the classroom. Each station is designed to aid children in a particular area and contains educational materials chosen collectively by consultants and school personnel. Additional materials that encourage acquisition of reading skills are made available to the class as a whole. Parent aides are trained to teach at different stations and work closely with the children. Each child is rotated among the stations according to a schedule most relevant to his or her needs.

The Social Skills Units. Social skills curriculum units are innovative teaching strategies designed to fuse social and academic skills development as an integral part of the regular curriculum. Social skills include relating to others in a mutually acceptable caring way, developing social amenities, and learning the skills necessary to deal successfully with social institutions such as banking, the political process, and securing employment. The process of engaging teachers in the development of the units (i.e., identifying curriculum needs, utilizing consultants and resources, and developing appropriate teaching programs) is stressed.

The school Development Program, then, is based on the assumption that educational improvement can be achieved more efficiently and effectively at an institutional level. The entire school must be the focus of attention. All aspects of school functioning must be part of an ecological approach to educational improvement, curriculum planning, social, and psychological services, extracurricular activities, classroom management, and the myraid of personal interactions that take place between and among staff, parents, and students on a day-to-day basis.

Like the Effective School Movement, the School Development Program emphasizes the importance of school climate but in a more basic sense. While

Effective School literature defined climate in terms of rules, discipline, and teacher expectations, the SDP model defines it in terms of an "ethos" or profound organizational structure in which groups of individuals engage in collaborative decision making. While the Effective Schools approach minimized the role of parents, the SDP model emphasizes the importance and essential nature of parental involvement. The parent program is a key element of the model.

PROGRAM ASSESSMENT STUDY

Essential to the implementation of an intervention such as the School Development Program is some evaluation or assessment of its impact. An important aspect of these authors' work is an ongoing assessment of the program's operation and effects. A report of a study conducted by the authors' research staff conducted to assess program impact follows.

The study sample included 306 randomly-selected black students in grades 3-5 who attended 14 different elementary schools. Of the total sample, 176 attended seven experimental schools, 91 attended four control schools, and 39 attended three special schools. All schools were located in low socioeconomic areas. The control schools were very similar to experimental schools in terms of achievement, behavior, and attendance: Those schools had no specially-structured activities but followed a regular schedule and curriculum. The special schools were schools in which specially designed curricular activities occurred. The three special schools included a creative arts academy, a gifted and talented program, and a Montessori program.

The sample also included 98 teachers who taught the children in the sample, and 276 parents of those children. Of the 98 teachers, 56 were from experimental schools, 29 from control schools, and 13 from special schools. Of the 276 parents, 155 were from experimental schools, 85 from control schools, and 36 from special schools.

The dependent measures used in the study were:

Classroom Climate—Measured by the Classroom Environment Scale (CES) (Trickett and Moos, 1974).[35] This scale requires children to assess the climate of their classroom along nine dimensions: (1) Involvement; (2) Affiliation; (3) Task Orientation; (4) Competition; (5) Rule Clarity; (6) Innovation; (7) Teacher Control; (8) Order and Organization; and (9) Teacher Support. A two-point rating scale was used.

School Climate—Measured by a scale called the School Climate Survey (SCS), developed by the School Development Program staff for this study. It was completed by both teachers and parents. The wording on the parent's version is slightly different from the wording on the teacher's version, but the content of both versions is essentially the same. A three-point rating scale was used.

Attendance—Measured by the percentage of days students were absent during the study period.

Achievement—Measured by classroom grades on reading and math.

To design the study, pretest data on the above measures were collected in the fall of 1985. Post-test data on the same measures for the same sample were collected at the end of the school year (spring 1986) after a full year of the School Development Program was in effect.

Written consent was obtained from the parents or guardians of all children who participated in the study. Procedures were instituted to protect the confidentiality of participants. Teachers and parents were also required to provide written assessments prior to their participation in the study.

The analysis consisted of t-test procedures for repeated measures to examine whether significant changes occurred between pretests and post-tests on the dependent measures among the three groups. The level of significance for rejecting the null hypothesis was set at .05.

Results were prepared according to the respective dependent measures.

Assessment of classroom climate by children in the experimental schools showed significant improvement along the following dimensions: Involvement, $t(175) = 6.98$, $p.000$; Affiliation, $t(175) = 4.3$, $p < .000$; Innovation, $t(175) = 8.2$, $p < .000$; Order and organization, $t(175) = 10.0$, $p < .000$; Teacher support, $t(175) = 10.0$, $p < .000$, Total Scale, $t(175) = 4.3$, $p < .000$. A significant negative change was noted on the competition dimension, $t(175) = 2.8$, $p < .000$. Assessment of classroom climate by children in control schools showed significant positive improvement on task orientation, $t(90) = 3.6$, $p < .001$ and competition, $t(90) = 1.8$, $p < .05$. Assessment of classroom climate by children in the special schools showed no significant change of any dimension.

The assessment of school climate by teachers in experimental schools and control schools showed no significant change. However, a significant positive change occurred in special schools, $t(12) = 3.2$, $p < .002$. The assessment of school climate by parents in experimental schools showed a significant positive change $t(154) = 6.8$, $p < .000$. The assessment of school climate by parents in control schools, $t(84) = 5.9$, $p < .000$ and special schools, $t(36) = 1.9$, $p < .053$, showed significant negative changes.

The percentage of days absent among children in experimental schools declined significantly, $t(175) = 2.0$, $p < .047$. No significant change occurred among children in control and special schools.

Children in the experimental schools showed significant improvement on classroom reading grades, $t(175) = 3.3$, $p < .010$, but not in math. The control and special children showed no significant changes.

Generally, children who were selected from schools where the School Development Program was implemented showed significant improvement in attendance and achievement in classroom reading grades. In addition, significant improvements were noted in children's assessments of their classrooms and parents' assessments of the climate in their children's schools. The control and special sample showed considerably less positive changes in these areas and in some instances showed significant negative changes. These results indicate that the School Development Program had a positive effect on school climate, as well as on student behavior and achievement. Because the SDP targets the entire school for change, it was expected that in the short term the most significant changes would occur in school climate, followed by significant positive changes in student behavior and achievement.

The lack of significant change in teachers' perceptions of their school climate in the experimental school may be explained by the fact that teachers' expectations for climate change were quite high and were not met within the study period. However, it is important that a significant positive change in their perceptions of school climate occurred among parents in the experimental schools, while no such significant changes occurred among parents in the control and special schools. This appears to indicate that the meaningful involvement of black parents in their childrens' schools began to bridge the gap between home and school and that it had a beneficial impact on school climate.

CONCLUSION

The task of educating America's youth rests mainly with the public schools. Coleman and Hoffer[36] reported that over 90 percent of all children in America are educated in public schools. Black children are disproportionately represented among this group because very few of them attend private schools. Yet, it appears that the black students who do attend private schools tend to do better academically than their peers in public schools. Dropout rates among students in public schools also repeatedly exceed that of students in private schools. Thus, the picture that emerges is one in which the large numbers of children in public schools, and especially black children, fail to achieve the levels of academic performance demonstrated by their peers who attend private schools.

Coleman and Hoffer attribute the apparent superiority of private schools to what they call the "social integration" provided by Catholic schools. This social integration stems from the human and social capital fostered by Catholic schools. Human capital is the development of skills and capabilities in individuals. Social capital is the relationship that exists among individuals. Comer[37] made this point many years ago, implicating the lack of an integrated and synergistic human service delivery system sensitive to the unique needs of black children in the failure of public schools to motivate such children. The School Development Program builds "human capital" through its emphasis on staff development training, which equips teachers and staff to deal with instructional and socio-cultural issues with competence and flexibility. SDP builds "social capital" through its emphasis on school management philosophy in which administrators, teachers, and parents work together to determine the climate, priorities, and objectives within their schools.

For black children in particular, school climate plays a significant role in their adjustment to school and the ability to perform well. Other research by these authors[38] has reported significant correlations between achievement and perceptions of classroom climate among black children. Other researchers[39] have reported similar results. Thus, the School Development Program, with its strong emphasis on changing attitudes, values, and ways of interacting among the adults and children in schools, seeks to create a climate, an ethos if you will, that is sensitive, challenging, and conducive to high academic achievement among black children in public schools.

Private schools are not inherently better than public schools. They appear to be better because they are organized differently and promote different attitudes and values. Public schools can succeed just as well and even surpass private schools. With active involvement by parents, local communities can work with educators to improve the quality of education in public schools and thereby enhance the achievement of the majority of black children who attend these schools. *(This article is reprinted from The Urban League Review, Summer 1987/ Winter 1987–88, Vol. 11, Nos. 1, 2, 1988.)*

Dr. JAMES P. COMER, a nationally renowned scholar, is the Maurice Falk Professor of Child Psychiatry and Director of the Yale Child Study Center. He is also the Associate Dean of the Yale School of Medicine. Dr. NORRIS M. HAYNES is an Assistant Professor and Director of Research and Evaluation of the School Development Program at the Yale Child Study Center. Dr. MURIEL HAMILTON-LEE is the former Associate Research Director of the School Development Program at the center.

Chronology of Events 1989*

Politics

Jan. 1: Chicago Mayor Eugene Sawyer and two other mayoral candidates call for an investigation into charges that the staff of Cook County State's Attorney Richard M. Daley, the front-runner in the race, submitted illegal petitions during a 1985-86 referendum drive. Had the petition drive been successful, it would have put on the ballot a measure to create a nonpartisan general election for mayor as opposed to a party primary.

Jan. 3: Retired schoolteacher Emma Gresham wins reelection as Mayor of Keysville, GA, defeating white candidate Joseph Cochran by a vote of 127 to 61. Cochran also loses his registration challenge claiming that 84 African-American voters did not live within Keysville's boundaries.

Jan. 7: The chief rival to Los Angeles Mayor Tom Bradley, who is seeking his fifth term in office, withdraws from the April 11 Democratic primary. City Councilmember Zev Yaroslavsky's pullout leaves no major challenger to Bradley in the primary and the June 6 general election.

Jan. 9: Bronx (NY) District Attorney Robert Johnson says during his inauguration ceremony that he will establish a policy of seeking a minimum one-year sentence for people convicted of dealing drugs within a block from a school. Johnson becomes the first African-American District Attorney in the state of New York.

Jan. 10: DC Mayor Marion Barry is threatened with a recall drive by Mitch Snyder, advocate for the homeless. Snyder issued the warning to Barry during a City Hall news conference, stating that the mayor would face a citizens' effort to remove him from office if the quality of government in the city does not improve.

Jan. 11: Washington lawyer Ronald Brown receives a major boost from the AFL-CIO in his campaign to become Chairman of the Democratic National Committee. Brown's campaign manager, Carl Wagner,

This chronology is based on news reports. In some instances, the event may have occurred a day before the news item was reported.

239

says the endorsement represented the support of a major force in American politics.

Jan. 15: The congressional press aide to Rep. John Miller (R-WA), Anna Perez, is chosen by First Lady Barbara Bush to be her press secretary. Perez, an African American, was chosen after Mrs. Bush made it known that she was interested in naming a black or Hispanic to the position.

Jan. 15: Two surveys, released by the *Detroit Free Press* and the *Detroit News,* show that Mayor Coleman Young should retire. Young was elected Detroit's first African-American mayor in 1973. The survey also showed that Young would be favored against most well-known potential challengers.

Jan. 18: William Burney, Jr., a city councilman in Augusta, Maine, is elected the first black mayor in that state. The senior program officer with the Maine State Housing Authority defeated his nearest rival by almost a 2-to-1 margin.

Jan. 20: DC Mayor Marion Barry appears at a federal grand jury closed hearing and tells reporters prior to the session that he has done no wrong and that he is not the target of the investigation into allegations of drug dealing and misuse of government funds.

Jan. 20: George Herbert Walker Bush is sworn in as the 41st President of the United States, as some 140,000 people watch the ceremony at the West Front of the Capitol in Washington.

Jan. 24: During the release of the National Urban League's annual *The State of Black America* in Washington, John E. Jacob, President and Chief Executive Officer, says the Bush White House is likely to be a very different place than the Reagan White House. Jacob also says that the disparity in economic well-being between America's white and black citizens is widening.

Jan. 25: Chicago Mayor Eugene Sawyer, a candidate for the Democratic mayoral nomination, is endorsed by Rev. Jesse Jackson. Jackson says that a Sawyer victory "will show our strong resolve to go forward in unity with a multiracial coalition of workers who are determined to conquer the present odds." Sawyer was selected by Chicago's board of aldermen to succeed the late Harold Washington until the special election could be held.

Jan. 25: President Bush comes to the defense of Dr. Louis Sullivan, his choice to be Secretary of Health and Human Services, after Sullivan expressed views on abortion differing from those of the president. His views became an issue following an interview in an Atlanta newspaper where he said that he personally believed that a woman should have the right to choose to have an abortion.

Jan. 26: Virginia's Lieutenant Governor, L. Douglas Wilder, launches his campaign to become the first black elected governor, announcing a "three-for-Virginia" plan. The proposal includes a permanent tax relief, a fight against drugs and drug-related crime, and creation of jobs and housing for rural Virginians.

Feb. 2: Jesse Jackson brings his crusade for justice to earthquake-stricken Armenia, urging hundreds of homeless Armenians to "keep hope alive." Jackson also discusses the plight of the 12 Armenian dissidents who were arrested in December in the latest series of crackdowns by party leaders against activists.

Feb. 11: Ronald Brown becomes the first African American to head the Democratic National Committee. "I promise you, my chairmanship will not be about race; it will be about the races we win," Brown said in his victory speech.

Feb. 14: Manhattan Borough President David Dinkins announces his candidacy for Mayor of New York City, stating that he is running because the city has become sharply polarized and that "we need a mayor who can transcend differences so we can work together to solve our problems."

Feb. 16: Former Atlanta Mayor Maynard Jackson announces that he is seeking his old post. Jackson was first elected mayor in 1973, becoming the first black ever elected to the position. Michael Lomax, Chairman of the Fulton County Commission, announced his candidacy last month.

Feb. 23: ˹ New York City Mayor Edward Koch says that he is aiming for 25 percent of the black vote in the September 12 primary. Koch also hopes that Jesse Jackson will not come to New York to campaign for black mayoral candidate David Dinkins.

Feb. 28: Richard Daley, Cook County prosecutor, is victorious over Chicago's Acting Mayor Eugene Sawyer in that city's Democratic courtordered primary election. Daley, the son of legendary Mayor Richard J. Daley, defeated Sawyer 484,424 to 385,029.

Feb. 28: Two black lawmakers of the Louisiana House of Representatives walk out when David Duke, a former Grand Wizard of the Ku Klux Klan, is sworn in. At the same time, several lawmakers—many of them black—take turns to warn Duke that they would be watching him closely.

March 8: Lee Atwater, Chairman of the Republican National Committee, resigns from the board of trustees of Howard University following a sit-in protest by students seeking his ouster. The students were protesting what they described as racist overtones in Atwater's management of George Bush's 1988 presidential campaign.

March 10: The Mayor of East Orange (NJ), John Hatcher, Jr., is indicted on charges that he and the former director of the East Orange golf course took $75,000 in membership and rental fees paid into the course. Hatcher was elected mayor in 1986.

March 20: Newly elected Chairman of the Democratic National Committee Ronald Brown urges Chicago Democrats to unite behind the mayoral candidacy of Richard Daley in the April 4th general election.

March 31: Lt. Gen. Colin Powell, the first African American to serve as White House National Security Adviser, is promoted to full general. Powell is also assigned to Ft. McPherson (GA), where he will command all Army troops inside the continental United States, including reserves, and play a key role in determining how they are trained and equipped.

April 4: Richard Daley, son of the late Richard J. Daley, longtime Mayor of Chicago, wins election to the mayor's office. He defeated Timothy Evans, who had sought to extend the black leadership at City Hall left vacant by the death of Harold Washington. Daley earlier defeated Acting Mayor Eugene Sawyer in the special Democratic primary.

April 7: L. Douglas Wilder, campaigning for the Democratic gubernatorial nomination in Virginia, crisscrosses the state as he seeks to liven interest in his candidacy. The Lieutenant Governor is running unopposed for his party's nomination and is hoping to become the first African American elected governor in the U.S. Three Republicans are vying for their party's nomination in the June primary.

April 12: Los Angeles Mayor Tom Bradley gets elected to a fifth term by a narrow margin, saying that voter concern over his ethics could have contributed to his slim lead. Prior to the election, an ethics investigation was launched by the City Attorney's office after it was learned that Bradley had performed consulting work with Far East National Bank, which did business with the city. Bradley called the charges politically motivated and returned the $18,000 consulting fee.

April 30: The news that Jesse Jackson is considering a race for mayor of the District of Columbia in 1990 is applauded by his supporters around the country. The *Washington Post* reported in an interview with the former Democratic presidential candidate that he had yet to determine if he would seek the job held by Marion Barry, and that he would not oppose Barry "under any circumstances." Jackson did make it clear that he is actively considering the race if Barry, who is faced with investigations and political problems, decides to step down.

May 3: President Bush announces plans to nominate Gwendolyn King as head of the Social Security Administration. King, a native of East Orange (NJ), served as deputy assistant to President Reagan and director of the White House Office of Intergovernmental Affairs.

May 3: Fayette (MS) Mayor Charles Evers loses his bid for a fifth term, by a vote of 390 to 248. Evers is defeated by Kennie Middleton, a lawyer and longtime opponent.

May 5: Former HUD Secretary Samuel Pierce testifies before a House subcommittee that he was betrayed and lied to by senior aides who had made awards in a $225 million housing subsidy program for political reasons and without his knowledge.

May 23: The Congressional Black Caucus is invited to the White House for the first time in eight years. Meeting with President Bush, Vice President Dan Quayle, and several Cabinet members, the black Congressmen tell the president that, despite his oft-stated desire to be known as a president who promotes education and equality, he will not succeed unless he can do something "dramatic" to stop the decline of inner cities.

May 25: A group of business and community leaders who have supported DC Mayor Marion Barry in the past tells him that it would be best for the District if he did not seek reelection. The leaders praised Barry but told him bluntly that he had made too many personal and political mistakes in order to govern effectively.

May 27: After Virginia's Lt. Governor L. Douglas Wilder returned from Boston from a fund-raiser for his gubernatorial campaign, Republicans claim that the Massachusetts event and other recent fund-raisers in the Los Angeles area indicate that Wilder is less conservative than he asserts. Michael Salster, a GOP spokesman, says that Wilder was playing the "darling of the glitterati" up north and on the West Coast while playing conservative back home in Virginia.

May 28: Bishop H. Hartford Brookins, the newly assigned bishop of the AME Church's Washington district, urges Rev. Jesse Jackson not to run for DC mayor. Brookins says that he would not like to see Jackson and DC Mayor Marion Barry at each other head-on. "I personally would like to see Jackson stay where he is," Brookins told reporters.

June 4: Rev. Jesse Jackson announces plans to move his legal residence from Chicago to Washington in August. Jackson sources say the move is the next step towards a possible run for DC mayor in 1990.

June 4: Less than two months after winning his fifth term as Mayor of Los Angeles, Tom Bradley is the subject of four local, state, and federal inquiries. Among the allegations: he improperly helped financial institutions and investors with whom he had personal dealings.

June 11: Virginia Lieutenant Governor L. Douglas Wilder wins the Democratic gubernatorial nomination. Wilder is seeking to become the nation's first African American to be elected governor.

June 14: Rep. William Gray III (D-PA) is elected Majority Whip, the third highest post in the U.S. House of Representatives. Gray's election comes on the heels of reports that the Justice Department is investigating his office. Colleagues say the reports backfired, rallying support behind Gray.

June 21: New York City mayoral candidate David Dinkins gets backing from the leadership of the city's most politically potent labor unions. The endorsement marks the first time the Central Labor Council has backed a successful mayoral candidate since 1973.

June 23: Black public officials in Alabama claim they are being selectively prosecuted for political reasons. The dispute comes amid continuing investigations of several black officials.

June 30: *The New York Times* inquiry into the financial affairs of mayoral front-runner David Dinkins discloses that he owed more money in back taxes than he acknowledged in 1973. The newspaper reports he failed to pay any taxes for the four years on his earnings from his private law practice, his largest source of income.

July 11: Earl Andrews, Jr., a black Republican investment banker from New York, is in the race for Manhattan Borough President, the position currently held by mayoral candidate David Dinkins. Andrews says that he is running in order to help keep minority representation in municipal government and to break one-party politics in the city.

July 13: A New York *Daily News* and Channel 7 Eyewitness News mayoral poll shows that Manhattan Borough President David Dinkins has a wide enough lead in the Democratic mayoral race to win the nomination over incumbent Ed Koch and two other rivals.

July 14: DC Mayor Marion Barry, speaking through aides, says that he will seek a fourth term. The mayor's press secretary, John White, says Barry intends to run for reelection and that he intends to announce formally this fall. Barry's popularity has suffered recently because of charges of corruption in his administration, the District's high murder rate, and his visits to the hotel room of a convicted drug dealer.

July 14: A federal judge orders Baltimore and Maryland state officials to negotiate methods of relieving tense overcrowding in the city's jails, thereby blocking a move by Mayor Kurt Schmoke to release up to 500 inmates. State officials say that Schmoke does not have the authority to release the inmates; that action is reserved for judges.

July 15: A former aide to Sen. John Heinz (R-PA), Gwendolyn King, is nominated by President Bush to head the Social Security Administration. She was formerly director of Pennsylvania's Washington office when Attorney General Dick Thornburgh was governor of Pennsylvania.

July 19: New York City Mayor Edward Koch says that mayoral candidate David Dinkins is guilty of tax evasion for failing to file tax returns from 1969 to 1972. Dinkins reacts by accusing Koch of "slander."

July 20: DC Mayor Marion Barry backs away from a firm timetable for announcing his reelection plans. Barry says he may wait until spring to do so. His hesitation continued to fuel speculation that Jesse Jackson wants Barry to step aside to clear the way for a Jackson campaign.

July 28: Atlantic City (NJ) Mayor James Usry, along with three city councilmen and nine others, was arrested on bribery and misconduct charges that included allegations of payoffs to win an exclusive franchise to operate motorized carts on the boardwalk. Usry is president of the National Conference of Black Mayors; he is charged with accepting cash from an undercover informer in exchange for supporting a license to allow a contractor to operate the boardwalk carts during the summer.

Aug. 2: The *Washington Post* reports Rep. Gus Savage (D-IL) cut short his official visit to China in 1986 so that he could fly to Hong Kong to buy custom-made suits. Savage is being investigated by a House panel for possible irregularities in the affair. The State Department is also looking into charges that the five-term Congressman sexually assaulted a Peace Corps volunteer in Zaire five months ago. Savage claims the charges are politically motivated.

Aug. 2:   DC Mayor Marion Barry says his decision to seek a fourth term in office is "irrevocable and unequivocal." Barry revealed his plans after learning that his announced opposition has already raised more than $400,000 for the 1990 political contest.

Aug. 4:   Fulton County Commission Chairman Michael Lomax portrays himself as the "now generation" candidate who should succeed Atlanta Mayor Andrew Young this fall. Despite those efforts, the *Atlanta Constitution* reports Lomax lags more than 30 points behind front-runner Maynard Jackson, Atlanta's first black mayor.

Aug. 4:   Former presidential candidate Jesse Jackson officially registers as a Democrat in the nation's capital, just five days after moving there from Chicago. His quick action spurs rumors that he may run for mayor, although he says his goal is winning statehood for the District.

Aug. 5:   Former Housing and Urban Development Secretary Sam Pierce reportedly did personal favors for his law firm colleagues, despite pledging not to do so when he was confirmed as the only black member of the Reagan cabinet. *The New York Times* reports a House inquiry is underway to determine the propriety of Pierce's actions.

Aug. 7:   The State Department reports a small plane carrying Rep. Mickey Leland (D-TX) and his party of eight Americans and seven Ethiopians failed to arrive when expected at Fugnido, a refugee camp near the Sudanese-Ethiopian border. Leland chairs the House Select Committee on Hunger and is on another one of his inspection missions. The State Department is concerned about the delay, but Leland's aides suggest he may have spent the night at another camp.

Aug. 8:   President Bush tells more than 3,100 people attending the annual conference of the National Urban League in Washington that his administration is committed to providing opportunity, education, and advancement to inner cities and urban Americans. Bush asserts that the gap between white and Black America has narrowed; he pledges his administration "is committed to reaching out to minorities and to striking down barriers to free and open access."

Aug. 8:   Rep. Charles Rangel (D-NY) expresses his concern over the sincerity of the Bush administration to end the scourge of drugs in America to conferees attending the National Urban League's annual conference in Washington. Rangel challenges the war on drugs in America, stating that "when a nation declares war on drugs, it is the president's responsibility to assign generals to fight such a war." Rangel, who chairs the House Select Committee on Narcotics Abuse, says the general should not be exclusive to one drug czar.

Aug. 9:   Republicans say they will woo blacks, Hispanics, and anyone else to keep Democrats from "gaining a legislative lock for the next decade," based on the anticipated realignment of congressional and state legislative districts resulting from the 1990 census. With Congress and most state legislatures in Democratic hands, the GOP is determined to shift the balance of power through redistricting, according to party leaders meeting in Tulsa (OK) to devise reapportionment strategies.

Aug. 9:   The staff of Texas Congressman Mickey Leland remains hopeful, even though the plane with Leland and his party is still missing days after it disappeared in a thunderstorm destined for an African refugee camp near Ethiopia.

Aug. 9:   National Urban League President and CEO John E. Jacob joins members of the Congressional Black Caucus in a midnight prayer vigil for Rep. Mickey Leland (D-TX).

Aug. 9:   Fulton County Commission Chairman Michael Lomax says he has "fought the good fight," but he is pulling his hat out of the Atlanta mayoral campaign ring, almost guaranteeing that former mayor Maynard Jackson will succeed Andrew Young in the city's number-one post.

Aug. 10:   President Bush names four-star general Colin Powell as the new Chairman of the Joint Chiefs of Staff, making Powell the first black and the youngest man to hold the nation's top military post. Because of a recent Pentagon reorganization, Powell—whom Bush described as a "complete soldier"—will be more powerful than any previous Joint Chiefs Chairman.

Aug. 10:   The *Star Ledger* reports Atlantic City Mayor James Usry and six other city officials facing state bribery charges want their legal tabs picked up by the city if they are not convicted. A city ordinance allows such payments if the officials are acquitted or exonerated, or if the charges are dropped.

Aug. 11: U.S. surveillance and transport planes have been allowed by Ethiopia to join in the search for missing Congressman Mickey Leland (D-TX), whose plane disappeared in a thunderstorm four days ago on its way to a refugee camp on the Ethiopian-Sudan border. Two of Leland's House colleagues also traveled to the area to show their support for the mission.

Aug. 13: Detroit Congressman John Conyers (D-MI) tells *The New York Times* he is counting on the "ABC vote"—"Anybody But Coleman" voters—to help him defeat four-term Mayor Coleman Young in next month's primary.

Aug. 13: The Pentagon sends more aircraft to Ethiopia to search for missing Rep. Mickey Leland and his party of 15, after Leland's staff complained that the U.S. search was "slow and inadequate."

Aug. 14: American military planes find the charred wreckage of Rep. Mickey Leland's plane which crashed into a rugged mountainside in southwestern Ethiopia six days ago. All 16 people on board are believed dead. On Capitol Hill, Leland is hailed as a "one-man army who tried to end world hunger."

Aug. 16: Campaign financial reports show Virginia GOP gubernatorial candidate Marshall Coleman raised twice as much money last month than his Democratic opponent, Lt. Governor L. Douglas Wilder. But for the next 12 weeks of what's expected to be the state's most expensive governor's race ever, Wilder has $800,000 more in the bank than Coleman does for the fall race.

Aug. 16: Ethiopian and American rescue workers recover the remains of Rep. Mickey Leland and the other 15 people on board with him who were killed when their twin-engine plane crashed last week in the jungle.

Aug. 18: City Councilman Hosea Williams announces he is running for mayor of Atlanta, challenging Maynard Jackson, who is seeking to regain his former post. Last week, Fulton County Chairman Michael Lomax withdrew, leaving Williams as Jackson's only serious challenger.

Aug. 18: DC Mayor Marion Barry urges President Bush to declare war on drugs with a "real army." At a news conference, Barry told reporters an "international drug eradication army . . . including people with helicopters and tanks" is needed to destroy drug crops in foreign countries.

Aug. 19: Rep. Mickey Leland (D-TX) is eulogized as a martyr for the cause of world hunger at a funeral mass in his hometown of Houston.

Rev. Jesse Jackson told the hundreds of mourners "Mickey is not in that box, just as Jesus was not in that tomb. And because Mickey is not in that box and Jesus is not in that tomb, death has not freed us of the burden of Mickey's mission."

Aug. 26: Virginia Attorney General Mary Sue Terry clears Democratic gubernatorial hopeful Douglas Wilder of an accusation that he violated the commonwealth's conflict-of-interest law. Republicans had accused Wilder of failing to report real estate and stock on his financial disclosure forms.

Aug. 31: Los Angeles Mayor Tom Bradley may face civil fines for serving as a consultant for banks doing business with the city. But *The Los Angeles Times* quotes unnamed informers as saying Bradley did nothing criminal in accepting the $18,000 fee for his services; Bradley returned the fee.

Sept. 5: DC Mayor Marion Barry refutes allegations that he used drugs, his first public denial since former District employee Charles Lewis told a federal grand jury that he smoked crack cocaine with the mayor.

Sept. 7: The New York *Daily News* endorses mayoral candidate Richard Ravitch—his first from a major daily—after executives and the editorial staff failed to agree on backing front-runners Ed Koch, the current mayor, and David Dinkins, Manhattan Borough president, in the Democratic mayoral primary.

Sept. 9: With less than six weeks to go before Election Day, the gubernatorial race in Virginia begins to resemble the Bush-Dukakis presidential race of '88. *Washington Post* political analysts say GOP candidate Marshall Coleman is portraying his challenger as someone "soft on crime." Lt. Gov. Douglas Wilder, trying to become the nation's first black elected governor, rebuts immediately by attacking Coleman's credibility in TV spots which say Coleman is a man "we just can't trust."

Sept. 10: Detroit Mayor Coleman Young says he is confident he will win his fifth four-year term as the city's top official. With the Democratic primary a mere 48 hours away, Young blames the flight of whites and upwardly mobile blacks for the city's high crime rate and shrinking financial base. His principal opponent, Congressman John Conyers, counters Young's argument by saying the city "cannot endure four more years of this."

Sept. 11: National Democratic party leaders convene in Washington to try to identify a message all party faithfuls can rally around in the 1990 midterm and 1992 presidential elections. Their goal: to return a Democrat to the White House in January 1993.

Sept. 12: Manhattan Borough President David Dinkins sweeps past Mayor Ed Koch in the Democratic primary, becoming New York's first black mayoral nominee of a major party. Dinkins promises he will be the mayor who "heals New York," once he defeats GOP challenger Rudolph Guiliani, who won his primary election by a 2-to-1 margin, in November.

Sept. 12: The *Washington Post* reports Lt. Gov. Douglas Wilder spent hundreds of taxpayer dollars on private and partisan political matters. The Democratic gubernatorial nominee—a lawyer—told reporters he did not do "any legal business" in his state office; his former chief of staff admitted some "small number of expenditures were inadvertently billed" to the state account.

Sept. 14: Health and Human Services Secretary Louis Sullivan calls for improved health care for blacks and other minorities, whose death rates from major diseases are considered excessively high by public health experts. Sullivan told a congressional panel that $110 million has been added to his budget for the next fiscal year earmarked for minority health programs.

Sept. 14: Connecticut state senator John Daniels appears headed for becoming New Haven's first black mayor. He edged out his nearest opponent by more than 4,000 votes; in a town where Democrats outnumber Republicans 10 to 1, Daniels is virtually assured of a November victory.

Sept. 18: In the few weeks leading up to Election Day 1989, the Republican and Democratic gubernatorial candidates in Virginia say race is "not an issue." Democratic hopeful Douglas Wilder says "Virginia has gone beyond race"; his GOP challenger, Marshall Coleman, says the race issue was "put to rest" when Wilder was elected Lieutenant Governor with half the white vote four years ago.

Sept. 22: With only seven weeks before the general election, NY Democratic mayoral candidate David Dinkins is reportedly changing his stripes. The *New York Times* describes Dinkins as a "liberal and proud of it" in the Democratic primary; but now, the newspaper says, Dinkins is challenging GOP contender Rudolph Guiliani for the title of New York's "toughest crime fighter" as he strives to widen his constituent base.

Sept. 24: A *Washington Post* poll shows Douglas Wilder and Marshall Coleman are in a dead heat in the Virginia gubernatorial race. Wilder, who hopes to become the first black elected governor in America, holds a fragile 45 to 42 percent edge over his Republican challenger.

Sept. 26: Former DC police chief Maurice Turner reportedly is close to announcing he will enter next year's mayoral race. The *Washington Post* says Turner gave a thumbs-up at a testimonial dinner when asked if he would run. The newspaper says Turner, who switched from the Democratic to the Republican party this summer, has told friends in private that he will be on the ballot.

Sept. 26: New York City Police Commissioner Benjamin Ward announces his resignation effective next month, citing continuing problems with asthma. The city's first black to hold the post, Ward increased the number of minorities and women on the police force, raised educational standards for officers, and tried to institute programs to combat the city's escalating drug problem during his six-year tenure.

Sept. 27: Former HUD Secretary Samuel Pierce invoked his Fifth Amendment protection against self-incrimination when he appeared on Capitol Hill to face questions about hundreds of millions of dollars in federal housing assistance being diverted to projects handled by major Republican backers.

Sept. 29: Former Democratic presidential candidate Jesse Jackson is inadvertently playing a role in the New York mayoral campaign. GOP contender Rudolph Guiliani is now running a full-page ad in the nation's largest Yiddish newspaper with two photos: one of Guiliani with President Bush; the other, with Democratic candidate David Dinkins and Jackson warmly embracing. The caption: "Let the people of New York choose their own destiny."

Sept. 29: Democratic National Committee chairman Ronald Brown declares the "Bush honeymoon is over," that it's time for Democrats to end the 16-year gap since they won the White House. *The New York Times* describes Brown as being "obsessed with winning" as he seeks to end the factionalism within his party and to forge a coalition between now and 1992 that will spell victory from the "courthouse to the White House."

Sept. 30: Trailing badly in the New York mayoral campaign, GOP contender Rudolph Guiliani attacks Democratic hopeful David Dinkins more aggressively. The former U.S. attorney accuses Dinkins of associating himself, as the *Washington Post* put it, "with the philosophy, programs, and policies of Jesse Jackson . . . which would bankrupt this city." In a related development, the newspaper reports Virginia's gubernatorial hopeful, L. Douglas Wilder, believes there are "compelling political reasons" to put as much distance between himself and Jackson as the Democratic candidate stumps for votes in generally conservative Virginia.

Oct. 6: Jesse Jackson announces he plans to host a weekly television program beginning next fall. At a New York news conference, the former presidential candidate said his show, "Voices of America with Jesse Jackson," will "make room for those voices that make up the real America." Composer-producer Quincy Jones will be executive producer of "Voices."

Oct. 20: Federal district judge Alcee Hastings is convicted by the U.S. Senate of engaging in a "corrupt conspiracy" to obtain a $150,000 bribe. After the decision, the 53-year-old judge, who served in the Southern District of Florida, called the trial unfair and immediately announced that he would run for governor of Florida.

Oct. 28: Former Housing and Urban Development Secretary Samuel Pierce declines to testify before a congressional subcommittee investigating events during his tenure at HUD. Pierce invokes his constitutional right to avoid self-incrimination by refusing for the second time to testify.

Nov. 2: Three months after Rep. Mickey Leland (D-TX) was buried in his hometown of Houston, the city is reeling from a debate over how to create a lasting memorial to the late Congressman. Blacks in Houston protest city councilmember Jim Westmoreland's racial slur that he made in connection with a proposal to rename the Houston Intercontinental Airport for Leland.

Nov. 7: Virginia's Lt. Gov. L. Douglas Wilder becomes that state's first black elected governor by narrowly defeating his Republican opponent, J. Marshall Coleman. Appearing at a news conference, Wilder says that Virginians are "prepared to move on" beyond the racial tensions of the past.

Nov. 7: Manhattan Borough President David Dinkins is elected Mayor of New York, becoming the first black ever to head the nation's largest city. Dinkins defeated Republican Rudolph Guiliani, winning about 30 percent of the white vote in a city where Democrats outnumber Republicans by a 5-to-1 ratio.

Nov. 7: Mayor Coleman Young of Detroit is elected to a fifth consecutive term in office, while Ohio state senator Michael White becomes Cleveland's first black mayor since Carl Stokes left office in 1971.

Other blacks elected as mayors are John Daniels, New Haven (CT), and Norman Rice, Seattle (WA).

Dec. 7: Leroy Rountree Hassell is named by Virginia Governor Gerald Baliles to the Virginia Supreme Court. Hassell will succeed John Charles Thomas, the first black ever to serve on the court.

Dec. 10: State senator Craig Washington, elected to succeed the late Rep. Mickey Leland (D-TX), refuses to take his new seat until the Texas legislature settles the issue of workers' compensation. Washington is a key supporter of revisions favored by labor.

Dec. 15: Ernest "Dutch" Morial, former mayor of New Orleans, announces he will not seek to regain the mayoralty, the office he had held for eight years. Morial's supporters had urged him to enter the nonpartisan primary February 3, 1990.

Dec. 19: Houston Police Chief Lee P. Brown is named by New York City Mayor-Elect David Dinkins as the new Police Commissioner. Brown, who holds a doctorate in criminology, was once Atlanta's Public Safety Commissioner.

Dec. 25: Ernest "Dutch" Morial, the first black mayor of New Orleans, dies of an apparent heart attack after collapsing outside the home of a friend. Morial, a lawyer, was regarded as one of New Orleans most accomplished politicians and served two terms as mayor (1978-1986). He was also a former president of the U.S. Conference of Mayors.

Civil Rights

Jan. 9: The owner of the only movie theater in Philadelphia, MS, says she will not show the film "Mississippi Burning." The newly released movie is a fictionalized account of the deaths of three civil rights workers killed in the town 25 years ago.

Jan. 11: A district judge in Alabama convicts the head of the state NAACP and 13 other black legislators who tried last year to remove the Confederate flag from atop the state capitol. The protesters are expected to appeal the $100 fine plus court costs.

Jan. 14: Interviewed on the CBS program "60 Minutes," President Reagan suggests some civil rights leaders exaggerate the degree of racism in the U.S. to keep their cause alive and to maintain their own prominence. Rev. Jesse Jackson quickly retorts, saying Reagan may be the "worst civil rights president we've had in recent memory."

Jan. 15: Memorial services and celebratory masses are held around the country in honor of Rev. Dr. Martin Luther King, Jr. on the 60th anniversary of his birth. President-Elect Bush pledges to "make it his mission as president to pursue King's dream of equality." In Memphis, where the civil rights leader was slain 21 years ago, the NAACP considers boycotting the local McDonald's, which issued a calendar with the King holiday noted as "National Nothing Day." McDonald's blames its advertising agency for the "terrible mistake."

Jan. 16: Dexter Scott King is named the new head of the Martin Luther King, Jr. Center for Non-Violent Social Change in Atlanta. When asked if he was qualified to be the new president, King responded: "I am the son of a son of the civil rights movement. I have grown up with [it]."

Jan. 16: A civil rights advocate in Long Beach, CA, says he was beaten up and his head pushed through a store window by police merely because he was "black in the wrong neighborhood." Don Jackson says he arranged the sting operation to prove that local police harass blacks.

Jan. 18: The *Washington Post* reports a group of civil rights leaders expect President Bush and his administration to take positive steps toward ending systemic discrimination. The Citizen's Commission on Civil Rights—a bipartisan group of lawyers, policy analysts, and religious leaders—is challenging Bush to establish a Cabinet-level task force to "deal with the causes and results of bigotry and prejudice."

Jan. 23: Clarence Norris, the last of the Scottsboro Boys rape case defendants, dies in Bronx Community Hospital at the age of 76. The case epitomized racial injustice in the Deep South during the 1930s.

Jan. 27: Attorney General Dick Thornburgh asks civil rights leaders to submit names of candidates to direct the enforcement of civil rights laws.

Feb. 7: The Lorraine Civil Rights Museum Foundation breaks ground at the Memphis (TN) hotel where Dr. Martin Luther King, Jr. was assassinated 21 years ago. When the museum opens in 1991, it will hold exhibits "depicting the sights, sounds, outrage, danger, and emotion of the civil rights movement," according to Foundation chairman D'Army Bailey.

Feb. 10: As the Bush administration settles in, one question it faces is what to do about the U.S. Civil Rights Commission. *The New York Times* reports Bush's civil rights advisor, Thaddeus Garrett, does not want the commission to die, which it almost did during the Reagan years.

March 15: Four major banks in New York discriminate against blacks and Hispanics who want to open checking accounts, according to a study published in *The New York Times* by two state legislators. The report says Citibank, Chemical, Chase Manhattan, and Marine Midland required minorities to live close to the banks' branches three times more often than they required it of whites. The banks denied the charge.

March 19: The chairman of the U.S. Civil Rights Commission says the days of the panel are over and its members should resign. The move by William Barclay Allen was, in the word of commissioner Mary Frances Berry, "bad judgment by the chairman and bad timing."

March 20: The student president of the Michigan State University NAACP chapter says he received a threatening phone call warning him to leave. Jeffrey Robinson told reporters the caller identified himself as "the KKK" and told him, "We're not going to put up with any spear-chucking moolies or any thick-lipped niggers. We will burn your room down."

March 20: Civil rights advocates criticize President Bush's choice for the next head of the Justice Department's civil rights division. The leaders say William Lucas, a black Republican from Michigan, lacks the experience and sensitivity to hold down the key post.

March 22: *The New York Times* quotes administration officials as saying President Bush is considering replacing William Barclay Allen as chairman of the Civil Rights Commission. Allen was involved last month in a controversial custody case involving a 14-year-old Apache girl. A Senate committee is investigating whether Allen had the authority to get involved in that case. Allen says he will not step down; he has apologized to the affected parties for the way he handled the matter.

March 28: The U.S. Supreme Court unanimously rules that people who bring civil rights lawsuits in federal court can win reimbursement of their legal fees, even if the suit is only partly successful. Civil rights advocates view the ruling as a victory for justice.

March 30: The Newark (NJ) NAACP sues the city's housing authority in order to stop it from demolishing more than 1,800 low-income apartments. In the class action suit, the civil rights group, along with other activists, argues the demolition would cause a "staggering loss of public housing while increasing segregation" in the state's largest city. The housing authority has asked the court to void the suit, saying the housing is uninhabitable.

March 31: *The New York Times* reports civil rights organizations and Senate investigators will closely review two court decisions in which black Republican William Lucas—named to head the Justice Department's civil rights division—was accused of tolerating brutality and overcrowding in county jails he oversaw in Detroit.

April 3: Criticism mounts over the choice of William Lucas as the next head of the Justice Department's civil rights division. The *Washington Post* reports Lucas's critics charge he is unqualified, his background in civil rights law being limited to a mere four months as a legal assistant to the division 25 years ago.

April 4: Fugitive Herman Ferguson reveals he will return to New York, ending his 18-year odyssey to avoid prosecution for allegedly conspiring to murder moderate civil rights leaders. Now 68, Ferguson says he believes he will be exonerated, based on data he has secured through the Freedom of Information Act.

April 14: The Detroit NAACP joins the chorus of those opposed to the nomination of William Lucas as chief of the Justice Department's civil rights division, citing his lack of experience as a lawyer and his "lack of involvement in the civil rights field."

May 15: National civil rights leaders are split over the administration's choice for head of the Justice Department's civil rights division. In *The New York Times* tally of support for William Lucas: Rev. Jesse Jackson, SCLC president Joseph Lowery, Rep. John Conyers (D-MI); the noted opponents: NAACP Executive Director Benjamin Hooks, Leadership Conference on Civil Rights head Ralph Neas, and Rep. William Gray III, House Majority Whip.

May 19: Michigan state legislators approve a bill to create a commission to protect the rights of blacks in the state. If the senate approves the measure, the governor will ask the Urban League, the NAACP, and other groups to submit nominees for the commission, which will survey the black population, monitor public and private programs, and coordinate with other minority commissions for women and Hispanics.

June 15: Baseball Hall of Famer William "Judy" Johnson dies at a nursing home in Wilmington, DE, following a stroke; he was 88. Johnson became the first black coach in the major leagues when the Philadelphia Athletics signed him as assistant manager in 1954.

July 1:   President Bush promises aggressive enforcement of civil rights laws and support for affirmative action as he marks the 25th anniversary of the 1964 Civil Rights Act. Bush says in a Rose Garden ceremony he will be content with "nothing less than equality of opportunity for all Americans."

July 10:   NAACP Executive Director Benjamin Hooks describes recent decisions of the U.S. Supreme Court as "more dangerous to this nation" than the segregationist foes of the civil rights movement. At the opening of the NAACP annual meeting in Detroit, Hooks said the Court "seems to be hell-bent on destroying the few gains that women and minorities have made."

July 10:   Housing and Urban Development Secretary Jack Kemp is cheered when he tells the NAACP annual meeting conferees gathered in Detroit that it is time for South Africa to "let our people go." Kemp adds it is also time for changes in the Republican party which, he says, was "nowhere to be found" in the civil rights struggles of the '60s.

July 13:   Vice President Dan Quayle gets a lukewarm response from attendees at the NAACP annual convention underway in Detroit when he says the Bush administration has kept its pledge on civil rights. After his speech, Quayle told reporters "doubters will eventually be aware that Mr. Bush has a heart and soul for the cause of civil rights."

July 15:   U.S. Civil Rights Commission Chairman William Barclay Allen accuses the Bush administration of leaving the future of the agency and civil rights in general in the hands of "country club Republicans . . . and their caddies." The *Washington Post* reports Allen is displeased that "no one in the White House will talk" to him as he tries to steer the troubled agency.

July 20:   Former Wayne County (MI) executive William Lucas tells the Senate Judiciary Committee he "resents being treated as if he were a potted plant along the way of advancement of civil rights." The black Republican's comments mark the first time he has publicly responded to charges that he is unqualified to head the Justice Department's civil rights division.

July 21:   Michigan Congressman John Conyers withdraws his endorsement of William Lucas as the next chief of the Justice Department's civil rights division, just one day after introducing him to the Senate panel considering the Lucas nomination. Conyers says he was "astounded" when he heard Lucas testify that recent Supreme Court decisions that set back some civil rights gains were "sound."

July 30:	A federal judge orders the records of the Mississippi Sovereignty Commission be opened to the public, ending a 12-year battle by civil rights groups to gain access to the records. The Commission, now defunct, was a public agency that tried to thwart civil rights groups in the '50s and '60s.
Aug. 1:	The Senate Judiciary Committee rejects William Lucas as the assistant attorney general for civil rights. Sen. Howell Heflin (D-AL), who cast the critical vote, says Lucas is "lacking in experience and qualifications, his managerial accomplishments are debatable." Sen. Minority Leader Bob Dole (R-KS) urges President Bush to name Lucas to the post on an interim basis, which would not require Senate approval.
Aug. 2:	Columbia University names Jack Greenberg as the dean of its undergraduate college. For 23 years, Greenberg headed the NAACP Legal Defense and Educational Fund, during which time he argued more than 40 cases before the U.S. Supreme Court, including the landmark *Brown v. Board of Education* desegregation case.
Aug. 6:	John E. Jacob, President and Chief Executive Officer of the National Urban League, urges President Bush and the Congress to restore civil rights protections lost because of recent U.S. Supreme Court rulings. Describing the Court as being "hijacked by the Reaganites" in his opening remarks at the annual League conference in Washington, Jacob said the court "we once looked to as the protector of minority rights has itself become a threat to our rights."
Aug. 8:	Using tactics that are throwbacks to the civil rights movement, blacks and Hispanics in Dallas are nonviolently protesting a proposed redistricting that would alter the number and shape of council districts. One protester calls the plan "a sharecropper's agreement . . . with the power structure telling minorities what is good for them."
Aug. 12:	Black Republican William Lucas, who was recently rejected by the Senate as the nation's top civil rights enforcer, is named as Attorney General Dick Thornburgh's "personal representative" to law enforcement groups and state and local governments.
Aug. 13:	Jesse Hill, Jr., chairman of the board of the Martin Luther King, Jr. Center for Nonviolent Social Change, announces Dexter Scott King has resigned as president. Hill refused to elaborate why King is resigning after only four months, but published reports indicate his

part of a family dispute on how to manage the center, fueled by a generation gap.

Aug. 16: Vice President Dan Quayle tells the annual meeting of the Southern Christian Leadership Conference in Atlanta that they and the Bush administration might differ over "the course the nation must travel" on racial issues but agree on "the ultimate destination. . . . We can work together and build an America we all envision."

Aug. 22: *The New York Times* reports a gas canister in a parcel detonated at the regional office of the NAACP in Atlanta when the package was opened, injuring 15 people.

Aug. 23: Black Panther Party co-founder Huey Newton is shot to death in an Oakland, CA neighborhood where he began his organizing. Authorities say they have no suspects and no motives for the murder.

Aug. 27: Civil rights demonstrators, led by the NAACP, march to the steps of the U.S. Supreme Court in a silent protest over the Court's recent rulings regarded as setbacks to hard-won civil rights gains.

Sept. 9: Supreme Court Justice Thurgood Marshall tells a group of federal judges meeting in New York that recent Supreme Court decisions have "put at risk not only the civil rights of minorities but also the civil rights of all citizens." In a stinging critique of the last Court term, Marshall said "we are back where we started."

Sept. 25: *The New York Times* reports a new law in Arizona establishing a holiday honoring Dr. Martin Luther King, Jr. is being challenged by conservatives who contend King had links to communist groups.

Sept. 29: Staunch conservative Sen. Jesse Helms (R-NC) hires James Meredith, the first black to enroll in the University of Mississippi. Meredith will be a "special assistant" to Helms, who has long been at odds with the civil rights movement.

Oct. 16: *The Washington Post* reports a recent suggestion by Smithsonian Secretary Robert McC. Adams to limit an African-American museum at the National Museum of History is sparking lively debate in the black community and on Capitol Hill. At the heart of the matter is whether to have a separate, freestanding museum to chronicle African-American gains versus one that would be added to a current museum.

Nov. 5: More than 600 family members and thousands of others gather in Montgomery (AL) for the unveiling of a new memorial that honors 40 men, women, and children representing all those killed in the violence from 1954 to 1968. Designed by Maya Lin, who also designed the Vietnam Veterans Memorial in Washington, the granite table-top contains the 40 names, interspersed with dates from the civil rights movement. Water bubbles from its center, reflecting the words of Dr. Martin Luther King, Jr., which serves as a backdrop: the struggle will continue "until justice rolls down like waters and righteousness like a mighty stream."

Nov. 18: The Senate approves a 22-month extension of the embattled U.S. Civil Rights Commission that would avert the panel's demise at the end of the month. The measure now goes back to the House, which earlier approved a six-month extension.

Nov. 20: *The Washington Post* reports the Supreme Court decision that sharply restricted the reach of a major civil rights law has resulted in the dismissal of 96 racial discrimination claims. According to a study by the NAACP Legal Defense and Educational Fund, nearly one claim per business day has been dropped since the opinion was issued.

Nov. 29: Administration sources tell the *Washington Post* President Bush is expected to nominate former New York state senator John Dunne as the nation's top civil rights enforcer . . . his second attempt to fill the post that has been vacant for nearly a year.

Dec. 16: The NAACP celebrates its 80th birthday at New York's Waldorf Astoria. Executive Director Benjamin Hooks tells the 1,800 prominent attendees that "it's good for those who normally see us in the trenches kicking and in the courts litigating to see us in a beautiful setting like this." President Bush, speaking to the group by telephone hookup, apologized for his laryngitis, which was the cause of his cancelling as keynote speaker.

Federal Budget

Jan. 2: House Minority Leader Bob Michel (R-IL) says President-Elect George Bush will have to accept a tax increase to get spending reductions as part of an overall deficit-reduction package. Sen. Majority Leader George Mitchell (D-ME) agrees, saying Bush may find a way to increase taxes without admitting it, the same as President Reagan did. Both lawmakers were interviewed on ABC's "This Week with David Brinkley."

Jan. 3: In a *Washington Post* analysis of the agenda for the 101st Congress convening this month, the newspaper predicts the deficit-ridden budget will be priority-one. The newspaper says President Bush and

Congress need to come up with roughly $35 billion in savings to meet the $100 billion deficit target for the new fiscal year as mandated by the Gramm-Rudman-Hollings budget-balancing law.

Jan. 5: The Congressional Budget Office projects the federal budget deficit will be $141 billion for the next fiscal year—$14 billion larger than the Reagan administration's estimate, because the budget outlook has deteriorated since last summer.

Jan. 5: Budget Director-Designate Richard Darman unveils the Bush administration's strategy for dealing with the federal budget. In several meetings with congressional leaders, Darman is pushing for no tax hikes, but says the president is willing to negotiate over spending for key national priorities.

Jan. 6: The *Washington Post* reports President Reagan—in his last days in the White House—is asking members of Congress to support pay increases of 50 percent for themselves and top federal political appointees. Reagan is quoted as saying that fair compensation is "critical" to the smooth functioning of government.

Jan. 7: White House spokesman Marlin Fitzwater predicts President-Elect George Bush's new fiscal budget will not differ on "any grand scale" from the one President Reagan will send to Capitol Hill next week. Both spending plans call for a $35 billion savings in spending to reach the $100 billion dollar deficit level mandated by the budget-balancing law for the next fiscal year.

Jan. 7: In his last radio address to the nation, President Reagan says he is leaving office as he came in: "dead set against any new taxes."

Jan. 7: The Reagan administration's budget headed for Congress will include a 30 percent increase in spending on AIDS. *The New York Times* reveals the administration's plans after securing a copy of the budget before its delivery to Capitol Hill. The newspaper also notes more than half of the money for the budget for health and human services—$260 billion—is earmarked for Social Security.

Jan. 10: The *Washington Post* reports President Reagan's new budget includes the administration's first formal admission that the government does not have enough money to close or merge hundreds of thousands of insolvent savings and loan associations in the U.S. The amount needed: $100 billion; the amount targeted in the budget: $64 billion.

Jan. 10: Democrats on Capitol Hill criticize President Reagan's new $1.15 trillion budget as "Draconian and unrealistic." The lawmakers are particularly upset over plans to cut spending for emergency shelter grants for the homeless and Amtrak operating subsidies.

Jan. 11: The *Washington Post* quotes administration and congressional sources as saying more than $53 million is earmarked to pay for the expected increase in official mailings by members of Congress next year, an election year. The publicly funded mailings are not supposed to be used for campaign materials, but members of Congress regularly almost double the amount of "official business" material they mail to constituents in election years.

Jan. 13: *Washington Post* financial writers discover a surprising admission buried in the President's new budget: that the 1986 rewrite of the tax laws will unexpectedly worsen the federal budget deficit by about $20 billion a year over the next four years.

Jan. 14: Twenty-one employees of the Justice Department are out of work unexpectedly because of "severe budgetary constraints" in the department. *The New York Times* reports the deputy attorney general gave the employees—some with more than 20 years of experience—one month to find new employment.

Jan. 20: At his confirmation hearing on Capitol Hill, Budget Director-Designate Richard Darman says he would recommend a tax increase only if the nation faced a crisis so severe that there was no alternative. He added that if a tax hike is needed, the administration will call it just that, not hide behind euphemisms in the manner of the Reagan administration.

Jan. 22: In his first full day as President, George Bush invites congressional leaders to the White House next week for their first talks on the budget, a part of his plan to seek bipartisan solutions to national problems.

Jan. 25: AFL-CIO president Lane Kirkland says President Bush's refusal to consider anything other than a flexible-freeze approach to reducing the budget deficit has doomed the work of the National Economic Commission, a blue-ribbon panel named to find a bipartisan strategy for reducing the $150 billion deficit. Kirkland tells the *Washington Post* the situation is a "missed opportunity."

Jan. 25: In his first meeting with congressional leaders over the budget, President Bush promises to outline his spending priorities when he addresses Congress next month. He suggests weekly bipartisan budget negotiations between the White House and Capitol Hill to work out a quick compromise.

Jan. 26:   *The New York Times* quotes budget experts from the White House and Congress as predicting the deficit limit can be met this year without raising taxes, thereby fulfilling President Bush's campaign promise of "no new taxes." But the experts agree that higher taxes are unavoidable next year.

Jan. 27:   A panel headed by former Secretary of State Edmund Muskie is recommending a broad tax increase as part of the plan to balance the federal budget. The Center for National Policy, in releasing the results of its yearlong study, "America Tomorrow, the Choices We Face," says new taxes will be "unavoidable, not only to achieve a net deficit reduction of $100 billion, but also to cover infrastructure problems."

Jan. 28:   At his first news conference, President Bush endorses a 50-percent pay hike for members of Congress and political appointees, saying such an increase "is overdue." In answering reporters' questions, Bush sidestepped the controversy over a savings and loan bailout plan and continued to oppose an increase in the minimum wage unless it is linked to a new subminimum wage for youths.

Feb. 7:   Congress kills the proposed 50-percent pay hike for federal officials, leaving what Rep. Vic Fazio (D-CA) calls a "national crisis" in which judges and federal executives are still underpaid. The lawmakers scuttled the proposal only hours before the midnight deadline when the increase would have become effective.

Feb. 8:   *The New York Times* quotes administration officials as saying President Bush will propose that military spending in the next fiscal year rise only enough to keep pace with inflation. That is about $2 billion less than President Reagan's farewell budget plan.

Feb. 9:   President Bush proposes more than $250 million in education spending above former President Reagan's budget. In a nationally televised address before Congress, Bush also calls for increases in aid to the homeless, research and development, and the environment.

Feb. 10:   Democrats criticize portions of President Bush's revised spending plans for the new fiscal year, saying he failed to make hard decisions on how to reduce the deficit, sticking instead to the broad outlines for squeezing domestic programs laid out by President Reagan.

Feb. 15:   In the face of sharp congressional criticism over the lack of details in President Bush's budget proposals, Budget Director Richard Darman promises his staff will meet with budget experts on Capitol Hill to provide more information on how the administration would like to finance particular programs. House Budget Committee Chairman Leon Panetta (D-CA) told Darman, "You can't negotiate when most of the lines are blank."

Feb. 17: President Bush calls budget negotiations a "two-way street," telling reporters he is not trying to shift to Congress the responsibility for proposing unpopular cuts.

Feb. 20: The National Weather Service may have to close as many as 62 local weather offices this year and 77 more next year because it faces a $10- to $20-million shortfall. Congressional sources tell the Associated Press the Bush administration may be reconsidering whether such sharp cuts can be averted.

Feb. 22: President Bush urges congressional leaders to join him in serious budget negotiations, but Democrats are holding out. Senate Budget Committee Chairman Jim Sasser (D-TN) claims, "We've got an administration here that wants to embrace the concept of a line-item veto but won't give us a line-item budget."

Feb. 23: Budget Director Richard Darman refuses to reveal what spending levels President Bush wants next year for programs such as care for poor pregnant women, veterans' education, and mass transit. Testifying before the House Budget Committee, Darman says Bush's position is that "he wants to negotiate the answer to that, and you don't like that apparently."

Feb. 28: *The New York Times* reports the National Economic Commission has been unable to reach a consensus on how to devise a politically acceptable way to cut the budget deficit. After a year of meeting over the politically sensitive issue, the blue-ribbon panel is expected to file a final report divided along party lines.

March 1: Federal Reserve Board Chairman Alan Greenspan tells the Senate Budget Committee that President Bush's proposed 1990 budget, if adopted, will trigger lower interest rates even if it eventually produces a deficit higher than the $100 billion allowed under the Gramm-Rudman-Hollings budget-balancing law.

March 1: Treasury Secretary Nicholas Brady tells the Senate Budget Committee how the administration plans to bail out the insolvent savings and loan industry—through a $123 billion, three-part proposal that will end what he calls a "national catastrophe."

March 17: The Washington area's congressional delegation calls on the federal government to provide $2.16 billion to complete construction of the 103-mile Metrorail system. Administration officials call the request unrealistic at a time when Congress is struggling to balance the budget and reduce the deficit.

March 20: *The Wall Street Journal* reports House Budget Committee Chairman Leon Panetta (D-CA) plans to propose that the fiscal 1990 deficit be reduced with a 50-50 mix of additional revenue and spending cuts in both defense and nondefense programs. The newspaper says Senate Democrats are holding out on revealing their strategy: "we want to see how Budget Director Richard Darman responds to this."

March 26: *The New York Times* reports a consensus is forming among politicians and economists, liberals and conservatives, that the only practical way to make a fundamental assault on the federal budget is for Republicans and Democrats to relinquish their strongest political weapons. The newspaper says the emerging view is that President Bush and congressional Republicans will have to accept part of the responsibility for raising taxes and that congressional Democrats will have to share the blame for limiting hikes in Social Security and other retirement benefits.

March 30: *The Wall Street Journal* quotes Treasury Secretary Nicholas Brady as saying that measures to close loopholes in the tax system will not necessarily violate President Bush's promise of "no new taxes."

April 12: The *Washington Post* reports White House and congressional negotiators are nearing agreement on a broad blueprint for reducing the federal budget deficit in the next fiscal year. The newspaper quotes congressional sources who say the accord will leave many details unspecified and will not address the longer-term deficit problem.

April 13: New York and New Jersey port officials are asking Congress to prov le 12 times the $600,000 in the 1990 federal budget for impro ements in the New York-New Jersey Harbor. The delegation acknov 'edges that current deficit reduction requires limiting all spending, but defends its request by saying that lives may be endangered if the harbor is not rid of drift from sunken hulks and decaying shore structures. More than 18,000 commercial, public, and recreational vessels annually collide with drift in the port, resulting in economic losses of more than $48 million.

April 17: Administration and congressional budget negotiators defend their deal to cut the 1990 budget deficit to $99.4 billion. Senate Budget Committee Jim Sasser (D-TN) says it is the "best that could be done," denying critics' charges that it is unrealistic and based on accounting gimmicks.

May 5:	The House and Senate adopt similar versions of a $1.17 trillion budget for the next fiscal year. The *Washington Post* reports some lawmakers are unhappy with the proposals, but say it is a first step towards later, more substantive negotiations with the White House.
May 12:	House and Senate negotiators hammer out a compromise $1.17 trillion budget for fiscal year 1990. The *Washington Post* summarizes the proposal as one that constrains the Pentagon, treats many domestic programs generously, and leaves many prickly decisions for later.
May 18:	The Senate gives final approval to a measure that would raise the minimum wage by $1.20 to $4.55 an hour over three years. But the measure failed to pass with a large enough margin to override a threatened veto by President Bush.
May 25:	The House approves a $3.7 billion "dire emergency" spending bill that most likely will face a presidential veto. Included in the measure are $822 million for anti-drug programs and $1.2 billion for veterans' health care services that are rapidly running out of money.
Aug. 5:	The House agrees to $286.4 billion in military spending for fiscal 1990. Wrapping up its budget bills before the August recess, the lawmakers approve the bill, which reflects sweeping changes in strategic and conventional programs earlier authorized by the House affecting the stealth bomber, the MX and Midgetman missile systems, and the Strategic Defense Initiative antimissile system.
Aug. 14:	Budget Director Richard Darman says the Bush administration will consider raising taxes next year unless Congress agrees to cut Medicare and other domestic programs, excluding Social Security. Appearing on NBC's "Meet the Press," Darman also complains that the Federal Reserve Board is holding interest rates too high, saying the central bank will be to blame if a recession occurs.
Aug. 18:	The Congressional Budget Office says that despite efforts by Congress and the White House to cut government spending, the federal budget deficit will average $140 billion over the next several years.
Sept. 20:	Senate Finance Committee Chairman Lloyd Bentsen (D-TX) postpones a planned vote on revising the 1988 Medicare catastrophic-illness benefits law because Health and Human Services Secretary Louis Sullivan failed to appear before the panel to state the administration's position. The law has come under heavy criticism by many elderly people who dislike paying up to $800 a month in premiums for the benefit. Says Bentsen in killing the vote: "This is the most important issue facing Dr. Sullivan, and I expected him to

be here." An HHS spokesman says the administration opposes changing the law.

Sept. 21:   House Democratic leaders agree to support a deficit reduction plan that would increase taxes on the wealthy, restore Individual Retirement Accounts (IRAs), and earmark surplus revenues for cutting the deficit. The *Washington Post* quotes several lawmakers who say the plan is an alternative to the capital gains tax cut favored by the White House.

Sept. 26:   The battle between the White House and Congress over the best way to reduce the federal deficit intensifies. Budget Director Richard Darman is quoted in the *Washington Post* as saying congressional Democrats are embracing "kamikaze tactics" aimed at engineering a budgetary crisis and a tax increase next month when the new fiscal year begins.

Oct. 15:   More than $16 billion in automatic federal spending reductions technically go into effect at midnight. The *Washington Post* reports most government employees and beneficiaries are not worried about the cuts because they expect the monies to be restored once the White House and Congress agree on a budget-balancing plan within the next few weeks.

Nov. 2:   The Bush administration and some key congressional Republicans say they are prepared to accept as permanent the $16 billion across-the-board spending cuts imposed last month under the Gramm-Rudman-Hollings budget-balancing law. The *Washington Post* quotes various officials who feel the cuts do less harm to the Pentagon than would a current controversial spending plan before Congress.

Nov. 3:   President Bush abandons his quest for a capital gains tax cut this year after realizing it could not get through Congress successfully. In a released statement, the president demanded a stringent deficit reduction package that does not contain new taxes nor spending measures that increase the federal deficit in the future. Bush threatened to veto any legislation that fails to meet these tests, leaving in place the $16 billion automatic across-the-board cuts imposed last month, which affect virtually every government agency and countless government programs.

Nov. 4:   The *Washington Post* reports the District of Columbia stands to lose roughly $40 million this year if across-the-board federal spending cuts remain in place. President Bush has already vetoed the 1990

DC appropriations bill, prompting one DC councilmember to say that the city is "in for a rough year."

Nov. 7:   Congress is preparing to raise the federal debt ceiling to more than $3 trillion this week so that the government can pay its bills. If the debt limit is not increased within 48 hours, the federal government would default on more than $13 billion in Treasury securities, throwing financial markets into chaos.

Nov. 9:   The Pentagon says it will be forced next year to cut 229,000 active duty men and women from the armed forces—roughly 10 percent of all U.S. military personnel—if automatic across-the-board budget cuts triggered last month are not restored. The *Washington Post* quotes senior military officials who told the Senate Armed Services Committee that it is "too mind boggling to contemplate" how the Pentagon would try to restructure worldwide military forces and reduce weapons acquisitions.

Nov. 20:   The *Washington Post* reports congressional budget negotiators are still deadlocked over a deficit reducing package that the White House says does not pass muster. Hanging in the balance is President Bush's threatened veto if the lawmakers adopt a bill he doesn't like, or—with no bill at all—slashing all government programs across the board as mandated by the budget-balancing law.

Nov. 21:   *The New York Times* quotes administration officials as saying the Army has proposed eliminating as many as 200,000 civilian, reserve, and military employees and giving up on the long-sought modernization of its main battle tank—the M1. The newspaper says the proposal outlines potential cuts totaling $180 billion in the years 1992-1994. Other sources tell the newspaper such cuts would be unusually difficult to make, adding the Pentagon's budget "has been cut to the bone."

Nov. 22:   After nine months of haggling, the White House and Congress are near agreement on a deficit reduction package that relies heavily on new taxes and a continuation of across-the-board cuts to trim more than $14 billion from the deficit this year. *The New York Times* reports the budget negotiators agreed on the compromise after a daylong, closed-door bargaining session that lasted until the wee hours of the morning. Congress is expected to act on the compromise before adjourning until January 23.

Nov. 23:   Congress ends the first half of its 101st session by enacting a $14 billion budget bill and by repealing the 1988 law protecting Medicare beneficiaries from the costs of catastrophic illness. The lawmakers agreed to consider the myriad of unfinished legislative items when they return in January.

Nov. 30: Health and Human Services Secretary Louis Sullivan is accusing the Office of Management and Budget of refusing to approve funding increases for social programs that President Bush has identified as national priorities. The *Washington Post* reports Sullivan wrote OMB Director Richard Darman that "the president and I have identified infant mortality, AIDS research, and biomedical research as high priorities" that should not be subject to current deficit reduction cutbacks.

Nov. 30: The White House budget office is proposing an $8 billion savings in Medicare spending that would otherwise be required in the next fiscal year. *The New York Times* reports some lawmakers plan to oppose the reductions in the health program when Congress next reconvenes.

Dec. 6: The *Washington Post* discloses details of the Office of Management and Budget's "high risk list" of 73 government programs that threaten to cost taxpayers billions of dollars unless serious management weaknesses are corrected. Among the examples on the list is the financial system at the Environmental Protection Agency which some officials say is so unreliable that 40 percent of its accounts receivables do not balance.

Dec. 7: *The New York Times* reports President Bush has decided to propose a Pentagon budget of $295 billion for the 1991 fiscal year, substantially less than the Defense Department had hoped to receive. The newspaper quotes administration officials who say the overall package meets deficit requirements of the budget-balancing law without raising taxes or cutting basic federal programs.

Dec. 24: Administration officials tell *The New York Times* President Bush will encourage personal saving and modest spending increases for drug control, education, science, research, and the environment in his budget message to Congress next month.

Affirmative Action

Jan. 11: New York City Mayor Edward Koch says he does not believe an affirmative action program he established more than five years ago has turned into an operation that systematically dispenses patronage jobs on behalf of top political leaders. *The New York Times* quotes the mayor as testifying before the State Commission on Government Integrity that his administration does not deal in patronage, refuting the testimony the day before from two former administration officials who allege the program, called the "Mayor's Talent Bank," does just that.

Jan. 13: Despite the involvement of minority officers in helping to prepare a new promotion examination for the New York City Police Department, 94.7 percent of the latest group of officers promoted to sergeant is white.

Jan. 18: The U.S. Supreme Court hears arguments in a lawsuit that some suggest could "open the floodgates" in hundreds of other affirmative action rulings. At issue is whether white Birmingham (AL) firefighters have the right to challenge the city's affirmative action program which, they claim, makes them the victims of reverse discrimination.

Jan. 19: Boston officials are questioning the assertions of 11 firefighters that they are members of minority groups and, thus, are qualified for preferential treatment in hiring and promotions. The Massachusetts Department of Personnel Administration is investigating the assertions, after realizing that two of the 11 firefighters claimed they were black after failing qualifying tests for whites; the pair passed the exams as blacks.

Jan. 20: New York City Mayor Edward Koch claims the city is exceeding its 20 percent goal of employing minorities and women on the largest redevelopment project in Harlem. After Koch's pronouncement at a breakfast meeting of businessmen, several minority contractors challenge the mayor's statement, according to the New York *Daily News,* saying that the jobs Koch referred to are all nonskilled positions.

Jan. 20: Even though the number of black and Hispanic workers in New York City government has increased, whites still continue to hold a disproportionate share of the highest-paying jobs. *The New York Times* quotes a study by the Community Service Society which finds whites employees are more likely to receive high salaries in the police and fire departments as well as in other lower-paying agencies such as Social Services and the Health Department.

Jan. 23: The U.S. Supreme Court invalidates a law in Richmond (VA) that channeled 30 percent of public works funds to minority-owned construction companies. The high court ruled that the city ordinance, which is similar to minority set-aside programs in 36 states, violates the constitutional rights of white contractors to equal protection of the law. In a stinging dissent, Justice Thurgood Marshall writes that governmental actions intended to help blacks overcome past discrimination should be judged by a more flexible standard that takes the country's racial history into account.

Jan. 24: *The New York Times* quotes city and state officials around the country who promise to continue their efforts to aid minority contractors, despite the Supreme Court's ruling yesterday that invalidated a Richmond law that channeled 30 percent of public works funds to businesses owned by minorities.

Jan. 26: Atlanta city officials say their affirmative action program will not be affected by a recent Supreme Court decision invalidating part of such a program in Richmond. Mayor Andrew Young asserts his city's program meets the strict standards outlined in the high court's decision; at the same time, he claims, minority contractors still win 37 percent of the city's contracts.

Jan. 28: At his news conference, President Bush denies the recent Supreme Court ruling affecting a minority set-aside ordinance in Richmond kills such programs. He told reporters the decision "didn't kill affirmative action," to which he says he is committed.

Feb. 2: An opinion by the State Attorney General in Georgia challenging the legality of a provision to assure the hiring of minority contractors has thrown a roadblock in front of plans to build a $210 million domed stadium in Atlanta. *The New York Times* reports the opinion is perhaps the first major offshoot of a Supreme Court ruling last week affecting minority set-asides. A suit contesting Atlanta's program is pending before the state supreme court.

March 3: Georgia's supreme court overturns a widely copied program that has guided Atlanta construction contracts to minority groups. The court ruled that the program, which sets a goal of 35 percent minority participation in city-financed construction contracts, fails to meet the standards of a U.S. Supreme Court decision in January involving a similar program in Richmond. Mayor Andrew Young responds to the decision by saying he will immediately impose a moratorium on letting any new contracts for city construction.

March 4: The U.S. Supreme Court refuses to revive an affirmative action program in South Bend, IN, that called for hiring more blacks and Hispanics as firefighters and police officers. Without comment, the high court let stand a ruling that struck down the plan after it was challenged by a white man denied a job as a firefighter.

March 5: Political powers in Detroit are putting pressure on the Detroit Symphony Orchestra to hire more blacks. *The New York Times* reports several state legislators withheld more than $1 million in state aid and threatened to boycott and picket the orchestra's concerts if it does not hire more blacks. As a result, the financially strapped orchestra waived its stringent audition requirement and hired the first black musician it has hired in 14 years, bringing the total of black musicians in the 98-member orchestra to three.

March 7: In its latest effort to gut affirmative action programs—as some critics charge, the U.S. Supreme Court declares unconstitutional a Michigan law requiring that seven percent of all state contracts be awarded to minority-owned businesses and five percent to businesses owned by women. In a related development, the Court tells a federal appeals court to consider dismantling a Miami (FL) plan requiring five percent participation of businesses owned by women or minorities in the construction of a rail transit system.

March 17: The New York City Health and Hospitals Corporation approves a new employment plan to address repeated charges by black and Hispanic workers that its hiring and promotion practices are discriminatory. *The New York Times* quotes officials as saying the plan does not set numerical goals or timetables that would be vulnerable to challenge under a recent U.S. Supreme Court ruling.

March 20: The Federal Bureau of Investigation promises to fight charges of racial harassment within the bureau by promising to increase the number of minorities on its staff. Appearing before a House Judiciary subcommittee, FBI Director William Sessions says his agency "must reflect more closely America's work force, . . . that the FBI must engage in a catch-up program."

March 20: According to a study by Black Career Women, Inc., black women are poorly represented in managerial positions nationwide. Published reports on the study claim that black women have been in the work force for more than 200 years, yet they make up only two percent of managers and administrators in state and local governments.

March 24: A group representing several hundred salaried black employees at General Motors announces it plans to file a petition opposing a proposed $3 million settlement of a lawsuit charging GM with discrimination. According to a report in *The New York Times,* the group—Concerned Black Salaried Employees—feels the terms of the settlement are "vague and evasive" and do not address its concerns. The group specifically objects to areas involving promotions, pay raises, and benefits as well as to performance appraisals.

April 20: The *Washington Post* reports the State Department is acknowledging that it discriminated against its female Foreign Service officers in hiring, assignments, and honors between 1976 and 1985. The department sent cables to U.S. embassies around the world and notifications in Washington that 600 women may be entitled to court-ordered relief, including reassignment to some of the department's most prestigious positions. A State Department spokesperson refused comment on the issue because it is still involved in litigation.

May 3: An affirmative action plan at the Columbia Law Review that goes far beyond similar plans at similar student legal publications has renewed a debate over how to preserve the quality of the prominent review while remedying discrimination. *The New York Times* reports the Review will set aside up to five extra places on its enlarged staff of 40; those slots will be targeted for gay, handicapped, and poor applicants, as well as for women and members of minority groups. Opponents say the plan, adopted last month, would lower the standards for those aspiring to be involved in the prestigious publication.

May 5: The *Washington Post* reports a study by the DC Commission for Women and the Business and Professional Women's Clubs finds that Washington women work hard for their money, do not earn as much as men, and have employers who do not offer them enough support. The survey notes that Washington women fare better than most of their counterparts around the country, but that they still lag behind their male counterparts in the nation's capital.

May 14: A federal judge in New York state lifts his court order imposing strict quotas for hiring minorities and women by state police. *The New York Times* quotes Judge James Foley as saying that there has been a "remarkable change over the years in the black and Hispanic representation in the New York State Police Division." Judge Foley disagreed with the superintendent of state police who had asked the judge to maintain quotas imposed a decade ago but to reduce them to about 20 percent of each training class from the initially imposed quota of 40 percent.

June 8: The Justice Department asks Fairfax County (VA) government for new statistics on its minority hiring and promotion practices, after black police officers and other minority county employees allege a lingering pattern of racial discrimination.

June 12: The U.S. Supreme Court rules that court-approved affirmative action settlements can be challenged by white workers. In a five-to-four decision, the justices permit white firefighters in Birmingham (AL) to contest an eight-year-old, court-approved settlement intended to increase the number of blacks hired and promoted in the department.

June 13: Rep. Don Edwards, who chairs the Judiciary Committee's civil and constitutional rights subcommittee, calls yesterday's Supreme Court ruling a major setback for civil rights. Quoted in *The New York Times,* Edwards accuses the high court of dealing "blow after blow to 25 years of progress in civil rights law." In a related development, advocates of blacks' and women's rights assailed the high court, saying that it has made it more difficult to carry out programs to redress past discrimination against women and minorities.

June 20: The city of Atlanta is authorizing a $517,000 study to help the city develop a program aimed at overcoming recent U.S. Supreme Court objections to minority set-aside programs.

July 9: District of Columbia officials say that, after three years and $340,000 spent, there is still no successful race-blind test for hiring and promoting firefighters. The *Washington Post* quotes city officials who say that their efforts to satisfy both black and white firefighters have failed, and that they will seek other methods that do not involve consultants to resolve the allegations of discrimination regarding promotion practices by both black and white firefighters.

July 11: The Metropolitan Washington Airports Authority suspends its affirmative action requirements for contracting in a response to recent Supreme Court rulings. But the *Washington Post* quotes officials as saying the authority threatens to reimpose those requirements if firms owned by minorities and women do not win enough of the three area airports' business.

July 13: Vice President Dan Quayle tries to soften the blow of recent Supreme Court rulings that civil rights advocates claim gut hard-won gains. Speaking to the NAACP in Detroit, Quayle says the Bush administration is committed to "fostering good and better relations with the civil rights community."

July 13: The New York State court system is perceived by minorities as a bastion of white employment. *Newsday* quotes the Judicial Commission on Minorities' recent study, which finds that the perception of racial bias is pervasive among minorities. The commission is calling for urgent action to adopt an affirmative action hiring plan.

Aug. 1: Supporters of the Federal Communications Commission's affirmative action plan say they are "batting .500" this year. In one case, a three-judge federal panel in DC struck down one of the agency's affirmative action policies. Three days later, a similar panel upheld those same policies. Pluria Marshall, chairman of the National Black Media Coalition, tells *Black Enterprise* magazine that the conflicting rulings are "frustrating reminders . . . that the struggle to protect these policies may be a long one."

Aug. 1: The NAACP Legal Defense and Educational Fund is slapping one of the nation's richest men with the largest private employment discrimination suit in U.S. history. According to a report in *Black Enterprise* magazine, the Fund—in a class-action suit—is charging Ray Danner, chairman of the board of Shoney's, Inc., with instigating discrimination policies that have been carried out among the restaurants in the chain.

Aug. 1: *The Star-Ledger* reports the NAACP is filing lawsuits against five northern New Jersey communities, charging them with discrimination against blacks in the hiring of municipal employees. The municipalities named in the suit: West Orange, Clifton, Harrison, Kearny, and Fort Lee.

Dec. 1: The head of a minority business development group tells Congress that Supreme Court decisions this past term have been "devastating." The *Washington Post* quotes Tony Robinson, president of the Minority Business Enterprise Legal Defense and Education Fund, as saying that the January decision by the high court restricting when minority set-aside programs are constitutional has resulted in four similar programs being declared unconstitutional and in court challenges to 28 set-aside programs and voluntary termination to 15 other efforts.

Dec. 5: A federal appeals court upheld San Francisco's agreement to hire and promote women and minorities in the fire department. The court rejected arguments that the plan violated the rights of white men, an argument frequently used recently by whites who have been spurred to legal challenges in the wake of U.S. Supreme Court decisions that such challenges are constitutionally sound.

Dec. 6: A federal court in Georgia has ordered the state to seek federal approval for any changes it has made in the past 30 years in the way it elects its judges. Civil rights advocates welcomed the order, which could pave the way for more blacks to become judges.

Education/Desegregation

Jan. 3: One of two major college admission tests will be redesigned for the first time in its 30-year history. Researchers overhauling the American College Testing Assessment (ACT) will emphasize a wider range of mathematical knowledge and more abstract reading skills. About one-million high school juniors and seniors annually take the ACT. Critics charge the current test is biased against minorities and females.

Jan. 5: School board officials in Prince George's County (MD) may fight the federal government's demand that they stop transferring teachers from one school to another to maintain racial quotas. The Justice Department claims the practice violates the civil rights of white teachers with seniority; the NAACP and similar groups in the predominantly black county insist the guideline is crucial to the system's overall desegregation effort.

Jan. 6: Elizabeth Duncan Koontz, the first black president of the National Education Association, dies of a heart attack in her Salisbury (NC) home; she was 69. President Richard Nixon named Koontz, a Democrat, as Director of the Labor Department's Women's Bureau, where she stood up for equal pay for women.

Jan. 11: New York City Schools Chancellor Richard Green announces a $19 million savings in the central board's budget. He pledges to use the windfall—gained primarily through staff attrition—to buy more metal detectors and equipment for the city's high schools, and to hire more drug counselors so that every student receives drug education. Dr. Green added that local school districts, under fire as being "patronage machines," would be closely monitored.

Jan. 12: The National Collegiate Athletic Association (NCAA) reverses itself overnight at its annual convention in San Francisco and narrowly agrees to tighten the athletic scholarship eligibility requirements for incoming freshmen. By a nine-vote margin, the NCAA rules that, for a freshman to be eligible for an athletic scholarship, beginning in 1990, he or she must have completed high school with a C average and must have scored a set minimum on standardized college admission tests (Proposition 42). Since 1983, a student was eligible if either requirement was met (Proposition 48).

Jan. 14: Georgetown University basketball coach John Thompson announces he will protest the new NCAA rule governing athletic scholarship eligibility by walking off the court when his team plays Boston College tonight. Thompson claims standardized tests are biased against minorities and that Proposition 42 will *de facto* deprive them of a college education. About 90 percent of the 600 students a year who will be affected are black.

Jan. 14: Nearly all of the ninth graders in Montgomery County, MD, pass a state-required reading test for graduation. The new results are basically unchanged from last year. Despite efforts to improve their performance, black and Hispanic freshmen still lag behind their white and Asian classmates.

Jan. 14: NC State University Chancellor Bruce Poulton announces the NCAA will investigate charges that grades for some of the school's basketball players are fixed. In a related development, school officials say they will conduct an in-house probe into allegations published in *Personal Fouls* by Peter Golenbock. NCSU basketball coach Jim Valvano calls the charges "preposterous."

Jan. 15: A Joint Center for Political Studies poll finds that blacks, like most whites, give money to charity, but their donations tend to be smaller, in part, because they have smaller average incomes. The study, conducted by the Gallup Poll, comes on the heels of the $20 million donation by entertainer Bill Cosby to Spelman College in Atlanta. Cosby calls the gift a challenge to other black professionals to support black colleges.

Jan. 16: The American Council on Education reports the number of black male college students has declined "alarmingly" in the past decade. The national organization says that total college enrollment grew by more than a million students between 1976-1986, but enrollment for black males fell by 34,000 during the same period, marking the largest decline for any racial or ethnic group.

Jan. 16: All four black members of the Boston (MA) School Committee oppose a plan to end 15 years of court-ordered busing. They contend the plan could send the weakest schools into a "tailspin" of declining enrollments, lower budgets, and loss of motivated students and teachers.

Jan. 17: Former Wimbledon Champion Arthur Ashe says he supports the new NCAA ruling tightening eligibility requirements for college athletic scholarships. Disputing critics of the controversial rule—including Georgetown basketball coach John Thompson—Ashe insists colleges do a "disservice when they accept athletes who can't meet academic demands."

Jan. 18: Black financier Reginald Lewis, head of TLC Beatrice International, donates one-million dollars to Howard University for scholarship aid to disadvantaged students. The gift, which will be matched by federal funds, is part of $2 million Lewis recently donated to 20 cultural and educational institutions.

Jan. 18: Georgetown basketball coach John Thompson boycotts the second game in a row, this one against Big East Conference team Providence, continuing his protest of that controversial new NCAA rule governing eligibility requirements for athletic scholarships to incoming freshmen.

Jan. 19: Newly elected President George Bush pledges before a national teachers' group he will be the "education president." At his first inaugural event, Bush acknowledges the budgetary crunch will make it difficult to increase federal aid to education.

Jan. 21: Georgetown basketball coach John Thompson returns to the bench, ending his one-week protest of a controversial NCAA rule that restricts athletic scholarships for freshmen. Thompson returned after meeting with top NCAA officials, who agreed to recommend delaying the enactment of the new provision until 1992, allowing an extensive reevaluation of its impact.

Jan. 27: Four school board members and a former district superintendent in the Bronx (NY) are indicted on corruption charges. The indictments are the first in a city-wide scandal stemming from the arrest last November of an elementary school principal on crack charges.

Jan. 31: The South Orange-Maplewood (NJ) Board of Education defeats a reorganization proposal to eliminate overcrowding in grades K-5 and to solve racial imbalance in the middle schools by requiring all fifth and sixth graders to attend one school; seventh and eighth graders, another one. Parents and community leaders urge that task forces be created to find solutions to resolve the dilemmas.

Feb. 2: The North Plainfield (NJ) Board of Education approves a desegregation plan to house all sixth graders in one school and K-5 grade students in three others. The new plan, effective next September, is designed to achieve racial and ethnic enrollment balance.

Feb. 7: School officials in racially split Boston (MA) say they will consider a new assignment plan that eliminates busing elementary students. Critics charge busing has not worked since the courts ordered it 16 years ago to achieve integration. School superintendent Laval Wilson maintains it is now "time to focus on quality."

Feb. 8: Black students from Ivy League and Boston-area colleges develop strategies on overcoming the subtle and overt barriers to success for blacks. The 400 students at the Harvard three-day conference will form a network to improve the future of blacks in America.

Feb. 8:   Middlebury (VT) College sends a corps of professors and admissions officials to DeWitt Clinton High School in New York City, the first act of a partnership formed by the small, liberal arts college and the urban high school to improve the educational quality of predominantly black and Hispanic students.

Feb. 8:   Critics of college entrance exams renew their debate over the validity of such tests after a federal district judge in New York rules they discriminate against high school girls. Supporters of the Scholastic Aptitude Test (SAT) say scholarships to boys (who score higher) and girls will be awarded on criteria other than the tests. Opponents argue colleges that use additional criteria first develop their pool of eligible applicants solely from SAT scores.

Feb. 28:   Nationally acclaimed high school principal Joe Clark of Paterson (NJ) says he will start a nonprofit foundation called CLOUT. Through it, Clark says he will teach principals how to use his drill-instructor tactics to restore discipline in their schools. One of Clark's critics, who recently visited Eastside High, accused him of not having an instructional program, adding that he can only teach "how to use a bullhorn, baseball bat, and whip."

March 3:   About 100 students at the New York University Law School stage sit-ins and rallies, demanding a better climate for minority groups. The multiracial coalition presented Dean John Sexton an 11-point proposal which includes establishing a committee to investigate racial bias, increasing the number of minority students and faculty, and offering a course on relations in the law.

March 8:   A 15-year-old federal desegregation lawsuit against Louisiana's colleges and universities appears close to being settled. Lawyers representing black and white educational institutions in the state delayed a hearing with the court-appointed special master overseeing the effort after a whirlwind set of talks. Blacks fear a compromise settlement that would eliminate traditionally black schools.

March 8:   Republican National Committee Chairman Lee Atwater resigns from the Howard University Board of Trustees after students occupy the main administration building. More than 1,000 students and black leaders called for Atwater's removal because of his role in a controversial Bush presidential campaign ad featuring convict Willie Horton, who murdered a MD couple while out on parole from a MA prison. Atwater told Howard Board Chairman John E.

Jacob he resigned because he could "never forgive himself" if someone were hurt in the protest.

March 10: Howard University students end their five-day protest after officials agree to their demands. The university promised not to punish students for their actions, which prompted former Bush campaign manager Lee Atwater to resign from the board of trustees. Other demands include adding more black studies programs, improving financial aid procedures, and making various improvements in dormitories and campus security.

March 10: Eastside High School principal Joe Clark, nationally renowned for his tough-guy tactics at his Paterson (NJ) campus, is suspended for five days because of a school variety show featuring male and female stripteasers. Clark says he may retire at the end of the school year.

March 20: The state of Arkansas agrees to pay $118 million over the next 10 years and to encourage desegregation statewide under a proposed settlement in federal court. The money will fund educational programs for blacks in three school districts, including Little Rock, where illegal segregation has existed for the past 30 years.

March 20: Entertainer/philanthropist Bill Cosby receives an honorary Doctor of Laws degree from Howard University. Cosby included Howard among four black institutions to which he donated $1.3 million last year.

March 21: Controversial New Jersey principal Joe Clark announces he will take a leave of absence from Eastside High School. Clark, whose bullhorn-and-baseball bat tactics are the subject of a hit movie, "Lean On Me," says he is involved in preliminary talks with new federal drug czar William Bennett.

March 23: The first black school superintendent in Boston (MA) may lose his job, if critics have their way. Laval Wilson has headed the racially divided system since 1985; now that his contract is up for renewal, his opponents insist he should be let go. Even his backers admit the 30-year educator "lacks the vision for the position."

March 28: The NAACP ends an eight-year battle to desegregate the school district of Los Angeles—the nation's second largest. NAACP lawyers assert their suit has merit, but that the agency can no longer afford to pursue it.

March 31: Joe Clark, the New Jersey high school principal known nationwide for patrolling Eastside High School with a baseball bat and a bullhorn, announces he will sue the Paterson City Council and school board for $10 million. The officials passed a resolution earlier this month recommending Clark's ouster for driving away up to 150 teachers and harassing and humiliating those who remained. Clark calls the charges "egregious."

April 5: An NCAA poll finds seven out of 10 black college athletes feel they are perceived as necessary but not entirely welcome in football and basketball programs, adding they feel "racially isolated." The study also reports universities seem more interested in recruiting black athletes than black students who are not athletes.

April 6: President George Bush sends a seven-point, $422 million proposal to Congress to make educational excellence a "classroom reality." Features include programs to reward successful schools, teachers, and students; more magnet schools; and grants for drug education programs.

April 6: Boys and Girls High School principal Frank Mickens reportedly succeeds in reversing his Brooklyn (NY) school trend. Following similar "tough-guy" tactics of nationally recognized New Jersey principal Joe Clark, Mickens has greatly decreased the school's dropout rate while dramatically increasing the rate of graduates attending four-year colleges.

April 12: Education Secretary Lauro Cavazos tells states they are obliged either to improve center-city schools or to close them down and transport students to better schools elsewhere.

April 13: Boston schools superintendent Laval Wilson is hired for two more years. But his hotly contested contract includes a clause to evaluate the city's first black superintendent every six months.

April 19: Public school and health care systems in America lag far behind those in other prosperous countries, according to a study released by the congressional Joint Economic Committee. Ironically, the U.S. spends more on these systems than do her industrialized counterparts.

April 20: Major changes are announced today to desegregate state universities in Louisiana. A court-appointed special master recommends establishing a single board of higher education to replace the current four boards, and providing more money to enhance traditionally black schools, alleviating minority concerns.

April 29: In Nashville (TN), hospital officials debate a proposal to merge predominantly black Meharry/Hubbard Hospital and predominantly white Nashville Metropolitan General Hospital. Meharry, a private facility, needs more patients to be economically viable; Metropolitan General, a public hospital, needs additional patient space. Race, turf, and pride are at the heart of the debate between the two century-old hospitals.

May 3:   Candidates for doctoral degrees are taking longer than ever to complete their dissertations, which may result in a shortage of college professors, scientists, and other highly skilled professionals. The Council of Graduate Schools says students earned their doctorates in five-and-a-half years in the sixties, compared with seven years today.

May 11:   New York City Schools Chancellor Richard Green dies after an asthma attack in his home at age 52. Dr. Green served as the first black to head the nation's largest school system for only 14 months. His successor faces staggering problems including high dropout rates, racial tension, deteriorating buildings, and drugs.

May 15:   First Lady Barbara Bush receives an honorary doctorate from Bennett College in Greensboro, NC. She admonishes graduates of the all-black women's college to help the young "enslaved by ignorance to learn their ABCs."

May 19:   President Bush praises the dramatic turnaround at Wilson High School in Rochester. Thanks to a coalition headed by the Urban League and Eastman Kodak, the high school that once led the district in suspensions, dropouts, and truancies is now ranked the ninth best magnet school in New York state.

May 20:   Education Secretary Lauro Cavazos announces the creation of a task force to promote and study choice programs, saying choice is "the cornerstone to restructuring elementary and secondary education" in the U.S.

May 23:   Black public school students remain "largely isolated" and receive an inferior education, despite federal and local efforts to provide equal opportunities in the 35 years since the U.S. Supreme Court ordered the end of segregated schools. That's the finding of a panel of 29 prominent black scholars commissioned by the Joint Center for Political Studies to assess the state of education for blacks.

May 26:   The Washington, DC school system operates schools it does not need, wastes money hiring bureaucrats of little use, and often fails to meet the academic and social needs of the 88,000-student school district. A panel of distinguished civic leaders suggests closing nearly a dozen schools, extending the school year, and toughening graduation requirements among its recommended overhauling of the system.

June 2:   *The New York Times* reports more than a dozen prominent leaders would fit the mold for the successor to New York City Schools Chancellor Richard Green, who died last month. The search committee, in its first meeting, says it is committed to finding a black or Hispanic to head the nation's largest school system.

June 17:   Orthopedic surgeon Augustus White III is named president of the University of Maryland-Baltimore, becoming the second black to serve recently as head of a historically white university in the state. He will oversee the professional schools of medicine, law, dentistry, social work, pharmacy, and nursing.

June 23:   The Howard County (MD) NAACP charges an "aura of negativism" exists for black students in the county school system. It wants school officials to increase the number of minority teachers and administrators and to develop clearer policies about black academic achievement.

June 30:   Slightly more than half of New York City's public school students are unable to read at the level expected of their grade. The School Board is using tougher reading standards for testing students, who did show a small improvement over last year.

July 3:   Mary Hatwood Futrell, the outgoing president of the National Education Association, calls for a "massive, systemwide restructuring" of the nation's schools. In her farewell address, the head of the country's largest union says it's "too late for tinkering" with the system, that it must be completely transformed.

July 3:   More than 300 friends gather for the retirement reception of Howard University President James E. Cheek. During his 20-year tenure, he tripled the university's graduate programs, started a radio and TV station, and added several major buildings to the city-wide campus.

July 12:   A model school aimed at improving academic excellence and race relations will open next fall in Pittsburgh. The principal of the Prospect Middle School Center for Multiracial, Multicultural, and Multiethnic Education says courses will be offered to encourage students to respect each other.

July 15:   The Paterson (NJ) school board names Charles Lighty to succeed Joe Clark as the new principal of Eastside High School. Clark, who became nationally known in the Warner Bros. movie depiction of his life, "Lean on Me," announced his retirement plans after his recent open-heart surgery.

Aug. 2:   Four black parents in Kansas City, MO, sue the state and city school boards, charging the current desegregation plan denies their children access to the best public schools, thus victimizing them rather than removing the barriers of illegal discrimination. The parents are seeking vouchers for their children to attend parochial or private schools at taxpayer expense.

Aug. 6:   A Sri Lankan woman, seeking to buy 108-year-old Bishop College in Dallas, forfeits $75,000 worth of sapphires that she put up as a deposit, after failing to secure the money needed to buy the school. A bankruptcy court shut down the historically black school last year because of its $18 million deficit.

Aug. 6:   Officials and alumni of Southern and Grambling State Universities are trying to block a federally ordered desegregation plan that they say would dilute and ultimately destroy both historically black schools in Louisiana.

Aug. 10:   College tuition and fees will cost five to nine percent more for the 1989-1990 academic year than for last year. The College Board's annual survey of college prices shows tuition rises outpacing inflation for the ninth consecutive year.

Aug. 12:   The black superintendent of schools in Chicago is not expected to be rehired when his contract expires next spring. Dr. Manford Byrd's critics accuse him of failing to provide leadership over the nation's third-largest school system.

Aug. 15:   The newly hired president of the University of Maryland's professional schools complex in Baltimore quits before his first day on the job. Augustus White III decided to keep his post at Harvard Medical School after learning that the university's board of regents planned to remove the schools of law and social work from his campus. White had been hailed by university officials as a preeminent physician and scholar and a "sterling black role model."

Aug. 15:   Associate Justice Byron White blocks a federal court order intended to desegregate Louisiana's public colleges and universities. Under the federal plan, the board of Southern University, the state's largest predominantly black school, would have been eliminated.

Aug. 16:   Calling it a "painful but necessary process," DC school superintendent Andrew Jenkins shifts 73 top officials to local schools in an effort to end the frequent criticism that the system administration was bloated and inefficient. In the largest reshuffling of executives in more than a decade, Jenkins said he will also ask 88 others to seek early retirement.

Sept. 3: As the new school term begins in Chicago, parents—not the board of education—take control of the nation's third-largest school system. Education experts say it's "the most radical attempt" to revamp a big-city school system . . . "absolutely precedent-breaking" . . . "close to an educational meltdown."

Sept. 7: Officials in southeastern Mississippi are trying to reverse the resegregation pattern developing in the public school system by cracking down on whites who claim residence in areas where they don't live so that their children can avoid predominantly black classrooms.

Sept. 25: Leaders in government, business, and education say America is developing into a nation of educational haves and have-nots, who are fast becoming employment haves and have-nots; that this polarization follows racial lines; and that the effect on the economy and the country could be devastating.

Sept. 25: Joseph Fernandez is named as the new Chancellor of New York City Schools, heading the nation's largest public school system. While heading the fourth-largest system in Miami, Fernandez earned a national reputation as an innovator and risk-taker.

Oct. 2: Nearly half of all black children in this country live in poverty, according to a new congressional study. And, by the year 2010, one of three children in America will be from a minority group; as a result, a steadily growing proportion of the child population will be disadvantaged.

Oct. 21: The fund-raising drive begins for the Sister Thea Bowman Black Catholic Educational Foundation, which will provide scholarships for minority students. The foundation is named in honor of a 51-year-old black nun with bone cancer who nevertheless has been active in minority education.

Nov. 1: Five colleges and universities from around the country announce their new consortium, which will recruit and train minority teachers. The pilot program hopes to be a model for areas with large minority populations.

Nov. 15: The ACLU and NAACP in Seattle (WA) reportedly will go to court if school board officials end busing to achieve racial balance. An initiative that allows the board to use six percent of the city's tax dollars for magnet schools if busing is stopped barely won approval—primarily through absentee ballots.

Nov. 22:   The alma mater of the nation's first elected black governor will name its new library in his honor. Governor-Elect L. Douglas Wilder says he is "humbled and flattered" that the $6.5 million learning resource center at Virginia Union University will bear his name.

Dec. 7:   Newly hired NY City schools chancellor Joseph Fernandez appoints Amina Abdur-Rahman as deputy schools chancellor for programs. The 41-year-old businesswoman has no college degree, but developed a successful track record as a teacher in the city's Urban League street academies for high school dropouts and later as director of its education programs.

Dec. 13:   A federal judge approves a $130 million settlement of an Arkansas desegregation case, ending a seven-year-old legal battle to integrate Little Rock and its neighboring schools.

Dec. 14:   The Atlanta (GA) school board reprimands superintendent J. Jerome Harris for failing to inform them he has yet to meet state certification requirements for his post—even though he's been on the job for 18 months. He has until next month to do so or face other action. The *Atlanta Constitution* also reports the board is withdrawing the contract for Harris's top aide who also lacked sufficient credentials to hold his job.

Dec. 14:   A federal appeals panel declares Topeka (KS) has not done enough to desegregate the city's schools since the landmark *Brown v. Board of Education* decision 35 years ago. The opinion overturns a 1987 ruling which said Topeka was not responsible for lingering segregation because the school board did not intend to promote the practice.

Race Relations

Jan. 1:   Pope John Paul II calls on all "men of good will" to help build a world of peace and justice in 1989. In a sermon at St. Peter's Basilica, the pontiff emphasizes the need to defend the rights of minority groups.

Jan. 1:   As the new year begins, *The New York Times* reports that "skinheads" are a growing population in the city. These young men, who say they are anti-drug, anti-gay, anti-communist, and militantly pro-American, are joining forces with old-line racist groups like the

Ku Klux Klan and newer neo-Nazi groups in a score of states and have been charged with racist violence.

Jan. 4: The Anglican community is moving a step closer to having its first female bishop. The *Washington Post* reports the Episcopal Diocese of Massachusetts has received majority approval of Rev. Barbara Harris from the church's 119 dioceses and expects approval by a majority of the nation's bishops. Her consecration is scheduled for February 11 in Boston.

Jan. 5: The only cable television franchise in Howard County (MD) has decided to discontinue two channels with programming geared to blacks, Asians, and several ethnic groups. The *Washington Post* reports community leaders are protesting the decision and are considering a move to ask the county not to renew its contract with Howard Cable Television Associates. The company says its decision is "purely business-based."

Jan. 6: The Montgomery County (MD) Council may renew its threat to withhold money from the Hyattstown Volunteer Fire Company in light of reports that the company has reinstated the white volunteer chief who called a black firefighter "nigger boy" nine months ago.

Jan. 7: The *Washington Post* reports a disproportionate number of whites are awarded work release and other privileges at Maryland's Patuxent Institution, apparently buttressing some lawmakers' contentions that the counseling and therapy techniques used at the predominantly black prison are biased against minorities.

Jan. 11: Harris Trust and Savings Bank in Chicago has agreed to pay $14 million in back pay to female and minority employees as part of a record settlement of federal charges of sexual and racial discrimination. *The New York Times* reports the bank still denies that the employees had faced discrimination.

Jan. 12: A national survey has found that blacks and whites are "worlds apart" in their perceptions of race relations, with large majorities of whites believing that blacks are treated equally in America and similarly large majorities of blacks disagreeing. The NAACP Legal Defense and Educational Fund also finds that there is a decline nationwide in white opposition to school busing.

Jan. 13: The NAACP and the New York Open Housing Center, an organization that advocates fair housing, are suing *The New York Times,* asserting the newspaper carries racially discriminatory housing advertisements. The suit claims that display real estate advertising in the newspaper has included white models almost exclusively for more than two decades. A spokesman for *The Times* says it has not had time to study the complaint thoroughly but that "a first reading would indicate that it is without merit."

Jan. 13: A team of researchers have found one of the strongest indications so far of racial differences in the kind of medical care Americans receive. *The New York Times* reports Harvard University researchers found that a significantly higher proportion of white people admitted to Massachusetts hospitals with heart problems undergo coronary bypass operations and cardiac catheterizations than do blacks. The study suggests that "racial inequalities exist in the provision of cardiac care in Massachusetts," say Dr. Mark Wenneker and Dr. Arnold Epstein.

Jan. 13: Bernhard Goetz, the New York man who shot four blacks in a subway five years ago, was sentenced to one year in jail for possessing an unlicensed gun which he used in the shooting.

Jan. 15: Blacks in Mississippi say the newly released film, "Mississippi Burning," revives painful memories of a time they would rather forget. The movie is a fictionalized account of the murder of three civil rights workers in Philadelphia, MS, during the height of racial violence in the '60s.

Jan. 15: The NAACP has suspended its involvement in a lawsuit charging *The New York Times* with publishing racially discriminatory housing advertisements. Executive Director Benjamin Hooks told reporters the organization had not talked with the newspaper before filing the suit, which Hooks called "an administrative oversight" that was unfair to the newspaper.

Jan. 17: Allegations of racism and excessive force have been leveled against Long Beach (CA) police officers in the wake of a violent confrontation—secretly taped by an NBC television crew—that showed an officer apparently shoving a black police officer activist into a store window, shattering the glass. The *Washington Post* reports the man, Don Jackson, said he was conducting a "sting operation" aimed at uncovering police racism.

Jan. 17: A crowd threw stones and bottles and set fire to cars in a predominantly black section of Miami (FL) after the police shot and killed an unarmed black man who was fleeing police on a motorcycle. Published reports claim more than 1,000 off-duty policemen were called in to help quell the riots in Overtown and Liberty City.

Jan. 18: A second day of disturbances continues in Miami, with blacks saying they are outraged at the police shooting an unarmed black man in a poor section of the city. A second black died from head injuries. Authorities are calling for calm and an end to the rioting and looting. An independent panel is investigating the shooting.

Jan. 20: Calm begins to return to Miami after four days of rioting and looting. National Football League Commissioner Pete Rozelle predicts the violence will have no impact on Super Bowl XXIII, scheduled to be played this Sunday in Miami.

Jan. 21: The *Washington Post* reports Southern Baptists meeting at a race relations conference in Nashville (TN) are asking their followers to "hire more blacks and publicly repent of their racist past."

Jan. 22: Six white supremacists march through downtown Atlanta surrounded by National Guard troops in riot gear as hundreds of angry counterdemonstrators hurl rocks, bricks, and insults at them. The *Washington Post* reports no marchers were hit, but at least six law enforcement officers were injured by the projectiles.

Jan. 23: Black NAACP members in Howard County (MD) say they may protest the county's granting water and sewer service to Turf Valley Country Club, whose manager called a black NAACP member a "nigger" in a taped telephone conversation last year. The blacks say that even though the manager was dismissed, the racial slur still rankles.

Jan. 24: Police officer William Lozano has been charged with two counts of manslaughter and released after posting $10,000 bond for shooting an unarmed black man last week that touched off a week of rioting and looting in the Miami neighborhoods of Overtown and Liberty City.

Jan. 24: More than 10 years after a group of Klansman blocked a Southern Christian Leadership Conference march in Decatur (AL), federal officials have finally sentenced the six Klansmen. *The New York Times* reports the federal sentences range from a few months to two years for their roles in the violence in which two black marchers and two Klansmen were wounded.

Jan. 25: The *Washington Post* reports the chief of local airports police force has ordered an investigation into complaints of racial discrimination against black officers at Dulles International Airport. The black officers say they routinely receive poor job performance evaluations, are passed over for promotions, and are not rotated among assignments fairly.

Jan. 27: A militant New York Jewish organization has threatened to disrupt the campaign of former Ku Klux Klan leader David Duke for a seat in the Louisiana legislature. *The Star Ledger* reports the Jewish Defense Organization vows to "meet force with force" in trying to defeat Duke. Local Jewish groups in New Orleans say they are outraged by the New York group's threats.

Jan. 27: The *Washington Post* quotes health officials in the District of Columbia as saying blacks living in the city are twice as likely as whites to die prematurely. The Centers for Disease Control studied the differences in the health status between the races in Washington and found that heart disease accounted for the largest percentage of the premature deaths.

Jan. 29: The Justice Department has launched an investigation of the Holiday Spa health club organization, one of the largest in the metropolitan Washington area, after allegations of bias against blacks. The *Washington Post* says the probe focuses on alleged attempts to discourage blacks customers from joining Holiday clubs that are described as more upscale and mostly white.

Jan. 30: Commercial bank branch closings in the New York metropolitan area over the last three years have made it more difficult for blacks and other minorities to gain access to banking services. *The New York Times* quotes a recently released study that shows the problem affected not just poor black areas, but also those with relatively high median incomes as well.

Jan. 31: The New York *Daily News* has learned that National League owners have zeroed in on longtime Yankee broadcaster Bill White as their new president. The league has been seeking a black to be their new leader since Bart Giamatti was elected to a five-year term to replace Peter Ueberroth as Commissioner.

Feb. 8: Two black members of baseball's Hall of Fame say that Bill White's selection as president of the National League is a "milestone" in race relations. Bob Gibson and Lou Brock, both former teammates of White, say the full impact of White's selection cannot be judged until it becomes clear that White is not alone as a black executive in the major leagues.

Feb. 10: Angrily labeling New York Police Commissioner Benjamin Ward a "nonentity," Hispanic leaders are asking Mayor Ed Koch to deal personally with charges that the police department is insensitive to their needs. *The Star Ledger* quotes the leaders as saying Ward's "insensitivity toward Latinos is too offensive to permit further dialogue."

Feb. 24:   Manhattan Borough President David Dinkins is accusing New York Mayor Ed Koch of using a "double standard" by spotlighting the race issue in the mayoral campaign. Dinkins is quoted by the *Daily News* as saying Koch told a Washington breakfast group earlier this week that he—Koch—would seek to win at least 25 percent of the black vote and that he hoped national black leaders like Jesse Jackson and Atlanta Mayor Andrew Young would not campaign in New York for Dinkins.

March 1:   Morristown (NJ) black leaders are reiterating their call for changes in the police department's performance. *The Star Ledger* reports the town council and the mayor vow to meet in small groups with black residents and to investigate calls for more police training and a citizen's complaint panel to review police conduct.

March 2:   Five black teenagers have been arrested in the beating of a 39-year-old white man in the Bronx. The police say the beating was racially motivated, adding the youths shouted "whitey" and other racial slurs as they attacked the man.

March 2:   FBI Director William Sessions has launched efforts to erase job bias against blacks, Hispanics, and women within the bureau and is promising measurable results within a year. Sessions told a House Judiciary subcommittee he will not only combat hiring bias but also racial harassment and a practice under which Hispanic agents sometimes do not advance because they are constantly thrown into stopgap duties requiring Spanish speakers, thereby building up little in-depth investigative experience.

March 20: The time to start rearing an unbiased child is at age two, when he or she is beginning to notice that people come in different shapes, colors, and sexes. That's the finding of the National Association for the Education of Young Children, quoted in *Jet* magazine. The 65,000-member group advises: "Don't assume simple exposure to diversity is enough to kill the seeds of prejudice, but, on the other hand, don't pretend such differences do not exist."

March 20: U.S. Civil Rights Commissioner Mary Frances Berry says recent racial unrest on college campuses may have been caused by white students who believe they have suffered reverse discrimination. She adds, however, that in many cases the opposite is true.

March 23: Blacks in Howard County (MD) are dissatisfied with a report from the county's Office of Human Rights which, the blacks charge, did a "woefully inadequate" probe of investigating racial slurs from a white country club owner at blacks. One of the blacks told the county council that if that's the best the officials can do, then the "governmental process really needs to be looked at."

March 29: The Black Student Union at the University of Maryland-College Park is upset with the college administration over conditions it is imposing on the group to bring in Nation of Islam leader Louis Farrakhan. The officials are demanding the student union pay an estimated $14,000 to build a fence around the coliseum where Farrakhan is speaking, bring in metal detectors, and keep on duty 43 additional campus police officers to ward off trouble from demonstrators hostile to Farrakhan's views. The student union president calls the demands "outrageous."

March 31: A former Black Panther convicted in one of the most politically charged cop shootings of the '70s is seeking to have his conviction dismissed. The New York *Daily News* reports lawyers for Richard (Dhoruba) Moore are basing their request on FBI documents showing massive amounts of evidence were withheld from his trial.

April 4: A former manager for a Wall Street brokerage firm has filed a $15 million class-action suit, charging the company with race and sex discrimination. Sheila Eileen Venable claims that Dean Witter Reynolds consistently discriminated against her because of her race and sex from July, 1981, when she was hired as a management trainee, until January 4, 1984, when she was dismissed. Officials at Dean Witter have declined comment on the suit.

April 5: About 250 outraged students have converged on the administration building at State University at Stony Brook (NY) to protest the arrest and suspension of a popular basketball player on rape charges. The New York *Daily News* reports the accused student claims he was at home during the time the alleged rape occurred.

April 6: White women are nearly twice as likely as black women to be awarded alimony, according to a Census Bureau report. The report also indicates that white women were also more likely than black women to receive property settlements.

April 7: A crowd of 300 black faculty members and students rallied in support of University of Maryland basketball coach Bob Wade. Wade's program is being investigated by the university and NCAA officials for possible violations involved in transportation provided to former Terrapins guard Rudy Archer. Wade has acknowledged that the rides occurred, but has said he was not involved nor did he authorize them.

April 9: A conference on black-Jewish relations became unruly in New Orleans when some participants clashed over whether blacks had an obligation to denounce anti-Semitic remarks made by other blacks. *The New York Times* reports that despite the controversy, many conferees left feeling as if they had gained a better understanding of each other as well as tools for improving the dialogue between the two groups.

April 10: Three months after racial unrest broke out in Miami, city officials say the aftershocks and effects are still there. The Benevolent and Protective Order of Elks has dropped its plans to hold its national convention in the city next year, and officials fear that tourism will continue to drop off as long as hostility remains among whites and nonwhites.

April 11: A former Miami police officer whose acquittal in the death by beating of a black man led to race riots in 1980 has been arrested on drug charges. Alex Marrero was charged, along with a federal agent, with conspiring to distribute cocaine and to commit bribery.

April 13: Former world middleweight boxing champion Sugar Ray Robinson is pronounced dead at the Brotman Medical Center in Los Angeles; he was 67. Officials say the cause of his death could not be immediately determined, but Robinson had been ill in recent months.

April 19: Volkswagen of America, Inc. has agreed to pay $670,000 and the United Auto Workers $48,000 to settle claims that they discriminated against black employees. *The New York Times* reports about 800 blacks could share in the money from the settlement, which ends a six-year-long case.

April 27: Hispanics in Gaithersburg, MD, claim they are the victims of a string of racially motivated attacks over the past two months. A Hispanic civic leader says the assaults have all been by white teenagers.

May 1: Twenty years after black students took over the student union at Cornell University in Ithaca (NY), students and faculty members find themselves faced with some of those same problems that prompted the disturbance in 1969. Students are demanding more black studies programs and more open-enrollment policies. The biggest sticking point is Cornell's continued investment in companies that do business in South Africa.

May 3: A Portland (OR) man has pleaded guilty to murder in the racial slaying of a black man whose head was struck so hard with a baseball bat that the bat split. Prosecutors plan to seek a life sentence with a mandatory minimum term of 20 years on the murder conviction.

May 12: Two New York City police officers have been charged with beating a black man and subjecting him to racial abuse, the latest indictment in an investigation of allegations of brutality by white officers against minorities in Queens.

May 22: A federal judge refuses to dismiss a racial discrimination suit brought by a light-skinned black female against her darker-skinned black supervisor in Atlanta (GA). The supervisor's attorney requested the dismissal, arguing discrimination cases must be between two different races; the presiding judge disagreed.

May 25: The president of the Greater Houston Convention and Visitors Bureau has resigned after weeks of criticism over derogatory remarks he made about minority-group members of the Houston City Council. Don Vaughn resigned, according to *The New York Times,* after the local NAACP chapter threatened to pull the group's national convention out of Houston in 1991.

June 11: The northward migration of blacks has begun to reverse itself after 100 years, with blacks returning to their southern roots. The Census Bureau reports it expects the pattern to come into sharper focus after the 1990 census.

June 15: Michigan black leaders are still waiting for a new strategy that would include more lottery advertising dollars for black-owned media and put more blacks in policy- and budget-making executive decisions. *The Detroit News* reports representatives from the Michigan Legislative Black Caucus, the National Urban League, the NAACP, and Operation PUSH say lottery officials want more time to study the 78-page report outlining the blacks' grievances and requests.

June 20: A prominent black Roman Catholic priest announces he plans to start an independent African-American Catholic congregation. The *Washington Post* quotes Father George Stallings, Jr., as saying he and "several hundred black Catholics" will launch the new church next month because the established church has "failed to meet the spiritual and cultural needs of African-American Catholics."

June 21: James Cardinal Hickey of Washington is sharply criticizing the plans of Father George Stallings to start an unauthorized African-American Catholic congregation. The *Washington Post* reports Cardinal Hickey is warning faithful Catholics to stay away from it.

June 22:   Blacks in the broadcasting business say they are wondering when what they consider the so-called "closed-door, old-boy network" will change. The *Washington Post* surveyed the numbers of blacks in broadcasting and found that most blacks are in lower-level, low-profile positions. The paper also quotes network officials who say they seldom hear from qualified blacks, but they are now committed to more aggressive minority hiring.

June 23:   A *New York Times*/WCBS-TV News poll finds black and white New Yorkers agree on many issues facing the city, including a generally pessimistic view of race relations. The poll indicates blacks and whites differ, however, in their preferences for candidates in the upcoming mayoral election. Among registered black Democrats, Manhattan Borough President David Dinkins is first choice; among white registered Democrats, current Mayor Ed Koch ranks first.

June 23:   The mayor and police chief in Annapolis (MD) say they have asked two state law enforcement agencies to investigate allegations of criminal misconduct by members of the city's police department. The probe will focus on charges that white officers have not cooperated with, and in some cases undermined, efforts of an elite drug-fighting squad composed mostly of black officers.

June 24:   The Washington Lawyers' Committee for Civil Rights Under Law is suing thee Washington cab companies and eight drivers, alleging violations of civil rights and of the DC Human Rights law. The lawyers say that blacks in the district are almost seven times as likely as whites to be passed while trying to hail a cab.

June 25:   A state court judge in Mobile (AL) has sentenced a former Ku Klux Klansman to life in prison for the 1981 beating and hanging death of a black teenager. A lawsuit stemming from the killing resulted in a $7 million judgment that bankrupted one Klan organization, the United Klans of America.

June 25:   James Cardinal Hickey, the Archbishop of Washington, has forbidden black Catholic priest George Stallings, Jr., to celebrate Mass. *The New York Times* reports Hickey issued the order because Stallings has charged the church with racism and announced plans to form his own African-American congregation. Stallings responded by saying, "Ain't nobody going to turn me around."

June 25:   Southern Democrats are trying to devise a strategy that will bring white males back into the party. Many conservative Democrats say they are switching parties because they are troubled by what they call the "liberal tilt" of the Democrats.

July 2:	The Justice Department has ended a probe of allegations that white FBI agents in Chicago racially harassed a black colleague. The *Washington Post* quotes a department spokesman as saying in a written statement that "no prosecutable violations" were established.
July 3:	In defiance of the Archbishop of Washington, Roman Catholic priest George Stallings, Jr., celebrates Mass and establishes what he terms an African-American Catholic congregation, the Imani Temple. Thousands pack the Howard University campus in Washington for the service.
July 3:	Reaction is mixed among blacks over the new Spike Lee movie, "Do the Right Thing." *The New York Times* reports some blacks are troubled about the movie depicting the hottest summer day in a single block of Bedford-Stuyvesant, where racial tensions erupt among racial groups. The newspaper quotes others as being elated by the movie, that it "tells it like it is."
July 5:	The Archbishop of Washington has suspended Father George Stallings for defying his orders not to celebrate Mass and form his own African-American Catholic church. James Cardinal Hickey wrote Stallings that his actions were "destructive" and a "public act of disobedience," according to published reports.
July 9:	A group of black investors led by Bertram M. Lee is buying the Denver Nuggets in a move that would make the National Basketball Association team the first minority-owned major league sports franchise. *The New York Times* reports Lee and his group are completing negotiations to buy the Nuggets for a reported $65 million.
July 11:	The new black coach of the New York Knicks tells reporters at a news conference that he sees himself as the coach of the Knicks for the '90s. Stu Jackson has signed a three-year deal worth $325,000 a year, according to the *New York Post*.
July 11:	The 13 black Roman Catholic bishops in the U.S. have sharply rebuffed Father George Stallings for establishing a separate African-American congregation. *The New York Times* reports the bishops issued a statement calling Stallings' actions "precipitous and ill-advised."
July 12:	New York State courts are staffed so overwhelmingly by whites that minorities have lost confidence in the justice system. That's the finding of the New York State Judicial Commission on Minorities, which traced what it calls a long pattern by New York court officials of ignoring warnings about racial bias.

July 13: New York State's Chief Judge and the Chief Administrator of the Courts say they are awaiting the recommendations from a Judicial Commission on Minorities to determine what action they should take to "confront the apparent perception among some citizens that minorities are not treated fairly in the courts," according to *The New York Times.*

July 13: A Federal Reserve economist says the home mortgage lending study being conducted by the Federal Reserve Bank of Boston will show that a disproportionately low number of loans are being granted by local banks and thrifts in minority neighborhoods. The *Boston Globe* quotes Karl Case as saying the long-anticipated study will reveal loan patterns "not dramatically different" from those indicated in a preliminary study by the central bank in January.

July 13: The hundreds of bias-related crimes reported each year in New York are all referred to one of the police department's tiniest units, with only 18 investigators and no assigned budget. Yet, according to New York *Newsday*, civil rights groups say the Anti-Bias Unit has been strikingly effective in defusing neighborhood tensions, involving local communities, and making quick arrests in some major cases.

July 13: Prince George's County State's Attorney Alex Williams, the county's first to hold the post, is involved in a dispute with police officers over what he calls a bungled case. At the heart of the controversy is how Williams handled the latest in a series of police brutality cases in the predominantly black county. Williams sought a manslaughter indictment for the murder of a black man recently, and blamed white police officers for tainting the investigation and obstructing justice when only a misdemeanor indictment was handed down. Police union officials accuse Williams of yielding to political pressure from blacks, according to the *Washington Post,* and say he owes the force an apology.

July 16: The Kansas City (MO) city council has voted to restore a local cable television company's public access channel that the city shut off last year after the Ku Klux Klan applied to use it for broadcasts. *The New York Times* reports the council amended its agreement with American Cablevision and restored the channel because city officials concluded they could not win a court action filed against them by the Klan, which charged their First Amendment right to free speech was violated.

July 17: A widening health gap between blacks and whites is due in part to low self-esteem among blacks who react adversely to the stresses of racism. *The New York Times* quotes panelists at the National Medical Association's annual convention in Orlando (FL) as saying they also found that high rates of cancer, substance abuse, and hypertension among poor blacks can be linked to such self-defeating behavior as overreacting to a perceived threat, poor eating habits, and self-medication with drugs and alcohol for depression.

July 18: The U.S. Census Bureau has agreed to conduct a random survey of 150,000 homes along with next year's total population tally that could lead to the first adjustment in the census for any undercounting of racial, ethnic, and other groups. *The New York Times* reports the agreement could lead to greater political representation and more federal aid for cities across the country.

July 20: The Grand Dragon of the Maryland Knights of the Ku Klux Klan pleads guilty to racial harassment and assault with intent to commit murder against a black man in Baltimore, but insists he intended neither murder nor racial harassment. A former exalted cyclops of the Klan, faced with the same charges, freely admits the assault and racial slurs, according to the *Washington Post,* then apologizes to the black men he attacked while in the same courtroom with them.

July 25: The owner of the Padres donates a letter written in 1959 by President John F. Kennedy to Jackie Robinson to the Hall of Fame in Cooperstown (NY). The *New York Post* says when Joan Kroc when heard about the letter, she knew it should be in the Hall of Fame. In the letter, Kennedy promises to help fight racial injustice.

Aug. 1: A New York State appeals court has upheld the manslaughter and assault convictions of three young white men in the Howard Beach attack three years ago. *The New York Times* reports the court refused a defense request to reduce the prison sentences imposed on them, saying their actions were "vicious and wanton . . . which cannot be condoned or trivialized."

Aug. 4: A second black Roman Catholic priest has joined Father George Stallings in setting up a separate African-American Catholic church. *The New York Times* reports Father Bruce Greening has been dismissed from his job as principal of St. Mary's Academy in Norfolk (VA). Greening says he will assist Stallings as a minister and in forming a school at the month-old Imani Temple.

Aug. 5: Racial segregation in 10 of the nation's largest cities is more deeply entrenched and takes more forms than social scientists previously thought. That's the finding of a study by the University of Chicago reported in today's edition of *The New York Times*. Another finding is that racial segregation is more pronounced in Northeastern and Midwestern cities, with Chicago being the most segregated.

Aug. 5:   Cardinal John J. O'Connor, one of the most powerful figures in the Catholic church in the U.S., tells a national gathering of black Catholics in Atlanta that their presence is critical to the church. The *Washington Post* quotes O'Connor, who is white, as challenging the group to join in the continuing battle against racism.

Aug. 6:   Gaps between blacks and whites in employment, income, education, and other social and economic areas are so broad that parity is unlikely until after the year 2000. That's the finding of the National Urban League, reported in a new research paper that analyzes black-white parity. In releasing the report at its annual conference meeting in Washington, the League said that despite advances by blacks in recent decades, "African Americans in the contemporary period continue to experience severe disadvantages."

Aug. 8:   President Bush tells the National Urban League conferees meeting in Washington that his administration is "committed to reaching out to minorities, to striking down barriers to free and open access. We will not tolerate discrimination, bigotry, or bias of any kind." After the president's speech, League president and chief executive officer John E. Jacob told reporters that the first six to eight months of a new president's administration is the rhetoric period, that "we will use the next 12 months to determine how well he does."

Aug. 17:   New York State's highest court has decided to hear the appeals of the three young men who were convicted of manslaughter in the Howard Beach racial attack. A lower court unanimously upheld the convictions just two weeks ago, but the high court says there are "questions of law" to review.

Aug. 18:   Four star general Colin Powell tells the National Association of Black Journalists meeting in New York that the armed forces is making strides "that regrettably do not exist in every part of our society, even within your own profession." Powell has been named by President Bush to be the next Chairman of the Joint Chiefs of Staff, which would make him the first black and youngest officer to hold the nation's top military post.

Aug. 25:   A black teenager was shot and killed after he and three companions were chased out of a predominantly white Brooklyn neighborhood where they were looking to buy a used car. The *Washington Post* quotes police officers who say as many as 30 white teenagers chased the youths, apparently seeking revenge for a spoiled romance. The death of Yusef Hawkins is under investigation.

Aug. 31:   Two white youths have been indicted by a Brooklyn (NY) grand jury for second-degree murder, riot, assault, and other charges in the racially motivated shooting of Yusef Hawkins, a black youth, last week.

Sept. 1:   The Federal Reserve Bank of Boston is criticizing mortgage lenders in the city, saying the percentage of loans for properties in predominantly black neighborhoods was substantially lower than that in white neighborhoods. After studying lending patterns in Boston, the Board said real estate agents, developers, lenders, and others share responsibility for the racial pattern of the mortgage loans.

Sept. 1:   A light-skinned black woman in Denver wins her battle to stop the illusion that she is white, even though her parents listed her as white on her birth certificate in an attempt to help her overcome racial bias. Mary Walker says she feels emancipated because now she will not have to be "put in a box I don't fit in."

Sept. 1:   About 20 police officers and an unknown number of demonstrators are injured when a mile-long protest march from Brooklyn turns into a scuffle as more than 7,500 mostly black demonstrators try to cross the Brooklyn Bridge into Manhattan. *The New York Times* reports the demonstration, billed as a "Day of Outrage and Mourning," had been called to protest the killing of a black youth by a white gang last month.

Sept. 3:   In the fourth such protest since the killing of a black teenager 11 days ago, about 300 demonstrators bearing African liberation flags and chanting "Yusef, Yusef"—the name of the teenager—marched through the streets of the Bensonhurst section of Brooklyn. As they had done on two previous marches, residents along the route taunted the marchers with obscenities such as "niggers, go home," "you savages," and "long live South Africa." *The New York Times* reports more than 400 police officers flanked the marchers; there was no violence.

Sept. 5:   Virginia Beach officials and NAACP leaders strongly disagree about what touched off two nights of looting and racially tinged violence as 100,000 people converged on the resort town over Labor Day weekend. The NAACP and the revelers, most of whom were black, dispute the mayor's suggestion that renewed looting yesterday preceded the decision to clear the streets forcibly in a 40-block resort area. The students were in town for the annual Greekfest, which officials say they may cancel in the future.

Sept. 7: Rev. Al Sharpton says he plans to lead a march through the Bensonhurst of Brooklyn, despite arguments that a demonstration might detract from David Dinkins's campaign in next Tuesday's mayoral primary. Quoted the flamboyant minister, "If Dinkins wins on the 12th, it does not solve racism on the 13th."

Sept. 7: President Bush says he will nominate Evan Kemp, Jr., a commissioner of the Equal Employment Opportunity Commission, to become chairman of the agency. Kemp, who has used a wheelchair since being stricken with a polio-like illness at the age of 10, says his nomination proves that Bush "is going to practice what he preaches, that he believes in mainstreaming . . . and has appointed disabled people in the administration."

Sept. 9: Religious leaders in New York are calling for interracial harmony in the wake of the killing of a black teenager last month. At a discussion on race held at *The New York Times,* however, the leaders had trouble understanding each other. Both black and white leaders participating in the setting felt that greater communications is needed among people of different ethnic and racial backgrounds, yet they failed to find a common way to provide such communications.

Sept. 13: An instructor at the University of Maryland-College Park has resigned after allegations that he had made sexist and racist comments to a student on the first day of class. John Strenge reportedly turned in his resignation—at the university's request—after an engineering student complained that Strenge said she "had two strikes against her" because she is female and black. The student, Danita Thomas, told the *Washington Post* she was "insulted and shocked."

Oct. 14: Paul Trotman, a 19-year-old black male, is mourned at his funeral as another victim of New York City's racial and ethnic violence. *The New York Times* reports Trotman died eight weeks after he was struck on the head by a bat-wielding assailant in the Windsor Terrace section of Brooklyn. Police say they are not sure the attack was racially motivated.

Oct. 21: Supporters of former federal judge Alcee Hastings are accusing the Senate of racism after his being impeached on bribery charges. The Afro-American Legal Defense Fund told the *Washington Post* that the Senate had held Hastings to a standard never imposed on whites when it ousted him from office in a rare trial. NAACP Executive Director Benjamin Hooks called Hastings's impeachment double jeopardy, but said he did not find the action racist: "When the vote is 20 to 3 [including the yea vote of black Congressman John Conyers], it's hard to say it's racism."

Oct. 22:   About 800 chanting demonstrators, protesting police brutality, march through Chicago Mayor Richard Daley's home neighborhood of Bridgeport without incident. The march was called to protest the beatings of two black teenagers in August and what the march organizers said is an increase in police brutality since Daley became mayor last April.

Oct. 24:   A forum between Jewish civic and religious leaders and David Dinkins in Queens—intended to reassure the audience about the Democratic mayoral nominee's support for Jewish causes—turns nasty when some attacked him for his friendship with Jesse Jackson. *The New York Times* reports Dinkins refused to denounce his friendship with the civil rights activist, saying he does not believe Jackson is anti-Semitic, that if he were, he would not support him.

Oct. 31:   The percentage of blacks among the nation's military recruits has dropped since 1980. A congressional study published in the *Washington Post* finds that the rate of black military recruits still continues to be higher in the U.S. armed forces than their percentage in the nation's overall population.

Nov. 2:   Baltimore Orioles manager Frank Robinson is named the American League manager of the year. The *Washington Post* reports the first black manager in the league received 23 of 28 first-place votes in balloting announced by the Baseball Writers Association of America.

Nov. 9:   Voter surveys for this week's elections in Virginia and New York City are producing widely divergent and largely inaccurate results. *The New York Times* reports poll takers are divided over whether the survey methods were flawed or people simply lied about voting for a black candidate to avoid seeming biased. The polls predicted a far greater victory margin for both Douglas Wilder, the Governor-Elect of Virginia, and David Dinkins, the Mayor-Elect of New York.

Nov. 15:   Howard University students say they will travel by chartered bus and cars to Virginia Beach in a show of support for a student who alleges he was beaten by riot police there during the Greekfest Labor Day weekend. Quinton Stovall says he will plead not guilty at his nonjury trial on a charge of violating a riot control ordinance.

Nov. 17:   The Raynor racing team, which competes on the Championship Auto Racing Teams Indy-Car Circuit, has hired Willy Ribbs as its driver in a three-year deal that includes Bill Cosby as a backer. If Ribbs qualifies for the Indianapolis 500 next May, The New York

Times reports, he will become the first black driver to compete in this country's most famous auto race.

Nov. 20: A rising tide of racial incidents across the South, including attacks and cross burnings, has provided a sour counterpoint to a decade of electoral progress by blacks. *The New York Times* quotes the Southeastern Regional Director of the NAACP as saying the group is finding a "very great and vehement resurgence of racial incidents in the South . . . . We're still putting out fires, still fighting the old battles over and over again, not because we want to, but because there's no choice."

Nov. 22: The head of the Virginia NAACP says lack of leadership on the part of Virginia Beach officials—not racism—was the most important factor contributing to the outbreak of violence over the Labor Day weekend. Speaking to the Labor Day Review Commission, Jack Gravely is quoted in the *Washington Post* as saying city leaders failed to act on proposals made by black leaders and college students as far back as last year.

Nov. 30: New Jersey's judicial system subtly discriminates against African-American and Hispanic defendants and those of other racial and ethnic minorities. That's the finding of a state Supreme Court task force, which, according to *The New York Times,* is recommending 33 changes including sensitivity training for judges and other judicial employees and bail policies that give more weight to the ability to pay.

Dec. 2: The Prince George's County (MD) police union has elected its first black president. The *Washington Post* reports the election of Corporal Darryl Jones comes at a time when the union is the target of criticism from the county NAACP and members of the black community.

Dec. 3: Montgomery County (MD) NAACP members are confronted by racist slogans spray-painted on trucks belonging to a restaurant where the group is celebrating its founding 52 years ago.

Dec. 5: A group of public housing tenants are suing the federal government, the city of Buffalo, and a suburban town over what they say is widespread segregation in public housing and a rental subsidy program. *The New York Times* reports the lawsuit contends the city of Buffalo and its housing authority caused 22 of the city's 25 housing projects to become racially segregated by discouraging minorities from applying for housing in white areas and vice versa.

Dec. 7: The Miami police department has canceled all vacations and days off and put its 1,100 officers on 12-hour shifts as it prepares for the possibility of rioting when a jury renders its verdict in the case of a Hispanic officer accused of manslaughter in the killing of two unarmed black men. Court officials say that once a verdict is reached, the announcement will be delayed for three hours to give the police time to position their forces.

Dec. 8: Miami police officer William Lozano is convicted of killing two black motorcycle riders after a lengthy, high-profile trial that has become the symbol of the racial tension plaguing the city for more than a decade. Lozano faces up to 45 years in prison.

Dec. 12: New York's most prestigious lawyers' organization, the City Bar Association, is preparing to name its first black president. *The New York Times* reports Conrad Harper, a partner in Simpson, Thatcher & Bartlett, heads a slate of candidates the organization's nominating committee will announce this week; in the past, nomination on the slate has been tantamount to election.

Dec. 19: A Savannah lawyer is killed when a letter bomb explodes in his office, while a similar device is found in a federal court building in Atlanta. Both events occur just two days after a federal appeals court judge is killed with a letter bomb in Birmingham. FBI agents are investigating all three to determine if they are racially motivated and possibly done by the same person or group.

Dec. 20: Federal investigators in Washington say they have found "hard forensic evidence" linking package bombs, including one that killed a federal appellate judge in Alabama and a second that killed a lawyer in Georgia. *The New York Times* reports investigators are now studying civil rights cases involving the judge, Robert S. Vance, and the lawyer, Robert E. Robinson.

Dec. 20: A federal judge has cleared the way for a discrimination suit against *The New York Times* to proceed to trial. The *Washington Post* reports the Open Housing Center is suing the newspaper because it rarely uses nonwhite models in housing advertisements. The group is seeking a voluntary agreement similar to one it reached with the *Post* under which real estate advertisers are told that one of four display ads using human models must include blacks.

Dec. 21: Federal investigators are widening their search for whoever mailed package bombs to a federal judge, a city alderman, the judge's court headquarters, and an NAACP chapter, all of whom figured prominently in recent civil rights legislation in three southern states.

The investigators say they are no longer looking for a narrow motive that would link the four intended victims but are looking for anyone with a general animosity towards recipients of the package bombs, including racial terrorists.

Dec. 23: Concerned about a growing number of racial incidents on campuses, the State University of New York is planning several steps to defuse trouble before it gets out of hand. *The New York Times* quotes university officials who outlined those steps, which include appointing a SUNY "hit squad" to travel to racially troubled campuses and developing "racial climate" committees at each of the system's 64 campuses.

Dec. 24: The NAACP is asking Florida Governor Bob Martinez to send the National Guard to Miami. *The New York Times* reports that black communities fear they may be ignored by police officers loyal to a Hispanic officer who was convicted earlier this month of killing two blacks. The Governor's press secretary says Martinez has taken no action on the request, that he has faith in the Miami police department.

NOTES AND
REFERENCES

FOOTNOTES

[1] *Wards Cove Packing Co. v. Atonio,* 104 L.Ed.2d 733, 755; 109 S.Ct. 2115 (1989).

[2] *Brown v. Board of Education of Topeka,* 347 U.S. 483 (1954).

[3] For example, the Supreme Court upheld the constitutionality of voluntary affirmative action in certain job training programs in *U.S. Steelworkers v. Weber,* 443 U.S. 193 (1979). The Court also upheld minority business set-aside programs as constitutional in *Fullilove v. Klutznick,* 448 U.S. 448 (1980). There are numerous examples of broad, liberal, remedial readings of civil rights laws and the Constitution by the Supreme Court during the 1970s, including *Griggs v. Duke Power,* 401 U.S. 424 (1971); *Swann v. Charlotte Mecklenburg Bd. of Education,* 402 U.S. 1 (1971); *Alexander v. Louisiana,* 405 U.S. 625 (1972); and *Albemarle Paper Co. v. Moody,* 422 U.S. 405 (1975).

[4] Julius L. Chambers, "The Law and Black Americans: Retreat from Civil Rights," in Janet Dewart (ed.), *The State of Black America 1987* (New York: National Urban League, Inc., 1987), pp. 23–26.

[5] *Runyon v. McCrary,* 427 U.S. 160 (1976).

[6] *Griggs v. Duke Power Co.,* 401 U.S. 424 (1971).

[7] *Patterson v. McLean Credit Union,* 105 L.Ed.2d 132, 109 S.Ct. 2363 (1989).

[8] *Id.,* 105 L.Ed. 2d at 150.

[9] *Id.,* 105 L.Ed. 2d at 156.

[10] NAACP Legal Defense and Educational Fund, Inc., "Impact of *Patterson v. McLean Credit Union*" (Washington: November 20, 1989).

[11] *Ibid.*

[12] *Wards Cove Packing Co. v. Atonio,* 104 L.Ed.2d 733, 109 S.Ct. 1775 (1989).

[13] *Price Waterhouse v. Hopkins,* 104 L.Ed.2d 268, 109 S.Ct. 1775 (1989).

[14] *Martin v. Wilks,* 104 L.Ed.2d 835, 109 S.Ct. 2180 (1989).

[15] *City of Richmond v. J.A. Croson Company,* 102 L.Ed.2d 854, 109 S.Ct. 706 (1989).

[16] Data reported by Minority Business Enterprise Legal Defense and Education Fund, Inc., Washington, DC.

[17] *Lorance v. AT&T Technologies, Inc.,* 104 L.Ed.2d 961, 109 S.Ct. 2261 (1989).

[18] The Court reasoned in *Lorance* that the discriminatory seniority system caused harm to the plaintiffs when it went into effect, which meant that the statute of limitations began running when the system was adopted. In *Wilks,* the Court didn't specifically address the statute of limitations issue. However, the broad language of the opinion may be interpreted as extending greater protection and a more liberal interpretation of Title VII to white male firefighters than was extended to the women in *Lorance.*

[19] *Crawford Fittings v. J.T. Gibbons, Inc.,* 482 U.S. 437 (1987).

[20] *Independent Federation of Flight Attendants v. Zipes,* 105 L.Ed.2d 639, 109 S.Ct. 2732 (1989).

[21] Additionally, plaintiffs' attorneys in Title VII cases and other civil rights litigators increasingly face the threat of the discriminatory application of Rule 11 under the Federal Rules of Civil Procedure, which authorizes judicial sanctions against attorneys who file cases deemed to be frivolous. Rule 11 has discouraged a number of civil rights attorneys from undertaking *any* civil rights cases. See Gerald Solovy et al., *Sanctions Under Federal Rule of Civil Procedure 11* (Chicago: Jenner & Block, 1989).

[22]Thurgood Marshall, Remarks at the Second Circuit Judicial Conference, September 1989.

[23]Data reported by the Joint Center for Political Studies, Washington, DC.

[24]*Thornburgh v. Gingles,* 474 U.S. 808 (1986).

[25]*McNeil v. Springfield Park District,* 851 F.2d 937 (7th Cir. 1988).

[26]*Collins v. City of Norfolk, Va.,* 816 F.2d 932 (4th Cir. 1987).

[27]*Martin v. Mabus,* 700 F.Supp. 327 (S.D. Miss., 1988).

[28]*LULAC v. Mattox,* Civ. Ac. No. 88-CA-154 (W.D. Tex., November 15, 1989).

[29]*Clark v. Edwards,* Civ. Ac. No. 86-435 (M.D. La., Aug. 15, 1988).

[30]*Chisom v. Roemer,* 853 F.2d 1186 (5th Cir. 1988), *rehearing and rehearing en banc denied.*

[31]*Whitfield v. Clinton,* Civ. Ac. No. 88-1953 (E.D. Ar., December 1989).

[32]Data reported by United States Census Bureau, Washington, DC.

[33]*Mississippi State Chapter, Operation PUSH v. Allain,* 674 F.Supp. 1245 (N.D. Miss., 1987).

[34]Steve Suitts et al., "How Congressional Redistricting May Change National Politics In the 1990s," Briefing Paper #2, Project 1990 (Atlanta: Southern Regional Council, 1989), p. 5.

[35]Robert G. Schwemm, "Federal Fair Housing Enforcement: A Critique of the Reagan Administration's Record and Recommendations For the Future," *One Nation, Indivisible* (Washington: Citizens' Commission on Civil Rights, 1989), p. 272.

[36]Testimony of John J. Knapp, General Counsel, U.S. Department of Housing and Urban Development, in *Issues in Housing Discrimination,* Vol. 2 (Washington: U.S. Commission on Civil Rights, November 13, 1987).

[37]Schwemm, *op. cit.,* p. 270.

[38]42 USC § 3610.

[39]42 USC § 3613.

[40]Schwemm, *op cit.,* p. 271.

[41]The House passed the Fair Housing Amendments Act on June 19, 1988 (H 4931). The Senate passed an amended version of this bill on August 2 (S 10562). The House concurred in the Senate version on August 8 (H 6501).

[42]*Id.* at § 810(g) (2) (A).

[43]*Id.* at § 812(a), § 812(o).

[44]*Id.* at § 810(a) (1) (B) (iv), § 810(f), § 812(b), and § 812(g) (1).

[45]Data reported by Department of Housing and Urban Development, Washington, DC, December 15, 1989.

[46]*Ibid.*

[47]Data reported by Department of Justice.

[48]Data reported by Low Income Housing Information Service.

[49]*Ibid.*

[50]No accurate national statistics on the percentage of blacks among the homeless population are available. However, in a systematic study of homelessness in Chicago, blacks comprised 53 percent of the homeless population. See P. Rossi, *Minorities and Homelessness,* reprinted in *Divided Opportunities: Minorities, Poverty and Social Policy* (Chicago: 1988).

[51]Fact Sheet on HOPE (Homeownership and Opportunity for People Everywhere) from United States Department of Housing and Urban Development, Washington, November 14, 1989.

[52]Jerry DeMuth, "Fair Housing Complaints Inundate HUD," *Washington Post,* October 16, 1989, p. E2.

[53]According to a 1988 National School Boards Association study, there has been no significant progress in school desegregation since the mid-1970s, and there are "severe increases in racial isolation in some areas." In a fifth of our nation's largest urban districts, three out of four black students attend schools in which minorities comprise over 90 percent of the student body. See Gary Orfield and Franklin Monfort, *Racial Change and Desegregation in Large School Districts: Trends Through the 1986-1987 School Year* (Washington: National School Boards Association, 1988), pp. 2-3, 31-32.

[54]For example, the annual per pupil expenditures in Massachusetts schools range from $5,013 in the best-funded school district to only $1,637 in the district with the least funding. In Texas, the top 100 school districts spend an average of $5,500 per child, while the bottom 100 spend an average of $1,800. See National Coalition of Advocates for Students, *Barriers to Excellence: Our Children At Risk* (Washington: National Coalition of Advocates for Students, 1985), pp. 73-74.

[55]*Dowell v. Board of Education of Oklahoma City Public Schools,* 887 F.2d 1438 (10th Cir. 1989).

[56]*Pitts v. Freeman,* 755 F.2d 1423 (11th Cir. 1985).

[57]*Jacksonville Branch of NAACP v. Duval County School Board,* 883 F.2d 945 (11th Cir. 1989).

[58]*United States and Nichols v. Natchez Special Municipal School District,* Civ. Ac. No. 1120-W (S.D. Miss., July 24, 1989).

[59]*Monroe v. Madison County School Board,* Civ. Ac. No. C-2209-E (W.D. Tenn., July 13, 1989).

[60]*Brown v. Board of Education of Topeka,* No. 87-1668 (10th Cir., December 11, 1989).

[61]*Riddick v. School Board of Norfolk,* 784 F.2d 521 (4th Cir. 1986), *cert. denied,* 107 S.Ct. 486 (1986).

[62]*U.S. v. Yonkers Board of Education,* 837 F.2d 1181 (2nd Cir. 1987), *cert. denied,* 108 S.Ct. 2821 (1988).

[63]*Jenkins v. Missouri,* 855 F.2d 1295 (8th Cir. 1988), *rehearing and rehearing en banc denied, cert. granted,* 109 S.Ct. 1930 (1989).

[64]*Women's Equity Action League v. Cavazos,* 879 F.2d 880 (DC Cir. 1989).

[65]*United States v. Louisiana,* 692 F.Supp. 642 (E.D. La., 1988); *United States v. Louisiana,* 718 F.Supp. 499 (E.D. La., 1989).

[66]See Ron Edmonds, "Effective Schools for the Urban Poor," 37 *Educational Leadership* 15, (1979), pp. 15-24; Gary Ratner, "A New Legal Duty for Urban Public Schools: Effective Education in Basic Skills, 63 *Texas Law Review* 787 (1985), p. 779.

[67]See generally, David Kirp and Mark Yudoff, *Kirp and Yudoff's Educational Policy and the Law* (2nd Ed., 1982).

[68]*Edgewood Independent School District v. Kirby,* No. C-8353 (October 2, 1989).

[69]Data reported by NAACP Legal Defense and Educational Fund, Inc., Capital Punishment Project *Death Row U.S.A.,* July 1989.

[70]*McClesky v. Kemp,* 481 U.S. 279 (1987).

[71]*Id.,* 481 U.S. at 321 (Brennan J., dissenting).

[72]*Waye v. Murray,* No. 89-00442-R (E.D. Va., 1989).

[73]NAACP Legal Defense and Educational Fund, Inc., "Execution Update," September 1, 1989.

[74]See S. Rep. No. 1760, 101st Cong., 1st Sess. (1989).

[75]*Ibid.*

[76]See S. Rep. No. 1757.

[77]*Powell v. Alabama,* 287 U.S. 45 (1932).

Budget and Tax Strategy: Implications for Blacks, *Lenneal J. Henderson, Ph.D.*

FOOTNOTES

[1]John L. Mikesell, *Fiscal Administration: Analysis and Applications for the Public Sector* (Chicago, Illinois: The Dorsey Press, 2nd Edition, 1986), p. X.

[2]Frank Sackton, "Financing Public Programs Under Fiscal Constraint," in Robert E. Cleary and Nicholas Henry (eds.), *Managing Public Programs: Balancing Politics, Administration, and Public Needs* (San Francisco: Jossey-Bass Publishers, 1989), pp. 147–166.

[3]On the issue of ethics and public finance, see B.J. Reed and John W. Swain, *Public Finance Administration* (Englewood Cliffs, New Jersey: Prentice-Hall, Inc., 1990), pp. 195–196.

[4]The Congressional Black Caucus, *The Quality of Life, Fiscal 1990 Alternative Budget* (Washington, DC, 1989), p. 1.

[5]Margaret C. Simms, editor, *Black Economic Progress: An Agenda for the 1990s* (Washington, DC: The Joint Center for Political Studies, 1988).

[6]For example, see Congressional Task Force on Federal Excise Taxes, *Analyzing the Possible Impact of Federal Excise Taxes on the Poor, Including Blacks and Other Minorities* (Washington, DC: Voter Education and Registration Action, Inc., July 1987).

[7]*State of Small Business, 1989* (Washington, DC: Government Printing Office, 1989).

[8]Georgia A. Persons, "Blacks in State and Local Government: Progress and Constraints," in Janet Dewart (ed.), *The State of Black America 1987* (New York: National Urban League, 1987), pp. 167–192; Georgia A. Persons, "Reflections on Mayoral Leadership: The Impact of Changing Issues and Changing Times," *Phylon,* Vol. 41, No. 3, September 1985), pp. 205–18; and Hanes Walton, *Black Politics: A Theoretical and Structural Analysis* (Philadelphia, Pennsylvania: J.B. Lippincott, Inc., 1972).

[9]Hanes Walton, *When the Marching Stopped: The Politics of Civil Rights Regulatory Agencies* (Albany, New York: State University of New York Press, 1988), p. 59.

[10]Lenneal J. Henderson, "The Impact of Military Base Shutdowns," *The Black Scholar,* September 1974, pp. 56–58.

[11]"The Peace Economy: How Defense Cuts Will Fuel America's Long-Term Prosperity," *Business Week,* No. 3137, December 11, 1989, p. 51.

[12]*Ibid.,* p. 52.

[13]Children's Defense Fund, *Children's Defense Fund Budget, FY 1989* (Washington, DC, 1989), p. 12.

[14]District of Columbia, *Operating Budget, 1990 Fiscal Year.*

[15]Section 641, 42 USC 7141.

[16]*Functional Interrelationships of the Office of Minority Economic Impact* (U.S. Department of Energy, 1989).

[17]William W. Ellis and Darlene Calbert, *Blacks and Tax Reform 1985–86* (Washington, DC: The Congressional Research Service, 1986).

[18]Mark S. Kamlet, David C. Mowery, and Tsai-Tsu Su, "Upsetting National Priorities: The Reagan Administration's Budgetary Strategy," *The American Political Science Review,* Vol. 82, No. 4, December 1988, pp. 1293–1307.

[19]Adapted from Irene S. Rubin, *Shrinking the Federal Government: The Effect of Cutbacks on Five Federal Agencies* (New York and London: Longman, Inc., 1985), p. 27.

[20]Paul David Schumaker, Russell W. Getter, and Terry Nichols Clark, *Party Responsiveness and Fiscal Strain in 51 American Communities* (Washington, DC: The American Political Science Association, 1983).

[21]Lenneal J. Henderson, *Proposition 13: Managing the Income Security Impacts* (Washington, DC: National Institute of Public Management, 1979).

[22]*Census of Governments, 1987* (Washington, DC: Bureau of the Census, 1988).

[23]Linda Williams, "Gramm-Rudman and the Politics of Deficit Reduction," *The Urban League Review,* Vol. 10, No. 2, Winter 1986–87, pp. 72–83.

[24]Carol E. Cohen, "State Fiscal Capacity and Effort: An Update," *Intergovernmental Perspective,* Spring 1989, Vol. 15, No. 2, pp. 15–23.

[25]Thomas W. Church and Milton Heumann, "The Underexamined Assumptions of the Invisible Hand: Monetary Incentives as Policy Instruments," *Journal of Policy Analysis and Management,* Vol. 8, No. 4, Fall 1989, p. 641.

[26]Lenneal J. Henderson, "Blacks, Budgets, and Taxes: Assessing the Impact of Budget Deficit Reduction and Tax Reform on Blacks," in Janet Dewart (ed.), *The State of Black America 1987* (New York: The National Urban League, 1987), pp. 76–78.

[27]*Ibid.,* p. 79.

[28]Raphael Thelwell, *Gramm-Rudman-Hollings Four Years Later: A Fable* (Washington, DC, unpublished paper, September 1989), p. 3.

[29]*Bowsher v. Synar,* 54 USLW 5064.

[30]Thelwell, *op. cit.,* p. 4.

[31]Lynn Burbridge, "Tax Reform: A Minimalist Approach for Assisting the Low-Income," *The Urban League Review,* Vol. 10, No. 2, Winter 1986–87, p. 105.

[32]William Darity, Jr. and Samuel Myers, Jr., "Distress v. Dependency: Changing Income Support Programs," *The Urban League Review, ibid.,* p. 24.

[33]Vincent Marando, "Revenue-Sharing and American Cities," paper delivered at the annual meeting of the American Political Science Association, Atlanta, GA, August 1989.

[34]Henderson, "Blacks, Budgets and Taxes," *op. cit.,* p. 84.

Housing Opportunity: A Dream Deferred, *Phillip Clay, Ph.D.*

FOOTNOTES

[1]See generally David Schwartz et al., *A New Housing Policy for America* (Philadelphia: Temple University Press, 1988). For update, see U.S. Bureau of the Census and HUD, *American Housing Survey 1985* (Washington: U.S. Bureau of the Census and HUD, 1988).

[2]For a proponent of this point of view, see Nathan Glazer, *Affirmative Discrimination* (New York: Basic Books, 1975), pp. 130–68. For an opposing view, see Reynolds Farley, *Blacks and Whites: Narrowing the Gap?* (Cambridge: Harvard University Press, 1984), p. 209.

3The bottom fifth of all families lost 10 percent of their income due to program cutbacks and loss of private income. See federal data cited in Isabel Wilkerson, "Society and Reaganomics Hurt the Poor," *The New York Times,* July 16, 1989, p. 70. A full analysis of this trend is documented in Sar Levitan and Isaac Shapiro, *Working But Poor: America's Contradiction* (Baltimore: Johns Hopkins Press, 1987), pp. 6–12.

4Schwartz et al., pp. 221–23.

5See the Bureau of the Census, *Statistical Abstract of the United States* (Washington: Department of Commerce, Bureau of the Census, 1988 and various years in the 1980s; Table 714 in 1988 edition).

6*Ibid.,* Table 717.

7While there is no census of the homeless, all the studies suggest that blacks are disproportionately represented and that blacks are especially prominent among homeless families, the fastest growing segment of this population. An estimated 800,000 people have signed up for housing in the 25 cities surveyed two years ago by the National Conference of Mayors. These and others who have basic housing needs and no long-term source of relief are the "pre-homeless." See National Alliance to End Homelessness, *Housing and Homelessness: A Report of the National Alliance* (Washington: The National Alliance, 1988).

8See Mary Jo Bane and Paul Jargowsky, *Urban Poverty Areas: Basic Questions Concerning Prevalence, Growth and Dynamics* (Cambridge, Mass: JFK School of Government/Harvard University, 1988).

9William J. Wilson, *The Truly Disadvantaged* (Chicago: University of Chicago Press, 1987).

10The Center for the Study of Social Policy, *A Dream Deferred: The Economic Status of Black Americans* (Washington: The Center for the Study of Social Policy, 1984). Data for 1986 were added from BLS data.

11See William Apgar, *The Nation's Housing: A Review of Past Trends and Future Prospects* (Cambridge: Center for Real Estate Development/MIT, 1988).

12For a discussion of these themes, see Phillip L. Clay, "Choosing Urban Futures: The Transformation of American Cities," *Stanford Law and Policy Review,* 1:1, Fall 1989, pp. 28–43.

13Irby Iredia, "Attaining the Housing Goal?," unpublished HUD paper, July 1986, in Schwartz et al., p. 33.

14The importance of this housing and the risks it faces have been documented. See National Low Income Housing Preservation Commission (Washington: NLIHPC, 1988.) The extent to which blacks benefit varies based on the city, but cities with large proportions of blacks depend heavily on this housing.

15The issue of overconcentration of public and subsidized housing in minority communities has been a major issue since the Supreme Court ruled in the *Gautreaux Case* (1972) that public and assisted housing ought not to reinforce segregation. In 1974, HUD attempted—with limited success, through site selection criteria—to spread assisted housing around. For a discussion of this issue, see John O. Calmore, "Fair Housing vs. Fair Housing: The Conflict Between Providing Low-Income Housing in Impacted Areas and Providing Increased Housing Opportunities Through Spatial Deconcentration, *Housing Law Bulletin,* 9:6, November/December 1979, pp. 1–12.

16There has been no comprehensive assessment of segregation patterns since the 1980 census, which documented extensive racial isolation. For an excellent source on this, see Harriet Newburger, *Recent Evidence on Discrimination in Housing* (Washington: Department of Housing and Urban Development, 1986). For a recent perspective, see Isabel Wilkerson, "Study Finds Segregation in Cities Worse than Scientists Imagined," *The New York Times,* August 5, 1989, p. 6.

17The current example is the disempowering influence of drugs in poor neighborhoods. Drugs pose difficulties for individuals who are addicted, but the crime, corruption, fear, and reaction caused by drugs interfere with community efforts at self-help. Congress has given HUD new authority in fighting drugs in public housing, and local efforts likewise target supportive services to communities affected by the drug situation.

18Over the years, there have been a host of housing bills, programs, and initiatives, including major bills in 1949, 1954, 1958, 1965, 1968, and 1974. While 1988 and 1989 were marked by a flurry of activity, the net result was some initially unfunded programs that then became active at a demonstration level. Included in this is implementation of the McKinney bill for the homeless and the Nehemiah program on low-income homeownership.

19Actually, the Tax Reform Act of 1986 should be considered an anti-housing initiative since it removed many of the financial incentives for private investors to produce rental housing, and it moderately reduced advantages of homeownership.

[20]The Community Reinvestment Act of 1975 and the Home Mortgage Disclosure Act of 1976 gave standing to communities to account for their lending and community investment activity (or lack of activity).

[21]Because of low income, blacks have few savings. Discrimination limits the options for upgrading to the best units left by those with higher income. Assisted housing often reinforced segregation.

[22]See William C. Apgar, *The Changing Utilization of the Housing Inventory: Past Trends and Future Prospects,* (Cambridge: MIT/Harvard Joint Center of Urban Studies, 1982).

[23]For a review of the literature on this subject, see Brian J. L. Berry, "Island of Renewal in Seas of Change," in Paul Peterson, *The New Reality* (Washington: Brookings Institution, 1985), pp. 33–68.

[24]Based on anecdotal information, we can expect, for example, to see the opening of selected suburban communities near major cities, and a reduction in isolation in selected middle-class areas in cities. Some closing of the North-South gaps are also suggested by the anecdotal information. The progress is balanced against more numerous concentration of very poor, all-black areas, the rise of low-income black suburbs, and the black suburbanization as reconcentration in some communities. For a discussion of the documented patterns of black suburbanization, see Phillip L. Clay, "The Process of Black Suburbanization," *Urban Affairs Quarterly,* Fall 1979.

[25]See Isabel Wilkerson, *op. cit.,* August 5, 1989, p. 6.

[26]See Clay, "Choosing Urban Futures . . .,"*op. cit.,* pp. 28–33.

[27]For the most recent study, see Allen Fishbein in testimony before the Subcommittee on Consumer and Regulatory Affairs of the Committee on Banking, Housing and Urban Affairs of the United States, October 24, 1989.

[28]Of special concern is how the nature of the program skews the incidence of benefit and whether programs by their nature (rather than intent) benefit blacks less than others. For example, programs that don't work in cities or that have a high income threshold are not likely to help blacks.

[29]See Leanne Lechman, *Decade to Decade: U.S. Real Estate Adapts to Revolution in Finance and Demographic Evolution* (New York: Schroder Real Estate Associates, 1988).

[30]The Local Initiatives Support Corporation and the Enterprise Foundation are two national housing intermediaries that perform this function for local neighborhood-based housing organizations.

[31]Many communities that can't or won't raise taxes will exact fees and impose restrictions that raise the cost of housing. Sometimes theirs is an environmental justification. See Frieden, Downtown, Inc.

[32]See National Congress of Economic Development, "Against All Odds: The Achievements of Community-Based Development Organizations," Washington: NCED, 1988. The organization has produced an estimated 125,000 units over the past decade.

[33]For example, cities like New York, Cleveland, Boston, and Chicago have dozens of community organizations with a development track record, while cities like Atlanta, Buffalo, and Topeka have little such capacity.

Understanding African-American Family Diversity, *Andrew Billingsley, Ph.D.*

FOOTNOTES

[1]W.E.B. DuBois, *The Philadelphia Negro* (New York: Schocken, first edition, 1895; current edition, 1967).

[2]Julius Lester (ed.), *The Seventh Son: The Thought and Writings of W.E.B. DuBois, Vol. II* (New York: Random House, 1971).

[3]*Ibid.*

[4]E. Franklin Frazier, *The Negro Family in the United States* (Chicago, IL: University of Chicago Press, 1966; first edition, 1939).

[5]U.S. Bureau of the Census, *Household and Family Characteristics,* March 1985 (Current Population Reports, Population Characteristics, Series P-20, No. 411), p. 9.

[6]*Ibid.*

[7]While some scholars find occupation to be a convenient index of social class, still others find combined family income to be more reliable. All scholars, however, are aware of the high degree of correlation among the three primary indexes of occupation, income, and education.

[8]Harriette McAdoo, "Factors Related to Stability in Upwardly Mobile Black Families," *Journal of Marriage and the Family,* 40 (4), 1981, pp. 761–776. See also McAdoo, "Upward Mobility and Parenting in Middle-Income Black Families," *The Journal of Black Psychology,* 8 (1), 1981, pp. 1–22, and McAdoo, "Transgeneral Patterns in Upward Mobility" ("Black Families," *op. cit.*).

William J. Wilson, *The Truly Disadvantaged* (Chicago: University of Chicago Press, 1987).

Barry Bluestone, *Deindustrialization of America* (New York: Basic Books, Inc., 1982).

[9]McAdoo, "Factors Related to Stability," *op cit.*

[10]U.S. Bureau of the Census, *Household Wealth and Asset Ownership: 1984 Census,* No. 7, 1986, p. 70.

[11]Walter L. Updegrave, "Race and Money," *Money,* December 1989, p. 152.

[12]Sara Lawrence Lightfoot, *Worlds Apart* (New York: Basic Books, 1978), p. 62.

The Rewards of Daring and the Ambiguity of Power: Perspectives on the Wilder Election of 1989, *Matthew Holden, Jr., Ph.D.*

FOOTNOTES

[1]Barbara Bryant Solomon, *Black Empowerment: Social Work in Oppressed Communities* (New York: Columbia University Press, 1976), p. 6.

[2]Mike Hardy and Jeff Schapiro, "Wilder Remains Mass of Contradictions," *Richmond Times-Dispatch,* October 8, 1989, p. 1.

[3]Larry J. Sabato, "Virginia's National Election for Governor—1989," report issued December 22, 1989.

[4]John J. Farmer, "Wilder Strikes a Virginia 'Traditionalist' Stance," *Newark Star-Ledger,* June 11, 1989.

[5]*Ibid.*

[6]Dwayne Yancey, *When Hell Froze Over* (Roanoke, VA: Taylor Publishing Company in association with the Roanoke *Times & World News,* 1989).

[7]Farmer, *op. cit.*

[8]*Richmond Times-Dispatch,* September 19, 1989, and Yancey, *op. cit.,* on the previous exchange between Robb and Wilder.

[9]*Richmond Times-Dispatch,* January 5, 1989.

[10]Commonwealth of Virginia, State Board of Elections, Candidate Campaign Contributions and Expenditures, "Friends of Doug Wilder" Report Covering Period November 10, 1987 to January 15, 1989 (amended).

[11]*Ibid,* "Wilder for Governor" Report Covering Period October 2–30, 1989.

[12]Jeff E. Schapiro, "Wilder Consults with Democratic Leaders," *Richmond Times-Dispatch*, September 17, 1989.

[13]*Ibid.*

[14]Sabato, *op. cit.,* p. 39.

[15]Sabato, p. 44.

[16]*Ibid.*

[17]*Ibid.*

[18]Charles V. Hamilton, "On Parity and Political Empowerment," in Janet Dewart (ed.), *The State of Black America 1989* (New York: National Urban League, 1989), pp. 114–115.

[19]Alexander J. Walker, "The Governor's Veto Power," in Thomas R. Morris and Larry Sabato (eds.), *Virginia Government and Politics* (Charlottesville: Virginia Chamber of Commerce and Institute of Government, University of Virginia, 1984), p. 149.

[20]Steven Johnson, "Charles S. Robb and the Reserved Governorship," unpublished Ph.D. dissertation, Government and Foreign Affairs Department, University of Virginia, 1989, pp. VII-26.

[21]*Ibid.,* pp. VII-28.

Health Status of Black Americans, *LaSalle D. Leffall, M.D.*

BIBLIOGRAPHY

American Cancer Society. *Cancer Facts and Figures,* 1989, p. 16.

Ansell, D.A., J. Dillard, M. Rothenberg et al. "Breast Cancer Screening in An Urban Black Population." *Cancer* 62:425–428, 1988.

Blendon, R.J., L.H. Aiken, H.E. Freeman, and C.R. Corey. "Access to Medical Care for Black and White Americans—A Matter of Continuing Concern." *Journal of the American Medical Association* [*JAMA* used hereafter] 261:278-281, 1989.

Brown, Lee P. "Crime in the Black Community." In Dewart, J. (ed.), *The STate of Black America 1988.* New York: National Urban League, 1988.

Callender, C.O. "The Results of Transplantation in Blacks: Just the Tip of the Iceberg." *Transplantation Proceedings* 21:3407-3410, 1989.

Cassel, J., S. Heyden, A.G. Bartel et al. "Incidence of Coronary Heart Disease by Ethnic Group, Social Class, and Sex." *Arch. Inter. Med.* 128:901-906, 1971.

Chasnoff, I.J., D.R. Giffith, S. MacGregor, K. Dirkes, and K.A. Burns. "Temporal Patterns of Cocaine Use in Pregnancy." *JAMA* 261:1741-1744, 1989.

Committee on Trauma Research Commission on Life Sciences, National Research Council, Institute of Medicine. "Injury in America: A Continuing Public Health Problem. Washington: National Academy Press, 1985.

Cooper, R.S., B. Simmons, A. Castaner, L. Prasad, C. Franklin, and J. Ferlinz. "Survival Rates and Prehospital Delay During Myocardial Infarction Among Black Persons." *American Journal of Cardiology* 57:208-211, 1986.

Curry, C.L., J. Oliver, and F.B. Mumtaz. "Coronary Artery Disease in Blacks: Risk Factors." *American Heart Journal* 104:852-864, 1982.

Curtis, J.L., F.C. Crummery, S.N. Vaker, R.E. Foster, C.S. Khayle, and R. Wilkins. "HIV Screening and Counseling for Intravenous Drug Abuse Patients. *JAMA* 261:258-262, 1989.

Edelman, Marian Wright. "Black Children in America." In Dewart, J. (ed.), *The State of Black America 1989.* New York: National Urban League, 1989.

Freeman, H.P. "Cancer in the Socioeconomically Disadvantaged." *CA-A Cancer Journal for Clinicians* 39:266–288, Sept.-Oct., 1989.

"From the National Institutes of Health;" "From the Health Resources and Services Administration;" "From the Health Care Financing Administration;" "From the Assistant Secretary of Health." *JAMA* 261(2), January 13, 1989.

Grant, W.M. and J.F. Burke. "Why Do Some People Go Blind from Glaucoma?" *Ophthalmology* 88:991–998, 1982.

Greene, M.G. "Abuse, Neglect Rising in DC" and "Boarder Babies." *Washington Post,* September 10–11, 1989.

Hagstrom, R.M., C.F. Federspiel, Y.C. Ho. "Incidence of Myocardial Infarction and Sudden Death from Coronary Heart Disease in Nashville, TN. *Circulation* 44:884–890, 1971.

Henschke, U.K., L.D. Leffall, Jr., C.H. Mason, A.W. Reinhold, R.L. Schneider, and J.E. White. "Alarming Increase of the Cancer Mortality in the U.S. Black Population (1950–1967). *Cancer* 31(4):736–768, April, 1973.

Hiller, R. and H. Kahn. "Blindness from Glaucoma." *American Journal of Ophthalmology* 80:62–69, 1975.

Hughes, D., K. Johnson, S. Rosenbaum, and J. Liu. *The Health of America's Children.* Children's Defense Fund, 1989.

Jaynes, G.D. and J.R.M. Williams, eds. *A Common Destiny: Blacks and American Society.* Washington: National Academy Press, 1989.

Keil, J.E., D.E. Saunders, D.R. Lackland et al. "Acute Myocardial Infarction: Period Prevalence, Case Fatality, and Comparison of Black and White Cases in Urban and Rural Areas of South Carolina." *American Heart Journal* 109:776–784, 1985.

Ki Moon Bang, J.E. White, B.L. Gause, and L.D. Leffall, Jr. "Evaluation of Recent Trends in Cancer Mortality and Incidence Among Blacks." *Cancer* 61:1255–1261, 1988.

Kitagawa, E.M. and P.M. Hauser. *Differential Mortality in the United States.* Cambridge: Harvard University Press, 1973.

Kleinman, J.C. and S.S. Kessel. "Racial Differences in Low Birth Weight." *New England Journal of Medicine* 317:749–753, 1987.

Leffall, L.D., Jr. "Cancer Mortality in Blacks." *CA-A Cancer Journal for Clinicians,* 24(1): 42–46, Jan.-Feb., 1974.

_____. "Challenge of Cancer in Black Americans." Keynote Address—Proceedings of the American Cancer Society National Conference on Meeting the Challenge of Cancer Among Black Americans, pp. 9–13, 1979.

_____. "Decreasing Cancer Mortality in Blacks—An Increasing Challenge" (editorial). *Oncology Times* 7(9):2, September, 1985.

Leske, M.C., A.M.S. Connell, and R. Kehse. "A Pilot Study of Glaucoma Prevalence in Barbados. *Invest. Ophthal. Vis. Sci.* 29 (supp.): 61, 1988.

Lotufa, D., R. Ritch, L. Szmyd, and J.E. Burris. "Juvenile Glaucoma, Race, and Refraction." *JAMA* 261:249–52, 1989.

McClellan, W. et al. "Racial Differences in the Incidence of Hypertensive End Stage Renal Disease (ESRD) Are Not Entirely Explained by Difference in the Prevalence of Hypertension." *American Journal of Kidney Disease* 12:285–290, 1988.

Martin, M.J., A. Sommer et al. "Race and Primary Open-Angle Glaucoma." *American Journal of Ophthalmology* 99:383, 387, 1985.

Mason, R.P., O. Kosoko, M.R. Wilson et al. "National Survey of the Prevalence and Risk Factors of Glaucoma in St. Lucia, West Indies." *Ophthalmology,* in press.

318

Primm, Beny J. "Drug Use: Special Implications for Black America." In Dewart, J. (ed.), *The State of Black America 1987*. New York: National Urban League, 1987.

Satariano, W.A. "Socioeconomic Status and Health: A Study of Age Differences in a Depressed Area." *American Journal of Preventive Medicine* 2:1–5, 1986.

Scott, R.B. "Whether Sickle Cell Disease in the 1980s?" *Journal of the National Medical Association* 73:307–308, 1981.

_____. "Advances in the Treatment of Sickle Cell Disease in Children." *Am. J. Dis. of Child.* 139:1219, 1985.

Seddon, J.M., B. Schwartz, and G. Flowerdew. "Case-Control Study of Ocular Hypertension." *Archives of Ophthalmology* 99:837–839, 1981.

Selik, R.M., K.G. Castro, and M. Pappaionou. "Racial Ethnic Differences in the Risk of AIDS in the United States." *American Journal of Public Health* 78:1539–1545, 1988.

Sempos, C., R. Cooper, M.G. Kovar et al. "Divergence of the Recent Trends in Coronary Mortality for the Four Major Race-Sex Groups in the United States." *American Journal of Public Health* 78: 1422–1427, 1988.

Simmons, B.E. et al. "Coronary Artery Disease in Blacks of Lower Socioeconomic Status." Angiographic Findings in the Cook County Hospital, Heart Disease Registry. *American Heart Journal* 116:90–97, 1988.

_____. Division of Adult Cardiology, Department of Medicine, Cook County Hospital 116:90–97, 1988.

"Substance Facts." Washington: The Psychiatric Institute of Washington, September, 1986.

U.S. Department of Health and Human Services. *Report of the Secretary's Task Force on Black and Minority Health*. Washington: Department of Health and Human Services, 1986.

Weisse, A.B., P.D. Abiuso, and I.S. Thind. "Acute Myocardial Infarction in Newark, NJ: A Study of Racial Incidence." *Archives of Internal Medicine* 137:1402–1405, 1977.

Wenneker, M.B. and A.M. Epstein. "Racial Inequalities in the Use of Procedures for Patients with Ischemic Heart Disease in Massachusetts." *JAMA* 261:253–257, 1989.

Wilensky, J.T., N. Gandhi, and T. Pan. "Racial Influence in Open Angle Glaucoma." *Annals of Ophthalmology* 10:1398–1402, 1978.

Wilson, R., T.M. Richardson, E. Hertzmark et al. "Race as a Risk Factor for Progressive Glaucomatous Damage." *Annals of Ophthalmology* 17:653–659, 1985.

Preventing Black Homicide, *Carl C. Bell, M.D. with Esther J. Jenkins, Ph.D.*

REFERENCES

Attorney General's Task Force on Family Violence. *Report of the Attorney General's Task Force on Family Violence*. Washington, DC: U.S. Department of Justice, 1984.

Batchelor, J. and N. Wicks. "Study of Children and Youth as Witnesses to Homicide, City of Detroit, 1985." Unpublished paper, 1985.

Bell, C.C. "Coma and the Etiology of Violence, Part 1. *Journal of the National Medical Association,* 1986, *78:* 1167–1176.

_____. "Coma and the Etiology of Violence Part 2. *Journal of the National Medical Association,* 1987a, *79:* 79–85.

_____. "Preventive Strategies for Dealing with Violence Among Blacks. *Community Mental Health Journal,* 1987b, *23:* 217–228.

Bell, C.C., K. Taylor-Crawford, E.J. Jenkins, and D. Chalmers. "Need for Victimization Screening in a Black Psychiatric Population." *Journal of the National Medical Association,* 1988, *80:* 41-48.

Bell, C.C., C.J. Hildreth, E.J. Jenkins, and C. Carter. "The Need for Victimization Screening in a Poor, Outpatient Medical Population." *Journal of the National Medical Association,* 1988, *80:* 853-860.

Berkowitz, L. and A. LePage. "Weapons as Aggression-Eliciting Stimuli." *Journal of Personality and Social Psychology,* 1967, *7:* 202-207.

Block, C.R. *Lethal Violence in Chicago Over Seventeen Years: Homicide Known to the Police, 1965-81.* Chicago: Illinois Criminal Justice Information Authority, 1985.

Centers for Disease Control. *Homicide Surveillance: High-Risk Racial and Ethnic Groups—Blacks and Hispanics, 1970 to 1983.* Atlanta: Centers for Disease Control, 1986.

Chicago Police Department. *Statistical Summary 1988.* Chicago: Public and Internal Information Division, Chicago Police Department, 1988.

Cooper, D., K. Tabadoor, W.A. Hauser, K. Schulman, C. Feiner, and P.R. Factor. "The Epidemiology of Head Injury in the Bronx." *Neuroepidemiology,* 1983, *2:* 70-88.

Dennis, R.E., A. Kirk, and B.N. Knuckles. *Black Males At Risk to Low Life Expectancy: A Study of Homicide Victims and Perpetrators.* Washington, DC: National Institute of Mental Health, Center for Studies of Minority Group Mental Health, 1981.

Dietz, P.E. "Pattern in Human Violence." In R.E. Hales and A.J. Frances (eds.), *Psychiatric Update: The American Psychiatric Association Annual Review, Vol. 5.* Washington, DC: American Psychiatric Press, 1987.

Dyson, J.L. "Family Violence and Its Effect on Children's Academic Underachievement and Behavior Problems in School? *Journal of the National Medical Association,* in press.

Federal Bureau of Investigation. *Crime in the United States: 1986.* Washington, DC: U.S. Department of Justice, 1987.

Flango, V.E. and S.L. Sherbinou. "Poverty, Urbanization, and Crime." *Criminology,* 1976, *14:* 331-346.

Frankowski, R.F., J.F. Annegers, and S. Whitman. "Epidemiological and Descriptive Studies, Part 1: The Descriptive Epidemiology of Head Trauma in the United States." In Becker, D.P. and J.T. Povlishock (eds.), *Central Nervous System Trauma: Status Report.* Washington, DC: National Institute of Neurological and Communicative Disorders and Stroke, 1985.

Gary, L.E. and G.L. Berry. "Predicting Attitudes Toward Substance Abuse in a Black Community: Implications for Prevention." *Community Mental Health Journal,* 1985, *21:* 42-51.

Gelles, R. *The Violent Home.* Newbury Park, CA: Sage, 1987.

Griffith, E.E.H. and C.C. Bell. "Recent Trends in Suicide and Homicide Among Blacks." *Journal of the American Medical Association,* 1989, *262:* 2265-2269.

Guttentag, M. and P.R. Secord. *Too Many Women? The Sex Ratio Question.* Beverly Hills, CA: Sage, 1983.

Hawkins, D.F. "Longitudinal-Situational Approaches to Understanding Black-on-Black Homicide." In Secretary's Task Force on Black and Minority Health, *Report of the Secretary's Task Force on Black and Minority Health, Vol. 5: Homicide, Suicide, and Unintentional Injuries.* Washington, DC: U.S. Department of Health and Human Services, 1986.

Hillard, J.R., W. Zung, D. Ramm et al. "Accidental and Homicidal Death in a Psychiatric Emergency Room Population." *Hospital and Community Psychiatry,* 1985, *36:* 640-642.

Jacobson, A., J.E. Koehler, and C. Jones-Brown. "The Failure of Routine Assessment to Detect Histories of Assault Experienced by Psychiatric Patients." *Hospital and Community Psychiatry,* 1987, *38:* 386-389.

Jaffe, P., D. Wolfe, S. Wilson, and L. Zak. "Similarities in Behavioral and Social Maladjustment Among Child Victims and Witnesses to Family Violence." *American Journal of Orthopsychiatry,* 1986, *56:* 143-146.

Jenkins, E. and B. Thompson. "Children Talk About Violence: Preliminary Findings from a Survey of Black Elementary School Children." Paper presented at the Nineteenth Annual Convention of the Association of Black Psychologists, Oakland, CA, 1986.

Jennett, B. and G. Teasdale. *Management of Head Injuries*. Philadelphia, PA: Davis, 1981.

Kalmus, D. "The Intergenerational Transmission of Marital Aggression." *Journal of Marriage and Family,* 1984, *46,* 11–19.

Kellerman, A.L. and D.T. Reay. "Protection or Peril? An Analysis of Firearm-Related Deaths in the Home." *New England Journal of Medicine,* 1986, *314:* 1557–1560.

Kotlowitz, A. "Urban Trauma: Day-to-Day Violence Takes a Terrible Toll on Inner-City Youth." *The Wall Street Journal,* October 27, 1987, pages 1, 26.

Lewis, D.O., E. Moy, and L.D. Jackson. "Biopsychological Characteristics of Children Who Later Murder: A Prospective Study." *American Journal of Psychiatry,* 1985, *142:* 1161–1167.

Lewis, D.O., J.H. Pincus, and M. Feldman. "Psychiatric, Neurological, and Psychoeducational Characteristics of 15 Death-Row Inmates in the United States." *American Journal of Psychiatry,* 1986, *143:* 838–845.

Linnoila, M., M. Virkunen, M. Scheinin et al. "Low Cerebrospinal Fluid 5-Hydroxyindolacetic Acid Concentration Differentiates Impulsive from Nonimpulsive Violent Behavior." *Life Sciences,* 1983, *33:* 2609–2614.

Loftin, C. and R.H. Hill. "Regional Subculture and Homicide." *American Sociological Review,* 1974, *39:* 714–724.

Lystad, M. (ed.). *Violence in the Home: Interdisciplinary Perspectives.* New York: Brunner/Mazel, 1986.

Mann, C.R. "The Black Female Criminal Homicide Offender in the United States." In Secretary's Task Force on Black and Minority Health, *Report of the Secretary's Task Force on Black and Minority Health, Vol. 5: Homicide, Suicide, and Unintentional Injuries.* Washington, DC: U.S. Department of Health and Human Services, 1986.

Masters, R., L.N. Friedman, and G. Getzel. "Helping Families of Homicide Victims: A Multi-Dimensional Approach." *Journal of Traumatic Stress,* 1988, *1:* 109–125.

Mendez, G.A. "Crime Is Not a Part of Our Black Heritage: A Theoretical Essay." In Dewart, J. (ed.), *The State of Black America 1988.* New York: National Urban League, 1988.

National Commission on Correctional Health Care. *Standards for Health Services in Jails.* Chicago: National Commission on Correctional Health Care, 1987.

National Committee for Injury Prevention and Control and Education Development Center, Inc. *Injury Prevention: Meeting the Challenge.* New York: Oxford University Press, 1989.

Office of Criminal Justice Plans And Analysis. "Homicide in the District of Columbia," Washington, DC: Office of Criminal Justice Plans and Analysis, 1988.

Ogintz, E. "Wounded Childhood." *Chicago Tribune.* May 24, 1989, Section 5, pages 1, 5.

Okun, L. *Woman Abuse: Facts Replacing Myths.* Albany, NY: State University of New York Press, 1986.

Police Foundation. *Domestic Violence and the Police: Studies in Detroit and Kansas City.* Washington, DC: Police Foundation, 1977.

Prescott, J.W. "Body Pleasure and the Origins of Violence." *Bulletin of Atomic Scientists,* November 1975: 10–20.

Prothrow-Stith, D. "Interdisciplinary Intervention Applicable to Prevention of Interpersonal Violence and Homicide in Black Youth." In Secretary's Task Force on Black and Minority Health, *Report of the Secretary's Task Force on Black and Minority Health, Volume 5: Homicide, Suicide, and Unintentional Injuries.* Washington, DC: U.S. Department of Health and Human Services, 1986.

Pynoos, R. and S. Eth. "Developmental Perspectives on Psychic Trauma in Childhood." In R. Figley (ed.), *Trauma and Its Wake.* New York: Brunner/Mazel, 1985.

Pynoos, R. and K. Nader. "Psychological First Aid and Treatment Approach to Children Exposed to Community Violence: Research Implications." *Journal of Traumatic Stress,* 1988, *1,* 445–473.

Ramos, S.M. and H.M. Delany. "Freefalls from Heights: A Persistent Urban Problem." *Journal of the National Medical Association,* 1986, *78:* 111-115.

Recktenwald, W. and R. Blau. "Chicago Bucking the Trend in Big City Slayings." *The Chicago Tribune,* January 8, 1989, Section 2, pages 1, 2.

Rivara, F.P. and B.A. Mueller. "The Epidemiology and Prevention of Pediatric Head Injury." *Journal of Head Trauma Rehabilitation,* 1986, *1:* 7-15.

Rose, H.M. *Black Homicide and the Urban Environment.* Washington, DC: U.S. Department of Health and Human Services, National Institute of Mental Health, 1981.

Rosenberg, M.L. and J.A. Mercy. "Homicide: Epidemiologic Analysis at the National Level." *Bulletin of the New York Academy of Medicine,* 1986, *62:* 376-399.

Rynearson, E.K. "Psychological Effects of Unnatural Dying on Bereavement." *Psychiatric Annals,* 1986, *16:* 272-275.

Secretary's Task Force on Black and Minority Health. *Report of the Secretary's Task Force on Black and Minority Health, Volume 1, Executive Summary.* Washington, DC: U.S. Department of Health and Human Services, 1985.

Shakoor, B. and D. Chalmers. "Co-Victimization of African-American Children Who Witness Violence and the Theoretical Implications of Its Effect on Their Cognitive, Emotional, and Behavioral Development." *Journal of the National Medical Association,* in press.

Sosin, D.M., J.J. Sacks, and S.M. Smith. "Head Injury-Associated Deaths in the United States from 1979 to 1986." *Journal of the American Medical Association,* 1989, *262:* 2251-2255.

Stark, E. and A. Flitcraft. "Medical Therapy as Repression: The Case of the Battered Woman." *Health and Medicine,* Summer/Fall 1982, 29-32.

Straus, M.A., S.K. Steinmetz, and R.J. Gelles. *Behind Closed Doors: Violence in the American Family.* Garden City, NY: Anchor Books, 1980.

Sulton, A.T. *National Symposium on Community Institutions and Inner-City Crime: Shaping the Future Agenda of Urban Crime Control Policy and Research.* Washington, DC: Police Foundation, 1987.

Surgeon General's Workshop on Violence and Public Health. *Surgeon General's Workshop on Violence and Public Health Report.* Washington, DC: Health Resources and Services Administration, U.S. Public Health Service, 1986.

"Tide of Drug Killing." *Newsweek,* January 16, 1989, p. 44.

Timnick, L. "Children of Violence." *Los Angeles Times Magazine,* September 3, 1989.

U.S. House of Representatives Select Committee on Children, Youth, and Families. "Down These Mean Streets: Violence By and Against America's Children"—a Fact Sheet. May, 1989.

"Violence: Public Health Enemy." *Medical Tribune,* February 6, 1985, p. 1 of news briefs.

Whitman, S., R. Coonley-Hoganson, and B.T. Desai. "Comparative Head Trauma Experience in Two Socioeconomically Different Chicago-Area Communities: A Population Study." *American Journal of Epidemiology,* 1984, *4,* 570-580.

Williams, K.R. "Economic Sources of Homicide: Re-estimating the Effects of Poverty and Inequality." *American Sociological Review,* 1984, *49:* 283-289.

Wilson, W. *The Truly Disadvantaged.* Chicago: The University of Chicago Press, 1987.

FOOTNOTES

[1]Bob Garfield, "Adnost: The Revolution in TV Commercials Just Keeps Going and Going . . .," *Washington Post,* November 5, 1989.

[2]Hermann Basinger, "Media, Technology and Daily Life," *Media, Culture and Society,* Vol. 6, No. 4 (October 1984), pp. 343–351.

[3]*Ibid.*

[4]*Ibid.*

[5]Leo Shapiro and Dwight Bohmbach, "Consumers Buy More If They Like the President," *Advertising Age,* January 25, 1988, p. 24.

[6]*Ibid.*

[7]*Ibid.*

[8]R. Craig Endicott, "Global Ad, Volume Soars for Top 500," *Advertising Age,* March 29, 1988, p. 1.

[9]Sheila Gadsen, "Blowing the Whistle on Media Placement," *Advertising Age,* December 19, 1985, p. 26.

[10]Marshall Johnson, "Marketing to Blacks Is A Minstrel Show—It's White Marketing in Blackface," *Advertising Age,* December 19, 1985, p. 21.

[11]William O'Hare, "Blacks and Whites: One Market or Two?," *Advertising in Society,* eds., Roxanne Hovland and Gary B. Wilcox (Chicago: NTC Business Books), p. 192.

[12]Lawrence Bowen, "Advertising and the Poor," *Journalism Monographs,* No. 75 (February 1982), pp. 1–36.

[13]O'Hare, "Blacks and Whites: One Market or Two?," *op. cit.,* p. 196.

[14]E. Fitch, "Using the Proper Signals Improves Ad Reception," *Advertising Age,* December 19, 1985, pp. 24–25.

[15]*Ibid.*

[16]Bowen, "Advertising and the Poor," *op. cit.,* p. 3.

[17]*Ibid.,* p. 4.

[18]O'Hare, "Blacks and Whites: One Market or Two?," *op. cit.,* p. 192.

[19]Alexander Alland, *Human Diversity* (New York: Columbia University Press, 1971), p. 160.

[20]*Ibid.,* p. 161.

[21]Bowen, "Advertising and the Poor," *op. cit.,* p. 1.

[22]Roland Barthes, *Mythologies* (New York: Hill and Wang, 1957; English Translation, 1972), p. 11.

[23]N. Postman, C. Nystrom, L. Strate, and C. Weingartner, *Myths, Men and Beer: An Analysis of Beer Commercials on Broadcast Television, 1987* (Washington, DC: AAA Foundation for Traffic Safety, 1987), p. 3.

[24]Bowen, "Advertising and the Poor," *op. cit.,* p. 2.

[25]*Ibid.,* p. 8.

[26]Cedric Watts, *The Deceptive Text: An Introduction to Covert Plots* (Sussex: The Harvester Press, 1984), p. 3.

27Alland, *Human Diversity, op. cit.,* p. 136.

28*Ibid.*

29*Ibid.,* p. 144.

30Harper W. Boyd, Jr. and Sidney J. Levy, *Promotion: Behavioral View* (Englewood Cliffs, NJ: Prentice-Hall, 1967), p. 34.

31*Ibid.*

32*Ibid.,* p. 35.

33*Ibid.,* p. 36.

34Debra Kent, "UniWorld Turns Trends into Crossover Appeal," *Advertising Age,* December 19, 1985, p. 16.

35*Ibid.*

36*Ibid.*

37Henry Allen, "How Life Went On in the '80s," *Washington Post,* November 14, 1989, p. C1.

38*Ibid.*

39*Ibid.*

40Alland, *Human Diversity, op. cit.,* p. 161.

41Allen, "How Life Went On in the '80s," *op. cit.,* p. C1.

42Alland, *Human Diversity,* p. 166.

43E. Fitch, "Using the Proper Signals," *op. cit.,* p. 25.

44*Ibid.*

45Katherine Newman, *Falling From Grace* (New York: The Free Press, 1988), p. x.

46*Ibid.,* p. 228.

47*Ibid.,* p. x.

48Barthes, *Mythologies, op. cit.,* p. 115.

Toward An African-American Agenda: An Inward Look, *Ramona Hoage Edelin, Ph.D.*

FOOTNOTES

1At the Republican National Convention, as a candidate for president, and later at his first talk before the joint houses of Congress as president, Mr. Bush made this observation.

2For example, the U.S. Bureau of the Census estimates that the total number of African Americans in 1995 will be 33,199,000 or 13 percent of the total population; that the total number of Hispanics will be 22,550,000 or nine percent of the total population of 260,138,000 Americans; and that the college-aged African-American population (ages 18–24) will be 3,703,000 or 15 percent of that total (24,281,000), as compared to 2,511,000 Hispanics (10 percent) in this age group. On the other hand, the National Science Board Commission on Pre-College Education in Mathematics, Science, and Technology projected in 1983 that more than 40 percent of all college-aged students available for the American work force in 1995 would be African American and Hispanic *(Educating Americans for the 21st Century: A Plan of Action for Improving Mathematics, Science, and Technology Education for All American Elementary and Secondary Students So That Their Achievement Is the Best in the World by 1995).*

[3]Dr. John Henrik Clarke has always said, "The Europeans decided long ago that whoever ruled the world, it would be one of them." However, European unification—the rule of *all* of them as one—would require an end to their long history of wars among themselves.

[4]"There is some evidence that increasing cooperation between East and West may not operate to the benefit of countries and peoples that are victims of racism and imperialism who historically have been exploited and oppressed. Indeed, we may not be able to look to the past supports from the traditional socialist and communist world leadership for continuing assistance. The development and expansion of other supports, therefore, is critical. To win our liberation, we must increase our reliance on ourselves and other victims of the same enemy: racism and imperialism. We must think and act globally to increase our power and ensure an equitable flow of resources to our people throughout the world as we move steadfastly towards liberation." Wilhelm Joseph, *NCBL Notes* (New York: National Conference of Black Lawyers, October–November 1989).

[5]"Racism is both overt and covert. It takes two, closely related forms: individual whites acting against individual blacks, and acts by the total white community against the black community. We call these individual racism and institutional racism. The first consists of overt acts by individuals, which cause death, injury, or the violent destruction of properly. . . . The second type is less overt, far more subtle, less identifiable in terms of *specific* individuals committing the acts. But it is no less destructive of human life. The second type originates in the operation of established and respected forces in the society, and thus receives far less public condemnation than the first type.

"When white terrorists bomb a black church and kill five black children, that is an act of individual racism, widely deplored by most segments of the society. But when in that same city—Birmingham, Alabama—500 black babies die each year because of the lack of proper food, shelter, and medical facilities, and thousands more are destroyed and maimed physically, emotionally, and intellectually because of conditions of poverty and discrimination in the black community, that is a function of institutional racism. . . ." Stokely Carmichael and Charles V. Hamilton, *Black Power: The Politics of Liberation in America* (New York: Vintage Books, a division of Random House, 1967), p. 4.

[6]See the preface to the 1988 reprint of *The Kerner Report: The 1968 Report of the National Advisory Commission on Civil Disorders* (New York: Pantheon Books), where Fred Harris unequivocally states: "Why did it happen? *Segregation and poverty have created in the racial ghettos a destructive environment totally unknown to most white Americans.* What can be done to prevent it from happening again? *It is time to make good the promises of American democracy to all citizens—urban and rural, white and black, Spanish-surname, American Indian, and every minority group.* [Italicized statements are quotes from the original report.] And, for a time after the Kerner Report, through the mid-1970s, America made progress on almost all fronts that the report had covered. Then came a series of recessions and other economic blows that were most severe for poor people and minorities; these were accompanied by federal cutbacks in jobs, training, and other social programs most important to the poor. Just a few years after the bitter lessons of the sixties, the government lost interest in, and even became hostile towards, affirmative action programs and civil rights laws.

"So poverty is worse today than it was twenty years ago. More people are poor. Poor people are poorer—and less able to escape their poverty. Unemployment is worse. There is a growing American urban underclass, principally black and Hispanic. 'Quiet riots' of high unemployment and poverty, segregation, family deterioration, social disorganization, narcotics use, and crime characterize today's central cities. These quiet riots are not as noticeable or alarming to outsiders as the violent riots of the 1960s, but they are more destructive of human life."

[7]"Ever have men striven to conceive of their victims as different from the victors, endlessly different, in soul and blood, strength and cunning, race and lineage. It has been left, however, to Europe and to modern days to discover the eternal worldwide mark of meanness—color. . . . The using of men for the benefit of masters is no new invention of modern Europe. It is quite as old as the world. But Europe proposed to apply it on a scale and within an elaborateness of detail which no former world ever dreamed. The imperial width of the thing—the heaven-defying audacity—makes it modern newness. Their theory of human culture and its aims has worked itself through warp and woof of our daily thought with a thoroughness that few realize. Everything great, good, efficient, fair, and honorable is 'white'; everything mean, bad, blundering, cheating, and dishonorable is 'yellow'; a bad taste is 'brown'; and the devil is 'black.' The changes of this theme are continually rung in picture and story, in newspaper heading and moving picture, in sermon and school book until, of course, the King can do no wrong—a White man is always right and a Black man has no rights which a White man is bound to respect." W.E.B. DuBois, *Darkwater: Voices from Within the Veil* (New York: Harcourt, Brace, 1920), pp. 42–43.

[8]"The past five decades have shown that purposeful actions and policies by governments and private institutions make a large difference in the opportunities and conditions of black Americans. Such purposeful actions and policies have been essential for past progress, and further progress is unlikely without them. Many blacks attained middle-class status because government and private programs enabled them to achieve better education and jobs, through employment and education programs and government enforcement of equal employment opportunity." Gerald David Jaynes and Robin M. Williams, Jr., editors, *A Common Destiny: Blacks and American Society*, Committee on the Status of Black Americans Commission on Behavioral and Social Sciences and Education, National Research Council (Washington, DC: National Academy Press, 1989), p. 9.

[9]At a meeting convened by the Reverend Jesse L. Jackson in December 1988, a group of 75 local and national leaders agreed to call our people together to set an agenda looking out to the year 2000 and beyond; and to provide a cultural context for our work by consistently referring to ourselves as African American rather than black, as proposed by this writer. Never a "name change debate" as portrayed by the media, this act was seen as the first step in a serious African-American cultural offensive. The African-American Summit '89, held in New Orleans in April 1989, initiated a formal process of national and local agenda-setting in the cultural context which has now to be implemented in cities and states around the nation.

[10]From "The Conservation of Races," provided by Julius Lester in *The Seventh Son, Vol. I* (New York: Vintage Books, a division of Random House), pp. 176–188.

[11]Cheikh Anta Diop, *The African Origin of Civilization: Myth or Reality*, trans. Mercer Cook (Chicago: Lawrence Hill Books, 1974), p. xiv.

[12]Egyptian civilization was more than 10,000 years old when Herodotus visited in the fifth century B.C. (Diop, *op. cit.*, p. 4).

[13]See John Hope Franklin, *From Slavery to Freedom* (New York: Vintage Books, a division of Random House, 1947, with several subsequent editions); and Lerone Bennett, Jr., *Before the Mayflower* (Chicago: Johnson Publishing Company, 1982 reissue).

[14]See Sterling Stuckey, *Slave Culture* (New York: Oxford University Press, 1987), p. 195.

[15]We can and should devote volumes of analysis to the very serious questions of what has been gained and what has been lost in the various compromise desegregation efforts we have experienced. The new 50-year study published by the National Research Council gives substantial data on African-American inclusion and exclusion in American society. See Jaynes and Williams, *op. cit.*

[16]See Basil Davidson, "The Ancient World and Africa Whose Roots?," in *Egypt Revisited*, ed. Ivan Van Sertima (New Brunswick and London: Transaction Publishers, 1989). Davidson says: "That the Ancient Egyptians were black . . . is a belief which has been denied in Europe since about 1630, not before. It is a denial, in short, that belongs to the rise of modern European imperialism, and has to be explained in terms of the 'new racism,' specifically and even frantically an anti-black racism, which went together with and was consistently nourished by that imperialism. I say 'new racism' because it followed and further expanded the older racism which spread around Europe after the Atlantic slave trade had reached its high point of 'take off' in about 1630. Was there no racism, then, before that? The point is complex and can be argued elsewhere: essentially, however, the answer to this is also in the negative. Before the Atlantic slave trade, and before its capitalism, there was plenty of ancient xenophobia . . ., but none of this was the racism that we know" (p. 40).

Those of Broader Vision: An African-American Perspective on Teenage Pregnancy and Parenting, *Georgia L. McMurray*

FOOTNOTES

[1]*Death Before Dying: The Tragedy of Infant Mortality*, The Report of the National Commission to Prevent Infant Mortality (Washington, August 1988).

[2]"Adolescent Male Responsibility in African-American Families," a paper presented by Robert B. Hill at the 1988 National Urban League conference on "Manhood and Fatherhood," in Detroit, MI.

³Toni Morrison, *Beloved* (New York: Alfred A. Knopf, 1987).

⁴*Teenage Pregnancy: An Advocate's Guide to Numbers* (Washington: January–March, 1988).

⁵Claudia Glenn Dowling, *Teenaged Mothers Seventeen Years Later* (New York: Commonwealth Fund Papers, 1987). Reports on the work of Frank Furstenberg, J. Brooks-Gunn, and S. Phillip Morgan, who followed the lives of 300 young mothers over 17 years.

⁶Dowling, *ibid.* Also: Jane C. Quint and James A. Riccio, *The Challenge of Serving Pregnant and Parenting Teens, Lessons from Project Redirection* (Manpower Demonstration Research Corporation, 1985)—an evaluation of teen parents in a highly publicized national program funded by the Ford Foundation. A majority of the participants were school dropouts prior to pregnancy and 70 percent were receiving Aid to Families with Dependent Children. See also: "Single Mothers—The Story Behind the Stereotypes," *RAND Research Review,* Vol. XII, No. 1, which reports on a detailed RAND study (*Beyond Stereotype: Who Becomes a Single Teenage Mother?*) by Abrahamse, Morrison, and Waite who tracked 13,000 high school females for two years, cutting across race and family income. Also, Joy Dryfoos, *Putting the Boy in the Picture.*

⁷Elizabeth Marek, "The Lives of Teenage Mothers, Schoolbooks, Boyfriends, and Babies," *Harpers Magazine,* April 1989.

⁸*RAND Research Review,* Vol. XII, No. 1.

⁹Dowling, *Teenaged Mothers Seventeen Years Later, op. cit.*

¹⁰*The Common Good* (New York: Ford Foundation, 1989).

¹¹Dowling, *op. cit.,* and Dryfoos, *Putting the Boy in the Picture.*

¹²Jacqueline Smollar and Theodore Ooms, *Young Unwed Fathers: Research Review, Policy Dilemmas, and Options, A Summary Report.*

¹³*Ibid.*

¹⁴According to a January 1989 Children's Defense Fund report, 2.7 million youths between ages 16 and 24 were unable to find work. Between 1973 and 1986, the earning power of males, 20 to 24, fell by 25 percent (adjusted for inflation).

¹⁵*The Crisis,* March 1986.

¹⁶*Ibid.*

¹⁷Dr. Walter Stafford, a senior research fellow at the Community Service Society in New York City, is among those near completion of an exhaustive study on this and related issues.

¹⁸*Teenage Pregnancy, op. cit.*

¹⁹Alvin F. Poussaint, M.D., "Black Children: Coping in a Racist Society," a paper presented at the University of Michigan School of Social Work, October 29, 1987.

²⁰According to the National Commission to Prevent Infant Mortality, Medicaid now helps only 40 percent of officially designated poor in the U.S., and only 50 percent of poor children. Although poverty grows, the number of Medicaid recipients declines because of low eligibility standards.

²¹*Author's Note:* Although this may raise questions of equity, I believe that young fathers should be targeted because the child's need for a positive father image is paramount. *GLM*

²²Poussaint, "Black Children: Coping in a Racist Society," *op. cit.*

The Unemployment Experience of African Americans: Some Important Correlates and Consequences, *Billy J. Tidwell, Ph.D.*

ENDNOTES

[1] Bureau of Labor Statistics, *Employment and Earnings* (Washington, DC: U.S. Government Printing Office, January 1989): Bureau of Labor Statistics, *Labor Force Statistics Derived from the Current Population Survey,* 1948–1987 (Washington, DC: U.S. Government Printing Office, August 1988); *Quarterly Economic Report on the African-American Worker,* Third Quarter 1989 (Washington, DC: National Urban League Research Department, November 1989).

[2] For discussion, see Billy J. Tidwell, "Black Wealth: Facts and Fiction," in Janet Dewart (ed.), *The State of Black America 1988* (New York: National Urban League, 1988), pp. 193–210. Also, Walter L. Updegrave, "Race and Money," *Money,* December 1989, pp. 152–172.

[3] For useful discussion and bibliography, see Katherine Hooper Briar, "Unemployment and Underemployment," *Encyclopedia of Social Work,* Eighteenth Edition, Volume 2 (Silver Spring, Maryland: National Association of Social Workers, 1987), pp. 778–788.

[4] Instructive findings on differences in duration as observed over an extended time frame may be found in Herbert S. Parnes, *The Distribution and Correlates of Unemployment Over A Decade* (Columbus, Ohio: Ohio State University Center for Human Resource Research, 1982).

[5] Briar, *op. cit.*

[6] The data were collected through the Census Bureau's ongoing Survey of Income and Program Participation, which interviews the same respondents at scheduled intervals over an extended period.

[7] Deficiencies in the unemployment insurance system are assessed in Isaac Shapiro and Marion E. Nichols, *Unprotected: Unemployment Insurance and Jobless Workers in 1988* (Washington, DC: Center on Budget and Policy Priorities, 1989).

School Power: A Model for Improving Black Student Achievement, *James P. Comer, M.D.; Norris M. Haynes, Ph.D., and Muriel Hamilton-Lee, Ed.D.*

FOOTNOTES

[1] J. Coleman, T. Hoffer, and S. Kilgure, *High School Achievement: Public, Catholic and Other Private Schools Compared* (New York: Basic Books, 1982).

[2] National Commission on Excellence in Education, *A Nation at Risk: The Imperative for Educational Reform* (Washington, DC: 1983).

[3] E.G. West, *Are American Schools Working: Disturbing Cost and Quality Trends: Policy Analysis No. 26.* (ERIC Research Document No. 235-885), 1983.

[4] National Institute of Education, *Violent Schools—Safe Schools* (Washington, DC: HEW, 1977).

[5] F. Parker, *Behind a Nation at Risk: The Imperative for Educational Reform* (ERIC Research Document No. 238-797), 1983.

[6] J. Bruce, *The Continuous Process of School Improvement: Learned From the Past* (Reston, VA: Association of Teacher Educators, 1980).

[7] R.R. Edmonds, "Improving the Effectiveness of New York City Public Schools," in *The Minority Student in Public Schools: Fostering Academic Excellence* (Princeton, NJ: Educational Testing Service, Office for Minority Education, 1981), pp. 23–30.

[8]S.T. Bossert, D.C. Dwyer, S. Rowan, and G.V. Lee, "The Instructional Management Role of the Principal," *Educational Administration Quarterly,* No. 3 (1982), pp. 34–64.

[9]P. Coleman, *Elementary School Self-Improvement through Social Climate Enhancement* (ERIC Research Document No. 251-961), 1984.

[10]M. Rutter, B. Maughan, P. Mortimore, J. Ouston, and A. Smith, *Fifteen Thousand Hairs, Secondary Schools and Their Effects on Children* (Cambridge, MA: Harvard Univ. Press, 1979).

[11]E.L. McDill, L.C. Rigsby, and E.D. Meyers Jr., "Educational Climates of High Schools: Their Effects and Sources," in D.A. Erickson (ed.), *Educational Organization and Administration* (Berkeley, CA: McCutchen, 1977).

[12]W.B. Brookover, L. Beamer, H. Efthim, D. Hathaway, L.W. Lesotte, S.K. Miller, T. Passalacqua, and L. Tornatsky, *Creating Effective Schools* (Holmes Beach: Learning Publications, 1983).

[13]C. Achilles et al. "Development and Use of a Replication and Evaluation Model to Track the Implementation Progress of Effective Schools Elements in an Inner City Setting. Paper presented at the annual meeting of the Mid-South Educational Research Association, New Orleans, LA, 1982.

[14]G. Weber, *Inner City Children Can Be Taught to Read: Four Successful Schools,* Council for Basic Education, Vol. 18 of Occasional Papers, 1971.

[15]R.R. Edmonds, "Programs of School Improvement: An Overview," *Educational Leadership* 39 (1983), pp. 4–14.

[16]J.I. Goodlad, "Can Our Schools Get Better," *Phi Delta Kappan* (Jan. 1979), pp. 342–47.

[17]D. Clark et al., "Factors Associated with Success in Urban Elementary Schools," *Phi Delta Kappan,* 61, No. 3 (1980), pp. 467–70.

[18]R.L. Venezky and L. Winfield, *Schools That Exceed Beyond Expectations in Teaching Reading* (Dover, DE: Univ. of Delaware Studies on Education, 1979).

[19]P. Purkey and M.S. Smith, *School Reform: The Policy Implications of the Effective Schools Literature* (ERIC Research Document No. ED 245-350), 1983.

[20]P. Berman and M.W. McLaughlin, *Federal Programs Supporting Educational Change: Factors Affecting Implementation and Continuation* (Santa Monica, CA; Rand Corp., 1977).

[21]J.W. Meyer and B. Rowan, "The Structure of Educational Organizations," in Meyer et al. (eds.), *Environments and Organizations* (San Francisco: Jossey-Boss, 1978).

[22]M.B. Miles, "Mapping the Common Properties of Schools," in R. Lehming and M. Kane (eds.), *Improving Schools: Using What We Know* (Beverly Hills: Sage Publications, 1981).

[23]S.B. Sarason, *The Culture of the School and the Problem of Change* (Boston: Allyn and Bacon, 1971).

[24]R.E. Weick, "Educational Organizations as Loosely Coupled Systems," *Administrative Science Quarterly,* 21 (1976), pp. 1–19.

[25]J. O'Toole, *Making America Work* (New York: Continuum Publishing Co., 1981).

[26]C.C. Selby, "Need for Top Down and Bottom Up Leadership," address delivered at the Forum on Excellence in Education, Indianapolis, IN, 1983.

[27]J.P. Comer, *School Power* (New York: The Free Press, 1980).

[28]A. Beck, L. Wyland, and W. McCourt, "Primary Prevention: Whose Responsibility," *American Journal of Psychiatry,* 128 (1971), pp. 412–17.

[29]L. Hartman, "The Preventive Education of Psychological Risk in Asymptomatic Adolescents," *American Journal of Orthopsychiatry,* 48 (1979), pp. 121–35.

[30]J. Reiff, "Mental Health Manpower and Institutional Change," *American Psychologist,* 21 (1966), pp. 540–48.

329

[31] J.G. Kelly, "Ecological Constraints on Mental Health Services," *American Psychologist,* 21 (1966), pp. 535-39.

[32] R. Lewin, *Principles of Topological Psychology* (New York: McGraw Hill, 1936).

[33] M. Weinstein and M. Frankel, "Ecological and Psychological Approaches to Community Psychology," *American Journal of Community Psychology,* 2 (1974), pp. 43-52.

[34] E.G. Wilkinson and W.A. O'Connor, "Human Ecology and Mental Illness," *American Journal of Psychiatry,* 139 (1982), pp. 985-90.

[35] E.J. Trickett and R.H. Moos, "The Classroom Scale," *American Journal of Community Psychology,* 2 (No. 1), pp. 1-12.

[36] J.S. Coleman and T. Hoffer, *Public and Private High Schools: The Impact of Communities* (New York: Basic Books, 1987).

[37] J.P. Comer, *op. cit.*

[38] N.M. Haynes, J.P. Comer, and M. Hamilton-Lee, "The Effects of Parental Involvement on Student Performance," *Journal of Research in Childhood Education* (in press).

[39] C. Woods, "The Effects of Parent Involvement on Reading Readiness Scores," in A. Henderson (ed.), *Parent Participation—Student Achievement: The Evidence Grows* (Columbia, MD: National Committee for Citizens in Education).

Acknowledgments

The National Urban League acknowledges with sincere appreciation the contributions of the authors of the various papers appearing in this publication. We also acknowledge Paulette Robinson, assistant editor; Johnnie Griffin, technical editor; Michele Long Pittman, proofreading assistant; and the special contributions of National Urban League staff, including Leslye L. Cheek, Ernie Johnston, Jr., B. Maxwell Stamper, Farida Syed, Faith Williams, Ralph Faust, and Denise Wright of the Public Relations and Communications Department; Daniel S. Davis and Betty Ford in the Office of the President; Washington Operations; the Research Department; and the Program Department.

Order Blank

National Urban League Publications
500 East 62nd Street
New York, N.Y. 10021

	Per Copy	Number of Copies	Total
The State of Black America 1990	$19.00		
Recent Volumes in series:			
The State of Black America 1989	$19.00		
The State of Black America 1988	$18.00		
The State of Black America 1987	$18.00		
The State of Black America 1986	$18.00		
Postage and handling:			
Individual volumes—$1.50 each Book Rate			
$3.00 each First Class			
Amount enclosed			

"The Reception" Lithograph

Limited edition, numbered lithography of "The Reception" by Jonathan Green, signed by the artist. "The Reception" is the third in the Great Artists series created for the National Urban League through a donation from the House of Seagram. Proceeds benefit the National Urban League.

Unframed lithograph 26" × 20". Full color. $1,000 each, includes postage and handling.

For information and to order, contact:

National Urban League, Inc.
Office of Development
500 East 62nd Street
New York, New York 10021

Please make checks or money orders payable to:
National Urban League, Inc.